A

An Exegetical Commentary

Joel, Amos, Obadiah

20
3.30
23.35
ETS
11-03

Thomas J. Finley
Chairman, Department of Old Testament and Semitics
Talbot School of Theology

About the Author

Thomas J. Finley (B.A., Biola University; M.Div., Talbot School of Theology; M.A., University of California at Los Angeles; Ph.D., University of California at Los Angeles) chairs the Department of Old Testament and Semitics at Talbot School of Theology in La Mirada, California. He has written both technical and popular articles for various publications.

Table of Contents

Preface

For several years it has been my privilege to ponder the prophecies of Joel, Amos, and Obadiah. Though it is an awesome responsibility to comment on God's holy Word, it is also necessary for each generation to find fresh answers from the pages of the inspired Scriptures to the questions that are troubling it.

The cultural and historical distance between the Old Testament prophets and their modern readers makes close study difficult. While these individuals spoke from God and therefore left a message that will always be relevant, God delivered His words through the vehicle of the prophets and their own situation in life. I have tried here to use the tools of language and history to help the reader grasp the meaning of each prophetic book in its original context as far as possible.

It is also my conviction that the individual books as they are known from the Hebrew Bible reflect accurately the prophet's own age. Some minor problems may have arisen through the process of textual transmission, but these are not so serious as to undermine the doctrine of an inspired (and inerrant) book. Where significant issues arise about whether or not a passage belongs to the prophet whose name is attached to the book, they are discussed. I have also attempted to be fair and courteous to those whose convictions on these matters differ from mine.

In my seminary training I was taught that good translation is the first step to good exegesis. Consequently, I have tried to interact frequently with modern translations, especially the *NASB* and the *NIV*. The process of making my own translations forced me to consider fine nuances of the text that I otherwise might have missed, though my own renderings seldom differ significantly from either of these fine versions. Great value is also to be gained, I discovered, from studying the ancient versions, especially the Aramaic Targum (*Tg. Jonathan* on the Prophets, also referred to as *Tg. Neb.*) because of its highly interpretive translations.

I gladly acknowledge the role students have had in stimulating my own thinking. Several significant contributions were made by students in a seminar on Amos. Three students wrote theses, Randy Haney who did two theses on Amos, Joel Robertson on Joel, and Joe Hellerman on Obadiah. Many other students in various classes have raised valid issues and had thought-provoking questions. Perhaps it is students I have had most in mind as I have tried to deal with the kind of problems they would find in attempting to understand the biblical text.

The editorial staff at Moody made excellent suggestions for improving the manuscript, and I want to express special thanks to them, especially to Joe O'Day.

Finally, I would like to thank Biola University and Talbot School of Theology for allowing me a sabbatical to accomplish the greater part of this work. Without this valuable time it would have been impossible to finish it.

This work was originally part of the series "Wycliffe Exegetical Commentary," published by Moody Press. The series was discontinued before it was completed, and the copyright is now owned by me. For this special version that is being made available on the Internet, I would like to thank Hampton Keathley for making it possible to post the manuscript electronically. Also, I would like to thank my student Jeff Wisdom for getting the Hebrew script into acceptable format and for helping me to update the research.

Joel

The prophet Joel speaks of a day of unparalleled blessing and judgment. Two events occupy center stage in the book of Joel: a great plague of locusts and the Day of the Lord. Joel calls the people of Judah to repent in light of the disastrous devastation brought by locusts. The Lord's promise to restore and bless anew His people when they repent serves as the backdrop for a sweeping message about the future Day of the Lord.

Introduction to Joel

Words both ancient and powerful enchant the reader who will take the time to become acquainted with the prophetic books of the Hebrew Scriptures. The men behind the books represent a variety of backgrounds. Some spoke in kings' palaces in eloquent tones; others were quite ordinary in speech and manner. Sometimes they saw elaborate visions and heard voices speaking; other times they report their message more simply, yet always noting that it was from God.

If the success of a man is measured by the impact he has on later generations, then all of these prophets were highly successful. In their own generation, however, they usually preached to plugged ears and hearts of stone. Their words, of course, were framed to have universal appeal, and while they originally spoke to Israel and Judah, they still speak as God's spokesmen to all people everywhere.

Joel is noteworthy because his audience responded to his preaching by a public demonstration of repentance. The Lord was gracious to His people because of it, but as with many revivals the spiritual effects were apparently short-lived and only penetrated to a portion of the population. Regardless of where the interpreter places Joel in history, it is clear that the people of the next generation needed to repent of their own rebellion against the Lord.

Historical Context

Joel remains a shadowy figure among the prophets. His name, a common one in Israel, means "the LORD (Yahweh) is God."[1] Possibly Joel was a priest; he had a strong interest in ritual fasting and prayer. In any case several other prophets were priests (cf. Jer. 1:1; Ezek. 1:3; Zech. 1:1 and Neh. 12:4 [if Iddo is the same person]), and Joel views the elders and priests as important leaders in the community.

Joel is perhaps the most difficult prophet to locate in history. Since his book does not state when it was written, interpreters are forced to rely on internal allusions. Joel deals with a locust plague, but such plagues were commonplace and could have happened at any time during the history of Israel. Other general conditions mentioned in the book offer some help but nothing that can decide the issue. The most important opinions about the date of composition are diverse:

1) 835-796 *B.C.*   During the time when Joash (835-796 *B.C.*)

---

[1] Since the commentary is exegetical, we will use "Yahweh" for the divine name יהוה. Most modern versions render "LORD" unless it is preceded by the Hebrew word for "Lord" (אֲדֹנָי). Then it is usually rendered "GOD." The modern versions are consistent with Jewish tradition (especially as seen in the LXX) and New Testament practice. "Jehovah" is less accurate than "Yahweh." For further information, see Kenneth L. Barker, "YHWH Sabaoth: *"The Lord Almighty"*," *The NIV: The Making of a Contemporary Translation*, ed. Kenneth L. Barker (Grand Rapids: Zondervan, 1986), pp. 106-9.

9

	was too young, so the High Priest Jehoiada governed the country (2 Kings 11; 2 Chron. 23-24).[2]
2) About 775-725 *B.C.*	Approximately contemporary with Hosea and Amos.[3]
3) About 500 *B.C.*	Approximately contemporary with Zechariah.[4]
4) About 400 *B.C.*	After Ezra and Nehemiah.[5]

Some have recently favored a fifth view, which makes Joel a contemporary of the prophet Jeremiah.[6] This does not seem possible in that the Judeans responded to Joel but failed to heed Jeremiah's call for repentance. Douglas Stuart entertains the possibility that Joel dates to the period of Jeremiah, but at the same time Stuart does not see a literal locust plague, nor does he think 2:18-19 refers to a positive response of the Lord in Joel's day.[7] In order to make an informed decision about any of these views, it will be necessary to examine historical allusions in the book, its language and theology, its position among the Minor Prophets, and its literary connections with other prophets.

Historical Allusions

In the first chapter priests and elders are prominent as leaders in Jerusalem (1:2, 9, 13, 14), and no king is mentioned anywhere in the book. The final chapter mentions, either historically or prophetically, a time when the inhabitants of Judah and Jerusalem were "scattered among the nations" and sold into slavery, while the land was "divided up" (3:2-3 [MT 4:2-3]).[8] Singled out for special mention are Tyre, Sidon, and Philistia because they took booty of gold and silver to their own palaces and sold the Judeans to the Greeks ("sons of Javan," i.e., Ionians; 3:4-6). Consequently, the descendants of these enemies will be returned to the Judeans who will sell them to "the Sabeans, a distant nation" (3:8). Finally, the Egyptians and Edomites will be judged in a special way, "Because of the violence done to the sons of Judah,/ In whose land they have shed innocent blood" (3:19).

---

[2] Ebenezer Henderson, *The Twelve Minor Prophets: Translated from the Original Hebrew with a Critical and Exegetical Commentary*, (Thornapple Commentaries; Grand Rapids: Baker, 1980 [repr. of 1858 edition]), pp. 89-90.

[3] Richard D. Patterson, "Joel," in *EBC* ed. Frank E. Gaebelein (Grand Rapids: Zondervan, 1985), 7:231-32.

[4] David Allan Hubbard, *Joel and Amos: An Introduction and Commentary* (TOTC; Downers Grove, IL: Inter-Varsity, 1989), pp. 25-27.

[5] Julius A. Bewer, *A Critical and Exegetical Commentary on Obadiah and Joel* (ICC; Edinburgh: T. & T. Clark, 1974 [repr of 1911 edition]), pp. 56-62.

[6] Wilhelm Rudolph, *Joel-Amos-Obadja-Jona*, (KAT 13:2; Gütersloh: Gütersloher Verlagshaus Gerd Mohn, 1971), pp. 26-27.

[7] Stuart, *Hosea-Jonah* (WBC 31; Waco, Tex.: Word, 1987), pp. 225-26, 232-34, 257-58.

[8] The Hebrew (MT) of Joel divides the chapters differently than the English. Chap. 3 of MT is 2:28-32 in the English, while chap. 3 in the English is chap. 4 of MT.

Since Judah and Jerusalem occupy the center of attention, it is clear the events of Joel took place there after the division of the kingdom. If one focuses on the importance of the priests and elders and the lack of reference to a king, two periods are most likely. First, many conservative commentators have preferred the era of the minority of Joash (835-789 *B.C.*), under the regency of the High Priest Jehoiada (2 Kings 11).[9] Second, others have thought of the postexilic period, after 515 *B.C.* when the Temple was rebuilt.[10]

The argument concerning a king is negative evidence. That is, it is based on the text not mentioning something. As Wilhelm Rudolph points out, Isa. 1-5 (exclusive of the heading in 1:1) is a longer section than Joel, yet it also does not mention a king in Judah, not even in 3:2-3 where various leaders are listed.[11] It could be that Joel simply had no special reason to refer to the king, whereas the elders had an important political role throughout the history of Israel (cf. 1 Kings 20:7, 8; 21:8, 11; 2 Kings 6:32; 10:1, 5; 23:1 [= 2 Chron. 34:29]; Ezra 10:8, 14; Isa. 3:14; 9:15 [MT 9:14]; 24:23; Jer. 19:1; 26:17; Ezek. 7:26).

More solid ground comes from comparing the constellation of foreign nations mentioned in chap. 3 with the history of Judah. Even here some ambiguity is apparent. Gleason Archer is sure that "at no time after the reign of Joash was the kingdom of Judah faced by this particular assortment of enemies," but Patterson, after a detailed analysis of chap. 3, concludes, "the early eighth century *B.C.* best harmonizes with the known data."[12]

The data do not rule out the possibility of a postexilic date. The failure to mention Babylon and Assyria could be because they had already fallen by the time of the Persian period.[13] The absence of Persia could simply reflect the generally positive relations with that nation, especially in the period of Zechariah (late sixth to early fifth centuries *B.C.*) or later under Ezra and Nehemiah.

Tyre, Sidon, and various Philistine cities are mentioned together in Zech. 9:2-6, and Zech. 14:16-19 singles out Egypt for special treatment. The similar configuration of nations seen in Zechariah could well argue for a date of Joel circa 500 *B.C.* While the mention of Greeks and Sabeans does not militate against a preexilic date, the reference would fit naturally with the postexilic period (cf. also Zech. 9:13). There are no compelling arguments for placing Joel any later than the traditional close of the OT canon about 400 *B.C.*

Joel refers to Jerusalem's wall (2:7, 9), but this is too vague to pinpoint a time either before 586 *B.C.* or after Nehemiah's reconstruction. Since he compares locusts to an army scaling the wall, it is not necessary to suppose that the wall was

---

[9] Gleason L. Archer, Jr., *A Survey of Old Testament Introduction*, rev. ed. (Chicago: Moody, 1975), p. 304.

[10] A minority view among those who accept the full inspiration and authority of Scripture, but see Roland Kenneth Harrison, *Introduction to the Old Testament* (Grand Rapids: Eerdmans, 1969), pp. 876-79; and Robert B. Chisholm, Jr., "Joel," in *BKCOT* ed. John F. Walvoord and Roy B. Zuck (Wheaton: Victor, 1985), pp. 1409-10.

[11] Rudolph, *Joel*, p. 27.

[12] Archer, *OT Introduction*, p. 305; Richard D. Patterson, "Joel," in *EBC* ed. Frank E. Gaebelein (Grand Rapids: Zondervan, 1985), 7:232.

[13] Rudolph's explanation for the lack of Babylon if Joel were contemporary with Jeremiah seems forced (*Joel*, p. 26).

in good condition. Some historians have even proposed that Jerusalem's walls had been reconstructed and destroyed again between Nebuchadnezzar's destruction and Nehemiah's return.[14]

Language And Theology

Linguistic analysis cannot yield firm data when no solid historical evidence exists to confirm the results. We have found no convincing evidence that Joel's language could not be preexilic, though some apparently late features are often mentioned.[15] Joel does use "Israel" to refer to God's people rather than to the northern kingdom (2:27; 3:2; 3:16) but not in a manner which differs from the usage of certain preexilic prophets (cf. Isa. 1:3; Jer. 2:14; Amos 9:14, 15; Mic. 1:13-15). The amount of poetic language found in Joel is unusual for a post-exilic prophet but certainly not unheard of (cf. Zech 9-10).[16]

Various theological arguments sometimes raised as evidence of lateness are also not decisive,[17] though neither can one prove an early date from the thoughts and ideas of the book. If it is postexilic, it is easy to understand the lack of any explicit reference to the salvation of the Gentiles, as in Isaiah and Micah (Isa. 2:1-4; 11:10; Mic. 4:1-5). The Lord encouraged the people who had suffered so much at the hands of the nations by focusing on a time of reckoning for all the peoples of the earth. Of course, Amos and Hosea are also largely silent about the Gentiles (yet cf. Amos 9:12), but neither do they discuss the final judgment of all the nations in the day of the Lord. Some interpreters see a positive word for the Gentiles in Joel 2:28-29 (MT 3:1-2; see exegesis).

Canonical Position

One argument raised by some concerns Joel's position among the twelve Minor Prophets. The end of the collection consists of late preexilic prophets (Nahum, Habakkuk, Zephaniah) followed by postexilic works (Haggai, Zechariah, Malachi), while the beginning consists of the early preexilic books of Hosea, Amos, Jonah, and Micah. Might one not expect Joel, positioned between Hosea and Amos, to be early also? This argument is important for many evangelicals,[18] so we will examine it in some detail.

In Hebrew the entire collection of Minor Prophets is considered one book, called "The Twelve." It is attested in this form as early as the apocryphal book of Ben Sirach (Ecclesiasticus, ca. 190 B.C.): "As for the twelve prophets, may their

---

[14] See J. Alberto Soggin, in *A History of Ancient Israel: From the Beginnings to the Bar Kochba Revolt, A.D. 135*, trans. John Bowden (Philadelphia: Westminster, 1984), pp. 272-73.

[15] Cf. Rudolph, *Joel*, p. 27; S. R. Driver, *The Books of Joel and Amos* CBSC; Cambridge: University, 1907), pp. 24-25.

[16] For a fine example of poetic analysis in a portion of Joel see Elias D. Mallon, "A Stylistic Analysis of Joel 1:10-12," *CBQ* 45 (1983): 537-48.

[17] See E. J. Young, *Introduction to the Old Testament* (Grand Rapids: Eerdmans, 1949), p. 256.

[18] Cf. Leon J. Wood, *The Prophets of Israel* (Grand Rapids: Baker, 1979), p. 267; Patterson, "Joel," 7:231.

bones flower again from the tomb" (49:10; *JB*). However, the sequence of the individual books does not appear to have stabilized until later. LXX attests the order Hosea, Amos, Micah, Joel, Obadiah, Jonah for the first six, with the same order as the MT for the remaining books.

Aside from Joel and Obadiah, whose dates are in dispute, a complete chronological ordering would be: Jonah,[19] Amos, Hosea, Micah, Nahum, Zephaniah, Habakkuk, Haggai, Zechariah, Malachi. Except for the question of whether Hosea precedes Amos or whether Zephaniah or Habakkuk comes first, this order should have been just as obvious to the ancient Jews as it is to modern scholars. Moreover, as we will argue later, Obadiah is most likely to be placed in the early exilic period (see Introduction to Obadiah). Thus, it seems that factors other than chronology operated here.

Haggai and Zechariah form a tight unit with their similar headings and the appearance of their names together in Ezra 5:1. Those who collected the individual prophetic books into one volume probably did so for thematic as well as chronological reasons.[20]

The LXX order has an interesting feature. Except for Malachi, the books that are dated by their headings (Hosea, Amos, Micah, Zephaniah, Haggai, Zechariah) bracket those that have no direct chronological information in their titles. This gives the sequence *dated-undated-dated* (with Malachi at the end). John Barton notes two other ancient variant orders (in *The Ascension of Isaiah* and in *The Lives of the Prophets*) and concludes that there was no "general consensus in ancient times on how the twelve were to be arranged."[21]

The undated books may be ordered by topical criteria. Jonah and Nahum both deal with Nineveh, Habakkuk and Zephaniah with Babylon. Also, Joel and Obadiah, in common with Amos, predict judgment on Edom. Possibly the LXX tended to group the undated books so as not to disturb the order of the first three or of the last four books. In the MT, on the other hand, the tendency to organize topically forced Joel and Obadiah into their present position on either side of Amos. Notice also Joel 3:16 and Amos 1:2.[22]

Jonah's position in the Hebrew is harder to explain. Was it perhaps placed after Obadiah to avoid too harsh a judgment against the Gentiles? Or was it

---

[19] At least for the setting of the book.

[20] Cf. Ronald W. Pierce, "Literary Connectors and a Haggai/Zechariah/Malachi Corpus," *JETS* 27 (1984): 277-89.

[21] John Barton, *Joel and Obadiah: A Commentary* (OTL; Louisville: Westminster John Knox, 2001), p. 117. He cites E. Ben Zvi (*A Historical-Critical Study of the Book of Obadiah* [*BZAW* 242; Berlin 1996]) for his information.

[22] See Hans Walter Wolff, *Joel and Amos* (Hermeneia; trans. Waldemar Janzen, et al.; Philadelphia: Fortress, 1977), pp. 3-4, for similar arguments. Cf. also Gerald T. Sheppard, "Canonization: Hearing the Voice of the Same God through Historically Dissimilar Traditions," *Int* 36 (1982): 21-33, who says, "Though historically the books of Joel and Amos are out of chronological order, they are now ordered and redacted with a hinge between them on the theme of the Day of the Lord" (p. 24). While it is not necessary to accept such thoroughgoing redaction as Sheppard does, his idea of thematic connections in the canon seems sound.

attached chronologically to the era of Amos because of 2 Kings 14:25 (see Amos 1:1)?

Incidentally, the doctrines of inspiration and canonicity deal with the original authors and the books to be included in the Bible, not their sequence. The order of books familiar to the English-speaking church is the product of some development over time.[23]

Literary Connections

One final argument which figures largely in both preexilic and postexilic theories about the date of Joel concerns literary relationships with other prophets. It soon becomes obvious to anyone who takes the time to make comparisons that many of the phrases and ideas in the book of Joel appear elsewhere. Wolff gives a comprehensive listing in his commentary.[24]

Walter Price felt this situation could only mean that Joel preceded the other prophets. Otherwise Joel's integrity would be called into question. Price reasons:

If Joel wrote later, there is no doubt but that he lifted much of his material from his predecessors and incorporated it into his book. He was guilty of plagiarizing Jewish eschatology, whose content was originated by other writers. He purloined their ideas, repeating them in his own book and sometimes using their exact words. If he is the last of the canonical prophets, then Joel trailed all of his predecessors, not only in time but also in the originality of his content.[25]

This would seem at first glance to be a serious objection to a late date for the book of Joel. However, though Price commendably seeks to guard the integrity of Scripture, he really overlooks the nature of OT prophecy. Prophets who are completely original in their expressions are difficult to find. The Hebrews valued traditional language and were not as concerned with originality as Western culture is. Looked at in another way, the Holy Spirit led the various prophets to develop different facets of similar truths in language that appealed to the people. For example, many of the prophets describe the day of the Lord in similar terms (cf. Isa. 13:6; Ezek. 30:2-3; Joel 1:15; 2:1-2; Amos 5:20; Obad. 15; Zeph. 1:15; Mal. 4:1, 5). This process extends even into the NT where the book of Revelation makes numerous allusions to various OT books, often using the same language (e.g., compare Rev. 9:20 with Deut. 4:28; Ps. 135:15-17; Jer. 1:16; Dan. 5:4; Mic. 5:13).

Whether Joel borrowed from other prophets or not, his book stands out as an original statement of the doctrine of the day of the Lord. Wolff, who dates the book even after 400 *B.C.*, says of Joel, "No other Old Testament witness gives it [the day

---

[23] See Otto Eissfeldt, *The Old Testament; An Introduction*, trans. Peter R. Ackroyd (New York: Harper and Row, 1972), pp. 568-70. It seems unlikely that the reference in the Prologue to Ben Sirach really means a three-fold division of the canon in the technical sense as in later Judaism.

[24] Wolff, *Joel and Amos*, pp. 10-11.

[25] Walter K. Price, *The Prophet Joel and the Day of the Lord* (Chicago: Moody, 1976), pp. 14-15.

of the Lord] as detailed and systematic a treatment as he does."[26] Moreover, Joel's language, if late, does not simply mimic what the other prophets say. Careful study shows many turns of phrase that are unique and fresh.

Another literary connection often cited in discussions of the date of Joel is the apparent quotation of Obad. 17 in Joel 2:32 (MT 3:5). If Joel used the formula, "as Yahweh has said," to refer to a quotation, then Obadiah must almost certainly be older. For those who date Obadiah to the period of Jehoram of Judah (848-841 B.C.), the reference would have no effect on the date of Joel. No one has suggested a date earlier than this. However, if Obadiah wrote after 586 B.C. (which seems probable), the quotation would argue strongly for the postexilic date of Joel.

Note, however, that the key here is whether Joel's language actually has to represent a quotation formula. Overt indicators of the quotation of previous material are rare in the OT. Also, the wording between the two passages is not exact. Joel adds "and in Jerusalem." Rudolph (who dates Obadiah later than Joel) explains that when Joel says "just as Yahweh has said," he is referring back to 2:26-27.[27] In the latter passage, the Lord promised that His people would not be put to shame again. Hence, it would amount to the same thing as saying He will permit some in Judah to escape the judgment that comes with the "day of Yahweh."

Conclusion About The Date Of Joel

Calvin said, "as there is no certainty, it is better to leave the time in which [Joel] taught undecided; and, as we shall see, this is of no great importance."[28] That is, the interpretation of the book does not hinge on a precise determination of its date since it deals with such general material.

We know for certain that Joel prophesied sometime between the division of the kingdom and the end of the canonical period (ca. 400 B.C.). If a choice must be made for a more definite period, perhaps the most important evidence would point to a time close to 500 B.C.[29] For instance, the general concerns of the book and historical allusions parallel Haggai and Zechariah, and Temple worship is in place. It might be objected that Zechariah argues against ritual fasting (7:1-7), whereas Joel calls for it. However, Zechariah responds to the insincerity of the people who had turned a time for reflection upon sin and its consequences into a hollow ritual.[30] Joel speaks of a fast due to a special crisis and makes it plain that God expects a heart attitude of repentance. Also, it would appear from an exegesis of Joel 3:1-6 that the prophet refers to the events surrounding the fall of Jerusalem in 586 B.C. as past history.[31]

---

[26] Wolff, *Joel and Amos*, p. 12.

[27] Rudolph, *Joel*, p. 73.

[28] John Calvin, *Joel, Amos, Obadiah* (Commentaries on the Twelve Minor Prophets 2; trans. John Owen; Grand Rapids: Baker, 1981), p. xv.

[29] Cf. G. W. Ahlström, *Joel and the Temple Cult of Jerusalem* (VTSup 21; Leiden: E. J. Brill, 1971), pp. 111-29.

[30] See Kenneth L. Barker, "Zechariah," in *EBC* 7:643-44.

[31] For further analysis of the various possibilities, see John Alexander Thompson, "The Date of Joel," in *A Light unto My Path: Old Testament Studies in Honor of Jacob M. Myers*

Literary Context

Literary Form

Joel, like most of the OT prophets, consists largely of vivid poetry. Only the heading and 3:4-8 are in prose. He probably preached his message before he transcribed it, though he might have adjusted the material some in writing the book.

By means of his well-constructed poems, Joel calls his audience to consider a recent disastrous locust plague, then pleads with them to repent, and finally warns them of dark days ahead. He delivers glad tidings of the Lord's renewed desire to bless them and proclaims a prophecy concerning the last days. His dramatic images draw the reader into personal participation. The passage in 2:1-11 is a poetic allegory, which describes the locusts as a great army under the command of the Lord Himself.

Included among forms that are easily recognizable in the book are "a call to communal lamentation" (1:5-12), a cry of alarm (2:1), a summons to repentance (2:12-17), and an oracle of salvation (2:21-27).[32] The prophet, in common with many other men of God, was capable of delivering both threats of judgment and promises of salvation and blessing. Joel 3:9-12 (MT 4:9-12) apparently reflects language associated with a call to war, but it is used ironically. Much of the language of Joel, as pointed out earlier, was probably traditional in nature. This would be true wherever the book is placed in history, though an earlier date would allow for a higher degree of originality of expression.

Joel moves his readers from horror and hopelessness to mourning and repentance, dread and awe, joy and assurance, hope and expectation. Through Joel the Lord promises dreams and visions with the coming of the Spirit, and already in the book itself one sees visions of locusts that are like lions and an invading army, a Temple that stands empty, a landscape stark as the surface of the moon, a darkness that overwhelms all light, a sky with perplexing signs, mountains with wine and milk pouring down their slopes, and a great judgment of nations in a large valley. Obviously one needs to approach the book with imagination and sensitivity for its poetic features.

A deeper question arises at this point concerning the relationship between the form of the book and its message. Already reference was made to the original oral setting of the presentations. Should we not expect, then, a strong homiletical style in which vivid word pictures prevail and a powerful current of emotions at times overwhelms the teaching? Joel pictures a world perched precariously on the brink of chaos, with nothing to hold it back but the grace of God alone. The reader will do well to reflect long on the utter suitability between forms of expression in Joel and the urgency of his message.

(Gettysburg Theological Studies 4; ed. Howard N. Bream, et al.; Philadelphia: Temple Univ., 1974), pp. 453-64.

[32] For the "call to communal lamentation" and the "cry of alarm," see Wolff, *Joel and Amos*, pp. 21, 39. For the other forms, see Eugene March, "Prophecy," in *Old Testament Form Criticism*, ed. John H. Hayes (San Antonio: Trinity Univ., 1974), pp. 163, 168-69.

Message Of The Book

The prophecy of Joel can be compared to two wheels turning on an axle. The wheels are history and eschatology, while the axle is the day of the Lord. Joel tells us in the first two chapters about a great locust plague and a consequent drought devastating the land of Judah. The effects were so severe that sacrifices could not be provided for the Temple. Was this a sign that God's covenant with Israel had been broken? Did it mean that Judah herself would be swallowed up in the day of the Lord? Joel called on the people to repent based on the covenant characteristics of the Lord – He is gracious, compassionate, slow to anger, abounding in lovingkindness, ready to relent (2:13). If the Lord would relent, the people could hope for a replenishment of the discontinued grain offerings and libations. When the Lord responded to the people's repentance, He renewed the covenant by promising restoration and future blessing.

The last part of the book (2:28-3:21 [MT chaps. 3, 4]) turns to a future time when the Lord will judge the nations and restore Judah and Jerusalem to great prosperity. The locust plague had represented this future day of the Lord as a type. By intertwining the concepts of judgment and the Lord's response to repentance, Joel stresses that, while that day will be utter blackness, God will hear those who call on Him. Thus, the response of the Lord to Judah's repentance during the locust plague also *prefigures* His response to all Israel in the last days. God will destroy the nations who have harmed Judah just as he destroyed the locusts, and he will restore the fortunes of His people just as He made up for the devastation of the locusts.

Outline

I. Locusts in the Land (1:1-14)
    A. Heading (1:1)
    B. Call to Attention (1:2-4)
    C. Call to Mourning (1:5-14)
II. Judgment in the Land (1:15-2:11)
    A. Aftermath of the Locust Invasion (1:15-20)
    B. Invasion of the Lord's Army (2:1-11)
III. Mercy in the Land (2:12-27)
    A. A Call to Repentance (2:12-17)
        1. Appeal to the Character of the Lord (2:12-14)
        2. Appeal for a Solemn Assembly (2:15-17)
    B. The Lord's Response (2:18-27)
IV. Wonders in the Earth (2:28-3:21 [MT 3:1-4:21])
V. Judgment in the Earth (3:1-21 [MT 4:1-21])
    A. The Nations Judged for Their Treatment of Israel (3:1-3 [MT 4:1-3])
    B. Tyre, Sidon and Philistia Sold to the Judeans (3:4-8 [MT 4:4-8])
    C. The Nations Defeated by the Lord but Israel Delivered (3:9-17 [MT 4:9-17])
    D. Judah Blessed but Egypt and Edom Desolated (3:18-21 [MT 4:18-21])

Flow Of The Argument

I. Locusts in the Land (1:1-14). The bipartite structure of Joel derives from two contrasting foci. In the first part Joel concentrates on the land of Judah in the historical present, but in the second part his perspective shifts to the whole earth in the eschatological future.

A. Heading (1:1). The heading of the book informs the reader that the Lord revealed the material to Joel, the son of Pethuel. No reference is made to any historical situation within Israel; the prophet deals with a locust plague and with the coming day of the Lord. Attention focuses immediately on the message itself, not the messenger.

B. Call to Attention (1:2-4). The first part of Joel is organized around a series of commands he gives to the people. First, he asks his audience to listen (1:2-4) to an astonishing report of complete devastation by hordes of locusts.

C. Call to Mourning (1:5-14). Second, Joel calls for a general state of mourning because of what the insects and an accompanying drought have done to the land (1:5-14). As the book progresses, it becomes clear that the sorrow is appropriate not only because of the disaster but also because of sin. Thus, Joel demands fasting and a general assembly to accompany the repentance.

II. Judgment in the Land (1:15-2:11). A lengthy narration intervenes between the first call for fasting and assembly and the final summons to repent (2:12-17). In it Joel envisions the coming of the day of the Lord and describes the locust plague as an invasion by the Lord's army (1:15-2:11). In this way the prophet shows that the condition of the nation is so severe as to signal God's utter rejection of His people. Perhaps they will be overwhelmed and destroyed by this judgment from the Lord.

III. Mercy in the Land (2:12-27). Finally a word of reassurance arrives (2:18-27). The Lord has responded; the land will be restored to its former state. At this point the prophecy consists of calls to rejoice and not to fear, and of the Lord's personal reassurance that He desires to bless the land and its people. God affirms His covenant; the people will know that He is the Lord in their midst.

IV. Wonders in the Earth (2:28-3:21 [MT 3:1-4:21]). How do the historical events at the time of the locust plague relate to the "great and awesome day of Yahweh" in the latter days? If God's people were threatened by the locust plague, how will they fare when He comes to judge all the nations? Judah is small because many of the covenant people live in exile. Will the Lord restore her position among the peoples of the world just as He restored her land after the locust infestation? These are the questions Joel turns to in the second half of his book.

Repentance was necessary before the Lord could remove from the land the damage of the locusts and drought. In the end times He will pour out His Spirit over all Israel (2:28-32 [MT 3:1-5]), bringing His people into a new relationship with their God. Then a fresh outburst of prophetic activity will usher in the day of the Lord with its miraculous displays of divine power in heaven and on earth. The power of the Spirit will draw those who receive Him to call on the Lord's name and thereby escape the judgment that will overtake the nations.

V. Judgment in the Earth (3:1-21 [MT 4:1-21]). When Joel turns to the fate of the world in the latter days, he draws a series of contrasts between Israel and the nations. The Lord desires to bless His people but to judge those who have mistreated them.

   A. *The Nations Judged for Their Treatment of Israel (3:1-3 [MT 4:1-4])*. Four scenes reveal the details of how the Lord will both bless the righteous and judge the wicked. In the first of these Joel announces the basis for judgment: how have "all the nations" treated the Lord's "inheritance" (Israel)? This is, of course, in light of Israel's reception of the Spirit. Since judgment comes for mistreatment of Israel, it is plain that the Lord's people will not themselves be judged.

   B. *Tyre, Sidon and Philistia Sold to the Judeans (3:4-8 [MT 4:4-8])*. In the second scene Phoenicia and Philistia are singled out for special judgment. Because they sold the Judeans into slavery to the Greeks, they in turn will be sold to the former slaves for further sale to the Sabeans. This prophecy of an incident that will happen in history prior to the judgment on all the nations interrupts the general flow of the context, but it highlights the main thought that God will treat the nations differently from Israel. It brings to a climax the emotional tensions felt by Joel's audience. The atrocities described were probably fresh in the minds of the people, and they were longing for the vengeance described to take place.

   C. *The Nations Defeated by the Lord but Israel Delivered (3:9-17 [MT 4:9-17])*. The high point of the third scene finds the Lord roaring from Zion against the nations assembled at the valley of Jehoshaphat for battle. At the same time He is a refuge and stronghold for His people. The time for God's wrath against the nations of this world has arrived at last, and the righteous Israelites inherit the kingdom.

   D. *Judah Blessed but Egypt and Edom Desolated (3:18-21 [MT 4:18-21])*. In the final scene Joel sees the land of Judah overflowing with an abundance of wine and milk. In contrast Egypt and Edom, two traditional enemies, are wastelands. So the reversal in Judah's lowly condition comes about through the physical productivity that had been threatened by the locust plague. The abundant blessings of the millennial kingdom will demonstrate that, at last, justice has been accomplished.

Structural Relations

   The second part of Joel has some interesting correlations with the first part, demonstrating a carefully planned structure. Certain specific comparisons will be brought out in the exegetical discussion, but the broad pattern, which is meant only to be suggestive, is as follows:

Call to Repent (1:2-14)	Gift of the Spirit (2:28-29)
Day of the Lord (1:15-2:2a)	Day of the Lord (2:28-32)
The Lord's Army (2:2b-11)	The Nations' Armies (3:1-3)
The Lord's Covenant Mercy (2:12-14)	The Lord's Covenant Concern (3:4-8)
Call to Repent (2:15-17)	Call to Holy War (3:9-11)
The Lord's Response (2:18-20)	The Lord's Response (3:12-17)
Renewed Blessing (2:21-27)	Renewed Blessing (3:18-21)

   The correspondences depend especially on the principle of reversal. The locusts brought devastation on the land of Judah, but the Spirit will bring a new age of prophecy and blessing. The day of the Lord in the first part of the book threatens to engulf Judah, but in the second part it overwhelms the nations.[33]

Contemporary Context

Joel's discussion of the "latter days" and his emphasis on the day of the Lord contribute to the doctrine of last things (eschatology). His words form part of a larger series of revelations that give substance to the believer's expectations for what the Lord will do in the future. Even though the details will apply specifically to the Jewish people, there is comfort for Christians as well. God makes His Spirit abundantly available in these last days, and He will be a refuge to all who call upon Him (cf. Acts 2:14-39). The practical value of prophecy is discovered when God's people live righteously in the face of opposition and struggle. Prophets like Joel show us the cosmic dimensions of life. God's people can cling to the general and universal promise of Joel that they will find deliverance when the powers of this world are judged.

Yet the value of Joel's prophecy extends beyond its merely prophetic aspects. Several other themes have universal significance. The first half of the book especially brings out the way in which God is actively at work in all aspects of life. Even seemingly "natural" disasters are a part of His plan. Joel does not attempt to explore the precise reasons for the plague. It must be God's work because He controls everything. In the same way, renewed productivity of the land is a sign that God is blessing the people.

The church does not have the same type of covenant relationship with the Lord by which physical prosperity is an automatic sign of His blessing and disaster a sign of His displeasure. However, the believer can see how all things accomplish the purposes of the Lord (Rom. 8:28), working toward a conclusion in the return of Jesus Christ and the setting up of His kingdom. Joel helps to underline God's control of the physical aspects of life in an age that increasingly seeks more scientific explanations. Such explanations are helpful, but Joel would point out that they do not really explain *why*, only *how*.

Joel also teaches the importance of repentance and of regular communication with God. The greatest tragedy of the locust plague consists not in the loss of daily bread but in the breaking of fellowship with God. In a similar way Jesus reiterated the words of Deut. 8:3, "Man shall not live on bread alone" (Matt. 4:4). Can there be any greater tragedy than for those in the church to find their prayers hindered by sin and unrighteousness?

---

[33] For a different structural analysis of Joel see Duane Garrett, *Hosea, Joel* (NAC 19A; [Nashville]: Broadman & Holman, 1997), pp. 301-304. Larry R. McQueen's division of Joel into lament (1:1-2:17), salvation (2:18-3:5), and judgment (4:1-21) is interesting especially for how it ties together 2:18-3:5. However, he seems to oversimplify the "lament" section, which cannot be reduced to one concept so easily (*Joel and the Spirit: The Cry of a Prophetic Hermeneutic* [Sheffield, England: Sheffield Academic Press, 1995], pp. 21-23). See also the detailed analysis of Joel's structure in James L. Crenshaw (*Joel: A New Translation with Introduction and Commentary* [AB 24C; New York: Doubleday, 1995], pp. 29-34).

Finally, it is important to notice Joel's words of joy as well as of woe. Rampant suffering and sorrow in the land indicated to Joel that something was wrong. Gladness and joy ought to be the normal condition of God's people. The products of the land that come through cultivation and work are meant to be abundant and life sustaining. Still, the Christian experiences a deeper joy which goes beyond outward physical circumstances. Nevertheless, all that God provides in life is meant to eventuate in happiness and lasting satisfaction. The conclusions to both parts of Joel's book highlight the God who longs to show His lovingkindness and mercy through good gifts to His people.

1
Locusts in the Land
(Joel 1:1-14)

A. Heading (1:1)

Translation

The word of Yahweh which came to Joel son of Pethuel. (1:1)

Exegesis and Exposition

The heading of the book reveals only two things: this is God's word, and it was delivered through a certain Joel son of Pethuel. As indicated in the introduction, nothing further is known of Joel, though we may speculate he was a priest. Since so many of the prophets give more details in a heading (but cf. Obadiah, Nahum, Habakkuk, and Malachi), it would be appropriate to ask why Joel's is so abbreviated.

Perhaps it simply stresses the general nature of the message. Locusts plagued the land; a prophet called the people to repentance; the Lord responded positively. This pattern of repentance followed by the Lord's mercy holds for any historical circumstance, even for the great day of the Lord when all the world will fall under His judgment.

Many formal devices were used in biblical Hebrew for marking off sections. Since these form part of the biblical text itself, as opposed to later chapter and verse divisions, it is best to follow them for structural information about the text. All of the "Latter Prophets" (the Hebrew division of the canon consisting of Isaiah, Jeremiah, Ezekiel, and "The Twelve") begin with a clearly marked heading which stands apart from the remainder of the book.

Joel's title follows the general structure of several other prophetic books. Observe especially Hos. 1:1; Mic. 1:1; and Zeph. 1:1. דְּבַר יְהוָה (*dĕbar YHWH*, "the word of Yahweh") decisively identifies the divine source of Joel's message. He was not speaking on his own authority but only at the impulse of the Spirit of the Lord. But Joel gives no indicators of the method by which he received the Lord's message. Since *dĕbar* applies to the whole book, here it means something like "message."

The first part of Joel's book (1:1-2:27) is organized around various commands and descriptions which accompany them. The surface structure that results looks something like the following:

Hear this! Pay attention! Tell! (1:2-3) —› Locusts have devoured (1:4)
Awake! (1:5) —› Wine cut off by the invaders (1:5-7)
Wail! (1:8) —› Offerings and libations cut off (1:9-10)
Be ashamed! (1:11)—› All plants and trees have perished (1:11-12)

23

> Wail with sackcloth! Fast! Cry out to yahweh! (1:13-14)
> —› Offerings and libations cut off (1:13b)
> —› The day of yahweh upon us (1:15-2:11)
> Blow a trumpet! Sound an alarm! (2:1) —› A great and mighty people
>   (2:2-11)
> Return to Yahweh! Fast! Weep! Mourn! Rend your garments! (2:12-13)
>   —› He is gracious and compassionate (2:13b-14)
> Sound the alarm! Fast! Proclaim assembly! Gather the people! Set aside
>   a meeting! Gather elders! Assemble everyone! (2:15-17) —›
>   Yahweh responded (2:18-19)
> Fear not! Be glad and rejoice! (2:21) —› Yahweh has done great things
>   (2:21)
> Fear not! (2:22) —› Pastures and trees have come back (2:22)
> Be glad and rejoice! (2:23) —› Yahweh has given a sign of restoration
>   (2:23-27)

The second half of the book (2:28-3:21 [MT 3-4]) is organized rather around phrases more typical of prophetic books:

> And it will come about afterward ... (3:1)
> For behold! In those days and at that time ... (4:1)
> And it will come about in that day ... (4:18)

The reason is clear enough. In the first part Joel calls the people to repentance, while in the second part he delivers messages about the future by quoting Yahweh directly. Only in 3:9-13 do we find commands, but they are issued by Yahweh Himself. Notice also the unique segment in 3:4-8 where Yahweh interrogates the guilty nations.

B. Call To Attention (1:2-4)

Translation

Hear this, elders,
and give ear, all who live in the land.
Has this ever happened in your days?
or in the days of your fathers?
³Tell about it to your children,
and your children to their children,
and their children to a later generation.
⁴What has been left by the gnawing locust the swarming locust has eaten;
What has been left by the swarming locust the creeping locust has eaten;
What has been left by the creeping locust the stripping locust has eaten.
(1:2-4)

Exegesis and Exposition

Joel's call for the leaders of the people to listen to his words and repeat them to their children brings to mind the instructions of Moses in Deut. 6. The Israelites were perpetually to tell their children about the great commandment to love the Lord with all one's heart. Thus, the book of Joel has a didactic function. The locusts and drought threatened the existence of Judah, but repentance would make it possible for God to restore them. Therefore, the severity of the catastrophe and the greatness of the deliverance were to be imprinted on the minds of all future generations.

The literary structure of the book of Joel should be noted carefully. The calls for mourning and fasting must have been given during Joel's preaching ministry. At the end of that initial ministry, a narrative section (2:18-19)[1] informs us that God took pity on the people and removed the plague from their land. A possible implication from the context is that Joel's preaching led to national repentance. Thus, the locust plague, the preaching of Joel, and the Lord's response in renewing the land comprise the full sequence of events that Joel calls the people to consider in his opening words.

Our prophet engenders a certain tension by plunging immediately into the preaching without any narrative framework. Yet vv. 2-3 presuppose the entire account. How can the people hope to tell these things to future generations unless it has been established that there will be a future? The locust plague brought the nation so close to destruction it foreshadowed the imminent onset of the day of the Lord. The command to make these events a part of the traditions means the judgment has been stayed for now.

1:2a When Joel calls his listeners to "hear ... and give ear" (וְהַאֲזִינוּ...שִׁמְעוּ, šimeʿû ... weha'ăzînû), he follows a pattern familiar from prophetic and other forms of elevated speech (Gen. 4:23; Num. 23:18; Deut. 32:1; Judg. 5:3; Ps. 49:1 [MT 49:2]; 84:8 [MT 84:9]; Isa. 1:2, 10; 32:9; Hos. 5:1). It is striking to see זְקֵנִים (zĕqēnîm, "elders") combined this way with כֹּל יוֹשְׁבֵי הָאָרֶץ (kōl yôšĕbê hā'āreṣ, "all inhabitants of the land"; cf. 1:14). The parallel construction implies, "Let all the leaders hear what I have to say. In fact, let the whole community listen."

Rudolph applies zĕqēnîm to old people rather than to the leadership.[2] It does mean "old men" in Joel 2:28 (MT 3:1) and possibly 2:16, but in those passages other classifications based on age occur. "Leaders/people" seems a more natural combination than "old people/people." The same term in Joel 1:14 also means "elders."

1:2b After summoning the attention of his audience, Joel proceeds to summarize his message with a rhetorical question by which he strengthens the impression of complete devastation found in the following verses. The question can be resolved into something like, "This is the worst thing that has ever happened to us." Also, the ambiguity of זֹאת (zō't, "this") when as yet it has no referent heightens the tension.

1:3 The events are so stunningly evidential of the Lord's work in the nation that the people must pass them down from generation to generation. Historical memory of the deeds of the Lord is a significant part of what parents are required to

---

[1] There is dispute about whether these verses narrate the past or predict future events (cf. NASB and NIV). See the exegesis on 2:18-19 for detailed argumentation in favor of the narration view.

[2] Wilhelm Rudolph, *Joel - Amos - Obadja - Jona* (KAT 13:2; Gütersloh: Gütersloher Verlagshaus Gerd Mohn, 1971), p. 41.

pass along to their children. For Christians this includes not only the events of Scripture but also God's more recent actions in the church.

1:4 Verse 1:4 contrasts with 2:14. The locusts leave nothing, but as for the Lord, "Who knows? Perhaps He will turn and relent, and leave a blessing behind Him." The stripping away of everything from the land shows that God's covenant blessing has been withdrawn.

The repetition of the pattern, "what has been left by X, Y has eaten," makes the reader think of a progression of different types or stages of locusts. Since 2:25 refers to "the years" that these various locusts ruined, the catastrophe must have occurred over an extended period of time. Wolff gives a detailed discussion of biological as well as contextual factors here.[3] His translations, based on the idea of separate developmental stages of the locusts, are as follows: "biter" for גָּזָם (gāzām); "locust" for אַרְבֶּה ('arbeh); "hopper" for יֶלֶק (yeleq); and "jumper" for חָסִיל (ḥasîl). Compare also Douglas Stuart: "full-grown locust ... adult locust ... infant locust ... young locust."[4]

Many commentators agree that Joel describes a literal locust plague in the first chapter, though there is much more dispute about the second chapter. The suggestion has also been made (Stuart) that even in the first chapter the locusts stand for an invading army, either the Assyrians or the Babylonians.[5] While there may be elements of hyperbole in Joel's description of the locust plague, as when he asks rhetorically whether anything like this has happened before, the poetic language reflects a manner of expression common among the Hebrews (cf. 2 Kings 18:5 and 23:25).[6] Locust plagues were greatly feared, and this particular one could have been unusually severe.

In our view, then, the details of the description in chap. 1 call for a real infestation of locusts, though Joel sees the harsh consequences of the plague as a foreshadowing of worse things to come. Today the people need to contend with locusts; tomorrow they may need to suffer the woes of the day of the Lord.

C. Call To Mourning, Fasting, And Public Assembly (1:5-14)

Translation

Awake, drunkards, and weep.

---

[3] Hans Walter Wolff, *Joel and Amos* (Hermeneia; trans. Waldemar Janzen, et al.; Philadelphia: Fortress, 1977), pp. 27-28.

[4] Stuart, *Hosea-Jonah* (WBC 31; Waco, Tex.: Word, 1987), p. 237.

[5] Ibid., pp. 232-34.

[6] G. B. Caird, *The Language and Imagery of the Bible* (Philadelphia: Westminster, 1980), p. 110, observes that "hyperbole or overstatement is a figure of speech common to all languages. But among the Semitic peoples its frequent use arises out of a habitual cast of mind, which I have called absoluteness – a tendency to think in extremes without qualification, in black and white without intervening shades of grey." One must be cautious not to overestimate the principle of hyperbole when interpreting the text, but it was a figure of speech used often by Jesus (cf. Matt. 5:29-30).

Yes, wail, all drinkers of wine,
for the new wine,
because it is cut off from you.
[6]For a nation has come up against My land,
mighty and without number.
Its teeth are lion's teeth;
even the fangs of a lioness it has.
[7]It has made My vine a waste,
and My fig tree splinters.
It stripped it bare and cast it aside;
its tendrils turned white.
[8]*Wail like a virgin clad with sackcloth
for the husband of her youth.
[9]Cut off are grain offering and libation
from Yahweh's house.
The priests mourn,
the ministers of *Yahweh.
[10]The field is ruined;
the ground parched.
Indeed the grain is ruined;
the new wine completely dried up;
the fresh oil exhausted.
[11]Be ashamed, farmers.
Wail, vinedressers,
for the wheat and for the barley,
because the field's harvest is lost.
[12]The vine has completely dried up,
and the fig tree has withered.
The pomegranate, also the date palm and apricot –
all the trees of the field are dry.
Indeed, rejoicing has completely dried up
from the sons of men.
[13]Gird yourselves and lament, priests.
Wail, ministers of the altar.
Come stay the night in sackcloth,
ministers of *my God.
For withheld from the house of your God
is grain offering and libation.
[14]Consecrate a fast!
Call for a solemn assembly!
Gather the elders
and all who live in the land
to the house of *Yahweh your God,
and cry out to Yahweh.

Exegesis and Exposition

Joel begins his preaching with a series of commands to the people, calling them to a period of deep mourning, fasting, and public assembly. The devastation of the locusts demands such drastic action, for the people could not survive on what the locusts left behind, but neither could they continue to offer sacrifices to the Lord. Hence, the very bond between God and people provided by the covenant was threatened.

When fasting is mentioned, it is clear that the mourning is for sin as well as for the tragedy that has struck the nation. In his final appeal Joel calls explicitly for repentance and prayer to the Lord (2:12-17). Between the two parts of his admonitions, however, he compares the magnitude of the disaster to the day of the Lord (1:15-2:11). The only thing that might possibly avert such final judgment is a time of national lamentation and fasting; thus the urgency in the pleas to the people.

The section divides into two parts. First, vv. 5-12 call for grieving and mourning because of the tragedy, and second, vv. 13-14 introduce the burden of Joel's prophecy – the people of Judah must repent in response to what God has done.

1:5 In light of the remainder of the chapter, Joel's command to the drunkards in v. 5 functions primarily to describe the desperate situation. Its focus is on the paucity of produce, not on the nation-wide problem of drunkenness. Those addicted to wine go to great lengths to obtain it (cf. Prov. 23:35), but not even they are able to find any.

The parallel to the drunkards, "all who drink wine" (יָיִן שֹׁתֵי־כָּל, *kol-šōtê yāyin*), most likely refers to a broader audience than drunkards. The latter group will be the most adversely affected, but even the occasional wine drinker will need to bewail his loss. Such an interpretation illustrates the tendency in Hebrew poetry for the second of two parallel lines to intensify or extend in some way the first line (see below on v 6b).

1:6a At this point Joel anticipates the detailed description of the locust invasion in chap. 2. He speaks of a "nation" (גּוֹי, *gôy*), though the reference to locusts is clear. Eventually the prophet will reveal that the insects foreshadow the time when the Lord will bring an invading army during the "great and awesome day of Yahweh" (2:31 [MT 3:4]). Joel's language skillfully evokes both images.

Since God is the speaker in these verses (cf. 1:1), "My land" (אַרְצִי, *'arṣî*) identifies Judah and Jerusalem as uniquely the Lord's (cf. "My holy mountain," 2:1). The NASB evidently referred the phrase to Joel ("my" in lowercase). In defense of this, one could appeal to the occurrence of "my God" in v. 13. However, the Lord frequently designates Israel as "My land" in the prophets (Jer. 2:7; 16:18; Ezek. 36:5; 38:16; Joel 3:2).

עָצוּם (*'āṣûm*, "mighty") nearly always occurs in a context of great numbers (cf. Num. 32:1; Deut. 26:5; Ps. 35:18; Prov. 7:26; Isa. 60:22; Amos 5:12). The idea of might derives from the power of a collective force ("strength in numbers"). Locust plagues are destructive because of their great size.

1:6b Joel uses hyperbole when he says the locusts have teeth that are like those of lions. By this figure of speech he focuses upon the gnawing power of the

locusts. Since the lioness (לָבִיא, *lābî'*) actually kills the prey, her teeth (מַחְלְעוֹת,
metallĕ'ôt, "fangs") are more fearsome than those of the male lion.

These lines of poetry display an instance of "synonymous" parallelism.
Contrary to a popular misconception, this does not usually mean merely restating
"the same thing" in different words. In this case the rare and more specific term,
metallĕ'ôt, in the second line heightens the effect by focusing.[7] As one takes a
closer look at the insects, one sees not simply "lion's teeth," but the very sharp
"fangs" used by the lioness for dispatching her victim.

1:7 General descriptions of complete devastation of the trees precede a more
detailed picture of the locusts stripping off their bark, laying bare the white
interior. Even though the plague and its effects are literal, the sequence "My land
… My vine … My fig tree" was surely intended to evoke the thought of Judah and
the people who inhabited it.[8] Fruitful vines and fig trees represented the blessing of
the Lord on the land (1 Kings 4:25 [MT 5:5]; Mic. 4:4; Zech. 3:10). For example,
speaking through Isaiah, the Lord called Judah "My vineyard" (see 5:1-7). The
current devastation of the vineyard means that God has taken the blessing from His
people.

1:8 The text in v. 8 does not say who should wail, but אֱלִי ('ĕlî) has the form
for addressing a woman (see Additional Notes). The Targum interpreted this, "O
assembly of Israel, make lamentation!"[9] This gives a good clue to the correct
meaning, since the Israelites are often personified as a woman (Isa. 37:22; Jer.
14:17; 18:13; 31:4; Amos 5:2; Zech. 2:10 [MT 2:14]; 9:9).

The "virgin" (בְּתוּלָה, *bĕtûlâ*) could have a "husband" (בַּעַל, *ba'al*) in that the
man was legally her spouse once the bridal price had been paid to her father (Deut.
22:22-29).[10] Joel's simile envisions a tragic scene: while the virgin waited
expectantly for the day when her husband would "take" her to his home (Deut.
20:7), he suddenly died. That is the depth of the sorrow Joel attempts to bring out.

Sackcloth (שַׂק, *śaq*) was made of goat's or camel's hair and worn during a
time of mourning (cf. Gen. 37:34; 2 Sam. 3:31; Isa. 22:12; Amos 8:10). Goat hair
would often be black, and either material could feel rough and uncomfortable if
placed next to the body. Perhaps its simplicity also contributed to its symbolic
association with mourning or with social protest.[11]

1:9 The priests at the Temple depended on the grain offerings and libations
(Lev. 2:2, 9, 16), even as the virgin who needed a husband. She was now a widow
lacking support, and the priests were in similar straits. It may be also that the
reference in the previous verse to the "virgin" and the "husband" of her youth is

---

[7] See Robert Alter, *The Art of Biblical Poetry* (New York: Basic Books, 1985), p. 120.

[8] Cf. גופני עמי (*gûpnê 'ammî*, "the vines of my people") in some Targum
manuscripts. All quotations from the Targum (Tg. Neb.) represent the author's own
translations from Alexander Sperber, ed., "The Latter Prophets according to Targum
Jonathan," vol. 3 in *The Bible in Aramaic* (Leiden: E. J. Brill, 1962).

[9] כנשתא דישראל עבידי אליא (*kĕništā' dĕyiśrā'ēl 'ăbîdî 'ilyā'*).

[10] See Wolff, *Joel and Amos*, p. 30, for a detailed discussion.

[11] For further details, see L. G. Herr, "Sackcloth," *ISBE*, rev. ed., 4:256.

meant to evoke the relationship between the Lord and Judah. Then the plight of the priests in the Lord's house brings the figurative allusion into reality.

For the people as a whole, the lack of grain offerings (מִנְחָה, *minḥâ*) and libations (נֶסֶךְ, *nesek*) pointed to God's rejection of them. The grain offerings normally followed the burnt offering and probably signified the worshiper's thankfulness and acknowledgment of restored relationship with the Lord.[12] Libations of wine evidently were a frequent accompaniment to various types of offering (cf. Lev. 23:13; Num. 15:5; 28:7). For the average Judean, accustomed to presenting on a regular basis a portion of the harvest, it must have been quite a shock to be unable to supply the Lord's portion, let alone have enough left to live on.

מְשָׁרְתֵי יהוה (*mĕšārĕtê YHWH*, "ministers of Yahweh") describes the priests more closely (see Additional Notes for a variant in LXX). They are those who perform the service before the Lord in the Temple. Joel attaches the phrase here to focus the scene even further. The priests, who are no less than those who attend to the Lord through offering and libation, have gone into deep mourning (אָבְלוּ, *'ābĕlû*; cf. on v. 10 below). The Targum's rendering, "the priests who serve in the house of the sanctuary of the Lord,"[13] makes the parallel line descriptive.

1:10 For stylistic and thematic reasons, 1:10-12 can be regarded as a discrete unit within the larger section of 1:5-14. Verse 9 concludes with the introduction of the priests, and v. 13 returns to them. A high number of word plays and patterns based on sound further serve to bind the unit together and give it aesthetic appeal.[14] After Joel first introduces the problem of no agricultural products for sacrifices at v. 9, he then gives a detailed description of that agricultural disaster before making a plea for prayer and fasting.

The verb אָבְלָה (*'ābelâ*) is defined as "mourn" or "lament" in the BDB lexicon. However, the use of יָבֵשׁ (*yābēš*, "be dry") elsewhere as its poetic reflection (Jer. 12:4; 23:10; Amos 1:2), plus the related Akkadian term *abālu* ("dry up"), fully justify the KB lexicon's addition of the meaning, "*vertrocknen* dry up" (cf. NIV; also KBRev). The Targum has "dried up" or "ruined," while LXX and Peshitta follow the idea of "mourn."[15] Notice once more the intensifying power of the poetic structure. Not only are the fields ruined; even the very ground is parched.

It might appear as though כִּי (*kî*, "for"), which introduces the following line, would support the more traditional rendering of *'ābelâ*, "The land *mourns*, / *for* the grain is ruined" (NASB). However, while *'ābal* as applied to people can mean "mourn," it does not seem to have that meaning (in the qal pattern) when referring

---

[12] See Gordon J. Wenham, *The Book of Leviticus* (NICOT; Grand Rapids: Eerdmans, 1979), pp. 69-72.

[13] כהניא דמשמשין בבית מקדשא דיוי (*kāhănayyā' dimĕšammĕšîn bebêt maqdĕšā' daYWY*).

[14] Elias D. Mallon, "A Stylistic Analysis of Joel 1:10-12," *CBQ* 45 (1983): 537-48.

[15] Throughout the commentary, the edition of Joseph Ziegler, ed., *Septuaginta*, 2d ed. (G"ottingen: Vandenhoeck & Ruprecht, 1967), is followed for LXX. For the Peshitta, see *The Old Testament in Syriac according to the Peshitta Version* (Leiden: E. J. Brill, 1980).

to the land (see Additional Notes). Some recent commentators regard the *kî* as "emphatic," as in the translation given above ("Indeed the grain is ruined"; cf. *kî* in 1:12).[16] Movement from the general ("field" and "ground") to the particular (products of the ground) might also account for the use of *kî*. The lack of productivity evidences the dryness of the ground.

In the phrase, תִּירוֹשׁ שׁ הוֹבִישׁ (*hôbîš tîrôš*, "the new wine completely dries up"), *hôbîš* is best related to the root meaning "become dry" (יבשׁ, *ybš*). Leslie Allen argues for the sense "be ashamed" (root בושׁ, *bwš*), since the same word has that meaning in v. 11.[17] However, his translation, "the wine is in a sorry state," would seem to understate the current crisis. The point is that there is no wine, not that it is poor in quality. In line with this, Mallon sees the hiphil form of *ho'bîš* as elative, giving the sense "completely" or "thoroughly dried up."[18]

1:11 *Hobîšû* ("be ashamed") and הֵילִילוּ (*hê'lîlû*, "wail") can be interpreted either as commands or as statements (cf. NASB margin). The same ambiguity exists in the Targum and Peshitta, while LXX has a statement for the first verb but a command for the second. The close parallel in grammatical structure between vv. 5 and 11, however, argues convincingly for translating both verbs as imperatives. This fits well with the overall structure of the first part of Joel, as outlined above (see under A).

The failure of the harvest humiliates the farmers; they have nothing to show for their work. Consequently, they too should participate in ritual mourning, a rite that shows shame as well as sorrow (cf. Jer 48:1-5). Possibly, as Wolff suggests, the term for shame was chosen because of its similarity in sound to the Hebrew term for "dry up."[19] Likewise, the vinedressers need to wail because they have failed to harvest a crop.

1:12a-b Twice previous to v. 12 the hiphil pattern of the root יבשׁ (*ybš*) occurred with the meaning "dry up" (an intransitive use of the hiphil); now the same root is in the qal pattern. Aside from the "elative" use of the hiphil posited above, Mallon thinks the qal is used here in order to get a patterning of vowels with the two previous words.[20] In any case, the final statement sums up what has happened: the trees cannot produce any fruit because they have been destroyed by the locusts.

---

[16] Wolff, *Joel and Amos*, p. 19; Stuart, *Hosea-Jonah*, p. 237. Anneli Aejmelaeus notes that "emphatic" function is "hardly probable" for a connective particle. He follows W. T. Claassen, "Function and Interpretation of כי in Biblical Hebrew," *JBL* 105 (1986): 195, 203, in using the label "evidential," in that the *kî* states "the *reason for saying*" the main clause rather than "the cause for *what* is actually said." While Aejmelaeus's observation is linguistically sound, "indeed" as a *translation* for *kî* in some "evidential" uses still seems less misleading to an English reader than "for" or "because" (KBRev still lists an "emphatic" category, 2:470).

[17] Leslie C. Allen, *The Books of Joel, Obadiah, Jonah and Micah* (NICOT; Grand Rapids: Eerdmans, 1976), p. 47 n. 9.

[18] Mallon, "Stylistic Analysis of Joel 1:10-12," p. 542 n. 15.

[19] Wolff, *Joel and Amos*, p. 32.

[20] Mallon, "Stylistic Analysis of Joel 1:10-12," p. 544.

The terms for the pomegranate (רִמּוֹן, *rimmôn*) and the date palm (תָּמָר,
tāmār) have been identified, but תַּפּוּחַ (*tappûaḥ*) is less certain. Some modern
versions call it the apple tree (cf. NASB and NIV), but perhaps a better guess would
be the apricot (margin of NASB). Wild apple trees may have grown in ancient
Palestine, but the fruit would not have been very tasty. "Apricot" is itself uncertain
but seems to meet the botanical and contextual requirements.[21]

1:12c At the end of v. 12 the prophet once more brings out the close
relationship of the people to the land with a play on words. The term *hobîs* is used
alternately of either "shame" or of "drying up." Any joy (שָׂשׂוֹן, *śāśôn*) found in the
land dries up as surely as the trees and various plants of the field. Both sorrow and
shame fill the void that is left (cf. 2:26, 27).

1:13a Prior to v. 13 the priests or ministers were said to be in mourning (v. 9);
here they are commanded to take up the type of lamentation that is appropriate for
repentance and supplication. The present verse thus marks a turning point. Joel
addresses these individuals in order to draw the community into a demonstration of
humble dependence on God.

1:13b This attitude of mourning should continue throughout the night (לִינוּ,
lînû, "spend the night"). It is not a time for normal activities in the Temp le,
followed by a night of sleep. Twenty-four hour vigilance is necessary to meet the
emergency.

Some interesting distinctions may be observed in this verse. "Sackcloth" is
not mentioned immediately as the garment to be worn. The priests are first
commanded to "gird on," then later to "spend the night in sackcloth." In this way
all the actions are tied together as a tight unit. Also, the priests become "ministers
of my God" (see Additional Notes for a variant in LXX). Joel appeals to all,
including himself, through the pronouns selected: "my," "your" (see below), and
"our" (v. 16).

1:13c A close verbal similarity exits between vv. 9a and 13c. One important
difference is that the Temple is here called "the house of *your* God." This serves to
remind the priests of their responsibility to perform the sacrifices that maintain
God's relationship with His people. But if there are no grain offerings and
libations, God must be very displeased. נִמְנַע (*nimnaʿ*, "withheld") implies that the
Lord Himself has done it (cf. Neh. 9:20; Amos 4:7). Thus, Joel calls on the
religious leaders to set the example and stir up the people to similar action.

1:14a It is interesting that Joel should call for a fast in 1:14. The prophets
rarely mentioned fasting except to condemn it (Isa. 58:3, 4; Jer. 14:12; Zech. 7:5).
Though Jer. 36:6, 9 narrates an occasion of a national fast without making any
judgmental comment, note that even as the people are fasting, the king is burning
Jeremiah's book! The ritual of fasting had become a replacement for righteous
behavior. Admittedly Joel acts differently than the other prophets when he calls for
fasting rather than for repentance from specific sins, but he does call for a genuine
attitude of repentance to accompany it (2:12).

---

[21] *Fauna and Flora of the Bible* (Helps for Translators 11; London: United Bible
Societies, 1972), pp. 92-93. See also J. C. Trever, "Apple," *IDB* 1:175-76, who argues for
"quince" for *tappûaḥ*.

Joel's words balance some of the other prophetic statements. God is displeased when mere ritual is seen as a magical means of manipulating Him. Prophets such as Amos, Isaiah, and Zechariah rightly spoke against such misuse of established religion. Joel reminds the people, however, that rituals can be an appropriate method for demonstrating inward sorrow for sin and a desire to change. Fasting and the solemn assembly were proper ways for the community to show humility and submission to God in the face of national disaster, as long as they reflected reality faithfully.

1:14b Previously Joel called on the elders and all the inhabitants of the land to pay attention to the Lord's word (1:2). When he calls upon them again in the present verse, it serves as a literary device known as "inclusio." That is, it marks the beginning and ending of the segment, with v. 15 the start of a new section.

The lack of a conjunction (in the Hebrew) between the two segments of the population (elders and inhabitants) is an unusual construction. It has led some to think the command is directed to the elders. That is, "Assemble, O elders, all the inhabitants of the land."[22] But it is the priests who have been directed to proclaim the fast and solemn assembly. While the asyndeton is unusual, it is not impossible and may be present for dramatic effect. Syntactically, the clause should be understood as, "Gather the elders, (and gather) all the inhabitants." The Syriac Peshitta, like many modern versions, solved the problem by adding the word "and" before "all."

1:14c At the climax of this section, Joel calls on the people to "cry out" (זַעֲקוּ, za‘ăqû) to Yahweh. Zā‘aq could be used of a national plea for deliverance directed to God (Ex. 2:23; Ps. 22:4-5 [MT 22:5-6]). The narrator of Judges used it in describing the repentance of the people that preceded the appearance of a new judge (Judg. 3:9, 15; 6:6, 7; 10:10). The term occurs in the Psalms on a more personal level (Ps. 142:1, 5 [MT vv 2, 6]). As with fasting, the Lord would not respond if the attitude of the heart was insincere (Hos. 7:14; 8:2; Mic. 3:4).

Additional Notes

1:8 אֱלִי: In the Peshitta this *hapax legomenon* is glossed with a Syriac cognate meaning "to mourn." The cognate in the Targum occurs in the form of a noun: עֲבִידִי אֶלְיָא ("make lamentation"). LXX seems to have read the Hebrew as "to me" (θρήνησον πρός με), though it may be that a double interpretation of the same word is involved. Perhaps the lack of an addressee occasioned the peculiar interpretation found in LXX. Wolff proposes a rearrangement of MT, though he admits the tentative nature of his suggestion.[23]

בְּתוּלָה: The term probably indicates a young woman of marriageable age, though in some contexts it can include lack of sexual experience (Deut. 22:17).[24] עַלְמָה seems to have a similar semantic range, though it is a rarer term.

---

[22] So S. M. Lehrman, "Joel," in *The Twelve Prophets* (Soncino Books of the Bible; ed. A. Cohen; London: Soncino, 1969), p. 63. Cf. Rudolph, *Joel*, p. 39, who feels "elders" was added to the text later, with the understanding that they were to do the gathering.

[23] Wolff, *Joel and Amos*, p. 18 n. i.

[24] *TDOT* 2:340-42.

1:9 מְשָׁרְתֵי יהוה: LXX reads οἱ λειτουργοῦντες θυσιαστηρίῳ, presumably reflecting מְשָׁרְתֵי הַמִּזְבֵּחַ, a reading accepted by some commentators.[25] Possibly the second יהוה of MT was influenced by the first occurrence, but it could also be that the *Vorlage* of LXX was influenced by v. 13a. Except for the heading the name יהוה occurs for the first time in v. 9. The double reference to the covenant name would strengthen the anxiety Joel wants to arouse. Read with MT.

1:10 אָבְלָה אֲדָמָה: The correct understanding of אָבַל depends chiefly on its grammatical form. The hithpael and the verbal nouns אֵבֶל and אָבֵל always refer to mourning. If the subject of a qal form is human, the verb also means consistently "to mourn." When the subject is inanimate, however, none of the examples listed in BDB must be taken in this way, and many of them quite obviously are connected with the idea of dryness (e.g. Isa. 24:4; Jer. 4:22; Amos 1:2). In fact, all of the instances could be explained as "become dry" or the like. Only Lam. 2:8 and Ezek. 31:15 are listed for the hiphil, and while BDB translates "cause to mourn" one could just as easily render "cause to decline" for the former passage and "cause to dry up" for the latter.

תִּירוֹשׁ: It is uncertain whether תִּירוֹשׁ was fermented. In Hos. 4:11 it is included with "harlotry" and "wine," which "take away the understanding." On the other hand, in Joel 2:24 the vats "overflow with the new wine."[26]

1:11 הֹבִישׁוּ: It seems certain from the context that הֹבִישׁוּ, addressed to the "farmers" (אִכָּרִים), must mean "demonstrate shame." Yet the form suggests the root יָבֵשׁ rather than בּוֹשׁ. Evidently a biform of the latter root also meant "shame" in certain parts of the hiphil pattern (attested only with forms that have a prefixed *he*).[27] See BDB for further references, but note also that while they appear to claim that all the ancient versions have a form related to the root בּוֹשׁ, the Targum reads בהיתו ("be ashamed") for Joel 1:11 and LXX has ᾔσχυναν for 1:12. Possibly the pattern used by Joel developed by analogy from the hiphil of יָבֵשׁ in the meaning "wither" or "dry up."

1:13 אֱלֹהָי: LXX reads θεῷ, implying אֱלֹהִים. MT has the more difficult reading and should be accepted.

1:14 בֵּית יהוה אֱלֹהֵיכֶם: LXX omits any equivalent for יהוה, evidently on the pattern of בֵּית אֱלֹהֵיכֶם in v. 13.

---

[25] Wolff, *Joel and Amos*, p. 18 n. l; Stuart, *Hosea-Jonah*, p. 238.

[26] Cf. R. Laird Harris, *TWOT* 2:969.

[27] Cf. Francis I. Andersen, "Biconsonantal Byforms of Weak Hebrew Roots," *ZAW* 82 (1970): 273.

2
Judgment in the Land
(Joel 1:15-2:11)

Joel interrupts his call for national repentance with a description of the devastating effects of the locust plague and the drought which followed it. He also introduces the motif of the approaching day of the Lord. The aftermath of the catastrophes conjures up the image of the final destruction associated with this great and awesome day which is foreseen by various OT prophets (see exegesis of 2:31 [MT 3:4]).

Then, to heighten the sense that Judah herself might be swallowed up in that day, the prophet compares the locust infestation to an invasion by the Lord's army (2:1-11). If Joel wrote to a postexilic audience, his description would have evoked memories of the dreadful attack by the Babylonian army. Joel's listeners would be asking themselves, "Is the present catastrophe any less severe? Will the Lord destroy His people off the face of the earth?"

Several formal considerations mark off 2:1-11 as a distinct unit from 1:15-20. The verbs in the latter passage occur mostly as "perfects," either to describe current conditions ("How the beasts *groan!*" v. 18) or to refer to the damage as accomplished fact ("fire *has consumed* the pastures of the wilderness," v. 19). In 2:1-11 the verbs are mostly "imperfects." Generally, the modern versions translate with descriptive present tenses in these cases ("they run like mighty men," v. 7). Some prefer to explain the imperfects as future tense, a reference to a future invasion by an army (see exegesis below). However, perfects also occur ("a fire *consumes*," v. 3; "Yahweh *utters* his voice," v. 11), and the imperfects occur always with verbs that depict actions of the locusts or of the people of Jerusalem ("run," "skip," "tremble," "climb," and so on). For describing what fire, the land, the sky, the sun, or the moon does or what the faces do, either perfects or participles are used. Only one exception occurs. In v. 3 an imperfect in the second half of the line parallels a perfect in the first half: "Before it a fire *consumes* [perfect],/ And after it a flame *burns* [imperfect]." A pattern like this points to the descriptive nature of the passage. When Joel focuses on the actions of the chief characters, he uses the more vivid imperfect forms that capture the deeds in progress.

The extended metaphor found in 2:1-11 also sets it apart from 1:15-20. Our prophet deepens the sense of gloom by moving from a literal comparison between the disaster and the day of the Lord to a figure in which the locusts become the fearful army of Yahweh in the great day of His judgment.

Finally, one may note a contrast between the sharp focus on the day of the Lord in 2:1-11 and the more general reference to that time in 1:15-20. It is only mentioned once in v. 15. The rest of the passage resumes the description of 1:4-12, only without its numerous commands.

One could argue for a major break in the thought to be placed at 2:1 rather than at 1:15. Yet when Joel mentions the day of the Lord for the first time in 1:15, it surely indicates an important new thrust, especially since that day figures so prominently throughout the book. Thus, it appears better to see 2:1-11 as intensification of the motif introduced at 1:15.

A. The Aftermath Of The Locust Invasion (1:15-20)

Translation

Alas for the day!
For the day of Yahweh is near,
 and as destruction from the Almighty it comes.
[16]Is not food cut off before our eyes,
from the house of our God joy and gladness?
[17]The seeds shrivel
under their clods.
Storehouses are devastated;
granaries are torn down,
 because the grain has dried up.
[18]How the livestock groan!
The herds of cattle are in confusion,
 for they have no pasture.
Even the flocks of sheep are *devastated.
[19]To You, Yahweh, I call,
for a fire has devoured the wilderness pasture,
and a flame has ignited all the trees of the field.
[20]Even the livestock of the field pant for You;
for the water channels are dried up,
and fire has consumed the wilderness pastures.

Exegesis and Exposition

Joel surveys the devastation of his country and realizes how close final destruction from the Lord is. The lack of food has affected man and beast alike. Worst of all, it must be that the Lord has brought this judgment to show He has withdrawn His presence. No joyous sounds echo through God's house, and even the wild animals yearn for His presence.

Thus the tension rises: does this ruin mean the day of the Lord has arrived? Will the people become completely separated from their God? The stress is nearly unbearable when Joel identifies the locusts with the Lord's army, but then the rest of the book shows a way out of the dilemma. First, when the call for repentance is renewed and the Lord responds, God's grace and mercy become apparent. Second, when Joel turns to the "great and awesome day of Yahweh," it becomes clear that Israel, by the power of God's Spirit, will be delivered.

1:15 אֲהָהּ (*ăhāh*) normally expresses shocked dismay (cf. Josh. 7:7; Judg. 6:22; 2 Kings 3:10; Jer. 1:6; Ezek. 4:14). It imitates the sound someone makes when the wind is knocked out. Joel has this strong reaction as he contemplates "the day of Yahweh" (יהוה יוֹם, *yôm YHWH*). The repetition of "the day" heightens further the sense of awe and dread. Joel knows the terror of the locusts in his own day, but he sees an even more frightening day that is "near" (קָרוֹב, *qārôb*) but not yet present.

The awful present cannot be described in any more desperate terms: it is the harbinger of the day of the Lord. Joel first describes that coming era as a completion of the tragedy begun in the locust plague. "We are in a state of total ruin now," says Joel. "What will happen when the day of Yahweh comes upon us?"

The Hebrew at the end of v. 15, וּכְשֹׁד מִשַּׁדַּי (*ûkěšōd miššadday*, "and like destruction from Shaddai," The Hebrew is striking because of a play on words between "destruction" (*šōd*) and "the Almighty" (*šadday*). Perhaps something like "destruction from the Destroyer" would capture more of the flavor, though Shaddai as a divine name does not have to stress God's destructive might (see Additional Notes for further discussion of the etymology of Shaddai and its unique form in *BHS*).

The language chosen follows the wording of Isa. 13:6 closely. The day of the Lord was a traditional theme, and various prophets used a set of stock phrases to describe it. If Joel preceded Isaiah he could have coined the phraseology, but certainty about the date of the book cannot be attained. "For the day of Yahweh is near" fits more naturally after Isaiah's "Wail!" than after Joel's "Alas for the day!" One could infer either that Isaiah smoothed out Joel's expression or that Joel adapted Isaiah's wording to his own situation. The Isaiah passage lacks "and" before "it will come," a slight argument in favor of Isaiah's originality, since the conjunction tends to be added for clarification rather than deleted.

Ezek. 30:2 also has much similarity with Joel 1:15:

Wail, "Alas [הָהּ, *hāh*] for the day!"
For the day is near,
even the day of Yahweh is near.

Ezekiel directs his prophecy against Egypt, while Isaiah speaks to Babylon. So Joel knew that the doctrine of the day of Yahweh was connected with a future time of judgment on the nations.[1] He is afraid that the locust plague may be a sign that the Lord has rejected Israel and that she will be treated like any other nation.

1:16 When Joel sees "gladness and joy" removed from the Temple in v. 16, he resumes the theme of v. 12: "rejoicing dries up from the sons of men." When the people realize how the Lord has reacted to their sins, they lose the joy of their salvation. Later Joel will speak of the reversal of this situation (2:23) when the Lord accepts Israel again.

Joel's literary artistry may be seen in the repetition that ties together the flow of the argument: "my God" (v. 13a), "your God" (vv. 13b, 14), "our God" (v. 16). The first two relate to Joel's address to the priests in particular. Now in v. 16, he addresses the whole nation and includes himself.

1:17 Because of three Hebrew words that occur nowhere else in the OT, the first line of v. 17 is notoriously difficult to translate. Hence it is necessary to examine the context closely for a clue to the meaning. The end of the verse speaks

---

[1] For more on the "day of the Lord," see Kenneth L. Barker, "Zechariah," in *EBC*, ed. Frank E. Gaebelein (Grand Rapids: Zondervan, 1985), 7:619-20.

of granaries and barns falling into ruin because "the grain is dried up." Verses 16 and 17 are linked by the idea that plant foods are "cut off" from people. Then v. 18 extends the discussion to grazing animals, which cannot eat because "there is no pasture for them." Therefore, those ancient versions which speak of animals in the first part of v. 17 cannot be right. For example, LXX has "the cows stamp by their manger" (similarly Peshitta and Vulg.).[2]

Our rendering follows *NASB* (cf. *NIV* and *JB*) and points to some problem concerning plants rather than animals. "Shrivel" for עָבְשׁוּ (*'ābĕšû*) is based on comparison with "dry up" at the end of the verse as well as an Arabic etymology. The seeds (פְּרֻדוֹת, *pĕrudôt*) that have been planted do not sprout. They shrivel up under the clods of earth (מֶגְרְפֹת, *megrĕpōt*) which cover them. Reliance on the KB lexicon yields, "The figs have shrivelled under their shovels." Douglas Stuart has a rendering that makes more sense by a different interpretation of *megrĕpōtêhem*: "The figs have dried out under their casings."[3]

Rudolph translates, "The stored up provisions have spoiled,"[4] but this is unlikely for two reasons. First, the drought would make spoilage less likely. Second, the storehouses fall into ruin because there is nothing to go into them.

1:18 Turning from crops to animals in v. 18, Joel notes how much the various beasts will suffer because the locusts and drought have consumed their food. He mentions three categories: בְהֵמָה (*bĕhēmâ*, "livestock"), בָּקָר (*bāqār*, "cattle"), and צֹאן (*ṣō'n*, "sheep"). The distinction between *bĕhēmâ* and *bāqār* does not seem clear. Perhaps the former is meant here as a more inclusive term to cover both *bāqār* and *ṣō'n*. The latter two words often occur together, sometimes translated "herd" and "flock" respectively (Gen. 33:13; Ex. 34:3; Lev. 27:32). All three terms occur together in the same order in Jonah 3:7.

1:19a As Joel builds to a climax, he cries out to God for deliverance (v. 19). None can help the struggling people and beasts in Judah except God alone. The plea for mercy here foreshadows the opportunity to find salvation during the calamitous time of the "great and awesome day of Yahweh" by "calling on" Yahweh's name (2:32 [MT 3:5]).

1:19b In the final two verses of the chapter Joel closes out his general description of the damage by reiterating three areas of suffering: the pastureland with its low plants, the trees of the field, and the animals. The herdsmen in Judah concentrated their flocks in the wilderness area (מִדְבָּר, *midbār*), which extended from the top of the Judean ridge eastward to the Dead Sea. "Fire" (אֵשׁ, *'ēš*) should possibly be taken metaphorically for a severe drought following the locust infestation (cf. Amos 7:4), though it could refer to grass fires that swept over the dried-out pastureland. The insects devoured the grass, and the pastures could not recover without rain.

---

[2] Cf. Hans Walter Wolff, *Joel and Amos* (Hermeneia; trans. Waldemar Janzen, et al.; Philadelphia: Fortress, 1977), p. 19 n. z.

[3] Stuart, *Hosea-Jonah* (WBC 31; Waco, Tex.: Word, 1987), p. 238.

[4] "*Die aufbewahrten Vorrate sind verdorben*"; Wilhelm Rudolph, *Joel--Amos-- Obadja--Jona* (KAT 13:2; Gütersloh: Gütersloher Verlagshaus Gerd Mohn, 1971), p. 38. He has a detailed etymological discussion (pp. 39-40).

The trees are apparently the same as those of v. 14. שָׂדֶה (śādeh) often implies a cultivated field (Gen. 37:7; 47:24; Ex. 22:4; Ruth 2:2; Mic. 2:4). By setting the "pastures of the wilderness" and "all the trees of the field" side by side Joel includes the entire land of Judah in the scope of the disaster. This parallelism also serves to link the two parts of the chapter.

1:20 The language of v. 20 resembles closely Ps. 42:1 (MT 42:2): "As the deer pants for the water brooks,/ so my soul pants for You, O God." The comparison helps to highlight a unique feature of the Joel passage: the beasts pant for *God*, not for the water brooks. In this way the prophet stresses the dependence of all living things on their Creator. God has brought the calamity and only He can remove it.

Repetition of elements serves throughout Joel as a unifying device. The final phrase of the chapter, "and fire has consumed the wilderness pastures," closes out the petition that began with the same wording (v. 19), but it makes for an effective transition to the next chapter.

Fire occurs often in the OT as a means of divine judgment (e.g., Gen. 19:24; Lev. 10:2; Num. 11:1; 16:35; Deut. 9:3; Ps. 11:6; 21:9 [MT 21:10]; Jer. 4:4; Amos 1:4; Nah. 1:6; Zech. 11:1). The doubling of the statement about fire, then, highlights the judgmental nature of the locusts and drought. The calamity came because of God's anger. In the same way Joel tells us in chap. 2 that the army of locusts is God's army (v. 11), with a consuming fire before and behind them (v. 2).

Additional Notes

1:15 מִשַּׁדַּי: This reading has been explained by A. Dotan as an instance where Codex B omits a *dagesh* in certain consonants after a prefixed preposition מִן to prevent gemination in two adjacent consonants. This in turn is part of a larger pattern of omission of *dagesh* in two adjacent consonants under certain conditions.[5]

The etymology of the divine name Shaddai is uncertain. The more likely suggestions relate it to the root שָׁדַד, "to destroy" (cf. Ruth 1:20, 21; Job 6:4; 15:25; 21:15, 20; 23:16; 27:2; 31:2; 37:23; Ps. 68:14 [MT 68:15]; Isa. 13:6) or to Akkadian *šadû*, "mountain."[6] The rendering "Almighty" goes back to παντοκράτωρ, used by the LXX but only in the book of Job.[7] The occurrences of אֵל שַׁדַּי in Genesis (17:1; 28:3; 35:11; 43:14; 48:3) hardly place emphasis on the destructive power of God, but we often see God associated with a mountain in the OT. Strength and might could be strong overtones arising from the expression "God of the mountain," and that etymology seems most likely. However, since contextual usage takes precedence over etymology for determining meaning in a given

---

[5] "Deviation in Gemination in the Tiberian Vocalization," in *Estudios Masoreticos (V Congreso de la IOMS)*, ed. Emilia Fernandez Tejero (Madrid: Instituto "Arias Montano," 1983), p. 69.

[6] Victor P. Hamilton, *TWOT* 2:907. Claus Westermann, *Genesis 12-36: A Commentary*, trans. John J. Scullion (Minneapolis: Augsburg, 1981), p. 258, lists six suggestions, most of which seem unlikely. See also now KBRev 4:1421-22.

[7] Edwin Hatch and Henry A. Redpath, *A Concordance to the Septuagint and the Other Greek Versions of the Old Testament (Including the Apocryphal Books)* (Grand Rapids: Baker, 1983), p. 1053.

passage, it is possible that Joel uses the similarity of sound rather than sense to stress God's ability to bring destruction.

1:18 נֶאְשְׁמוּ: Usually the verb occurs in the qal pattern and means "be (held) guilty" (Hos. 4:15). The niphal form is unique to the present verse. The context indicates suffering (cf. *NASB*), though the sheep would hardly suffer because of their own guilt. The ancient versions uniformly render as though the Hebrew were נָשַׁמּוּ ("were devastated"), as in v. 17.[8] The context favors this reading so strongly that one should think either of an *aleph* inserted accidentally into the Hebrew (influenced by the same sequence of consonants in נֶאֶנְחָה or as a vowel letter?) or of a root אשׁם as a biform of שׁמם.[9]

B. The Invasion Of The Lord's Army (2:1-11)

Translation

> Sound a trumpet in Zion!
> And sound the alarm on My holy mountain!
> Let all who live in the land tremble.
> For the day of Yahweh comes.
> Indeed it is near!
> [2](It is) a dark and gloomy day,
> a day black with thick clouds.
> Like dawn spread out over the mountains,
> (there is) a great and numerous people.
> Like them there has never been from ancient times;
> and after them not again
>   to the years of many generations.
> [3]Before them a fire devours,
> and behind them a flame blazes.
> Like the Garden of Eden – the land before them;
> and behind them – a desolate wilderness.
> Not even a small group of survivors escapes them.
> [4]Like the appearance of horses is their appearance,
> and like steeds, so they run.
> [5]They sound like chariots
> leaping about on the mountaintops,
> They sound like a blazing fire
> consuming stubble.
> (They are) like a mighty people
> arrayed for battle.

---

[8] LXX uses ἠφανίσθησαν in both verses, while the Targum has צדיאו. Only Peshitta uses different verbs, though with roughly synonymous meaning. It has *ḥrbw* ("be destroyed") at 1:17 but *spw* ("come to an end") at 1:18.

[9] Suggested by Douglas Stuart, *Hosea-Jonah*, p. 239 n. 18c. Some linguistic principles for the formation of biforms are given by Francis I. Andersen, "Biconsonantal Byforms of Weak Hebrew Roots," *ZAW* 82 (1970): 270-74. None of Andersen's examples involves elision of *aleph*.

[6]At the sight of them nations writhe in anguish;
every face turns pale.
[7]Like warriors they run;
like men of war they scale a wall.
And each one marches in his own line,
and none deviates from their path.
[8]Yes, none jostles another;
each one marches in his own road.
When they burst through the defenses,
they do not break ranks.
[9]Into the city they surge;
on the wall they run;
into the houses they go up;
through the windows they enter like thieves.
[10]Before them the earth quakes;
the heavens shake.
Sun and moon darken,
and the stars lose their brightness.
[11]And Yahweh thunders before His army.
Surely very great is His camp;
surely mighty are those who carry out His command.
Indeed Yahweh's day is great
and very awesome.
And who can endure it?

Exegesis and Exposition

Joel, like other OT prophets, connects the day of the Lord with military action (3:9-12). Amos saw the day heavy with judgment for the northern kingdom of Israel (5:18-20), and he also predicted that a foreign army would invade the country (6:14). Zephaniah likewise foresaw invasions that would come with this day of judgment (1:16), and Ezekiel even applied "the day of the Lord" to the Babylonian onslaught against Judah in 586 B.C. (13:5).

Therefore, it is not surprising that Joel couches his description of the locust plague in terms of an army which the Lord Himself leads. Joel's point is not primarily to describe a future attack against Jerusalem, though other prophets predict such an event for the end times (Dan. 11:41; Zech. 14:1-2). Rather, he intends to motivate the people to repent by showing how the invasion of locusts represents the Lord's judgment against the land. For the wicked the day of the Lord can only mean complete destruction. If the Judeans remain in their sin, their end could be as final as that of the nations in the great period of God's wrath.

For Joel, then, the day of the Lord is "near." That is, the locusts show that the Lord's anger against His people must be turned aside if the nation is to survive. This is why the present section so vividly describes how the locusts enter the city. They bring divine judgment with them no less than the Assyrian or Babylonian armies or than the enemy forces that will assemble against Judah at the end of the age. There is no defense against an army brought by the Lord, but perhaps the full effects can be stayed through national repentance.

Patterson represents a different school of thought when he argues that Joel's language "goes beyond a literal locust plague in 2:1-11 (e.g., vv. 3, 6, 10), especially as amplified in the details contained in the spiritual challenge based on this event in 2:12-27 (cf. particularly vv. 17, 20, 26-27)." He also argues that "the time of 2:1-27 is future to that of chapter 1 but anterior to 2:28-3:21."[10]

There is certainly some hyperbole in Joel's description, but each detail can be related to the effects of a literal locust infestation (see exegesis below). Certain key phrases link 2:1-11 with chap. 1. The most important of these include "for the day of Yahweh is near" (1:15; 2:1), "a great and mighty people" (2:2; cf. 1:6), "there has never been anything like it" (2:2; cf. 1:2), and "a fire consumes before them" (2:3; cf. 1:19). Observe further that 2:25 explicitly calls the various kinds of locusts "My great army which I sent among you," a clear echo of 2:11, "And Yahweh utters His voice before His army."

The spiritual challenge that Joel gives after his description of the invasion simply heightens that which he had given earlier. The crisis of the locusts must not be taken lightly; it could mean utter destruction if the people do not turn to the Lord.

While references to a future blessing are found in chap. 2 (vv. 24-27), they are based on a historical notation that the Lord responded to the appeals called for by Joel (2:18-19). The verbs within 2:2-11 describe the invasion as though Joel is viewing it directly. Thus, the form coincides with the function: Joel wished to stir his audience to action.

All this is not to deny the aptness of the comparison between the day of the Lord and a military invasion. One might even go so far as to view Joel's description of the locust invasion as typological, with its correspondent in the latter days. The locusts are a harbinger of that day precisely because the Lord controls them in the same way that He will direct literal armies at that time. In fact, in the second half of the book Joel draws parallels between his own time and what will take place "afterward" (2:28 [MT 3:1]). Even so, it is not necessary to think Joel means *only* a real military incursion in 2:1-11.[11]

2:1 The first two verses of chap. 2 make an envelope structure (*inclusio*) with v. 11 to enclose the entire description within the topic of the day of the Lord. Joel amasses a number of traditional phrases to describe the gloom and danger of that time.

---

[10] Richard D. Patterson, "Joel," in *EBC*, 7:246; cf. Wolff, *Joel and Amos*, pp. 41-42.

[11] This analysis of the structure of Joel differs in this respect from that of Duane Garrett, *Hosea, Joel* (NAC 19A; [Nashville]: Broadman & Holman, 1997), pp 298-99. Garrett thinks that the position of the 2:1-11 in the book demands that it refer to a human army, else it would make Joel 3 and 4 "unintelligible" in the context of the book as a whole. The pivotal issue of the "day of the Lord," though, allows for some typological value for the locust plague. The nations of Joel 4 will be judged for the deeds described in 4:1-6. Amos warned that the day of the Lord would overwhelm Israel herself (5:18-20). Joel applies the invasion of the locusts to such a judgment but furthers the teaching by providing the way of escape through repentance and showing that the nations of the world will ultimately share in the judgment too. The locusts portray the severe judgment in its historical setting but also typify the future events. Indeed, now it is an army of locusts but in the future it will be an army of men who will carry out the Lord's plans.

First, he calls the people to prepare for an enemy invasion: תִּקְעוּ שׁוֹפָר (tiqĕ'û šôpār, "Blow a trumpet). The trumpet or shofar is a ram's horn, used as a signal to alert the population. Here the sudden command to sound the horn ties in with the previous chapter: "Hear! Awake and weep! Wail! Put on sackcloth! Set aside a time for fasting! Proclaim a solemn assembly! Blow a trumpet!" Also, both chapters indicate the need for action in the face of disaster.

The Hebrew (וְהָרִיעוּ, wĕhārî'û) is literally "raise a shout." The expression can be used of joy (Zech. 9:9) and of the triumph of anticipated victory (Josh. 6:16) as well as of an alarm (Hos. 5:8). Other prophets closely associate the blowing of the shofar and the cry of alarm with judgment from the Lord (Jer. 4:19; Hos. 5:8). Zephaniah describes the day of the Lord as "a day of trumpet and battle cry" (1:16). The term "battle cry" (תְּרוּעָה, tĕrû'â), in fact, is a noun form based on the same root as "raise a shout."

The sound of the horn and cry of alarm should strike fear into the hearts of the people. The "trembling" (יִרְגְּזוּ, yirgĕzû, "let them tremble") of "all the inhabitants of the land" also connects the message with chapter 1 (vv. 2, 14).

At the end of v. 1 Joel comes to his main thrust: כִּי־בָא יוֹם־יהוה כִּי קָרוֹב (kî-bā' yôm-YHWH kî qārôb, "for the day of Yahweh comes; indeed it is near"). The noise of trumpet and shout of alarm do not call upon the people to prepare for an ordinary invasion. It is the Lord Himself who is near at hand with the full fury of His judgment.

Many of the modern versions (e.g., *NASB*) give the second occurrence of *kî* an emphatic translation (see discussion of 1:10). The day of the Lord has not quite arrived, but the severity of the locust plague reminds the prophet of how close it is if the people will not repent.

The Peshitta joins the last phrase with v. 2, yielding, "For the day of the Lord comes, and the day of darkness … is near." Some commentators prefer this reading for metrical reasons,[12] but notice that Peshitta has substituted "and" for *ki* ("surely"). MT accords better with Isaiah 13:6, 9 and Zeph. 1:14-15.

2:2 The second verse concentrates on darkness and the sudden appearance of a great army. Darkness symbolizes the judgment and wrath of the day of the Lord (Isa. 13:10; Amos 5:18, 20; Zeph. 1:15). For Amos it would engulf all the Israelites who smugly believed that the judgment would not touch them. Isaiah applied the doom inherent in that day to the Babylonians, though he also spoke of "a day of reckoning" when the Lord will deal with Judah (2:12). Zephaniah saw its terrors engulfing the Judeans, who "have sinned against Yahweh" (1:17). Obadiah, however, concentrated only on the fact that the day will come on "all the nations," especially on Edom (v. 15). For Joel, the approaching day potentially threatens Judah but need not overtake any who "call on the name of Yahweh" (2:32 [MT 3:5]). Common to all these prophets is the idea that the Lord will judge sinners in an unprecedented manner.

Four separate terms describe the utter blackness of the day: חֹשֶׁךְ (ḥōšek, "darkness"); אֲפֵלָה ('ăpēlâ, "gloom"); עָנָן ('ānān, "cloud"); and עֲרָפֶל ('ărāpel, "thick darkness"). It may well be that the darkness is that which accompanies the

---

[12] Rudolph, *Joel*, p. 51 n. c.; Wolff, *Joel and Amos*, p. 37.

presence of the Lord Himself. When He spoke from Sinai, three of these terms –
"darkness [*ḥōšek*], cloud [*'ānān*] and thick darkness [*'ărāpel*]" – were present
(Deut. 4:11). The day of the Lord, then, includes that time when God will come
personally to deal with all sinners among the nations of the earth. It also
encompasses a period of blessing that follows the judgment,[13] but Joel does not
focus on this until chap. 3 (MT chap. 4). Could this great darkness apply also to a
literal locust plague? Many have described the swarm as like a dark cloud that
obscures the light of the sun.[14]

With so much talk of darkness, the third line of the verse
(כְּשַׁחַר פָּרֻשׂ עַל־הֶהָרִים, *kĕšaḥar pāruś 'al-hehārîm*, "like the dawn spread out
upon the mountains") seems surprising with its introduction of the "dawn." The
point of the comparison is suddenness. Anyone who has seen a sunrise in the
mountains knows how quickly the brightness appears on the face of the cliffs.
Perhaps even the jarring feeling the reader or listener gets when Joel so abruptly
switches from blackness to dawn contributes to this sense of suddenness. That
quickly has the vast army of locusts appeared (cf. Isa. 58:8);[15] that quickly will the
Lord appear in the day of His wrath. The phrase "great and mighty people" forms
an important connection with 1:6, the term *'āṣûm* ("mighty") appearing in both
places.

Leslie Allen translates this line, "like blackness covering the mountains,"
noting that the idea of darkness carries over from the previous lines.[16] However, it
is then necessary to emend "dawn" (*šaḥar*) to "darkness" (שְׁחוֹר, *šĕḥōr*). Allen also
brings in Ex. 10:15 as a parallel, but in that passage (which does not use *šĕḥōr*) the
darkness covers the land, not the mountains.

One should observe the close similarity between the end of the verse to the
question posed in 1:2. Both the locust plague and the day of the Lord are
unprecedented in their darkness and in their sudden, overwhelming arrival. Also
noteworthy are the collective singular pronouns that begin with כָּמֹהוּ (*kāmōhû*,
"like it") and extend to לְפָנָיו (*lĕpānāyw*, "before it") in 2:10. The army of locusts is
in focus. The verbs that describe the locusts are plural throughout the section (e.g.,
"they run," v. 3; "they scale," v. 7; "they fall," v. 8), though the singular participle
עֹשֶׂה (*'ōśeh*, "one doing") in 2:11 sums up the task of the army as "those who carry
out His command."

2:3a The precise meaning of the fire imagery is difficult to discern. Is it some
kind of "scorched earth" policy practiced by the invading army? Those who
connect the fire with the fact that this is the Lord's army are probably on the right
track. Allen observes, "It is almost as if a fiery aura emanating from the advancing

---

[13] For a good description, see Kenneth L. Barker, "Zechariah," in *EBC*, 7:619-20.
Georg Fohrer, ("Der Tag JHWHs," *Eretz-Israel* 16 (1982): 43-50, tries to show how various
prophets use the concept in different ways; but he assumes that Joel is not a unified work,
and he is not concerned to harmonize the various references.
[14] See S. R. Driver, *The Books of Joel and Amos* (CBSC; Cambridge: University,
1907), pp. 87-91.
[15] Wolff, *Joel and Amos*, p. 44.
[16] Leslie C. Allen, *The Books of Joel, Obadiah, Jonah and Micah* (NICOT; Grand
Rapids: Eerdmans, 1976), pp. 68-69.

locusts sweeps ahead of them."[17] Other passages of Scripture reinforce the thought that fire accompanies the Lord and His army, especially Ps. 97:3 – "Fire goes before Him,/ And burns up His adversaries round about" (cf. Ps. 50:3; Zeph. 1:18; Zech. 11:1; 12:6; Mal. 4:1 [MT 3:19]; cf. also Joel 1:19). The locusts have destroyed all vegetation as surely as though an army had gone through and torched the fields. Perhaps the burning flame behind the army refers to the drought that made it impossible for the land to recover.

2:3b The exaggerated description of the land as "like the Garden of Eden" before the locusts came heightens the contrast with the barrenness afterward. Joel is quite interested in "before and after" descriptions, and they form a motif throughout the book. The locust plague is unequalled in past experience, and people will talk about it for generations to come. The Lord will drive "the vanguard" (lit. "its face," פָּנָיו, *pānāyw*) of the locust army into the eastern sea (in Hebrew, the sea "in front," הַקַּדְמֹנִי, *haqqadmōnî*) and the "rear guard" (lit. "its end," סֹפוֹ, *sōpô*) into the western sea (the sea "in back," הָאַחֲרוֹן, *hā'aḥărôn*). Then the Lord will restore the damage done by the locusts, turning the land once again into a paradise with "plenty to eat" (2:24-25). Of course, repentance also represents a new condition, not only for the people but also, speaking analogically, for the Lord who responds by turning from judgment to salvation.

The theme continues into the second half of the book with the actual appearance of the day of the Lord. It will come about "after this" (2:28 [MT 3:1]) and will include spiritual blessings and salvation in great abundance. At that time also there will be awesome effects in nature and a great judgment, but God will deliver those of His people who call on Him. After the judgment Judah will become a land of unprecedented fruitfulness, while the nations who harmed her will become the "desolate wilderness" that she once had been (3:18-19 [MT 4:18-19]). What had been "before" will be reversed in the time "afterward."

2:3c Joel uses an interesting figure to close out his portrayal of the thorough scorching of the land by the locusts and drought. The Hebrew of 2:3 has the literal construction, "and even an escaped remnant [פְּלֵיטָה, *pĕlêṭâ*] there is not to it." The plants in the path of the locusts are personified as fugitives or refugees. The locust army bears down on them so that none can escape. The Targum resolved the figure and gave an application, "And also there is no escape in it for the wicked."

Joel makes structural connections between the various parts of his message both by repetition and by contrast. His reference to the vegetation recalls the direct statements of chapter 1 ("all the trees," "no pasture"). Later Joel brings out an important contrast. The plants cannot escape the locusts, but when the day of the Lord finally comes, there *will* be those who escape [*pĕlêṭâ*] on Mount Zion and in Jerusalem (2:32 [MT 3:5]).

2:4 When the army is compared in appearance to horses, it would seem that locusts are meant. It would be unusual to say that the "people" are "like" horses. An army would move swiftly because of horse-drawn chariots, but the language is less appropriate for the soldiers themselves. Locusts, on the other hand, do resemble horses, and their rapid movements could be compared to the speed of war horses.

---

[17] Allen, *Joel*, p. 70.

Garrett attempts to explain the use of Hebrew כְּ (kĕ-, "as" or "like") as the kaph veritatis.[18] However, this usage can only apply when the feature that serves as the point of comparison represents an ideal of the thing being compared. Thus, according to Ezek. 26:10, Nebuchadnezzar and his army will enter the gates of Jerusalem "as men enter a city that is breached." They will do it in a perfect, true, or ideal manner. If this function of kaph applied here, it would mean that the army has a true or ideal appearance as horses. Rather, the preposition should be taken in its usual, comparative function. See Additional Notes for a comment on the unusual form of יְרוּצוּן (yĕrûṣûn, "they run").

2:5a-b The passage moves on from physical appearance ("like horses") to motion ("like steeds") and then to sound (v. 5). Enemy chariots were heard many times jostling about on the Judean hills. The locusts made a similar sound as the swarms leaped (יְרַקֵּדוּן, yĕraqqēdûn) from hilltop to hilltop (cf. Nah 3:2).

The terrifying sound of the locusts crescendos as the people in the city first hear the crackling of their nearby fields falling to the insects and then the deafening roar of the swarm massed for the frontal assault. The sound of flames licking at stubble seems more appropriate as a description of locusts than of an army, though the figure is sometimes applied to military effectiveness (Obad. 18; Zech. 12:6). Literally, the Hebrew has "like the sound of chariots" and "like the sound of a flame of fire." The translation given above reflects the underlying sense. The terseness of the Hebrew is due to the poetic form.

2:5c The thought of sound possibly carries over to the last line of v. 5: "(They have a sound) like (that of) a mighty people arrayed for battle." It seems better to take it as a transitional line, summarizing both appearance and sound and preparing for the signs of fear and dread found in v. 6. Then the pronoun would be deleted in favor of the poetic form: "(They are) like a mighty people arrayed for battle."

2:6 Evidently v. 6 refers to a trembling and paleness that come to terrified people. פָּארוּר (pā'rûr), often translated "pale," is uncertain, though the same expression occurs in Nah. 2:10 (MT 2:11). Possibly it signifies something like "receive blackness" (cf. KJV), but a parallel phrase in Isa. 13:8 might argue for a flushing of the face rather than paleness. In any case, the terror shows both in the bodily movements and in the facial expressions of everyone in the city. Also, as Wolff points out, the language closely follows depictions elsewhere of the agonies of the day of the Lord (esp. Isa 13:8).[19]

Once again, Joel has an effective play on words, which can be obscured through an English translation. The people tremble "from the face of" (i.e., "before" or "at the sight of") the locusts, and all their "faces" gather blackness. One might say the appearance of the locusts makes the appearance of the people pale.

2:7a The mention in vv. 7 and 9 of a wall need not exclude the period between the first return from exile and Nehemiah's return for the date of composition of the book. If the army stands figuratively for the locusts, then Joel could be describing them as climbing over the remains of the preexilic walls. Not only do the locusts

---

[18] Garrett, "The Structure of Joel," JETS 28 (1985), p. 293. See also Hosea, Joel (NAC 19A; [Nashville]: Broadman & Holman, 1997), pp. 298-299.

[19] Wolff, Joel and Amos, pp. 46-47.

run like warriors, they climb walls like battle-hardened troops. It is also possible that the walls of Jerusalem were rebuilt and subsequently destroyed prior to Nehemiah's arrival (see Introduction to Joel, p. 6).

2:7b The second half of v. 7 has some difficulties, but the parallel structure of the line helps to establish the general sense of movement in tight formations. The first half of the line is clear enough, but the term יְעַבְּטוּן (yĕʿabbĕṭûn, "they deviate") is otherwise unattested and the meaning has to be derived only from this context (see Additional Notes for an etymological discussion). Locust swarms operate as a tight unit (cf. Prov. 30:27).

2:8 A difficulty arises in v. 8 from the obscure term שֶׁלַח (šelaḥ). Two different meanings have been suggested. The more traditional translation relies on the common idea of some type of weapon that is thrown. On the other hand, Allen follows Rudolph in referring the term to the water tunnel into the city (cf. Neh. 3:15, "Pool of Shelah," i.e., the Pool of Siloam).[20] According to this view the usual translation is unlikely because weapons were useless against locusts. However, the passage views the locusts under the figure of an invading army, so the general point is simply that the locusts continue despite all efforts at resistance. The idea of bursting through the defenses seems to fit better with not breaking ranks (יְבְצָעוּ, yibṣāʿû; lit. "they do (not) break off [their course]").[21]

KJV reads "and when they fall upon the sword they shall not be wounded." The preposition בְּעַד (bĕʿad, "through") and the use of the verb bāṣaʿ elsewhere do not support this interpretation.

Verses 7b and 8a have an interesting chiastic (A-B // B´-A´) structure.

| A And-each in-his-ways they-march | B and-not they-deviate their-paths. |
| B´ And-each his-fellow not they-jostle | A´ each in-his-road they-march |

All four parts speak generally of regular ranks, but A and A´ stress predetermined paths, while B and B´ refer to the lack of moving outside those roads. This is a nice example of how the poetic form underlines the meaning. The insects march on in wave after wave in perfectly aligned ranks.

2:9 Verse 7 spoke of scaling the wall; now in v. 9 the insects are inside the city. Houses were built close to or even right against the walls of cities in ancient times, so one should perhaps imagine the locusts scurrying around the walls to gain access to various parts of the city.

2:10 The term for the quaking of the earth (v. 10) is רָגַז (rāgaz), the same as in 2:1, "Let all the inhabitants of the land tremble" (cf. Amos 8:8). Since 2:2 goes on to mention heavenly portents (darkness and thick clouds), vv. 10-11 close off the segment of text beginning with 2:1.

The effects may be local or universal (cf. 2:30-31 [MT 3:3-4]). On a local level one should think of the huge swarms which send a quaking sensation through the land in their continual rhythm of alighting and rising. Also the beating of wings and

---

[20] Rudolph, *Joel*, p. 52; Allen, *Joel*, pp. 72-73 n. 47.

[21] See also Patterson, "Joel," p. 250 n. 8.

rapid, sharp turns of the formation make the sky itself shake. On the universal level the prophets apply similar language to the appearance of the Lord Himself, which causes an uproar in heaven and earth (cf. Jer 4:23-28). It is not that the text has more than one meaning. Rather, the local plague serves to stir up thoughts of the greater events of the end. The coherence of the passage as a description of the locust plague suggests that the local significance is primary.

Even the reference to the darkening of the sun and the moon could refer to the immediate event. Eyewitness accounts of locust infestations mention a thick cloud that blocks out even the light of the sun.[22] Yet once again Joel's language evokes images of the upheavals in the sky that accompany the final day of the Lord (cf. Isa. 13:10; Zeph. 2:14-15).

2:11a The most important connection between the locusts that overran Judah in Joel's day and the future day of the Lord is the personal presence of the Lord in both cases. In v. 11 that connection becomes prominent when Joel views the Lord as the Commander of the locust army. The Hebrew phrase קוֹל נָתַן (nātan qôl), literally "give voice," refers to a loud noise, whether of weeping (Gen. 45:2; Num. 14:1) or of shouting in the streets (Prov. 8:1). It can also be used of thunder (Ps. 77:17 [MT 77:18]), even of God's voice as thunder (Ps. 18:13 [MT 18:14]), and of the roar of lions (Jer. 2:15). Here Joel means to convey the shouting of the military commander to his troops in the heat of battle (cf. Jer. 4:16; Lam. 2:7). The Lord personally leads this army of locusts against Jerusalem and Judah; the element of judgment cannot be missed.

Later Joel will turn the tables and depict the Lord roaring like a lion from the midst of Jerusalem in wrath against the nations (3:16). "His people," however, will find "refuge" in Him at that time.

2:11b Since the locusts are Yahweh's "army" (חֵילוֹ, hêlô) they must also be the ones who "carry out His command" (עֹשֵׂה דְבָרוֹ, 'ōśēh dĕbārô). NASB translates the second clause, "For strong is He who carries out His word." That is, it makes the Lord the subject of the singular participle, 'ōśēh. However, the participle may still be applied to the insects even though it is singular. All the way through the passage singular (collective) forms refer to the "army." Comparison with 1:6 yields the observation that "mighty" ('āṣûm) should be taken in the sense of numerous. It is hardly suitable as a description of the Lord, and in fact never elsewhere refers to Him. The parallel description of the "camp" as "great" also supports this observation, in that רַב (rab) often indicates greatness in number (e.g., Josh 11:4, "a great [=many] people, like the sand"). Also, the immediate context makes it clear that the Lord stands at the head of His army and issues His command. Therefore, it seems most natural for the army to be the one that carries it out.

Since the description of the army as numerous adds to the force of the Lord's command rather than giving a reason for it, the two occurrences of kî should be taken as emphatic.[23]

---

[22] See S. R. Driver, *Joel and Amos*, pp. 87-91; Walter K. Price, *The Prophet Joel and the Day of the Lord* (Chicago: Moody, 1976), p. 33.

[23] Against C. F. Keil, *Minor Prophets* (COTTV 10; Grand Rapids: Eerdmans, 1973), p. 195; Rudolph, *Joel*, p. 57.

2:11c At the climax of his description, Joel refers once more to the terror of the day of the Lord. It is great because it will include unusual events that will result in unbearable distress (cf. Jer. 30:4-7; Zeph. 1:14-18). It inspires such terror that the prophet cries out, "who can endure it?" In like manner Amos saw Israel on the verge of destruction and exclaimed, "Lord Yahweh, please stop!/ How can Jacob stand, for he is small?" (Amos 7:5). Also, Amaziah uses similar language when he tells Jeroboam II how Amos has preached against the land: "the land is unable to endure all his words" (7:10). Joel means to say that if the locust plague blends into the great day of the Lord, Judah cannot survive.

In the second part of the book Joel once again raises the question of the inescapable terror of that day. None can avoid it by their own effort, but the Lord will deliver those who call on Him (2:31-32 [MT 3:4-5]).

Additional Notes

2:4 יְרוּצוּן: The final *nun* is called "paragogic" by Gesenius (GKC, par. 47m). It occurs most often in early books, though it is found in 2 Chron. 6:26; Jer. 10:11; 17:24; 21:3; 31:22; 33:24; 42:15; 44:28; and Zech. 6:15. Notice that Joel 2:4-9 contains eight instances, three of them with the verb "to run." Only יַעֲבֹטוּן אָרְחוֹתָם (2:7) does not occur in pause. See also יַחֲלֹמוּן at 2:28 (MT 3:1).

J. Hoftijzer recently claimed to find some functional difference in the use of forms with *nun*, and Ronald J. Williams had previously expressed the opinion that these forms are not archaisms but variants existing side by side with the forms without *nun* in all stages of the biblical language.[24] Hoftijzer says the examples in Joel 2:5, 7-9 fall under the category of "a description of facts and events presented as happening generally, normally or regularly," while Joel 2:28 (MT 3:1) describes "what will certainly happen in the future."[25] Hoftijzer admits that his data have many exceptions; he is only trying to point out general tendencies or patterns. The surprising concentration of these forms in Joel 2 might indicate a poetic device on the level of phonology.

2:7 יַעֲבֹטוּן: C. F. Whitley also follows A. Guillaume in relating the term to Arabic *ḥbt*, "striking or beating in a way that is not right." Whitley suggests other possible instances of *ḥ* > ʿ.[26] A relation with the root meaning "take or give a pledge" does not seem feasible.

---

[24] J. Hoftijzer, *The Function and Use of the Imperfect Forms with Nun Paragogicum in Classical Hebrew* (Studia Semitica Neerlandica 20; Assen, Netherlands: Van Gorcum, 1985); Ronald J. Williams, "Energic Verbal Forms in Hebrew," in *Studies on the Ancient Palestinian World Presented to Professor F. V. Winnett...*, ed. J. W. Wevers and D. B. Redford (Toronto: Univ. of Toronto, 1972), pp. 75-85.

[25] Hoftijzer, *Imperfect Forms*, pp. 67, 69.

[26] C. F. Whitley, "*bṭ* in Joel 2,7," *Bib* 65 (1984) 101-2.

3
Mercy in the Land
(Joel 2:12-27)

Having brought his listeners to the brink of the Lord's day of wrath, Joel
pleads with them to repent with sincere hearts. He knows that mere ritual cannot
sway the Lord, but he also recognizes the loving and forgiving nature of his God.
On that basis he calls for a national assembly of every man, woman, and child in
Judah to cry out for mercy. In response, the Lord promises to restore the land to its
former state and to bless it anew.

A. A Call To Repentance (2:12-17)

· At 2:12 the text shifts to a new thought, and some grammatical features mark
off its boundaries. First, certain terms and phrases in 2:1 are repeated in 2:10-11 to
mark the end of that section (2:1-11). Second, in like manner Joel reiterates the call
for weeping found at 2:12 in v. 17. Third, the topic of 2:12-17 changes from a
threat of judgment to a call for national repentance. Then at 2:18 the text begins to
report the Lord's response. Fourth, the forms used for the verbs vary in the
different segments of the chapter. *Descriptive* forms dominate 2:1-11, while a
series of *entreaties* occur in 2:12-17, in which Joel first appeals to the Lord's
gracious character (vv. 12-14) and then makes an impassioned plea for a national
outpouring of mourning for sin. Then the text moves to narration at v. 18, followed
by promises of renewed blessing in vv. 20-27.

1. Appeal To The Character Of The Lord (2:12-14)

Translation

"But even now," declares *Yahweh,
"return to Me with your whole heart
and with fasting and weeping and mourning.
¹³But rend your heart
and not merely your garments."
Yes, return to Yahweh your God,
for He is gracious and compassionate.
slow to anger, abounding in lovingkindness,
and relenting of calamity.
¹⁴Perhaps He might turn and relent,
leaving a blessing after His (visitation),
(a harvest with) a grain offering and libation
for Yahweh your God. (2:12-14)

51

Exegesis and Exposition

Joel's fresh call to repentance builds on the instructions he gave in chapter one (esp. vv. 13-14), but also some significant differences surface. Previously he dwelled on the element of distress. The people were to show signs of grief and cry out to the Lord, but no direct word was said about "returning" to Him. Now a new climax is reached when Joel calls for a genuine change of heart. He pictures a relentless destruction which builds up even to the consummation of the day of the Lord. But he says it is still not too late. Even *now* it is possible for the Lord to show His mercy.

2:12 The close dependence of Joel's language on the teaching of Moses in Deuteronomy can hardly be missed. "With your whole heart" (בְּכָל־לְבַבְכֶם, *bĕkol-lĕbabĕkem*) echoes the first and greatest command to love God above all else (Deut. 6:5), but it also describes how Israel was to obey the Law God gave them through Moses (Deut. 10:12; 26:16). Moreover, when the Lord answered Moses, He restated His former promise to send the various seasonal rains, crops of grain, new wine, olive oil, and pasturage for the cattle if the people would obey His commandments (Deut 11:13-15), even as the Lord responds in Joel's day (Joel 2:18-27). Finally, Joel also reminds the Judeans of God's promise to restore the people after they have been scattered among the nations and they "return to Yahweh your God and obey Him with all your heart and soul" (Deut. 30:1-3; cf. Joel 3:1-8).

In other words, at this point Joel appeals to the covenant God first made with Israel under Moses. The listeners would understand exactly what the Lord meant when He demanded repentance "with all your heart."

2:13a Signs of great sorrow and brokenness, such as fasting and mourning, were in order (v.12). Yet the right perspective was also necessary (v. 13). The Lord never commanded His people to rend their garments, but sometimes the action accompanied repentance (1 Kings 21:27; 2 Kings 22:11, 19; Ezra 9:3, 5; Jer. 36:24). Since Joel has just spoken of fasting, weeping, and mourning, we should interpret, "Rend your heart and not *merely* your garments." Nowhere else in the book is there any sign that the prophet intends to forbid outward demonstrations of religion. Rather they are encouraged.

The colorful phrase "rend your heart" (קִרְעוּ לְבַבְכֶם, *qirĕ'û lĕbabĕkem*) is unique to Joel; elsewhere we find rather the concept of coming before God with a "broken" (נִשְׁבָּר, *nišbār*) heart (cf. Ps. 51:17 [MT 51:19]). *JB* renders the Joel passage, "Let your hearts be broken." This misses the liveliness of the imagery. Of course, Joel does not mean for the people to literally tear apart their hearts, but the hyperbolic image would stress the severity of the situation. When Josiah heard the Law read before him, his first action was to tear his clothes (2 Kings 22:11). Later, the prophetess Huldah gave the Lord's response to the king, "because your heart was tender and you humbled yourself before Yahweh … and you have torn your clothes and wept before Me, I truly have heard you" (22:19).

2:13b Turning from the traditional language of the Lord Himself, Joel now (v. 13) adds his own admonition by reiterating the main thought of the opening command in v. 12: "Return." The careful student will note some interesting variations in v. 13. Now the preposition "to" has the form אֶל (*'el*) instead of עַד

('ad), and the object changes from "Me" to "Yahweh your God." 'el is the more common preposition for this idiom, but a similar sequence of 'ad followed by 'el also occurs in Hos. 14:1-2 (MT 14:2-3). The biblical writers made frequent use of repetition as a poetic device, but they also preferred to introduce subtle variations. Perhaps the alternation helps focus attention on the Lord, to whom the people must turn.

The call to repentance bears within it the seeds of hope. Having appealed to the people to return to keeping their part of the covenant, Joel focuses on the part of the covenant-keeping God. Once again he uses traditional language that goes back to Exodus (34:6) and Numbers (14:18) but also appears in several Psalms (86:15; 103:8; 145:8) and in Nehemiah (9:17). The closest parallel, however, is with Jonah's prayer of complaint after the Assyrians repented (4:2). Jonah could not understand why those characteristics of God by which He dealt graciously with Israel should also apply to the Assyrians.

God's "graciousness" (חַנּוּן, hannûn) means He is willing to respond even when His people do not deserve it. The Levites in Nehemiah's time spoke in their prayer of confession about how God had been gracious when the people were stubborn and committed the sin of idolatry (Neh. 9:17). Repentance must normally precede the outpouring of God's grace, but even repentance cannot force action by God because of merit. It is part of His character to show grace in response to genuine repentance. That He went to great lengths to make atonement for sin through the death of His Son is itself an infinite expression of His gracious nature.

When the Scripture writers say that God is "compassionate" (רַחוּם, rahûm), they highlight His emotional response. His mercy or compassion flows out of His deep love for His people who were chosen merely because of His grace. He is eager to forgive, ready to bless.

The Lord is "slow to anger" (אֶרֶךְ אַפַּיִם, 'erek 'appayim) in that His graciousness makes Him hold back judgment as long as possible. The time may come when punishment is inevitable, but it is in the nature of God to extend the offer of salvation for the repentant until the last possible moment.

Lovingkindness (חֶסֶד, hesed), like love, expresses itself in actions that are merciful and compassionate. As Nelson Glueck has demonstrated, the Lord's hesed has to be understood within the context of His covenant with His people.[1] The term stresses the Lord's loyalty or faithfulness to His covenant, demonstrated through His willingness to forgive when necessary (Ex. 34:6; Num. 14:18; Ps. 86:15). The Lord made an everlasting covenant with His people, Israel. In doing so, He bound Himself by oath (Gen 22:16-17) to bless the nation. At times punishment proved necessary in order to lead the people back to the laws God had graciously given for their benefit. He has always been faithful or loyal to that covenant, even though His people have often forgotten it. Throughout the history

---

[1] Nelson Glueck, *Hesed in the Bible*, ed. Elias L. Epstein (trans. Alfred Gottschalk; n.p.: KTAV, 1975), esp. p. 102. See also Norman H. Snaith, *The Distinctive Ideas of the Old Testament* (New York: Schocken, 1969), pp. 94-130; Katherine Doob Sakenfeld, *The Meaning of Hesed in the Hebrew Bible: A New Inquiry* (HSM 17; Missoula, Mont.: Scholars, 1978).

of Israel and Judah the Lord repeatedly exercised His lovingkindness through concrete actions on their behalf. Removal of the locust plague would be one more link in the series.

The phrase עַל־הָרָעָה וְנִחַם (*weniḥam 'al-hārā'â*, "and He might relent of calamity") contains two words that have more than one sense, depending on the context. "And repententh him of the evil" in KJV highlights the problem. First, *niḥam* can be used of people who repent from their sins (Job 42:6; Jer. 8:6; 31:19), though the usage is rare (more commonly שׁוּב, *šûb*). The basic idea, however, is to change from a certain course of action or to relent.

The second problematic term, translated "evil" in both KJV and *NASB*, refers to natural catastrophes as well as to moral evil (cf. *NIV*, "calamity"). Thus it is used of the judgment on Sodom and Gomorrah (Gen. 19:19) and of the Babylonian invasion of Judah (Jer. 1:14). Both incidents were brought about by the Lord but grounded in His righteous character. In the context of Joel, the thought is that the disaster brought by the locusts could be turned around even while the crisis was going on. More importantly, the judgment that will come with the day of the Lord can be turned back. God is not anxious to bring it; He would much prefer to bring a blessing. Hence, it is in His nature to relent or hold back from judgment, even when it is due.[2]

2:14 In v. 14 Joel applies the general truths about God's nature to the specific problem at hand. The question "Who knows?" (מִי יוֹדֵעַ, *mî yôdēa'*) is equivalent to "perhaps";[3] it expresses some hope that the Lord will hold back once again from the full force of His judgment.

Previously Joel warned that "grain offerings" (*minḥâ*) and "libations" (*nesek*) were cut off from the Temple because God had brought the locust plague and the famine (1:9, 13). Now he speaks of a possible new harvest from which an offering could be presented. If God chooses to be gracious in response to repentance, says Joel, perhaps there will once again be what is required for the Temple service. The renewal of sacrifice will be a sign that the Lord has heard.

The second half of the first line, בְּרָכָה אַחֲרָיו וְהִשְׁאִיר (*wěhiš'îr 'aḥărāyw běrākâ*), is literally "and leave behind Him a blessing." "Behind Him" implies that the Lord will visit the land afresh, leaving behind a blessing (cf. *JB*, "leave a blessing as he passes"). As Wolff notes, "behind Him" contrasts with "behind them" of v. 3, that is, the army of locusts.[4] The Hebrew is the same for both (*'aḥărāyw*), because of the collective singular pronoun for the army. The second line clarifies the nature of the blessing with an apposition: "a grain offering and a libation for Yahweh your God." Since the people do not have the plant products necessary to prepare these offerings, the offerings stand for a new harvest that will make them possible.

---

[2] For further discussion of the theological problem of God changing His mind, see *The New Scofield Reference Bible* on Zech. 8:14 and Marvin R. Wilson, *TWOT* 2:571.

[3] Hans Walter Wolff, *Joel and Amos* (Hermeneia; trans. Waldemar Janzen, et al.; Philadelphia: Fortress, 1977), p. 50.

[4] Wolff, *Joel and Amos*, p. 50.

Additional Notes

2:12 יהוה: LXX has ηύριος ὁ Θεὸς ὑμῶν ("the Lord your God"), probably by assimilation with the same phrase elsewhere in Joel (1:14; 2:14, 23, 26).

2. Appeal For A Solemn Assembly (2:15-17)

Translation

Sound a trumpet in Zion!
Consecrate a fast;
call for a solemn assembly.
[16]Gather the people;
sanctify the congregation;
assemble the elders.
Gather the children
and the nursing infants.
Let the bridegroom come out of his room,
and the bride from her chamber.
[17]Between the porch and the altar
let the priests weep,
those who minister to Yahweh.
And let them say,
"Spare Your people, O Yahweh!
And do not make Your inheritance a reproach,
(allowing) the nations taunt them.
Why should it be said among the peoples,
'Where is their God?'"

Exegesis and Exposition

With great urgency Joel exhorts the entire nation to come together for a time of national mourning and appeal to the Lord. All segments of the population are to be present; neither age nor prior responsibility can be an exemption. The priests are to intercede for all the people, calling on the Lord to remember His covenant relationship with them. As the Lord's unique possession, Israel must not be put to shame among the nations.

2:15 Previously (2:1) the trumpet sounded to give warning of the approaching day of the Lord. Now in v. 15 Joel calls for it to be blown to assemble the people so they might repent as a nation. Consequently, the passage harks back to the commands of 1:13-14.

The verb קִדֵּשׁ (*qiddēš*) normally has the idea to "make holy" or "sanctify." While this is its sense in v. 16 (i.e., prepare the congregation ritually for a religious service), with צֹום (*ṣôm*, "fasting") as its object, it must mean something like "set apart a time for fasting."

2:16 By way of climax, in v. 16 Joel draws out the thought of a complete assembly of *all* the people. Previously only the elders and "all the inhabitants of the land" were specified. The sense of urgency is heightened as Joel dwells on every single person within Judah and Jerusalem, regardless of age or prior commitment. The existence of the community is under a dire threat; all must come to plead before the Lord.

In light of the strong affinity with 1:14, it seems likely that "elders" is meant as a political or religious term rather than as a contrast between the old and the young. On the other hand, one might prefer to see a distinction from the very young children mentioned in the next line. If so, it seems strange that the parallel term is not rather בַּחוּרִים (bāḥûrîm, "young men"), as in 2:28 (MT 3:1).

The command to the bride (כַּלָּה, kallâ) and bridegroom (חָתָן, ḥātān) represents the most extreme example of the setting aside of a responsibility that might be expected under normal circumstances to have priority. For example, a man was exempt from military service for a year after his wedding (Deut. 24:5), but not even the anticipated intimacies of the wedding night could excuse the couple from participation in this solemn assembly.

2:17 The priests in v. 17 are to take up their position of intercession for the people between the entrance to the Temple (אוּלָם, 'ûlām) and the altar of burnt offering (מִזְבֵּחַ, mizbēaḥ). They weep on account of sins. The Hebrew actually places some emphasis on their location. Joel wants to be certain that the rituals performed are done both with a proper attitude of repentance and in the correct manner.

Joel frames a prayer for the priests to bring before the Lord. Notice how the reference to "Your people" appeals to the covenant that bound Israel and her God. The plea itself is to the Lord's tender feelings, in line with the description of Him as "abounding in lovingkindness" (v. 13). חוּסָה (ḥûsâ ("spare")) has the central idea of showing pity or compassion (cf. Deut. 7:16; Jonah 4:10, 11), but it is of the sort that motivates to action on behalf of another.[5] Nehemiah is the only other biblical author to use the term in a prayer: "For this also remember me, O my God, and *have compassion* on me according to the greatness of Your lovingkindness" (Neh. 13:22).

As Joel continues with the prayer of repentance, he again follows the example of Moses in appealing to the Lord's honor or glory. If Israel had perished while Moses led them in the wilderness, the other nations, which had already been impressed by the deliverance from Egypt, would say that the Lord did not have enough power left to also bring them into Canaan (Num. 14:15-16). Joel commands the priests to make their plea in a similar manner. If Judah, the nation that the Lord claimed as His "inheritance" (נַחֲלָה, naḥălâ), perishes altogether, then the nations will speak against them in a manner that will reflect upon the Lord Himself (cf. Neh. 4:4 [MT 3:36]).

KJV follows the ancient versions in rendering לִמְשָׁל־בָּם גּוֹיִם (limĕšol-bām gôyim): "that the heathen should rule over them." In isolation this would be the most normal interpretation of the Hebrew. However, the thought of the nations ruling the Judeans is too abrupt in this context. Wolff argues for the traditional interpretation on the basis that Joel really speaks of a foreign army rather than locusts.[6] Even if that were true, though, it would not change the demands of the

---

[5] S. Wagner, *TDOT* 4:272.

[6] Wolff, *Joel and Amos*, p. 52.

immediate context, which speaks of a "reproach" and of the nations talking derisively about the Lord's "possession."

Another possible interpretation is, "(Do not permit) the nations to raise a taunt against them." This less common meaning for the verb *māšal* occurs otherwise with the preposition ʿ*al* for the object of the taunt or byword (Ezek. 16:44), but Allen notes that other verbs of mocking sometimes use the preposition *beth* (2 Kings 2:23; 2 Chron. 30:10).[7] However, the examples are so few that it is impossible to make a definitive statement. Jeremiah juxtaposed "reproach" and "proverb" in a similar context (Jer. 24:9). The last line of the verse clarifies the sense, "Why should it be said among the nations, 'Where is their God?'"

Additional Notes

2:16 Some have thought that the call for every person in the nation, including young children, to assemble at the Temple must point to a postexilic date for the book. The reasoning is that in preexilic times there would have been too many people in Judah for such a massive meeting. Yet this does not seem convincing. Joel's language could be taken as hyperbole to stress the need for complete rededication to the Lord throughout the land. The "nursing infants," for example, could hardly participate meaningfully in a rending of the "heart."

2:17 וְיֹאמְרוּ: The poetic balance would be improved by taking מְשָׁרְתֵי יהוה as a preposed subject ("The ministers of Yahweh – yes, let them say"). The editor of *BHS* even goes so far as to propose a transposition so that the verb with the conjunction would occur before the subject. Perhaps, though, the verb receives greater stress by being the sole member of its verse unit. Everywhere else in Joel, מְשָׁרְתֵי יהוה occurs in apposition with הַכֹּהֲנִים, an interpretation supported here by the Masoretic accents. Possibly the poetic rhythm can be explained as an instance of enjambment.

B. The Lord's Response (2:18-27)

Translation

> Then Yahweh became zealous for His land,
> and had pity for His people.
> [19]So Yahweh responded and said:
> "Behold, I am going to send you
> grain and new wine and fresh oil,
> and you will be satisfied with them.
> And I will not make you again
> a reproach among the nations.
> [20]And the northern (army)
> I will remove far from you.

---

[7] Leslie C. Allen, *The Books of Joel, Obadiah, Jonah and Micah* (NICOT; Grand Rapids: Eerdmans, 1976), p. 77 n. 64.

I will drive it away to a dry and desolate land,
its vanguard into the eastern sea
and its rear guard into the western sea.
Its stench will rise up.
Yes, let its foul odor rise up,
for it has acted arrogantly.
[21]Do not be afraid, land.
Rejoice and be glad!
For Yahweh has done great things.
[22]Do not be afraid, beasts of the field,
for the wilderness pastures have sprouted grass,
for the trees have borne their fruit,
the fig and vine have yielded their abundance.
[23]So, sons of Zion,
rejoice and be glad
in Yahweh your God.
For He has given you
*that which instructs in righteousness.
For he has poured down for you the rain,
the *early and latter rain *as before.
[24]Now the threshing floors will be full of grain,
and the vats will overflow with new wine and fresh oil.
Then I will make up to you for the years
which the swarming locust devoured,
the creeping locust and the stripping locust and the gnawing locust, –
My great army which I sent out among you.
[26]So you shall eat freely until full;
and you shall praise the name of Yahweh your God,
who has worked wonders for you.
And My people will never be put to shame.
[27]And you shall know that I am in the midst of Israel.
For I am Yahweh your God and there is no other,
and My people will never be put to shame."

Exegesis and Exposition

The first part of Joel presents the reader with a crisis, the people's repentance in response to it, and finally the Lord's response to the people. From an overall standpoint the segment should be viewed as narrative, though within it are found earnest pleas and promises. The account forms a perfect illustration of the Lord's word through Zechariah (1:3), "Return to Me ... that I may return to you." Joel impresses on his listeners the good news that God is eager to show mercy and blessing, reluctant to send His judgment.

A fresh promise by the Lord to restore the nation from the effects of the locust plague forms part of His gracious response given in 2:18-27. The relationship between the Lord and His people is reaffirmed: they will know Him as Yahweh and He will live in their midst.

The response has three parts to it. First (vv. 18-20), the Lord promises to restore the crops and remove the army of locusts. In the second part (vv. 21-23), the people are called to rejoicing because the Lord has already begun to act. Evidently fresh rainfall was the sign that the Lord had relented. Finally (vv. 24-27), the Lord promises to make up for what the locusts have done and to live among His people.

2:18 At vv. 18 and 19 the verbs abruptly change to the forms normally used for narrating events that have taken place in the past (*waw*-consecutive with the "imperfect"):

וַיְקַנֵּא, *wayĕqannē'*, "and He became zealous";

וַיַּחְמֹל, *wayyaḥmōl*, "and He had pity";

וַיַּעַן, *wayya'an*, "and He answered";

וַיֹּאמֶר, *wayyō'mer*, "and He said."

Yet some versions (e.g., KJV, *NASB*, and *NIV*) translate as though Joel is making a prediction. Thus *NASB*, "Then the LORD will be zealous ... ,/ And will have pity ... ,/ And the LORD will answer and say. . . ." On the other hand, the marginal renderings in *NASB* and *NIV* as well as the modified rendering of the KJV in the *New Scofield Reference Bible* all have past tense forms. Obviously, then, it is difficult to decide on how best to render the meaning intended by Joel, though the evidence may support the past tense view the best.

First, recall how Joel pled for a national repentance so that *perhaps* (v. 14) the Lord would relent concerning the punishment. If He now turns around and promises that the Lord *will* respond, it seems inconsistent. That is, Joel calls for these actions with the hope that the Lord will respond. He does not say that, if the people do this, the Lord *must* respond.

Returning to the grammar for a moment, in v. 19 the verbs are of the type that indicate response within a narrative, "so Yahweh answered and said to His people." The idiom is so established within all of biblical Hebrew literature that it is hard to imagine a future interpretation without strong contextual arguments to the contrary (see Additional Notes).

Finally, the structure of the book of Joel is built on a comparison between what happened in the past and what will happen in the future. The fact that God did respond to His people in their crisis becomes the pledge that in the future day of the Lord all who call upon His name will be saved. If the Lord had not responded, who would be present to hear Joel's charge to teach these events to their children and grandchildren (1:3)?

One might object that if the people did respond, we cannot take literally the threefold promise given in this section: "I will never again make you a reproach among the nations" (2:19, 26, 27). This promise must be seen within the context of the covenant with Israel, which is eternal. The "reproach" refers apparently to God's abandonment of Israel. Thus, the promise given through Joel is roughly equivalent to that given to Abraham, and later to David, of an everlasting relationship with Israel. The Jewish people have suffered much, but God has still preserved them from complete destruction. They stand as testimony to the greatness of our God. Certainly we can also say that the applicability of the promise to individuals within the covenant community depends on individual faith and obedience.[8]

The full sequence of events in the narrative is: 1) the prophet announces a great catastrophe; 2) he calls for repentance; 3) the people repent; 4) God responds. The fact that Joel does not report explicitly that the people did repent calls for some explanation. Of course, when the text says the Lord "answered" (v. 19) His people, a response to some action on their part is implied. Still it is unusual that such a major event would be only implied. Would it not be a great thing to report a large scale response to the preaching of a prophet?

That which is so obvious that it needs no mention is also less important or less prominent. The book of Joel stresses what the Lord does. He brought the locusts and removed them; He will pour out the Spirit and judge the nations. The sovereign God chooses to maintain His eternal covenant with His people not because *they* have responded but because *He* is gracious and compassionate. The particular people contemporary with Joel must have responded, but the invitation to call upon God and receive His grace remains open forever.

The passage begins with יְהוָה לְאַרְצוֹ יְהוָה אֵ‍קַנֵּ‍א‍ ו‍ (*wayĕqannē' YHWH lĕ'arṣô* ("then Yahweh became zealous for His land"). The root *qn'* can refer to either jealousy or zeal. Here the idea is that the Lord, remembering His everlasting covenant with His people, determined to act swiftly on their behalf. Isaiah spoke of the Lord's zeal that would fulfill His promises to Israel (Isa. 9:7 [MT 9:6]; 37:32), but the closest parallel is found in Zechariah, who reports God's "gracious" and "comforting" words to His people: "I am very zealous for Jerusalem and Zion" (Zech. 1:14). That is, the Lord has noticed their lowly condition (vision of the myrtle trees, 1:8) but is now prepared to act.[9]

The Targum, Peshitta, LXX, and Vulg. use the past tense for the verb. The future tense is found as early as Theodotian. While the *waw*-consecutive form of the verb is almost never translated as future, it may be rendered that way if it is included with actions stated in the "prophetic perfect" (Isa 9:6 [MT 9:5]; see also Additional Notes). Some would find that form in Joel 2:23,[10] but see the exegesis below.

2:19 The Lord's answer becomes concrete through the promises in v. 19 to restore all the yield destroyed by the locusts and to remove the insects far from them. These two actions are linked by a word of reassurance: "And I will never again make you a reproach among the nations."

A representative occurs for each of the three categories of lost crops: grain, vine, and tree. The extent of the deprivation suffered will be matched by a sense of fullness and satisfaction with the abundant yield.

---

[8] Cf. Walter C. Kaiser, Jr., *The Uses of the Old Testament in the New* (Chicago: Moody, 1985), p. 166.

[9] For a slightly different emphasis on the interpretation of קָנָא in Zech. 2:14, see Kenneth L. Barker, "Zechariah," in *EBC*, ed. Frank E. Gaebelein (Grand Rapids: Zondervan, 1985), 7:612-13.

[10] P. Paul Joüon, *Grammaire de l'hébreu biblique* (Rome: Institut Biblique Pontifical, 1965), par. 118s.

2:20 The term "northerner" (הַצְּפוֹנִי, haṣṣĕpônî) in v. 20 provides the strongest argument for those who see a literal army behind the description of the locust invasion in chap. 2. Feinberg, for example, says, "Literal locusts ... would scarcely be called 'the northern army'."[11] On the other hand, at least one modern report notes a locust plague that did come from the north.[12] Also, the locusts are reported under the figure of an invading army. Because of the geographical setting of Jerusalem most foreign armies invade from the north regardless of their direction of origin (cf. Jer. 1:14).

Jerome observed about a locust plague in his day, "And when the shores of both seas (the Mediterranean and the Dead Sea) were filled with heaps of dead locusts which the waters had cast up, their stench and putrefaction was so noxious as to corrupt the air, so that a pestilence was produced among both beasts and men."[13] Of course, the dead of a defeated army also develops a stench (Isa. 34:3; Amos 4:10), and the military imagery still lies behind the passage. The similarities between locusts and an invading army form the basis for the military terms used in the passage (פָּנָיו, pānāyw, "its vanguard," lit. "its face," and סֹפוֹ, sōpô, "its rear guard," lit. "its end").

Locusts do not have motives, but they have acted like an army that would enter the land and destroy everything at will. The Hebrew construction הִגְדִּיל לַעֲשׂוֹת (higdîl la'ăśôt, "it acted arrogantly") is literally, "for it has shown itself great to act" (intransitive hiphil). This follows a well known pattern where a finite verb precedes an infinitive, with the latter expressing the main action while the former gives an adverbial modification.[14]

The same expression is repeated in v. 21 but is applied to the Lord: "For Yahweh has done great things." Evidently Joel intends to contrast the arrogant enemy (cf. Jer. 48:26; Dan. 8:4, 8, 11, 25; Zeph. 2:8, 10) and the Lord who has acted in a great manner (cf. Ps. 126:2, 3), with repetition highlighting the contrast.[15] Joel also uses similarity or repetition for contrast elsewhere in his book (e.g., "behind it/them" in 2:3 with "behind Him" in 2:14; "consecrate a fast" and "call for a solemn assembly" in 1:14 and 2:15 with "prepare for a holy war" [lit., "consecrate a war"] and "proclaim this among the nations" in 3:9 [MT 4:9]).

An alternative view is represented in the *NIV*: "Surely he has done great things." The *NIV* further divides the passage so that the statement is introductory to v. 21 rather than the conclusion to v. 20. As a result, the repetition of the same phrase in v. 21 makes for a closure, with the pronoun referent in v. 20 anticipating the reference to the Lord in the next verse. The ancient versions support the first

---

[11] Charles Lee Feinberg, *The Minor Prophets* (Chicago: Moody, 1976), p. 79.

[12] Walter K. Price, *The Prophet Joel and the Day of the Lord* (Chicago: Moody, 1976), p. 61, cites a 1915 report in the *National Geographic* by John D. Whiting. See also Allen, *Joel*, p. 88.

[13] Cited by Julius A. Bewer, *A Critical and Exegetical Commentary on Obadiah and Joel* (ICC; Edinburgh: T. & T. Clark, 1974), p. 113.

[14] See Ronald J. Williams, *Hebrew Syntax: An Outline*, 2d ed. (Toronto: Univ. of Toronto, 1976), par. 226.

[15] Cf. Robert B. Chisholm, Jr., "Wordplay in the Eighth-Century Prophets," *BSac* 144 (1987): 52.

phrase as a reference to the army (cf. Targum, "For he has shown himself great to do evil").[16]

2:21 The commands to rejoice in v. 21 balance the earlier calls to mourning and repentance. Also, the exhortations occur between two parts of the Lord's response (2:18-20, 24-27), much as 1:15-2:11 interrupts the call to repentance.

The invitation to joy comes first to the ground itself, then to the cattle, and finally to the people. Since the well-being of the people depends on the condition of the ground and the cattle, the whole unit really speaks to the Judeans. Yet the poetic personification of land and beasts lends vividness to the blessing of God. Perhaps the order is intended to replicate that of original creation: earth, beasts, man. It is as though the Lord re-created Judah after its terrible devastation.

The verse closes by repeating from v. 20 the phrase *kî higdîl la'ăśôt*. Only now Yahweh is inserted as the subject: "For Yahweh has done great things" (*kî higdîl YHWH la'ăśôt*). The Lord has acted creatively and brought blessing (cf. Ps. 126), contrary to the locusts which acted arrogantly and brought devastation. Rain and a revitalizing of the wilderness occur prominently in this section. Perhaps a fresh outpouring of rain was the physical sign that enabled Joel to say, in v. 18, "Then Yahweh was zealous for His land." Alternatively, some take the verbs in these verses as prophetic perfects.[17]

2:23 Joel uses a rare designation for the Judeans in v. 23, calling them "sons of Zion" (elsewhere only Ps. 149:2 and Lam. 4:2). Ps. 149 calls for glad praise to the Lord as King: "Let the sons of Zion rejoice in their King." The sequence of disaster-repentance-restoration makes it clear that the Lord, their God, has delivered them.

Rain apparently was a sign that the Lord accepted His people's cry for mercy. הַמּוֹרֶה לִצְדָקָה (*hammôreh liṣĕdāqâ*) is one of the most difficult phrases in the book to translate. In isolation the term *môreh* could be taken as "teacher," a rendering found as early as the Targum (actually, "your teachers in righteousness," מלפיכון בזכו, *mallĕpêkôn bizĕkû*). The immediate context of Joel gives no reason to expect the introduction of a person in such vague terms.

Môreh can also mean "early rain," but "He has given you the early rain" also raises a contextual problem. How do we explain the later reference in the same verse to "early rain" (*môreh*)? The term גֶּשֶׁם (*gešem*) is a more general word for rain; why then does *môreh* occur first in a summary statement as a more general term but later as a particular type of rain?

If teaching is implied by the term *hammôreh*, it is better to take it in an impersonal sense: "that which instructs."[18] Then the rain the Lord sends on the earth would be a sign to point people to the restoration of a right covenant relationship. Notice also how this view would solve the problem of the two occurrences of *môreh*. The same word would be used with two different meanings. In other words, we are dealing with a wordplay. The wordplay is strengthened by

---

[16] אסגי יוי למעבד ביך טבון לעמיה but in v. 20 אסגי למעבד ביש, "YHWY has shown Himself great to do good with you, for His people," in v. 21.

[17] C. F. Keil, *Minor Prophets*, (COTTV 10; Grand Rapids: Eerdmans, 1973), p. 204-5.

[18] Richard D. Patterson, "Joel," in *EBC*, 7:254.

the frequent association in the OT between teaching and rain (1 Kings 8:36; Isa. 45:8) or between the Lord and rain (Isa. 30:20-23; Hos. 6:3; 10:12).[19] In fact, the pouring out of rain as a sign of righteousness would also parallel the pouring out of the Spirit, which occurs later in Joel.

The "early rain" (מוֹרֶה, môreh, usually יוֹרֶה, yôreh; see Additional Notes) occurs in the fall, while the "latter rain" (מַלְקוֹשׁ, malqôš) comes in the spring. "That which instructs in righteousness" probably means the restoration of the proper cycles of rain. This teaches the people that God has taken steps to reestablish the normal operation of His covenant with Israel.[20]

2:24 The plant products (v. 24), which before had been completely destroyed, will now be in great abundance. בַּר (bār, "grain") occurs for the first and only time in Joel, though תִּירוֹשׁ (tîrôš, "new wine") and יִצְהָר (yiṣhār, "fresh oil") have appeared before (1:10; 2:19).

2:25 Going along with the promise of complete restoration to covenant harmony, the Lord purposes to "pay back" or make up for all the damage that the locusts had done (v. 25). So He speaks of a great abundance of crops that will completely fill the people's stomachs. What began as mournful sorrow because of emptiness ends with joy because of plenty.

But there are also spiritual blessings. Whereas before the people stood under judgment and the near loss of all hope, now they will praise God's name because of the miracles He has performed. The people will recognize that God is in their midst. Thus, the broken relationship between God and His people will be healed.

When Joel reiterates the list of locusts in this verse, he changes the order from that of 1:4. Actually, the only term that has changed position is גָּזָם (gāzām, the "gnawing locust"). Possibly the change also stresses the reversal of the fortunes of the people.

In this verse Joel also explicitly connects the locusts with God's army (הַגָּדוֹל חֵילִי, ḥêlî haggādôl, "My great army"). Therefore, the locusts would seem to be the primary figure behind the invading army of 2:2-11. The translator of the Targum even here could not be satisfied that the text spoke only of locusts, adding, "the years when the nations and foreign powers and kingdoms plundered you." Foreign nations will be mentioned later in the book, but they will be singled out for judgment. The first part of the book speaks simply of locusts under the figure of an invading army. The imagery no doubt dredged up memories of past invasions or fears of future conquest, but Joel concentrated on a particular, literal locust plague that was removed by the Lord in response to the repentance of the people.

2:26-27 Joel sums up God's actions by saying they are "wondrous" or "miraculous" (לְהַפְלִיא, lĕhaplî', "in a wondrous manner"). The events the prophet

---

[19] See G. W. Ahlström, *Joel and the Temple Cult of Jerusalem* (VTSup 21; Leiden: E. J. Brill, 1971), pp. 98-110. He demonstrates successfully that the concept of teaching need not seem strange in the Joel passage but is not so convincing in proving that a *personal* teacher is in view.

[20] The *waw*-consecutive with וַיּוֹרֶד (wayyôred) is apparently explanatory ("*for* He has poured down"). See Joüon, *Grammaire*, par. 118j., for other examples of explanatory *waw*-consecutive.

has recounted for Judah cannot be explained in any ordinary way. Only the Lord could have brought both the grievous punishment and the joyous relief that came with His deliverance. These wondrous dealings are told to make the people see the truth: "I [Yahweh] am in the midst of Israel." For Joel the transformation is complete. Woes have given way to a new glory.

The thrice-repeated promise of no more reproach among the nations is the last thing said in the first half of the book. It points the way forward to God's future dealings with Israel and the nations.

Additional Notes

2:18-19 וַיֹּאמֶר ... וַיַּעַן ... וַיַּחְמֹל ... וַיְקַנֵּא: For centuries grammarians have been debating the proper function of the Hebrew "imperfect" with *waw*-consecutive.[21] In 1981 I discussed the form in some detail,[22] concluding that the form would be better named *wayyiqtōl*, since in *function* it is more aligned with the "perfect" than with the "imperfect." Part of the evidence is the fact that sometimes *wayyiqtōl* forms can occur in place of "prophetic perfects." Even so, this usage is rather limited. Leslie McFall compared all the *wayyiqtōl* forms with their translation in the *RSV*, finding that of 14,972 instances 14,202 were translated as past. Of the remaining 770 cases, only 30 received a future translation. These included two in Exodus, one in Deuteronomy, five in Isaiah, two in Jeremiah, nine in Ezekiel, one in Hosea, one in Micah, and nine in the Psalms.[23] Some additional major works on the Hebrew verb include the following:

S. R. Driver, *A Treatise on the Use of the Tenses in Hebrew*, 3d ed. (1892; repr.; Oxford, Clarendon, 1969); G. R. Driver, *Problems of the Hebrew Verbal System* (Edinburgh: T. & T. Clark, 1936); Frank R. Blake, *A Resurvey of Hebrew Tenses* (Rome: Pontificium Institutum Biblicum, 1951); Frithiof Rundgren, *Das althebräische Verbum: Abriss der Aspektlehre* (Stockholm: Almqvist & Wiksell, 1961); Péter Kustar, *Aspekt im Hebräischen* (Basel: Friedrich Reinhardt Kommissionsverlag, 1972); T. Mettinger, "The Hebrew Verb System: A Survey of Recent Research," *ASTI* 9 (1973): 64-84; Michael H. Silverman, "Syntactic Notes on the *Waw* Consecutive," in *Orient and Occident: Essays Presented to Cyrus H. Gordon* ..., ed. H. A. Hoffner (AOAT 22; Neukirchen-Vluyn: Neukirchener Verlag, 1973); W. Gross, *Verbform und Funktion. wayyiqtol für die Gegenwart?* (Arbeiten zu Text und Sprache im Alten Testament 1; St. Ottilien: Eos, 1976); James A. Hughes, "Another Look at the Hebrew Tenses," *JNES* 29 (1979): 12-24.

---

[21] See Leslie McFall, *The Enigma of the Hebrew Verbal System: Solutions from Ewald to the Present Day* (Historic Texts and Interpreters in Biblical Scholarship 2; Sheffield: Almond, 1982). He includes a brief survey of grammatical thought from Saadia Gaon (882-942) to N. W. Schroeder (1721-1798) and a more detailed analysis of discussions between 1800 and 1954.

[22] Thomas J. Finley, "The *Waw*-Consecutive with 'Imperfect' in Biblical Hebrew: Theoretical Studies and Its Use in Amos," in *Tradition and Testament: Essays in Honor of Charles Lee Feinberg*, ed. John Feinberg and Paul Feinberg (Chicago: Moody, 1981), pp. 241-62.

[23] McFall, *Enigma of the Hebrew Verbal System*, pp. 18, 187.

2:23 הַמּוֹרֶה: The Peshitta and LXX have equivalents for "food" in the place occupied by the Hebrew term. Wolff feels that the versions offer a superior text,[24] but the evidence does not seem strong enough to depart from MT. The wordplay contained in MT argues for its originality. Possibly the meaning "food" was surmised from the context by the translators of both versions.[25]

מוֹרֶה: The term is unexpected for "early rain"; elsewhere it is rather יוֹרֶה (Deut. 11:14; Jer. 5:24). As noted in *BHS*, many Hebrew manuscripts actually have יוֹרֶה. However, the use of מוֹרֶה in Ps. 84:7 offers some support for the more difficult reading, though that passage is itself controversial. *Mu-ru-ú* in an Akkadian/Sumerian lexicon found at Ugarit with the meaning "rainstorm" is of interest,[26] though it is not necessarily connected with the Hebrew form.

S. R. Driver wants to remove this (second) occurrence of מוֹרֶה, because he sees three types of rain: הַמּוֹרֶה, the autumn rains; גֶּשֶׁם, the winter rains; and מַלְקוֹשׁ, the spring rains.[27] A better speculation than deletion would be to read מַרְוֶה (*marweh*), with metathesis of *waw* and *resh*, resulting in "copious rain."

בָּרִאשׁוֹן: The Targum has "in the month Nisan," that is, in the first month. In fact, this is the meaning of every other instance of the Hebrew phrase (cf. Gen. 8:13; Ex. 12:18). Yet in the other passages it is also linked with a further specification of the day. Additionally, the Targum's translation does not make much sense in the context. Therefore, most have followed the Peshitta and LXX, "as at the first." This would be a difficult understanding of the Hebrew, though perhaps not impossible. Many prefer to emend the Hebrew to כָּרִאשׁוֹן (cf. the marginal note in *NASB*).

---

[24] Wolff, *Joel and Amos*, p. 55 n. i. See also Douglas Stuart, *Hosea to Jonah* (WBC 31; Waco, Tex.: Word, 1987), p. 256 n. 23.a.

[25] For some issues and problems involved in agreements between Peshitta and LXX, see M. J. Mulder, "The Use of the Peshitta in Textual Criticism," in *La Septuaginta en la investigacion contemporanea (V Congreso de la IOSCS)*, ed. Natalio Fernandez Marcos (Madrid: Instituto "Arias Montano," 1985), pp. 37-53, esp. p. 53.

[26] *CAD*, "M," 2:229.

[27] Driver, *Joel and Amos*, p. 62.

4
Wonders in the Earth
(Joel 2:28-32 [MT 3:1-5])

The second part of Joel's book has certain characteristics that set it off from the first part of the book. First, it is framed almost entirely in the future. The only exception is found in 3:2-6 (MT 4:2-6), which states that the nations will be called to answer before God because of how they have treated His people, Israel. Here, in fact, is a second difference. In the first part of the book we hear nothing about what the nations have done to Israel, only about the havoc wrought by the locusts. Nor is there any word about the destruction of the nations in the first half. Third, the second part of Joel becomes more extravagant about physical and spiritual blessing for Israel when it speaks of the pouring out of the Spirit and of the mountains and hills of Judah flowing with sweet wine and milk.

The final portion of the book may be divided into two further sections. First, Joel speaks of the pouring out of the Spirit and the day of the Lord (2:28-32 [MT 3:1-5]). He had already preached the necessity of repentance in order to escape the judgment that will come with that day. Moreover, historical events had proven he was correct. The people repented and the Lord graciously responded by relenting from total destruction and restoring the land and people. Now it is revealed through Joel that, when the "great and awesome day of Yahweh" is near, the Spirit of God will be poured out on all the people of Israel. This will lead to a new era of prophecy with the result that many will call on the Lord's name and find deliverance. Joel's successful preaching in his own day foreshadowed this fresh period of prophetic utterance.

In the second section Joel turns to the fate of the nations in the day of the Lord, including Israel (3:1-21 [MT 4:1-21]). The foreign nations will be judged because they have mistreated God's people. Therefore, Joel sees a contrast between how the Lord will deal with Israel and how He will treat the other nations. Israel, as the Lord's special possession, will be saved and will receive the Spirit. The nations, on the other hand, will have to answer for how they have oppressed the covenant people. Their punishment will follow the pattern of their guilt. The Phoenicians and Philistines will be sold into slavery to the Judeans; all the nations will suffer defeat in battle at the hands of the Lord's army; and Egypt and Edom will be left desolate. The Israelites, on the other hand, will return from their captivity, find great deliverance, and experience unprecedented blessing in their land.

After the locust plague, the Lord poured out a blessing in the form of abundant rain to show He had accepted the repentance of the Judeans. Repentance also results in spiritual changes in the individual brought about by the Lord. The people were sadly unprepared for the locust invasion, but when the fearsome day of God's wrath finally arrives, He will accomplish a fresh spiritual work in them. The outward sign of the inner divine work will be prophecy, and deliverance will come through firm trust in the name of Yahweh. The very elements of the universe will collapse, but God's people will stand firm upon their land.

Translation

Now it will happen after this:
I will pour out My Spirit on all flesh,
and your sons and your daughters will prophesy.
Your old men will dream dreams;
your young men will see visions.
And even on *the servants and on *the maidservants
in those days I will pour out My Spirit.
Then I will display wonders in the sky and on the earth,
blood and fire and columns of smoke.
The sun will be turned to darkness
and the moon to blood
before the day of Yahweh comes,
that great and awesome (day).
Then it will happen (that)
all who call on the name of Yahweh will be delivered.
For on Mount Zion and in Jerusalem
there will be an escaped remnant,
just as Yahweh has said,
*even among the survivors whom Yahweh calls.

Exegesis and Exposition

In this section Joel deals with the spiritual and physical phenomena that will accompany the end times. The prophet looks through the broad sweep of history to the day when the Lord Himself will establish justice in the earth by judging the unrighteous and setting up a new kingdom for His people. As the final chapter of the book makes clear, Israel had suffered much injustice at the hands of the nations, but in that day all will be made right. The people will serve God from their hearts and have no fear for the terrifying effects of divine wrath upon the earth.

2:28a (MT 3:1a) Joel uses a striking expression to place the second part of his book in a later age. Though אַחֲרֵי־כֵן ('aḥărê-kēn) can be used for actions that follow immediately (Ex. 11:1; 1 Sam. 24:5), here it is prefaced by וְהָיָה (wĕhāyâ, "and it will come about"), a statement that often introduces new predictions in the prophetic books (e.g., Isa. 7:21; Jer. 17:24; Ezek. 38:10; Hos. 1:5; Amos 8:9; Mic. 5:10 [MT 5:9]; Zeph. 1:10; Zech. 13:2). The previous section also dealt with the future, but the sequence is, first, restoration of a state of blessing following the locust plague, then at a later time, the pouring out of the Spirit.

Jeremiah (46:26; 49:6) uses wĕ'aḥărê-kēn to refer to a time when the Gentile nations will be brought under God's blessing (cf. Isa. 1:26). Peter's citation of Joel's passage in Greek translates as, "and it shall be in the last days" (Acts 2:17), giving its general sense (see Excursus on the Citation of Joel 2:28-32 in Acts 2:17-

21). Feinberg cites Hos. 3:5 as a parallel passage.[1] It refers to a time "afterward" (אַחַר, 'aḥar) when Israel will "return and seek Yahweh their God and David their king," and the parallel phrase in the same verse mentions "the last days."

2:28b (MT 3:1b) Almost immediately Joel centers our attention on the key event of this section, the pouring out of the Spirit. כָּל־בָּשָׂר (kol-bāśār, "all flesh") can mean all animals and people on earth (Gen. 9:15; Dan. 4:12), but its sphere of application is restricted by the context. Since God here speaks of the pouring out of the Spirit, animals are obviously not in question. A more difficult issue is whether the prophet intends to include only all Israelites (cf. Num. 18:15 [also their cattle]; Jer. 12:12; 45:5; Ezek. 21:4, 5 [MT 21:9, 10]) or all people on earth (Gen. 6:12; Num. 16:22; 27:16; Job 34:15; Ps. 145:21; Zech. 2:13 [MT 2:17]). In two passages it is restricted to all the wicked (Isa. 66:16; Jer. 25:31).

While there is a certain abruptness about the new passage, there is no reason to think Joel is not still addressing the community of Judah and Jerusalem. Therefore, when he applies the results of the action to his audience ("your [plural] sons ... your young men"), we should also restrict the action itself to that community. Thus, those who escape the judgment brought with the day of the Lord are "on Mount Zion and in Jerusalem." Finally, other OT references to the pouring out of the Spirit refer especially to Israel (Isa. 32:15; 44:3-4; Ezek. 36:27; 37:14; 39:29; Zech. 12:10).

One side of the expression "all flesh" stresses inclusiveness within the sphere intended by the context, but another side sets living creatures apart from God. "All flesh is grass," proclaims Isaiah, "but the word of our God stands forever" (Isa. 40:7-8). Mankind could not even exist apart from that "breath of God" that gave him life (Gen. 2:7; Job 34:14-15). Yet there will be, says Joel, a new outpouring of God's Spirit resulting in a renewed community. The Targum heightens the contrast: "I will pour out My Holy Spirit on all flesh."

The image of pouring (אֶשְׁפֹּךְ, 'ešpōk, "I will pour out") refers to a liquid, making an interesting connection with the promise of rain in 2:23 (cf. Isa. 44:3). The point is that the Spirit will be available in abundance for anyone in Israel. Appropriation of the gift of God through faith would still be necessary, though the stress on universality would indicate a special work of grace by God to draw Israel to Himself (cf. Zech. 12:10; Rom. 11:25-26).

2:28c-e (MT 3:1c-e) Joel dwells on one result of God's new presence among His people – prophetic revelation. According to the Hebrew style of expression, this would not exclude other results. Isaiah views a new era of justice, righteousness, and peace that accompanies the coming of the Spirit (Isa. 32:15), while Ezekiel points to the obedience of those who have been cleansed and given a "new heart" (Ezek. 36:25-27). For Zechariah the new infusion of the Spirit gives a strong sense of sorrow over the time when the people rejected God's personal representative among them (Zech. 12:10). An element that accompanies all three, however, is a great regathering of God's people to their land (cf. Joel 3:1 [MT 4:1]). The common time reference leads us to connect these passages even though the prophets envisioned different (though certainly not conflicting) results.

---

[1] Charles L. Feinberg, *The Minor Prophets* (Chicago: Moody, 1976), p. 80.

When Joel speaks of those who prophesy, dream dreams, and see visions, the language must mean more than simply that, as Walter Price says, "everyone would be his own prophet. All would have a direct revelation from God."[2] Rather, it denotes a new era of revelation with the Israelites preaching to each other.

Is not the model Joel himself? He preached repentance and the whole community responded. As a result God's blessing came to all. In the future, says Joel, the entire population will become prophets, stimulating each other to serve the Lord. This prophetic revelation will be necessary because of the awesome signs that will accompany the day of the Lord. Israel will be delivered at this time, and God will use visions and dreams to reassure His people and give a warning to the world.

2:29 (MT 3:2) Walter Kaiser argues for a broader application of "all flesh" because the gift of the Spirit extends to slaves:

> Then by way of surprise the prophet abruptly declared "and also" or "and even" ($w^e gam$) menservants and maidservants would receive the Spirit of God. It is this epexegetical addition that was marked by the "and even" phrase that forces the interpreter to acknowledge that Joel had "all mankind" in mind here. Even the Gentile slaves in the Jewish households would benefit in this outpouring.[3]

Kaiser is correct that "menservants" and "maidservants" would include Gentiles (see also Additional Notes). Slaves could be obtained in Israel through war (Deut. 20:10-14) or acquired from foreign sources (cf. the "maids" of Rachel and Leah, Gen. 30:3, 9; also 2 Chron. 2:34-35). Yet it was also possible for Israelites to become slaves, though usually in a more temporary sense, by selling themselves (Ex. 21:1-6) or their children (Ex. 21:7-11; cf. 2 Kings 4:1).[4] Consider, however, that slaves would still be counted as under the covenant (cf. Ex. 20:10; Deut. 12:12, 18; 16:11, 14).[5] "All flesh" could be restricted to Israelites yet still include their (Gentile and/or Israelite) slaves.

One might suppose the element of surprise (וְגַם, *wĕgam*, "and even") lies in the breaking down of all social barriers (cf. Gal. 3:28). However, prophetic revelation was not restricted to any particular social class. Perhaps *wĕgam* simply makes the element of universality prominent to its greatest extent. It would probably be surprising to most Israelites to think of slaves as participating, in any general way, in an outburst of prophetic visions. Once large numbers of them begin to see revelations, the full extent of the miracle will be apparent to all.

The text also stresses equal participation in the prophetic activity by women as well as men. The OT priesthood was limited to Levite men, while the office of king was hereditary through the son in the line of David. The prophetic office, on

---

[2] Walter K. Price, *The Prophet Joel and the Day of the Lord* (Chicago: Moody, 1976), p. 74; cf. Hans Walter Wolff, *Joel and Amos* (Hermeneia; trans. Waldemar Janzen, et al.; Philadelphia: Fortress, 1977), pp. 66-67.

[3] Walter C. Kaiser, Jr., *The Uses of the Old Testament in the New* (Chicago: Moody, 1985), p. 97.

[4] For more details see I. Mendelsohn, "Slavery in the OT," *IDB* 4:383-91.

[5] See Wolff, *Joel and Amos*, p. 67.

the other hand, was always open to anyone, though the number of women who filled the position was small as far as can be discerned from the biblical materials. Deborah was an outstanding early example, and she contributed a chapter to canonical Scripture (Judg. 5; cf. Miriam, Ex. 15:20-21). At a later time the prophetess Huldah delivered a revelation to king Josiah about his personal future and the fate of the kingdom (2 Kings 22:11-20). The NT also knows of prophetesses (Luke 2:36). Joel's revelation puts emphasis on the fact that the prophetic gift will be common, perhaps even universal, among Israelite women, even among the female slaves.

The expression הָהֵמָּה בַּיָּמִים (bayyāmîm hāhēmmâ, "in those days") is another way the prophets indicate the end times when the Lord will intervene in history to deliver His people and set up His kingdom (cf. Jer. 33:15, 16; Zech. 8:23). Particularly important is the variety of terms Joel uses, as well as the way he gradually makes the time notices more explicit:

"after this" (2:28 [MT 3:1]);
"in those days" (2:29 [MT 3:2]);
"before the day of Yahweh, the great and awesome (day)" (2:31 [MT 3:4]);
"in those days and at that time,/ when I restore the fortunes of Judah and Jerusalem" (3:1 [MT 4:1]);
"the day of Yahweh is near" (3:14 [MT 4:14]);
"in that day" (3:18 [MT 4:18]).

2:30 (MT 3:3) The future community will face similar perils from the coming day of the Lord as the community in Joel's day. The blackness that accompanied the locusts corresponds to an even greater blackness in the sky itself. This will be, in fact, "the time of Jacob's trouble" (Jer. 30:4-9). The "blood, fire, and columns of smoke" evidently refer to the killing, pillaging, and burning that will accompany a great outbreak of war that will also engulf Israel (Zech. 12:2-9; 14:1-2).

The initial poetic line speaks in general terms of signs in the sky (שָׁמַיִם, šāmayim, "heavens") and on earth. Then the parallel line of v. 30 (MT 3:3) describes the effects on earth in more detail, while the heavenly manifestations are not depicted until v. 31 (MT 3:4). This gives a chiastic (A-B / B´-A´) structure to the unit.

A מוֹפֵת (môpēt) is a "sign" or "wonder" that points to the power of God who is able to bring it about, inspiring wonder and awe (cf. Ex. 4:21; 1 Kings 13:3, 5; 2 Chron. 32:24; Zech. 3:8). Here the signs will cause dread and fear as they anticipate the exact moment of the Lord's arrival on earth to carry out His judgment. These signs are similar to those of Rev. 6:12-17 wherein people say to the mountains and rocks, "Fall on us and hide us from the presence of Him who sits on the throne, and from the wrath of the Lamb; for the great day of their wrath has come; and who is able to stand?" (vv. 16-17; NASB).

2:31 (MT 3:4) The text does not specify exactly how the terrible effects in the sky will be accomplished. The sun could be darkened by eclipse, but heavy smoke in the atmosphere may be what turns the moon to blood-red. Perhaps the smoke will derive from volcanic and tectonic activity on the earth as well as through war.[6]

The signs in heaven and earth immediately precede the day of the Lord proper. This is because the key feature of that day will be the presence on earth of the Lord Himself (cf. Zech. 14:4). Then in His wrath He will judge the nations, which have mistreated His people (cf. Zeph. 1:18, "the day of Yahweh's wrath") but grant deliverance to all who call upon Him. Because the portents must accompany the day itself, other prophets include some of the prior events as well (Isa. 13:10; Zech. 14:1-2). Depending on the context, "day of the Lord" may include the broader period of the Lord's visitation, which culminates in the setting up of His kingdom on earth (Zech. 14), or it may stress (as in Joel) the central event of His actual appearance on earth to judge the nations. Of course, the same signs probably continue during the actual day. They serve as both harbinger and companion.

2:32 (MT 3:5) Just as the people in Joel's day called on the Lord and found deliverance, so none need perish in the day of the Lord. As long as Israel is in a state of apostasy from her God, she stands under the fear of His wrath. But Joel speaks of a God who is so gracious that He sends His Spirit to prepare His chosen people to turn back to Him and experience blessing rather than judgment.

Joel seems to quote or paraphrase כִּי בְּהַר־צִיּוֹן וּבִירוּשָׁלַיִם תִּהְיֶה פְלֵיטָה (*kî běhar-ṣiyyôn ûbîrûšālayim tihyeh pělêṭâ*, "For on Mount Zion and in Jerusalem there will be an escaped remnant"), in that it is followed by כַּאֲשֶׁר אָמַר יהוה (*ka'ăšer 'āmar YHWH*, "just as Yahweh has said"). The statement probably derives from Obad. 17 or possibly Isa. 37:31-32.[7] It is not impossible, however, that it reinforces previous promises in Joel (cf. Introduction to Joel).

Since *pělêṭâ* signifies an "escaped remnant" (see Exegesis on 2:3; cf. also Gen. 32:8 [MT 32:9]; 2 Kings 19:30; Ezra 9:13; Neh. 1:2) some of the Israelites will not escape the Lord's wrath – only those who turn back to Him. From the community that returns to the land, however, individuals will come to the Lord in unprecedented numbers because of the action of the Spirit.

Those delivered will "call upon" (יִקְרָא, *yiqrā'*) the Lord, but the Lord "calls" (קֹרֵא, *qōrē'*) the survivors. The verse reinforces the opening remarks about the gift of the Spirit. God's grace made it possible for Israel not only to obtain deliverance, but also to repent. Everything is ultimately wrapped up in His gracious election of His people (cf. 2:13; Eph 2:8-9).

In the phrase וּבַשְּׂרִידִים (*ûbaśśěrîdîm*, "and among the survivors") it seems best to take the *waw* as epexegetical ("even"), making the phrase qualify the *pělêṭâ* ("escaped remnant"). That is, the *pělêṭâ* consists of those whom the Lord has called. The structure of the whole verse is as follows:

---

[6] Cf. ibid., p. 68; Richard D. Patterson, "Joel," in *EBC*, ed. Frank E. Gaebelein (Grand Rapids: Zondervan, 1985), 7:256.

[7] See also John Day, "Prophecy," in *It is Written: Scripture Citing Scripture: Essays in Honour of Barnabas Lindars, SSF*, ed. D. A. Carson and H. G. M. Williamson (New York: Cambridge Univ., 1988), p. 49.

1. statement of deliverance – freely available for all who call on the name of Yahweh;
2. reason for deliverance – a previous promise of Yahweh;
3. further assurance of deliverance – Yahweh will call out the survivors.

Additional Notes

2:29 (MT 3:2) וְעַל־הָעֲבָדִים וְעַל־הַשְּׁפָחוֹת: Acts 2:18 has "upon My servants and upon My maidservants," whereas MT has "the servants and the maidservants." In isolation the Hebrew could be interpreted to allow the pronoun, but the context argues against it (yet note *NIV*). The earliest form of the LXX agrees with the MT, but later Greek revisions include the pronoun.[8] The Acts passage implies that the recipients of the Spirit are the Lord's servants. This does not contradict Joel's statement and is a legitimate extension of his general teaching.

2:32 (MT 3:5) וּבַשְּׂרִידִים: The LXX has "and those preaching good news" (και εὐαγγελιζόμενοι), evidently reading בשֹרים (although בשֹר does not elsewhere occur in the qal stem). Failure to recognize the epexegetical *waw* might have led the translator to such a forced translation. Of course, the missing letters could also have been dropped out of the LXX *Vorlage* through haplography, since *daleth* and *resh* so closely resembled each other.

Excursus on the Citation of Joel 2:28-32 [MT 3:1-5] in Acts 2:17-21

On the day of Pentecost Peter stood up to explain to a skeptical crowd exactly what had happened to the Christians. After denying that they were drunk, he cited the text of Joel: "This is what was spoken of through the prophet Joel" (τουτό ἐστιν τὸ εἰρημένον διὰ του προφήτου Ιωήλ, *touto estin to eirēmenon dia tou prophētou Iōēl*, Acts 2:16). Peter had no hesitation about connecting the two texts, but numerous questions arise because the passages do not completely overlap in their contexual meaning.

The differences seem obvious enough. Joel speaks of dreams and visions, whereas the Christians experienced the ability to speak in different languages. The sun did not darken at Pentecost, nor did the moon turn to blood; and the Lord did not appear with wrath against the nations.

There are also some significant similarities between the two passages. First, in each case the Lord pours out the Holy Spirit on the community of regathered Israel. At Pentecost Jews were present from all over the diaspora. Note also that Peter goes on to say that after Jesus rose from the dead and was exalted to the Father's right hand, He "poured forth [ἐξέχεεν, *execheen*] this which you both see and hear" (Acts 2:33). *Execheen* comes from ἐκχέω (*ekcheō*), the same verb used to translate "I will pour out" in the LXX of Joel 2:28-29 (MT 3:1-2).

Also, though Joel gives a prominence to prophetic activity that goes beyond the things happening in Peter's day, the NT came into existence in the first century through a new burst of revelation, and Luke stressed various prophetic activities in the early Christian community. Peter's sermon itself contained new revelation and could be called prophecy. The church community was then unified around the

---

[8] Wolff, *Joel and Amos*, p. 56 n. t.

"apostles's teaching" (Acts 2:42). Peter continued to preach prophetic sermons (Acts 3; 10:34-43), and Stephen (Acts 7) and Paul made their own contributions. The latter two also had visions of the risen Christ (Acts 7:56; 9:3-7), and Peter saw a vision and heard the Spirit direct him to Cornelius (Acts 10:9-20). Even Cornelius saw an angel who told him to send men to Peter (Acts 10:1-7). Many similar incidents abound in the book of Acts (8:26-40; 12:7-10; 13:2, 9-11; 16:6-10; 21:11).

Another item of interest is the presence of miraculous signs and wonders, even though they are not the same signs mentioned by Joel. Peter stressed that God had performed "miracles and wonders and signs" through Jesus while He was present on earth (Acts 2:22), "wonders and signs" (τέρασι καὶ σημείοις, *terasi kai sēmeiois*) being the same words Peter cited from Joel's prophecy. At least some of these signs were astronomical (Luke 23:44-45). The miracle of tongues given on the day of Pentecost was also a sign, and Luke continues to mention throughout the book of Acts various wonders and signs performed by Christians through the power of God.

Peter interpreted Joel's "after this" (*'aḥărê kēn*) as being "in the last days" (ἐν ταῖς ἐσχάταις ἡμέραις, *en tais eschatais hēmerais*). The following summarizes the equivalents for "in the last days" in LXX, MT, and the NT (Nestle-Aland):

Reference	Hebrew (MT)	Greek (LXX or NT)
Gen. 49:1	*bĕ'aḥărît hayyāmîm*	*ep eschatōn tōn hēmerōn*
Isa. 2:2	*bĕ'aḥărît hayyāmîm*	*en tais eschatais hēmerais*
Ezek. 38:16	*bĕ'aḥărît hayyāmîm*	*ep eschatōn tōn hēmerōn*
Heb. 1:2		*ep eschatou tōn hēmerōn*
1 Pet. 1:20		*ep eschatou tōn chronōn**
		*ep eschatōn tōn hēmerōn**
		*textual variant

From these references we note that "in the last days" may refer to a variety of events. In Gen. 49:1 it looks simply to Jacob's future. In Isa. 2:2 it applies to the millennium and in Ezek. 38:16 to Gog's future battle with Israel. According to 1 Pet. 1:20-21 and Heb. 1:2 the "last days" began with the first coming of Christ, and Peter's sermon in Acts 2 appears to make an important connection between Joel's prophecy and Christ's first coming. Thus, Peter's use of "last days" in his citation of Joel proves a further connecting link between the earlier prophecy and the events of Pentecost.

Admittedly, the note given by the *New Scofield* at Acts 2:17 represents a variant view that the "last days" are different for the Church than for Israel. While God will deal more directly with national Israel in the events surrounding Christ's second advent, it seems to this writer that the NT concept of "last days" includes both comings of Christ, in that the appearance of Jesus Christ on earth has such overwhelming significance to the program of God for both Israel and the Church.

What about the wrath that God will pour out on the nations? It is instructive to notice that both the Joel passage and Peter's sermon are written to encourage the listeners; God's wrath need not be directed at them. All that is necessary is to repent and call on the name of the Lord (cf. Acts 2:38). Peter did not know when the time of wrath would come; nor did Joel state precisely how much time would elapse between the coming of the Spirit and "the great and awesome day of Yahweh."

Finally, how do the Gentiles fit into God's plan? In the book of Acts, Luke shows the readers how it was only with great reluctance that the early Church, including Peter, concluded that salvation was for the Gentiles also. Therefore, it seems unlikely that Peter used the Joel passage to teach that "all flesh" extended to the Gentiles. Some have noted that he applied the "promise" to "all who are far off" (Acts 2:39) and concluded that this refers to the Gentiles.[9] More likely it refers to those Jews who were unable to get to Jerusalem for Pentecost, or possibly to distant generations of Jews (i.e., "your children and later generations," cf. Joel 1:3). Paul uses similar terminology for Gentiles in Eph. 2:13 and 17, but there he deals with the inclusion of Gentiles in the body of Christ, not the pouring out of the Spirit. He did cite Isa. 57:19, which would have been known to Peter, but Peter's sermon revolves around the Joel passage.

That the Gentiles did receive the Spirit at a later time has a simple explanation. While Joel's prophecy was given to the Jews, it does not suggest that it was impossible for the Gentiles to obtain the same deliverance. The extension of the promise of the Spirit to Gentiles was something new, but it was not inconsistent with Joel's vision. As Paul would explain later, the Gentiles were like a wild olive branch grafted into the cultivated olive tree which represents God's chosen people, Israel (Rom. 11:17). God's purposes for Israel as over against the Church will yet be accomplished. In the meantime, the Gentiles enjoy the blessings of the age of grace.

The OT does make it clear that the Gentiles had a place in the plan of God. This is especially true of the promise to Abraham: "In you all the families of the earth shall be blessed" (Gen. 12:3). Exactly how the Gentiles would participate in the promises of God remained a mystery until it was revealed to the NT writers.

Comparison demonstrates, then, considerable overlap between Joel's prediction that God would pour out His Spirit on "all flesh" and the situation of the Church at Pentecost and its early stages of growth. Actually, we might say that the latter events are a fulfillment "in miniature" of Joel's prophecy. The astronomical signs that accompanied the first coming of Christ will be intensified at the second coming. The Jews gathered from the diaspora to Jerusalem on Pentecost were but a small portion of the great and permanent return that will take place in the future. Finally, the Spirit will bring about the repentance of all Israel before the final day of the Lord. Though large numbers of Jews responded to Peter's call for repentance at Pentecost, the book of Acts demonstrates the increasing rejection of Christ by the Jews and the simultaneous offer of salvation to the Gentiles.

Walter Kaiser makes an important statement about the problem:

We conclude that the promise of the outpouring of the Holy Spirit in the last days has received a preliminary fulfillment in the series of events at Pentecost, Samaria, and Caesarea. But those events and the subsequent baptisms of the Holy Spirit that take place whenever

---

[9] E.g., Kaiser, *The Uses of the OT in the New*, p. 97.

anyone receives Christ as Lord and Savior and is thereby ushered into the family of God are all mere harbingers and samples of that final downpour that will come in that complex of events connected with Christ's second return. However, these events – past, present, and future – make up one generic whole concept, for in the prophet's view there is a wholeness and a totality to what he sees.[10]

To this we would add that Peter was given new insight when he took the event Joel foresaw and linked it with the beginning of the new age of the Spirit. In other words, Joel saw the end point of the whole process, while Peter fixed his eyes on the onset.

One final question: What is the implication of Peter's reference to Joel's prophecy for the relationship between Israel and the Church? If one assumes a literal fulfillment for the many prophecies of the OT to national Israel, it will not do to simply say that the Church is spiritual Israel. On the other hand, some stress the discontinuity to the point that the events of Pentecost cannot have been a fulfillment in any sense of the promised outpouring of the Spirit. A note in the *New Scofield* on Joel 2:28 says, for example, "Peter quoted Joel's prediction as an illustration of what was taking place in his day, and as a guarantee that God would yet completely fulfill all that Joel had prophesied." Charles Feinberg notes the lack of "the customary formula for a fulfilled prophecy" in Acts 2:16 in support of this interpretation.[11] To this latter argument Walter Kaiser responds, "The truth of the matter is that there is no single [fulfillment] formula used consistently in Acts or elsewhere in the NT for that matter."[12]

Robert B. Chisholm argues that "in the early chapters of Acts the kingdom was being offered to Israel once more." Thus, Peter thought that "the outpouring of the Holy Spirit signaled the coming of the Millennium. However, the complete fulfillment of the prophecy (with respect to both the extent of the Spirit's work and the other details) was delayed because of Jewish unbelief ..."[13] This idea has some strengths, especially in that it permits fulfillment in some sense *both* at Pentecost and in the Millennium. However, in our view more allowance needs to be made for the fact that Pentecost represents the inception of the Church. Thus, something more foundational must have happened than simply an offer which was "delayed because of Jewish unbelief."

Paul's analogy of the vine with Gentiles grafted in can be helpful here. The work that Christ accomplished at His first coming is just as foundational to the future work of God in national Israel as to His present work with the Church. The same is true for Jesus Christ's pouring out of the Spirit from heaven (Acts 2:33). There is one people of God, but the Lord's special dealings with the Church now

---

[10] Ibid., pp. 99-100.

[11] Feinberg, *The Minor Prophets*, p. 82.

[12] Kaiser, *The Uses of the OT in the New*, p. 91.

[13] Robert B. Chisholm, "Joel," in *BKCOT*, ed. John F. Walvoord and Roy B. Zuck (Wheaton: Victor, 1985), p. 1421.

and with national Israel in the future represent different phases or emphases in His overall plan.[14]

Perhaps Pentecost can be called the time of firstfruits. It was the inauguration of the age of the Spirit. Joel's prophecy can apply throughout the "last days." There is no inherent reason to restrict his statement about the gift of the Spirit to one particular occasion.[15] Even in the time of the final regathering of Israel there may be more than one occasion for the Spirit to be poured out upon God's people, as we may imply from the variety of other OT passages about the event. The NT reveals additionally that the "last days" will be extended to cover the Church age, and the Gentiles can enjoy the spiritual benefits previously reserved for Israel through the outpouring of the Spirit.[16]

---

[14] Cf. Walter C. Kaiser, Jr., *Toward an Old Testament Theology* (Grand Rapids: Zondervan, 1978), pp. 268-69; Kenneth L. Barker, "False Dichotomies Between the Testaments," *JETS* 25 (1982): 10-15.

[15] Barker, "False Dichotomies," p. 4 n. 5, refers to the type of interpretation advocated here as "progressive fulfillment," a label he says he borrowed from W. J. Beecher.

[16] See also Paul D. Feinberg, "Hermeneutics of Discontinuity," in *Continuity and Discontinuity: Perspectives on the Relationship Between the Old and New Testaments, Essays in Honor of S. Lewis Johnson, Jr.*, ed. John S. Feinberg (Westchester, Ill.: Crossway, 1988), pp. 108-28. He has a clear discussion of the hermeneutical issues, as well as a more detailed examination of Peter's use of Joel 2:28-32, generally affirming Walter Kaiser's views.

5
Judgment in the Earth
(Joel 3:1-21 [MT 4:1-21])

From a panoramic view of the last days when the Lord will renew His covenant with His people and pour out His Spirit on them, Joel turns to the Lord's final disposition of the nations of the earth. The time of this judgment continues to be that period of the "great and awesome day of Yahweh." For the Gentiles there remains the pouring out of His wrath, but for Israel there will be restitution to her former glory and increased blessing such as she has never known.

The last chapter of Joel has four parts. Similarities between the first and third and between the second and last sections make an A-B-A´-B´ structural pattern. The "A" elements both deal with the judgment of all the nations on the one hand, and the deliverance and general restoration of Israel on the other. In the "B" parts, however, Joel singles out specific nations, and their punishment consists of their submission to Israel. That is, they either become slaves to Israel, or their land becomes a desolation in contrast to the renewed fruitfulness of Judah (see Excursus on the Genuineness of Joel 3:4-8 [MT 4:4-8]).

A. The Nations Judged For Their Treatment Of Israel (3:1-3 [MT 4:1-3])

Translation

> For behold! In those days and at that time,
> when I *restore the fortunes of Judah and Jerusalem,
> ²then I will gather all the nations
> and bring them down to Jehoshaphat Valley.
> Then I will enter into judgment with them there
> because of My people and My possession Israel,
> whom they scattered among the nations;
> and they divided up My land.
> ³And *for My people they cast lots,
> traded a boy for a harlot,
> and sold a girl for wine to drink.

Exegesis and Exposition

In this first section Joel prophesies that Judah and Jerusalem will be restored but that the nations will be gathered for judgment in "the valley of Jehoshaphat." The Lord summons them there because they treated His chosen people like slaves, scattering them throughout the earth.

3:1 (MT 4:1) It is clear from v. 1 (MT 4:1) that Judah and Jerusalem will be restored when the nations are judged. The idiom "restore the fortunes of" (שְׁבוּת־

79

80   JOEL

אֶת שְׁבִיב הָ, *hēšîb 'et-šĕbût*) often occurs with reference to the Millennium (cf. Ps.
14:7; Ezek. 39:25; Amos 9:14; Zeph. 3:20), though some instances are found in a
non-eschatological context (Ps. 126:1; Lam. 2:14; Ezek. 29:14). The translation
"restore the fortunes" rather than the ancient versions' "restore the captivity" is now
generally accepted.[1]

3:2 (MT 4:2) According to v. 2, a broad plain is required where the nations
can be judged. "Valley of Jehoshaphat" is not currently known as a place name.
That the name is symbolic (cf. Targum, "plain of division") is confirmed by two
observations. First, "Jehoshaphat" means "Yahweh judges," and the verse
continues, "Then I will enter into judgment [וְנִשְׁפַּטְתִּי, *wĕnišpaṭtî*] with them there."
The play on words is obvious. Second, Joel 3:14 (MT 4:14) refers to the place as
the valley of "decision" (חָרוּץ, *ḥārûṣ*). Possibly "Jehoshaphat" was intended to call
to mind the time when God defeated the Ammonites, Moabites, and Edomites on
behalf of Jehoshaphat, king of Judah (2 Chr 20), though the text need not imply that
the judgment will happen at the same place.

Even though 3:16 [MT 4:16] views the Lord roaring like a lion from Zion, it is
not necessary to think that the valley must be near Jerusalem. For Amos, who also
spoke of the Lord's roaring, the burning heat of divine judgment reached all the
way to the top of Mt. Carmel (1:2). Zechariah mentions a "very large valley"
formed when the Lord's feet touch the Mount of Olives (14:4), but the main
purpose of that valley is for the Jews to escape from the nations. Of course,
judgment could occur there once the Lord's people have fled.[2]

All the nations will be judged at Jehoshaphat Valley, indicating that they are
all guilty of crimes against Israel. Specifically, they are said to have "scattered"
(פִּזְּרוּ, *pizzĕrû*) her among the nations. If Joel is dated in the preexilic period, then
the only specific instances of scattering would include certain raids against the
southern kingdom. During the reign of Rehoboam, the Egyptian Pharaoh Shishak
carried away much plunder, though the Bible says nothing of captives. Later the
Philistines and Arabs conducted a raid against Judah, taking treasure and captives
from the royal house of Jeroboam (2 Chron. 21:16-17).

Sennacherib was the first Assyrian to trouble Judah, but he was unable to take
Jerusalem. Hezekiah gave him tribute from his own palace and from the Temple (2
Kings 18:14-16), but again no mention is made of captives. Sennacherib himself
boasted of carrying away 200,150 people from the other towns of Judah and various
women from Hezekiah's court.[3] Whether the boast was accurate is hard to say.
Next we hear of Manasseh carried away to Babylon in chains by the Assyrians (2
Chron. 33:11). Probably other prisoners were taken at the same time.

---

[1] Hans Walter Wolff, *Joel and Amos* (Hermeneia; trans. Waldemar Janzen, et al.;
Philadelphia: Fortress, 1977), p. 76 n. 19; Leslie C. Allen, *The Books of Joel, Obadiah,
Jonah and Micah* (NICOT; Grand Rapids: Eerdmans, 1976), pp. 108-9 n. 12. In Hos. 6:11
the phrase should possibly be taken with 7:1, forming a parallelism (note the arrangement in
BHS): "When I would restore the fortunes of My people,/ When I would heal Israel."
[2] Cf. C. F. Keil, *Minor Prophets*, (COTTV 10; Grand Rapids: Eerdmans, 1973), p. 220;
Richard D. Patterson, "Joel," in *EBC*, ed. Frank E. Gaebelein (Grand Rapids: Zondervan,
1985), 7:260.
[3] *ANET* (3rd ed.), p. 288.

When Jerusalem fell in 586 B.C., the Babylonians deported a great part of the population to various parts of the empire. It is also clear from the biblical texts that other nations participated in the downfall of the Judean kingdom (cf. 2 Kings 24:2; Ezek. 25:2-3, 8, 12, 15-17; 26:2; Obad. 10-14). Slightly later a group of Judeans migrated to Egypt. Some Judeans returned to the land when Cyrus of Persia issued his decree in 538 B.C., but many remained in their scattered condition. During the reign of Xerxes (Ahasuerus, 486-465 B.C.), the Jews were still "scattered and dispersed among the peoples in all the provinces" of the Persian empire (Esther 3:8).

No activity against Judah prior to the fall of Jerusalem fits easily with the notation about the dispersal of the population as well as the scenes that depict the division of the land and the selling of some of the people into slavery. From a prophetic perspective these events could still lie within Joel's future. Keil, for example, thought that some of the happenings in the following verses could only have taken place under the Romans.[4] If this view is correct, then the passage teaches that all the nations, which in the meantime will have dispersed the Jewish population, will be judged when the distant day of the Lord arrives.

Some precedent could be found in Isaiah's oracle against Babylon (chap. 13) or in his later pronouncements about that nation (chap. 47; cf. esp. vv. 6-7). Yet the visit of Merodach-baladan to Judah served as the occasion for Isaiah's predictions concerning Babylon (Isa. 39, esp. vv. 5-7). The message of chaps. 40-66 then comforts the believing remnant that remained after the Assyrian invasion and that will remain after the coming Babylonian destruction.

For Joel it seems more natural to interpret the destruction of Jerusalem as an event in the prophet's past. If Babylon has already fallen, it would be possible for him to pass by that nation and dwell more particularly on nations that remain to be judged (vv. 4, 19). In any case, the wrath of the Lord will be poured out on all nations specifically because of the way they have treated Israel, His own possession (cf. Matt. 25:31-46). The events surrounding the Babylonian capture of Jerusalem become a paradigm, as it were, for the way nations throughout history have treated Israel. As Feinberg so aptly states, "Little do the nations realize how they incur the wrath of God when they lay violent hands upon His heritage and the plant of His choosing."[5]

The Babylonians did not bring new people into Judah to inhabit it. The division of the land (חִלֵּקוּ וְאֶת־אַרְצִי, wĕʾet-ʾarṣî ḥillēqû, "and they divided up My land") refers either to its incorporation into the Babylonian empire or possibly to the actions of neighboring countries. Since Tyre, Sidon, and Philistia are introduced as an additional case in vv. 4-8, the former explanation is more likely.[6]

---

[4] Keil, *Minor Prophets*, pp. 220-21.

[5] Charles L. Feinberg, *The Minor Prophets* (Chicago: Moody, 1976), p. 82. He says Joel is "probably one of the earliest of the minor prophets" (p. 71).

[6] But see Allen, *Joel*, p. 110, for the latter view. For the political situation of Judah during the exile see, with some caution, Bustenay Oded, "Judah and the Exile," *Israelite and Judean History* (OTL; ed. John H. Hayes and J. Maxwell Miller; Philadelphia: Westminster, 1977), pp. 476-80.

The language of the passage grows out of the very personal relationship between the Lord and His people. When He calls them "My possession" (נַחֲלָתִי, *naḥălātî*), He refers to the process of distributing the land as it was set up in the days of Moses and Joshua and continued in the institution of the year of Jubilee (Lev. 25). By the casting of lots each tribe down to its various families and households would receive a *naḥălâ* or portion for sustaining life. In the OT concept God, as the Creator, owns the entire earth, but Israel is His special *naḥălâ*. Thus the heinous crime of the nations: they took the Lord's *naḥălâ* and divided it up for themselves.[7]

3:3 (MT 4:3) Imagine the chaos after invaders have penetrated a great city. The soldiers are prone to mob action and atrocities (v. 3). They kill all the defending warriors but capture the defenseless for their own uses. So the dice are thrown to determine who gets the best women and the strongest slaves. A man sees a woman he wants and trades a mere boy for her.[8] Another wants wine and gives a young girl for it. These are commonplaces of war (Obad. 13-14; Zech. 14:2), yet the Lord does not consider them any less abhorrent because of this fact. The nations will have to answer directly to God for having treated His own personal possession, the "apple of His eye" (Zech. 2:8 [MT 2:12]), so lightly.

Additional Notes

3:1 (MT 4:1) אָשׁוּב: The *qere* changes the reading from אָשׁוּב to אָשִׁיב. MT fluctuates between the hiphil and qal for the verb "restore" in this idiom, with the latter form predominating. However, only the hiphil of the first person ("I") occurs with the imperfect, though two examples have exactly the same *ketib* / *qere* situation found here (Jer. 33:26; 49:39). The Hebrew scroll of the Minor Prophets from Wadi Murabbaat evidently follows the *ketib*. The editor marks the *waw* as uncertain.[9]

3:3 (MT 4:3) וְאֶל־עַמִּי: In Obad. 11 and Nah. 3:10 the expression "cast lots for" uses the preposition עַל. The scroll from Wadi Murabbaat also reads עַל in the present passage.[10]

B. Tyre, Sidon And Philistia Sold To The Judeans (3:4-8 [MT 4:4-8])

Translation

Moreover, what are you to Me, Tyre and Sidon,
and all the regions of Philistia?

---

[7] For the concept of land distribution in ancient Israel, see Jon Lee Dybdahl, *Israelite Village Land Tenure: Settlement to Exile*, diss. for Fuller Theological Seminary (Ann Arbor: University Microfilms, 1981).

[8] For the use of the preposition *beth* with זוֹנָה (*zônâ*, "harlot") and יַיִן (*yayin*, "wine"), see Ronald J. Williams, *Hebrew Syntax: An Outline*, 2d ed. (Toronto: Univ. of Toronto, 1980), par. 246.

[9] *DJD* 2:185.

[10] Ibid.

Are you paying Me back for something?
Or are you doing something to (harm) Me?
Swiftly, speedily
I will make your action return on your (own) heads.
[5]For it is My silver and My gold you took,
and My precious treasures you brought to your *palaces.
[6]Also the sons of Judah and the sons of Jerusalem
you sold to the sons of Greece,
in order to remove them far from their territory.
[7]Behold! I will stir them up from that place
where you sold them,
and I will cause your action to return on your (own) heads.
[8]Thus I will sell your sons and your daughters
into the control of the sons of Judah,
and they will sell them to the *Sabeans,
destined for a distant nation.
For Yahweh has spoken (it).

Exegesis and Exposition

Here Joel singles out Phoenicia and Philistia for special punishment because of their attempt to remove the Judeans far from their territory. The Lord will reverse the situation, enabling Judah and Jerusalem to sell the Phoenicians and Philistines to the Sabeans.

Should the passage be structured as poetry or prose? Many modern versions opt for prose (*NASB* and *NIV*; but see also *JB*), but a certain parallelism of lines occurs, though the balance in the number of thought units per line (the Hebrew equivalent of meter) would be more irregular than usual (mostly 4+4 or 4+3, with some shorter lines).[11]

Joel 3:4-8 (MT 4:4-8) is probably the one section of the book whose authorship is most frequently denied to Joel by modern commentators. See Excursus on the Genuineness of Joel 3:4-8 (MT 4:4-8) below for a more detailed discussion.

3:4a (MT 4:4a) The Lord's question is rhetorical and implies a feeling of importance on the part of the one interrogated that is denied by the speaker. Resolved into a positive statement the result would be, "You are of no special importance to Me." Thus, the verse shows the willfulness of these nations. They actually thought they could escape the same punishment reserved for all the rest of the nations.[12]

The phrasing of the question is rare, possibly even unique. A similar construction occurs in 2 Sam. 16:1, but the question is not rhetorical in that the speaker really seeks information. Literally, David's question is, "What are these to you?" Notice *NASB*'s rendering: "Why do you have these?" Perhaps the interrogative in Joel could likewise be taken as equivalent to "why" (normally לָמָּה,

---

[11] Wolff gives a similar poetic analysis to ours, though he also views the section as secondary to Joel's work (*Joel and Amos*, p. 72).

[12] Cf. Feinberg, *Minor Prophets*, p. 83.

lāmmâ), yielding the understanding, "Why are you against Me?" *NIV* has, "What have you against Me?" Allen takes Joel's wording as a variant of the Hebrew idiom, "What to me and to you?" That is, "What have you to do with me?"[13] Is it likely, however, that a common idiom would be varied in such an unusual way? Stuart translates, "what were your intentions toward me . . .?," indicating at the same time some uncertainty about the exact sense.[14]

Various nearby nations participated in the plundering of Judah at the time of the Babylonian conquest, leading the reader to wonder, Why single out Tyre, Sidon, and Philistia? Perhaps these nations were excessively bold in their hostility toward the Lord and His people. They were intimately involved with the trading of Hebrew slaves, as the following text makes plain (v. 6).[15] Or, the answer may have to do with Hebrew style, whereby a general subject is represented by a few specific examples. Tyre and Sidon belong together, and with the Philistine plain practically all the coastland is represented. Edom and Egypt also get special mention near the end of the chapter (v. 19).

Keil makes the historical background for the passage the raid by the Philistines and Arabians against Judah when Jehoram was king (2 Chron. 21:17).[16] However, the Chronicles passage says nothing about the Phoenicians, while Joel says nothing about Arabians.

3:4b-d (MT 4:4b-d) גְּמוּל (*gĕmûl*) evidently means some action directed toward the Lord to "pay back" (שִׁלֵּם, *šillēm*) for something He did. It is unclear whether the Phoenicians and Philistines would have in mind at this point a hostile or friendly action. That is, the Lord interprets it as hostile because of Judah's involvement, but these nations might think their actions against Israel are somehow going to do the Lord a favor. On the other hand, if the next question is rightly rendered as a parallel, the thought is: "Do you think mistreating My people this way will get back at Me for past victories they have had over you?"[17]

אִם (*'im*, "or," usually "if") can be used to coordinate questions (Joel 1:2), but many modern versions (including *NASB* and *NIV*) follow the Vulgate in making the second half conditional. The translation suggested here stresses the point that the Phoenicians and Philistines have done deeds that they believe somehow strike at God.[18] In their own exaggerated sense of importance they thought to defy Him and get away with it (cf. Deut. 32:6). For the use of גָּמַל (*gāmal*) by itself in the sense of "do something to" see Gen. 50:15, 17 and Prov. 3:30. The Lord is more powerful than the arrogant nations. His response will be swift and thorough. The very crimes they have done will boomerang on them (cf. Ps. 7:16 [MT 7:17]; Obad. 15).

---

[13] Allen, *Joel*, p. 112 n. 28. For מָה (*mâ*) as "why," see Williams (*Hebrew Syntax*, par. 126).

[14] Stuart, *Hosea-Jonah* (WBC 31; Waco, Tex.: Word, 1987), pp. 263, 265 n. 4a.

[15] Cf. Patterson, "Joel," 7:261.

[16] Keil, *Minor Prophets*, pp. 223-24.

[17] Cf. also K. Seybold, *TDOT* 3:32.

[18] Wolff, *Joel and Amos*, p. 72 n. g.

3:5 (MT 4:5) A problem arises in v. 5 with הֵיכָל (*hêkāl*), which can be either "temple" (as in LXX) or "palace" (Prov. 30:28; Isa. 13:22). "Temple" is appropriate for *hêkāl* with reference to the house of God in Jerusalem, though Ezra 5:14 (in Aramaic) is an exception. If the treasures are the Lord's because they are from the Temple in Jerusalem, then it would be most natural to think that they were deposited in foreign temples.[19] Historically, however, most of the Temple treasures went to Babylon (2 Kings 25:13-15), not Tyre, Sidon, and the Philistine cities. Therefore, we should think of booty left behind or shared by the Babylonians, which the Phoenicians and Philistines took for their own palaces.

The plunder is designated "Mine" by the Lord because Judah was His personal possession (v. 2). The crime of the nations was to despoil the Judeans and use the treasures for their own pleasure.

3:6 (MT 4:6) The Greeks appear in v. 6 as a people so far away from Judah that the slave dealers who sold to them would not think of the captives as ever being able to return. Ezek. 27:13 points out the trade relations between Phoenicia and Greece ("Javan").

The expression "sons of Jerusalem" is unique to this passage. It means something like "citizens of Jerusalem," but the repetition of בְּנֵי (*benê*; "*sons of* Judah," "*sons of* Jerusalem," "*sons of* Greece") underlines the personal tragedy of the slave dealing.

3:7 (MT 4:7) How appropriately the punishment fits the crime! From the very places these slave traders have driven away God's people (v. 7), the Lord will stir them up and bring them back to render judgment in kind.

3:8 (MT 4:8) The form of the punishment (v. 8) follows the pronouncement stated twice in the section: "I will return your recompense on your head." Unless we are to assume that enslavement to another nation would be a condition of the Millennium, the fulfillment of the punishment should be sought in history. Yet historical information about such a sale is scanty. Allen points to the selling of the Sidonians by Antiochus III in 345 B.C. and the enslavement of Tyre and Gaza by Alexander the Great in 332 B.C.[20] Possibly Jews purchased some of the slaves and then resold them to the Sabeans, though this is only speculation.

Chisholm argues that the historical fulfillment "prefigures" the passage's "eschatological significance." That is, "Philistia and Phoenicia represent all of Israel's enemies (much as do Moab in Isa. 25:10-12 and Edom in the Book of Obadiah). At that time God's people will gain ascendancy over their foes (cf. Isa. 41:11-12; Amos 9:12; Obad. 15-21; Mic. 7:16-17; Zeph. 2:6-7)."[21] Since the chapter falls within the scope of "the latter days," there is some point to Chisholm's view. Yet we would still maintain that a strictly literal fulfillment of the prophecy that Judeans will sell their former enemies into slavery to another nation must occur prior to the Millennium (and perhaps has already occurred; see also, Excursus on the Genuineness of Joel 3:4-8).

---

[19] See Allen, *Joel*, p. 112.

[20] Ibid., p. 114.

[21] Robert B. Chisholm, Jr., "Joel," in *BKCOT*, ed. John F. Walvoord and Roy B. Zuck (Wheaton: Victor, 1985), p. 1422.

The text indicates the Judeans as middlemen between God and the Sabeans. The Sabeans are located in Southwest Arabia near modern Yemen, but evidently they themselves send the Judeans on to another "distant nation." This interpretation would seem to be necessary because of the change in prepositions (*l* and *'el*; see also Additional Notes for a variation in LXX). Allen, on the other hand, discounts the argument from the prepositions and identifies Sabea with the "distant nation," based on the "artistic balance" and a parallelism between Sheba and "a distant nation" in Jer. 6:20.[22] Actually, "(destined) for a distant nation" nicely balances "in order to remove them far from their territory" of v. 6. Gen. 37:36 shows a similar change of prepositions: "To [*'el*] the Egyptians (and then) to [*l*] Potiphar" seems a nice parallel to the rendering given above. Further, that Sheba is paralleled with "a distant nation" in Jer. 6:20 does not mean that the same relationship has to be maintained in Joel.

Additional Notes

3:5 (MT 4:5) לִהֵיכָלֵכֶם: The manuscript from Wadi Murabbaat omits the *yodh* that marks the noun as plural. In all likelihood, it is simply a defective spelling.[23]

3:8 (MT 4:8) לִשְׁבָאִים: LXX has εἰς αἰχμαλωσίαν ("into captivity"), apparently reflecting לִשְׁבִי or לְשִׁבְיָה. As Allen correctly notes, "Sabeans" gives a better balance with "Greeks" in v. 6.[24] Possibly the translator had the same trouble with variation in the prepositions that modern translators have had.

Excursus on the Genuineness of Joel 3:4-8 (MT 4:4-8)

Joel 3:4-8 has some unique features that present distinctive problems. For example, it is the most difficult portion of the book to analyze as poetry; many think it is actually prose. Also, the Lord conducts the judgment at Jehoshaphat Valley in person at the end of the age. How is it, then, that Judah will sell the Phoenicians and Philistines to the Sabeans? As Rudolph sees it, "these verses contain nothing eschatological."[25]

For these reasons some commentators have proposed that the section was inserted into the book of Joel at a later date.[26] Yet when all the available versions and texts contain the passage, is it not important to probe deeper into how it fits the context?

---

[22] Allen, *Joel*, p. 114 n. 35.

[23] *DJD* 2:185.

[24] Allen, *Joel*, p. 114 n. 35.

[25] Wilhelm Rudolph, *Joel--Amos--Obadja--Jona* (KAT 13:2; G+tersloh: G+tersloher Verlagshaus Gerd Mohn, 1971) p. 80; " *diese Verse nichts Eschatologisches enthalten…* "

[26] Julius A. Bewer, *A Critical and Exegetical Commentary on Obadiah and Joel* (ICC; Edinburgh: T. & T. Clark, 1974), p. 130; Hans Walter Wolff, *Joel and Amos* (Hermeneia; trans. Waldemar Janzen, et al.; Philadelphia: Fortress, 1977), pp. 77-78; Rudolph, *Joel*, pp. 80-81.

In reality the section has all the earmarks of what R. E. Longacre calls a "peak episode" in the development of a narrative.[27] He calls the "markers" of these episodes "rhetorical underlining," "concentration of participants," "heightened vividness," "change of pace," and "change of vantage point and/or orientation."

First, Joel's passage lengthens the description ("rhetorical underlining") of the guilt of the nations that began at 3:2. Second, it concentrates the participants by introducing Tyre, Sidon, and "all the regions of Philistia," as well as the Greeks, Sabeans, and "the sons of Judah." Third, "heightened vividness" is obtained when God questions the nations, providing a courtroom-like atmosphere. Fourth, the shift in poetic style to something closer to prose provides a "change of pace." Finally, the "orientation" changes when God moves from speaking *about* the nations to speaking *to* them. Also, the focus on judgment in the day of the Lord changes to a time within the ordinary course of history when the Lord will cause these nations to receive their punishment from the Judeans and Jerusalemites themselves.

We should probably think of the segment ("episode") as itself extending the discussion in vv. 2-3 of how the nations have treated Israel. Why should this form a "peak" for Joel and his audience? Surely it must be due to the way the people felt they had been wronged and to their desire for vengeance. That is, it deals with an incident still fresh in the minds of the Judeans. They had strong emotions about what the Phoenicians and Philistines did, and the Lord seeks to offer reassurance that justice will be done.

Vengeance is a negative notion in modern Western thought, but it is a theme that runs throughout Scripture. It surfaces in the "imprecatory" Psalms (cf. Ps. 137:7-9) and even becomes a controlling idea in Obadiah and Nahum. Nor is it absent from the NT. According to John's Revelation, "The souls of those who had been slain because of the word of God" will cry out when the "fifth seal" is broken: "How long, O Lord, holy and true, wilt Thou refrain from judging and avenging our blood on those who dwell on the earth?" (Rev. 6: 9-10; *NASB*). The justice of God demands that the injustice of men and nations toward each other be redressed. The Scriptures teach, however, that vengeance belongs to God, not to individuals (Deut. 32:35; Rom 12:19). The individual should try to overcome evil with good. But, failing that, there remains the necessity for God to right all wrongs.

Also significant is the overall structure of the chapter, as discussed in the introduction to 3:1-21 (MT 4:1-21):

A   Restoration of Judah and Jerusalem and Judgment of All the Nations
    (3:1-3 [MT 4:1-3])
    B   Judgment of Specific Nations through Judah (3:4-8 [MT 4:4-8])
    A´   Judgment of All the Nations and Deliverance for Jerusalem
        (3:9-17 [MT 4:9-17])
B´   Restoration of Judah and Desolation for Specific Nations
    (3:18-21 [MT 4:18-21])

---

[27] Longacre, *An Anatomy of Speech Notions* (Lisse, Belgium: Peter de Ridder, 1976), pp. 217-28.

The reference to specific nations here balances the later mention of Egypt and Edom in 3:19. Thus, the episode may seem to digress from the main idea of the eschatological time of the end, but actually it fits its overall context quite well.

C. The Nations Defeated By The Lord But Israel Delivered (3:9-17 [MT 4:9-17])

Translation

Proclaim this among the nations:
Prepare for a holy war!
Rouse the warriors!
*Let them draw near to go up,
all the men of war.
[10]Beat your plowshares into swords,
and your pruning hooks into spears.
As for the one who is weak, let him say,
"I am a warrior!"
[11]Come quickly,
all nations from all sides,
and assemble yourselves there.
*Bring down, Yahweh, Your warriors!
[12]Let the nations rouse themselves and go up
to Jehoshaphat Valley.
For there I will sit down to judge
all the nations from all around.
[13]Put in the sickle,
for the harvest is ripe.
Come tread,
for the winepress is full;
the vats overflow,
for their wickedness is great.
[14]Tumults, tumults in the Verdict Valley!
For the day of Yahweh is near
in the Verdict Valley.
[15]The sun and the moon grow dark,
and the stars hold back their shining.
[16]Then Yahweh will roar from Zion,
and from Jerusalem He will utter His voice;
and heaven and earth will tremble.
But Yahweh will be a refuge for His people,
and a stronghold for the sons of Israel.
[17]Then you will know that I am Yahweh your God,
who dwells in Zion, My holy mountain.
So Jerusalem will be holy,
and foreign (armies) will pass through it no more.

Exegesis and Exposition

The theme of judgment in the valley of Jehoshaphat is resumed in vv. 9-17. In language reminiscent of Joel's plea for the Judeans to assemble at the Temple to fast and pray, the nations are summoned to the valley for a battle. But when they arrive, they will find the Lord prepared to judge them like a farmer commanding his servants to reap the harvest. This will be a time of intense darkness for the earth, but the Lord will save His people Israel.

3:9 (MT 4:9) A cry for war goes out among the nations. Once again Joel returns to a command as a means of structuring the book. The last summons given was a word of assurance for the land of Judah (2:21-23). This time an alarm is sounded, much like that which had earlier warned the Israelites of the approaching day of the Lord (2:1). No one in particular is addressed; a rhetorical device is used to inform the reader that the nations will be stirred up to war by God (cf. Obad. 1; Hag. 2:21).

The structure of the verse parallels closely the summoning of the people of Judah to the Temple (1:13; 2:15-16). The destruction caused by the locusts led to a general call to come for fasting and prayer. When the call was heeded, the Lord relented from the full force of the anticipated judgment and healed the land.

Now a call goes out to the nations. They are to come to Jehoshaphat Valley to do battle, where they will be destroyed by the full fury of God's wrath. A certain irony in the wording of the summons highlights the contrast. The Judeans came together for repentance and were delivered. The nations come together for war with God and are destroyed. The various terms that describe the gathering of the nations in vv. 9-12 prolong the suspense, even as in chap. 1 various groups are successively enjoined to wail and mourn.

The first two verbs of the summons, קַדְּשׁוּ ... קִרְאוּ (*qir'û ... qaddĕšû*; "sanctify a war"), correspond to those directed earlier to Israel, though in reverse order: "Proclaim ... consecrate." Use of the verb *qiddēš* probably implies that the enemies offer sacrifices or make other types of religious preparations when they muster the troops.[28] Allen recognizes an irony that calls the nations to a holy war that will lead to their own defeat by the Lord.[29]

הַגִּבּוֹרִים ... כֹּל אַנְשֵׁי הַמִּלְחָמָה (*haggibbôrîm ... kōl 'anšê hammilḥāmâ*, "the warriors ... all the men of war") makes another close parallel with 1:14 and 2:16. The "warriors" correspond to the "elders," while "all the men of war" echoes "all the inhabitants of the land."

3:10 (MT 4:10) Isaiah (2:4) and Micah (4:3) both predict that the nations will "hammer [וְכִתְּתוּ, *wĕkittĕtû*] their swords into plowshares/ and their spears into pruning hooks." How do we account for the contrast with Joel's statement in v. 10? Does he contradict these other prophets? Or do they contradict him? The solution lies in differing perspectives. Joel envisions the judgment that will take place *before* the Messianic kingdom is set up. Isaiah and Micah, on the other hand, view what happens *after* "the mountain of Yahweh's house" becomes established "as the

---

[28] Bewer, *Obadiah and Joel*, p. 134.
[29] Allen, *Joel*, p. 115. The translation above follows Wolff, *Joel and Amos*, p. 72.

chief of the mountains." Then the survivors of the nations that remain will go up to Jerusalem to worship the Lord, learning peace instead of war.

It cannot be established whether Joel or Isaiah and Micah have the more original form. It is not impossible that the form in Joel was a popular saying often used for making preparations for war. The other prophets then changed its common meaning to suit a different context. Also, Joel could have adapted it from Isaiah and Micah, especially considering the way he frames the appeal to the nations in terms of a summons from the Lord.

3:11 (MT 4:11) The verb עוּשׁוּ ('ûšû) in v. 11 is otherwise unknown in Hebrew. LXX reads "gather yourselves together" (συναθροίζεσθε, sunathroizesthe), an interpretation followed by the KJV. The Targum and Peshitta are similar, except that they make the command indirect ("let them gather together"). Vulg. has "burst forth" (erumpite), like the Greek and Hebrew, a direct command. The meaning "help" or "aid" found in the BDB and KB lexicons is based on an Arabic etymology. Rudolph presents an alternate Arabic derivation yielding the meaning "hasten," while Wolff prefers to view the Hebrew as a textual corruption from חוּשׁוּ (ḥûšû, "hurry") or עורוּ ('ûrû, "wake up").[30] The two coordinated verbs are literally "hurry and come." In this idiom, the second verb carries the main thought.[31]

MT phrases וְנִקְבָּצוּ שָׁמָּה (wĕniqbāṣû šāmmâ, "and assemble yourselves there"), "So assemble yourselves. There..." In general, modern commentators follow LXX in making "there" the last word of the sentence,[32] since the Hebrew line is then more balanced. Is the verb itself a rare form of the niphal imperative (cf. GKC, par. 51o)? Or does the Hebrew give an indirect command ("So let them be gathered")?

For the prophet to interject a prayer, הַנְחַת יהוה גִּבּוֹרֶיךָ (hanhat YHWH gibbôrêkā, "bring down, Yahweh, Your warriors"), into the midst of the Lord's instructions to the nations is difficult but not impossible, especially in a lively declaration concerning the day of the Lord. Also, the structural similarity of the passage with Joel 2:16-17 might help to explain the presence of a prayer. In both places the commands are followed by a petition.

The "warriors" (gibbôrîm) must refer to the angelic hosts who will assist God in the judgment (cf. Ps. 103:20; Zech. 14:5). The term fits the context of a battle scene well, though it does not elsewhere refer to angels. Notice how it is the same term used for "warriors" in v. 9. The nations bring their warriors, and the Lord will bring His army down from heaven.

3:12 (MT 4:12) The Lord sits to hold court, a scene similar to that of Dan. 7:9-14 and of Matt. 25:31-46 (cf. Matt. 24:29-31). The verse is pivotal to the structure of the section. Verses 3:9-12a (MT 4:9-12a) contain the message to the nations (except for the prayer at the end of v. 11), while in v. 13 the Lord issues

---

[30] Rudolph, Joel, p. 77; Wolff, Joel and Amos, p. 72 n. o.

[31] Williams, Hebrew Syntax; An Outline, p. 40, par. 223.

[32] S. M. Lehrman, "Joel," in The Twelve Prophets (Soncino Books of the Bible; ed. A. Cohen; London: Soncino, 1969), p. 76, is an exception, but he does not discuss the issue.

instructions to His angelic attendants. In the center of the action sits the Lord Himself, ready to decide the verdict.

3:13 (MT 4:13) In v. 13 the scene changes from one of war to harvest. The ripe crops, along with the full wine press and overflowing vats, mean that the nations are ready for judgment (cf. Jer. 51:33; Hos. 6:11; Amos 8:1). At last their wickedness is complete, and God must act. The commands in this verse, plural in form, are probably given to the "warriors" (v. 11). The NT also teaches that God's angels will participate in a harvest of judgment (Matt. 24:31; Rev. 14:14-20).

The clear connection with the agricultural imagery of the first part of Joel is unmistakable. The locusts and drought prevented any harvesting, but later God promised a renewed harvest of plenty after His people repented. For the nations, the harvest time means that they are ripe for judgment. Much of the same terminology occurs in both places.

3:14 (MT 4:14) The term "decision" (חָרוּץ, ḥārûṣ) in v. 14, like "Jehoshaphat," contains a play on words. חָרַץ (ḥāraṣ) can mean to render a judgment (1 Kings 20:40), so the meaning "verdict" or "decision" fits the context well. However, the noun can also mean that which is dug out or excavated ("moat" in Dan. 9:25). Aside from the legal context, then, the phrase might mean something like "a deep valley."

The nations are packed so tightly into the valley that they jostle each other and shout loudly. Not only do the peoples overflow with wickedness; their sheer numbers fill up the large area set aside by God to render their verdict. "Tumults" seems a better rendering for הֲמוֹנִים (hămônîm) than the traditional "multitudes," because the noise as well as the size is implied.

Here the nearness (qārôb) of the day of the Lord is virtually equivalent to its actual presence. The final moment toward which Joel has been building throughout the book has finally arrived.

3:15 (MT 4:15) In v. 15 Joel repeats the cosmic signs that accompanied the locusts. Now they will be on a much more universal and disastrous scale. The wicked will not be able to flee from the presence of the Lord seated on His throne. This judgment is to be distinguished from that held before "the great white throne," which will take place after the Millennium (Rev. 20:4-15).

3:16 (MT 4:16) The act of judgment itself is represented by a terrible roar, like that of a lion, issuing from the Lord's mouth. The same statement is found in Amos 1:2, where it applies to judgment on the northern kingdom of Israel. Commentators are divided as to which prophet borrowed the phrase; naturally it depends on the date assigned to Joel. At any rate, for Joel the Lord's roar reflects His earlier commands to His army of locusts (2:11).

Joel sees a great earthquake that follows the roar. It shakes the whole earth to its foundations and sets even the heavens tottering (cf. Zech. 14:4-5). Just as none could have endured the army of locusts apart from a special outpouring of divine grace, so all people on earth stand in danger from the appearance of God on Zion.

Only in the Lord Himself, who is "gracious and compassionate, slow to anger, abounding in lovingkindness, and relenting of calamity" (Joel 2:13), can His people seek escape from wrath. Those who have called on His name will find that nothing can harm them when they are under His protection.

3:17 (MT 4:17) God completes His act of grace by reaffirming His covenant with His people in v. 17. That relationship had been threatened in Joel's day by the devastation of the locusts and drought. At the brink of extinction, the people threw themselves on the mercy of the Lord. He relented and restored their land; then He confirmed His position as Israel's God (2:27).

The same cycle will be repeated in the future. That aspect of the day of the Lord that comes on the heels of the time of Jacob's trouble will appear to overwhelm the whole earth. But God will pour out His Spirit, motivating the elect to call on His name. Then all Israel will be saved and recognize their unique relationship to the Lord once again.

For thousands of years the Jews have heard the tramping of foreign boots (זָרִים, *zārîm*, "foreigners") through their holy city. The Assyrians were kept out by the Angel of the Lord, but later the Babylonian army marched in. When the exiles returned, they discovered strangers who frustrated their efforts to rebuild the Temple (Ezra 4). Throughout the coming years Greeks, Romans, Arabs, and Crusaders invaded the city. What a welcome sound to Jewish ears – "foreigners will pass through it no more."

Hebrew *zār* has a stronger meaning than "stranger" (as in *NASB*). For the latter meaning גֵּר (*gēr*) is the usual equivalent. "Strangers" or "sojourners" were always welcome in Israel, because the Israelites had themselves been strangers in Egypt (Lev. 19:34). A stranger or visitor could participate in the blessings of the Sabbath, but "foreigners" seek to wrest the land from God's people and enjoy its benefits for themselves (Isa. 1:7; Ezek. 7:21; Hos. 7:9; cf. Amos 5:11-12). It was even possible for the Israelites themselves to become "aliens" (*zārîm*) within their own nation by following after pagan cults (Hos. 5:7).[33]

Other prophets speak of a time when the nations will go up to Jerusalem to learn the ways of the Lord (Isa. 2:2-4; Micah 4:1-4). Joel does not mean to deny this. He speaks of foreigners, whereas Isaiah and Micah speak of those who *learn* the ways of the Lord. They no longer have aspirations to seize the land; they become more like sojourners than foreigners.

We call Jerusalem "the Holy City," but she will not really be holy (קֹדֶשׁ, *qōdeš*) again until God dwells in her midst. Then, as the prophet Zechariah puts it,

> There will be inscribed on the bells of the horses, "Holy to Yahweh."
> And the cooking pots in Yahweh's house will be like the bowls
> before the altar. And every cooking pot in Jerusalem and in Judah
> will be holy to Yahweh of hosts; and all who sacrifice will come and
> take of them and boil in them. (Zech. 14:20-21)

Everything and every person within the walls of the city will be pervaded with a sanctity because of God's presence.

Zechariah goes on to predict that the "Canaanite" or "merchant" will no longer be in God's house in those days.[34] The thought is very close to Joel's remark

---

[33] See L. A. Snijders, *TDOT* 4:52-58. He also discusses contexts where *zār* has a less negative connotation.

[34] Cf. Thomas J. Finley, "The Sheep Merchants of Zechariah 11." *Grace Theological Journal* 3 (1982): 51-65. But cf. also Barker's remarks in *EBC* 7:697.

about foreigners. Just as merchants had no place in the sacred precincts of the Temple (cf. Jesus' cleansing of the Temple), so those with the impure motive of conquest will have no part in the sacred city.

Additional Notes

3:9 (MT 4:9) יִגְּשׁוּ יַעֲלוּ: The LXX has imperatives instead of jussives.

3:11 (MT 4:11) הַנְחַת יהוה גִּבּוֹרֶיךָ: The LXX reads, "Let the meek be a warrior." Apparently this would presuppose a Hebrew text something like הַנֹּחַת יְהִי גִבּוֹר.[35] The interchange of ëäë ("let be") and Yahweh seems plausible enough (cf. 2 Chron. 36:23 and Ezra 1:3), but if LXX be original how can we explain the addition of "your" (or "their") to "warrior" in MT and the other versions? Since LXX so closely resembles in thought the end of v. 10, it would seem to smooth out MT. The Targum reads גיבריהון ("their mighty men"; "your [pl.] mighty men" in a variant text) and Peshitta *gnbrwtkwn* ("your [pl.] mighty men"). Evidently these versions had trouble with the abruptness of the prophet's interruption of the Lord's speech. Perhaps the trouble was even theological. Could a mere man, even a prophet, interrupt God? MT (supported by Vulg.) preserves better the structural similarity with the call to repent in 2:16-17. Finally, the scroll from Wadi Murabbaat supports MT.[36]

D. Judah Blessed But Egypt And Edom Desolated (3:18-21 [MT 4:18-21])

Translation

> Now it will happen in that day,
> the mountains will drip with sweet wine;
> and the hills will flow with milk;
> and all the streams of Judah will flow with water.
> Also a spring will come out from the house of Yahweh
> and water the valley of Shittim.
> [19]Egypt will become a devastation,
> while Edom will become a desolate wilderness,
> because of violence against the sons of Judah,
> in whose land they shed innocent blood.
> [20]But Judah will be populated forever,
> and Jerusalem for generation after generation.
> [21]*Thus I will avenge their blood which I have not avenged.
> For Yahweh dwells in Zion.

Exegesis and Exposition

The conclusion to the second half of Joel centers around the unprecedented blessing in the land of Judah that will accompany the Millennial Kingdom. Egypt

---

[35] After Allen, *Joel*, p. 107 n. 7.
[36] *DJD* 2:185.

and Edom enter the scene only as a contrasting background. The utter desolation of their land makes Judah's fruitfulness stand out more boldly.

The section corresponds to the conclusion of the first half of the book, which speaks of a restoration in extra measure for the devastation caused by the locust plague. According to both parts, the Lord will restore His close relationship with His people as He dwells in Zion. Yet in the Millennial Kingdom the blessings will be unusual in scope, and the Lord will make Judah and Jerusalem a home for them forever.

3:18 (MT 4:18) The Hebrew prophets used the phrase וְהָיָה בַיּוֹם הַהוּא (wĕhāyâ bayyôm hahû', "and it will happen in that day") to mark off a new section, as here in v. 18. As is so often the case in predictive portions of the OT, "that day" refers to the general events surrounding the day of the Lord. Judgment of the nations and deliverance for Israel do not exhaust God's purposes. He has planned a new blessing for the land that will be unsurpassed, even beyond the splendor of the kingdom of David and Solomon.

The covenant with Israel included a promise of land. That is why the prophets were so often concerned about the condition of the ground. Would it be productive or desolate? Who would own it? God reassured His people after He destroyed the locusts that the ruined land would once again overflow with wine, oil, and grain. Now Joel returns to the same theme, but with much more extravagant language.

Everything will grow in such abundance that the mountains will appear to have springs of wine dripping from them. The cattle will be so well-fed (cf. Joel 1:18) that the excess milk will pour down the hillsides into the valleys. Perhaps the extravagant language reflects also Jacob's blessing for Judah in Gen. 49:11-12.[37] And all will be made possible by a plenteous supply of water for the thirsty ground. It will even flow out from the house of God in Jerusalem itself (cf. Ezek. 47:1-12; Zech. 14:8).

Since the lower stretch of the Kidron valley would be the natural destination for all water flowing from the Temple area, the valley of Shittim should probably be located there.[38] The word for "valley" (נַחַל, naḥal) refers to a wadi or dry stream bed that has water only during the rainy season. By extension it also can be used for the depression that has been carved out by the rapidly flowing water. By a creative miracle the Lord will make a ceaseless spring of water flow out so that the usually dry area will be constantly wet. "Shittim" is the Hebrew term for acacia trees, evergreens with yellow flowers and useful wood that grow mainly in the valleys around the Dead Sea.[39]

3:19 (MT 4:19) Egypt and Edom are mentioned in v. 19 to highlight Judah's fruitfulness by way of contrast. The Nile overflows regularly and makes the land along its banks lush and fertile, but the judgment at Verdict Valley will reduce it to a wasteland. Writing from the perspective of a time after the Millennium has

---

[37] Derek Kidner, *Genesis: An Introduction and Commentary* (Tyndale OT Commentaries; Downers Grove, Ill.: InterVarsity, 1967), p. 219, applies the language of the blessing to "the golden age of the Coming One."

[38] E. D. Grohman, "Shittim," *IDB* 4:339.

[39] *Fauna and Flora of the Bible* (Helps for Translators 11; London: United Bible Societies, 1972), pp. 87-88.

begun, Zechariah also singled out Egypt. She will especially suffer God's plague of no rainfall if the Egyptians refuse to go to Jerusalem to celebrate the Feast of Booths (Zech. 14:18-19).

Perhaps Edom receives special mention because her people descended from Esau, Jacob's brother. There should have been a close feeling between the two; instead there was perpetual enmity (cf. Amos 1:11-12; Obad. 10). Edom will also become a desolate wilderness, dry and lifeless in comparison with well-watered Judah.

The indictment of violence against Judah applies to both Egypt and Edom, but especially to the latter nation. Obad. 10 contains a similar statement: "Because of violence done to your brother Jacob." The Edomites committed their worst crime against Judah when they betrayed their brother-nation during the Babylonian conquest (cf. Exegesis on Obad. 10-14). The most notable example of Egyptian violence was when Pharaoh Neco killed King Josiah at Megiddo (2 Kings 23:29). Of course there were other occasions when Egypt either invaded Judah (1 Kings 14:25-26) or proved to be a false ally (Isa. 36:6; Jer. 2:36; Ezek. 29:6-7).

3:20 (MT 4:20) Verse 20 tells us that when God establishes His kingdom, none will ever destroy it (Dan. 7:27). At this time the Lord Jesus Christ will sit on His throne to fulfill the promise to David of an everlasting dynasty (2 Sam. 7:13; Rev. 20:4).

3:21 (MT 4:21) The first part of v. 21 is notoriously difficult to interpret. Apparently both instances of וְנִקֵּיתִי (wĕniqqêtî) are in the piel pattern, with "their blood" (דָּמָם, dāmām) the object. But the usual piel meanings are "hold innocent," "acquit," "leave unpunished," or "exempt," none of which fits the context. "Their blood" most naturally means the Israelite blood that has been shed by the nations (cf. Rev. 20:4).

NIV takes "their blood" to mean bloodguiltiness that Israel had incurred: "Their bloodguilt, which I have not pardoned, I will pardon." Yet the context otherwise gives no clue that Israel has incurred such guilt. Allen ingeniously suggests the line be rendered as a question: "And shall I leave their bloodshed unpardoned? I shall not leave (it) unpardoned."[40] But it is doubtful that the second occurrence of the verb (which does not have *waw* prefixed to it) can be given a future sense. Jer. 25:29 (see also Jer 49:12), given by Allen as a parallel, contains a future form for both verbs.

The rendering we have given follows the ancient versions and the *NASB* (cf. also *JB*). This assumes that the crucial verb occurs in the niphal or passive pattern, a possibility that does not require a textual emendation. Even so, the meaning "avenged" would still be unique. The niphal can mean to be free from an oath or obligation (Gen. 24:8, 41), so the development in meaning may not be too far-fetched. To paraphrase, "And after I have judged the nations I will be free from my obligation concerning the blood of Judah."[41] Admittedly one would then expect the preposition "from" (מִן, *min*) before "their blood," though it could be implied (see also Additional Notes).

---

[40] See Allen, *Joel*, p. 117.
[41] Cf. Feinberg, *Minor Prophets*, p. 85.

In a final outburst of faith Joel proclaims, "Yahweh dwells in Zion." Judah was threatened by a locust plague, but the Lord was gracious and restored his nation. The inhabitants were scattered to the far corners of the earth and were roughly treated at the hands of the Gentiles. Yet the Lord promises to regather His people, to restore and bless their land, and to judge the nations from the top of Zion. Zion is a site of salvation for those who trust the Lord but of wrath for those who have harmed His personal possession. Joel states the gist of the eternal covenant between Israel and the Lord in the simple affirmation that Zion itself is His home.

Additional Notes

3:21 (MT 4:21) נִקֵּיתִי: Rudolph, following an Akkadian cognate, translates "and I will pour out their own blood which I have not (previously) poured out."[42] Yet to do this he must rearrange the verses so that "their blood" refers to the blood of the nations.

BHS cites the evidence of LXX and Peshitta for the reading וְנִקַּמְתִּי, which would more directly mean "I will be avenged." Yet the ancient versions could have relied on the context for the meaning as much as modern versions, and a change from an original mem to a yodh in two places would be rather drastic as a scribal change. MT clearly preserves the more difficult and superior reading.

---

[42] Rudolph, Joel, pp. 76, 78.

Amos

The prophet Amos speaks to people who were *religious* but who were not *righteous*. He focuses on the unjust practices of the rich and powerful against the poor and helpless in Israelite society. He strives especially to show how day-to-day living cannot be separated from true worship of the Lord. Words of judgment and condemnation dominate the prophet's message, but Amos concludes with a vision of Israel rejoined with the people of Judah in justice and unprecedented prosperity.

Introduction to Amos

Among the sixteen writing prophets found in the OT, only Amos tells what his occupation was before his divine call. He was a "herdsman" and a "grower of sycamore trees" when God encountered him (7:14). The beginning of his book is also unusual; the first phrase is "the words of Amos." This fixes attention immediately on the man and on what he had to say. Only the prophecy of Jeremiah has a similar introduction. Perhaps it is significant that both Amos and Jeremiah describe their firm loyalty to the call of the Lord to speak His message in the face of human opposition.

Historical Context

The Prophet Amos

Let us consider for a moment Amos the man. To know Amos and his times is to make the vital connection between the "words" and the personality who infuses life into the literary form, in order to grasp better what God would say through this man and his book. Amos was careful to point out that his words were really the words of the Lord; God desired to preserve a record of the historical situation accompanying the revelation.

Apparently Amos was prosperous and settled in life when the call of God came to him: "Go prophesy to My people Israel." The tenor of Amos's reply to Amaziah suggests such a "crisis experience." Nothing about the prophet hints at any formal preparation (see exegesis on 7:14 below). He had not sought his assignment.

The name Amos (עָמוֹס, 'āmôs) is unique to the prophet in the OT, but it is probably a shortened form of Amasiah (עֲמַסְיָה, 'ămāsyâ; 2 Chron. 17:16). The full form of Amos's name probably meant, "one sustained by Yahweh."[1]

Little else is known of the prophet, except that he was "among the sheepherders from Tekoa" (1:1). Tekoa sits on a hill located east of the Judean ridge. The town lies within the stark wilderness that descends to the Dead Sea on the east. Many deep valleys cut through the area. Amos left this part of Judah and went to Samaria, far to the north, to deliver a message of terrible import to the nation of Israel, led at the time by Jeroboam ben Joash.

---

[1] Johann Jakob Stamm, "Der Name des Propheten Amos und sein sprachlicher Hintergrund," in *Prophecy; Essays Georg Fohrer 1980* (BZAW; ed. J. A. Emerton; New York: Walter de Gruyter, 1980), pp. 137-42. Stamm also suggests etymological connection with Amashsai (Neh. 11:13) or Amasa (2 Sam. 17:25; etc.).

99

The Date Of The Book Of Amos

The ministry of Amos took place in "the days of Uzziah king of Judah, and in the days of Jeroboam son of Joash, king of Israel" (1:1). The overlapping regnal years of Uzziah of Judah and Jeroboam of Israel are 767-753 B.C.[2]

The general period is made more explicit by the mention of an earthquake, still remembered more than two centuries later (Zech. 14:5). Recent excavations at Hazor give evidence of a massive temblor that destroyed the sixth archaeological level sometime between 765 and 760 B.C. The excavator, Yigael Yadin, plausibly connects this event with the first verse of Amos. Corroborating evidence also comes from Beersheba.[3]

In the past some have preferred a date for Amos closer to 755-750 B.C. Supposedly the high living of some Israelites, which Amos describes (e.g., 6:1-7), was partly a result of Jeroboam II's military successes in the latter part of his reign.[4] The book of Kings, however, attributes the beginning of Israel's resurgence to the reign of Joash (also known as Jehoash), Jeroboam's father (2 Kings 13:25; 14:11-15). Jeroboam II merely continued this process of expansion (2 Kings 14:25-27). Whether his great military successes came early or late in his reign is unknown. J. Alberto Soggin now places the victories mentioned in Amos 6:13 in Jeroboam's early years.[5] Also, the great earthquake undoubtedly wreaked so much destruction that military and economic power was greatly reduced.

More recently John H. Hayes has placed Amos's preaching rather precisely in 750 B.C.[6] Hayes gives an original and intriguing reconstruction of Israel's history in the late ninth and eighth centuries, but several factors make his date for Amos's ministry unlikely. First, his chronology for the reigns of the various kings differs considerably from the system generally accepted (e.g., he assigns Jeroboam II the years 788 to 748 B.C., rather than the more usual 782-753).[7] Second, it seems unlikely that Amos 1:1 would fail to mention Jotham as one of the kings of Judah

---

[2] Gleason L. Archer, Jr., "The Chronology of the Old Testament," in *EBC*, ed. Frank E. Gaebelein (Grand Rapids: Zondervan, 1979), 1:371. For a discussion of chronological problems connected with a presumed coregency of Uzziah from 790 to 767 B.C., see exegesis of Amos 1:1 below.

[3] Yigael Yadin, *Hazor*, Schweich Lectures, 1970 (London: Oxford, 1972), p. 151; Yohanan Aharoni, "The History of the City and Its Significance," in *Beer-Sheba I: Excavations at Tel Beer-Sheba, 1969-1971 Seasons* (Tel Aviv University: Givatayim-Ramat Gan, 1973), pp. 107-8.

[4] S. R. Driver, *The Books of Joel and Amos* (CBSC; Cambridge: University, 1907), p. 98.

[5] J. Alberts Soggin, *The Prophet Amos: A Translation and Commentary*, trans. John Bowden (London: SCM, 1987), pp. 3-4.

[6] John H. Hayes, *Amos, The Eighth-Century Prophet: His Times and His Preaching* (Nashville: Abingdon, 1988), pp. 16-27, 45-47.

[7] Admittedly the chronology of the eighth century B.C. is quite difficult to sort out, and there are some disagreements about the details. Yet the dates for Jeroboam II and Uzziah/Azariah form the backbone for most systems. The most comprehensive treatment of the problems (though not necessarily to be accepted unquestioningly) remains Edwin R. Thiele, *The Mysterious Numbers of the Hebrew Kings*, new rev. ed. (Grand Rapids: Zondervan, 1983), esp. pp. 103-38.

when he was already coregent with his father (the superscriptions to the other writing prophets form a better parallel than dating formulas in Kings). Third, while Hayes discusses the earthquake mentioned in Amos 1:1, he ignores the excavation reports that attempt to give it an approximate date. Finally, Hayes's assumption that the ruler in the "Valley of Aven" in Amos 1:5 must be Pekah, the son of Remaliah, is too tenuous to accept (see exegesis below), yet this hypothesis is his major argument for placing Amos so late as 750 B.C.[8]

The Political Situation Of Israel

Jeroboam II, fourth king of the Jehu dynasty, brought about unusual political stability and expanded Israel's territory. During his reign of 41 years, which includes a ten-year coregency with his father Joash,[9] he restored Israel's borders to Lebo-Hamath ("the entrance to Hamath") in the north and to the Dead Sea ("the Sea of the Arabah") in the south (2 Kings 14:25). This followed up the earlier action of his father, who "recovered the cities of Israel" from Ben-hadad, son of Hazael and king of Aram (2 Kings 13:27; Aram in the OT is roughly equivalent to modern Syria).

The expansion was set against a background of bitter hostility between Israel and her northern neighbor, the Aramean (Syrian) kingdom of Damascus. David subjugated the Arameans (2 Sam. 8:3-8), but later Rezon ruled an independent realm at Damascus. The author of Kings states, "So he [Rezon] was an adversary to Israel all the days of Solomon" (1 Kings 11:25). From then on Syria and Israel were frequently at war (see 1 Kings 20; 22:1-36; 2 Kings 5:2; 6:8-19, 24-25; 8:28-29). Hazael of Damascus (843-801 B.C.) virtually overran Israel and put it under vassal status (2 Kings 10:32-33; cf. 2 Kings 8:12).[10] Hazael's son, Ben-hadad, also vexed Jehu's son, Jehoahaz (2 Kgs 13:3).

That Joash and his son Jeroboam II were able to regain control of Damascus and Hamath (2 Kings 14:28) and virtually restore the territory realized under David and Solomon, was partly due to the rise of Assyria. The heart of Assyria lay to the east and north of Israel, between the Tigris and Euphrates rivers in northwestern Mesopotamia. Frequently the nation would expand outward under the leadership of powerful kings. These expansions can be thought of as pulsations in which a period of growth would be followed by one of retraction to the central area, occasioned by the difficulty of administering a vast empire.

Tiglath-pileser I (1114-1076 B.C.; not mentioned in the Bible)[11] made a campaign to the Mediterranean Sea and forced Byblos, Sidon, and Arvad to pay tribute to him. Later Ashurnasirpal II (883-859 B.C.) and then Shalmaneser III

---

[8] Hayes, *Amos*, pp. 46-47.

[9] S. J. De Vries, "Chronology of the OT," *IDB* 1:587.

[10] Cf. Hayes, *Amos*, pp. 18-20.

[11] The Bible mentions Tiglath-pileser (2 Kings 16:7), Tilgath-pilneser (1 Chron. 5:6), and Pul (2 Kings 15:19), all three names referring to Tiglath-pileser III, who was king of Babylon, 745-727 B.C. The first two forms are spelling variants, and the king assumed the name Pul when he ascended the throne of Babylon (previously he had been king only of Assyria). See A. L. Oppenheim, "Tiglath-pileser (III)," *IDB* 4:641-42. The annals are translated in *ANET*, 3d ed., pp. 275-81.

(858-824 B.C.) carried out expeditions into Syria. A coalition of western kings, including Hadadezer and "Ahab the Israelite," met the latter Assyrian monarch at Qarqar on the Orontes river in 853 B.C. Shalmaneser III's annals describe a great victory, but many historians view it as a "draw."[12] For several years Shalmaneser held back, but later he again marched to the west numerous times. In his eighteenth year he received tribute from Jehu of Israel.

The next Assyrian king to apply pressure to Syria and Israel was Adad-nirari III (810-783 B.C.). He forced the king of Damascus and Joash of Israel to pay tribute.[13] After Adad-nirari came a period of weakness and contraction of the Assyrian empire following an attack by the kingdom of Urartu (the area of Armenia).[14]

These political events in Amos's day weakened Aramean power. In the wake of Assyrian ineffectiveness and of war by the Arameans among themselves, a capable ruler like Jeroboam II was able to reassert Israelite control. Peace with Judah led to great prosperity and unhindered commerce along the major trade routes through the two countries. Even so, Amos's oracles of chaps. 1-2 probably reflect some continued instability internationally.[15]

When Jeroboam II died almost all of his accomplishments came to an end. The dynasty of Jehu collapsed with the murder of Jeroboam's son Zechariah, and not long afterward the powerful Assyrian king Tiglath-pileser III (744-727 B.C.) applied pressure on the west. Eventually Shalmaneser V (727-722 B.C.) absorbed Israel into the Assyrian empire in 722 B.C. when he captured Samaria.[16]

Relations Between Judah And Israel

At the same time that Jeroboam II ruled Israel so ably, Uzziah (Azariah) sat as king in Jerusalem. The book of Amos implies a time of peace and cooperation between the two nations, symbolized most vividly by Amos himself, who as a prophet from Judah preached in Samaria and Bethel. Moreover, he spoke of free travel between the countries (see 5:5) and often linked them together in his pronouncements of judgment (1:2; 2:4-8; 3:1-2; 6:1). Amos foresaw ultimate hope only in a restoration of the Davidic kingdom that would reunite the divided people (9:11-12). Other eighth century B.C. prophets also dealt with both kingdoms as a unit (cf. Isa. 9:8-21; 28:1; Hos. 4:15; 5:5, 10; Mic. 1:1, 5).

---

[12] See Herbert Donner, "The Separate States of Israel and Judah," in *Israelite and Judean History* (OTL; ed. John H. Hayes and J. Maxwell Miller; Philadelphia: Westminster, 1977), p. 400. For the Assyrian annals, see *ANET*, 3d ed., pp. 275-81.

[13] *ANET*, 3d ed., pp. 281-82. A stele found in 1967 at Tell er-Rimah mentions tribute from Joash (M. C. Astour, "Joash, King of Israel," in *IDBSup*, p. 479).

[14] Soggin, *Amos*, pp. 2-3.

[15] M. S. Seale, "Jeroboam," *ISBE*, rev. ed., 2:997; John Bright, *A History of Israel*, 2d ed. (Philadelphia: Westminster, 1972), p. 240.

[16] The Bible ascribes the fall of Samaria to Shalmaneser V, (2 Kings 17:3-6), but Sargon II, his successor, claims the feat for himself in his annals. According to R. M. Talbert, "re-evaluation of the evidence indicates that [Sargon's] scribes altered the historical record" ("Assyria and Babylonia," in *IDBSup*, p. 75). But there is also the possibility that he at least engaged in "mopping-up" operations.

Perhaps the book of Amos sheds some light, then, on a puzzling statement in 2 Kings 14:28. Literally it reads, "[Jeroboam II] restored Damascus and Hamath to Judah in/by [ב, *b*] Israel."[17] Possibly the author recognized a close relationship between the kingdoms, thinking already of a near-restoration of the united monarchy in which Jeroboam II played a major role. In any case, significant cooperation and positive relations between Jeroboam II and Uzziah (Azariah) seems likely, evidently with Jeroboam II as the stronger of the two monarchs.[18]

Literary Context

Composition Of The Book Of Amos

Amos presumably delivered all or most of his messages orally. His encounter with Amaziah (7:10-17) implies a preaching ministry to which the priest objected: "the land is unable to endure all his words" (7:10). Since Amos's words come to us in written form, a preliminary question is, "How did the message get from sermon to book?" This is not an idle question. Issues of authenticity, accuracy, and the correct method of interpretation hinge on the answer one gives to it.

The school of thought known as "form criticism," for example, posits a series of editors or redactors who compiled the words of Amos and added their own organization, interpretations, or expansions to make the material relevant for their contemporaries.[19] These later reflections are not distinguishable from the words of the prophet in any clear manner, and at times they may give a different twist to or even contradict the prophet's meaning. The period when these additions were made was supposedly prior to the belief in the holiness of an inspired text that could not be altered. Thus, Robert B. Coote writes,

> In its present form the book of Amos was written by more than one author at more than one time. Like almost all the prophetic books, it is the end of a series of recompositions of the original words of a named prophet. …In between Amos and the final edition of the book of Amos there were other editions of his words, possibly several, composed by several different authors.[20]

---

[17] M. S. Seale ("Jeroboam," *ISBE*, rev. ed., 2:997) takes Israel as the instrument of restoration, while T. R. Hobbs follows a suggestion to read "to Judah and Israel" (*2 Kings* [WBC 13; Waco, Tex.: Word, 1985], p. 184). More recently, however, some have suggested that "Judah" may refer rather to the kingdom of Yaudi in Syria (cf. *NIV*; Richard D. Patterson and Hermann J. Austel, "1, 2 Kings," in *EBC*, 4:232).

[18] Hayes thinks Judah was a vassal to Israel throughout most of the period between Omri and Pekah (*Amos*, pp. 23-24).

[19] Perhaps "redaction criticism" would be a better term in view of conclusions about successive redactions or editings of the book. The methods used, however, are more typical of form criticism and are not to be confused, for example, with the methods of "redaction criticism" of the Gospels in the New Testament. The term "redaction criticism" is used by Robert B. Coote in his analysis of the successive stages of composition in Amos, *Amos among the Prophets: Composition and Theology* (Philadelphia: Fortress, 1981), p. 6. Hayes gives a summary of the various stages of critical scholarship on the book (*Amos*, pp. 29-38).

[20] Coote, *Amos among the Prophets*, pp. 2, 3.

Wolff posits a long process of formation for the book, which includes six stages and extends from Amos himself to the time after the Jews returned from exile.[21] The most significant objections have been raised with reference to the genuineness of 2:4-5; 3:7; 4:13; 5:8-9; 9:5-6, 11-15. These issues will be treated in more detail under the passages cited.

Several more general objections can be raised to this approach.[22] First, it lessens the authority of the OT books as attested to by Jesus Christ and the NT authors. Second, the text of the biblical books themselves does not support it. At least in the case of Amos, the introductory phrase, "the words of Amos," would be drained of much of its meaning. If some major portions are exceptions to this claim of the heading, one might reasonably expect some clear indication in the text. For example, books such as Proverbs and Jeremiah, which were composed in various stages, notify the reader (cf. Prov. 1:1; 10:1; 22:17; 24:23; 25:1; 30:1; 31:1; Jer. 1:1-3; 36:1-32; 51:64). No hints are given in Amos to show the reader where the opinions of a later age are to be found.

A third objection to the multiple layers approach is that no objective evidence (such as ancient manuscripts) is produced to support or weaken the analysis. Rather, alleged internal contradictions or abrupt changes in grammar or subject matter are used to make a case against the unity of the book. This approach often fails to consider that an apparent "difficulty" in the text may be important for the meaning in quite the opposite way. For example, it may signal an emphasis or a key point in the structure of the passage. Moreover, the danger of imposing an extraneous system of logic or grammar on the biblical material is ever present.[23]

When we turn to more objective internal evidence, we discover that most of the book is cast in first person narrative (in some cases representing God as the speaker), but some small portions are in the third person. These include:

1. the heading or superscription in 1:1;
2. the introduction to direct speech in 1:2; and
3. the narrative of the encounter between Amos and the priest Amaziah at Bethel (7:10-17).

Only two sentences indicate the change in chap. 7:

1. "Then Amaziah said to Amos..." (v. 12);

---

[21] Wolff, *Joel and Amos*, pp. 107-13.

[22] This is not to deny the value and even necessity of analyzing genres or literary forms. For an assessment of some more positive aspects of form criticism see Tremper Longman III, "Form Criticism, Recent Developments in Genre Theory, and the Evangelical," *WTJ* 47 (1985): 46-67; also very helpful is Kevin J. Vanhoozer, "The Semantics of Biblical Literature: Truth and Scripture's Diverse Literary Forms," in *Hermeneutics, Authority, and Canon*, ed. D. A. Carson and John D. Woodbridge (Grand Rapids: Zondervan, 1986), pp. 49-104.

[23] For further discussion, see Gleason Archer, *A Survey of Old Testament Introduction*, rev. ed. (Chicago: Moody, 1975), pp. 19-34; and Kenneth Kitchen, *Ancient Orient & Old Testament* (Downers Grove, Ill.: InterVarsity, 1966), pp. 112-31. More recently, Hayes rejects the form critical approach in favor of a more unified treatment of the book (*Amos*, pp. 38-39). Another recent scholar who accepts the essential unity of Amos is Shalom M. Paul (*Amos: A Commentary on the Book of Amos* (ed. Frank Moore Cross; Hermeneia; Minneapolis: Augsburg Fortress, 1992).

2. "Then Amos answered and said to Amaziah..." (v. 14).

Three explanations for this grammatical shift from first to third person are possible. First, Amos himself may have composed the passages in the third person. A similar change of person occurs in other biblical books (e.g., Deuteronomy; Ezra 7-10; Dan. 1-6 v. Dan. 7-12). It should not be assumed automatically that a writer may never refer to himself obliquely. The three sections in Amos that are in the third person serve to organize the book and introduce narrative background. Thus, the difference in content from the main part of the book could have motivated Amos to use the third person form.

Second, one might argue that Amos wrote the book and was responsible for the organization of the material, but the heading and the section about Amaziah were added by someone else where it seemed appropriate. A third possibility is that a disciple or a secretary (cf. Baruch and the book of Jeremiah) wrote the entire book. The words of Amos would either have been used as a written source or written down at dictation or from memory. The main difference in this third view would be that the actual writer could have imposed his own organization on the material even though the words were those of Amos.[24]

In any case there, is every reason to suppose that the written form o f the book came into existence either during the prophet's lifetime or shortly afterward. It seems best to take the statement that the "words" of the book belong to Amos at its maximum and assume that Amos was responsible even for their organization. This need not exclude in principle that some brief insertions could have worked their way into the text during the process of scribes making copies.

The Language And Style Of Amos

Nearly the entire book of Amos has been set off as poetry in modern translations. Most of the OT prophets, especially those of the period before the Babylonian exile, delivered their messages in verse. Apparently the poetic style made for words more vivid as well as easier to memorize. Amos uses mostly a balanced line of three thought units per half-line (3+3, as in 1:2), as well as the uneven rhythm sometimes known as "qinah" (3+2, as in 5:2) after the Hebrew term for "lament." It should not be thought, however, that Amos follows standard poetic patterns rigidly. Rather, he frequently inserts a longer half-line (cf. 3:4b and 3:5a, both with a 4+3 structure). Parallelism of thought sometimes occurs, though it does not seem to be characteristic (cf. esp. 1:2; 5:24).[25]

Vivid imagery, especially that of wild animals and agricultural life, also finds full expression in Amos. He sees rushing streams, withered fields, locusts, plant blight, hills dripping with sweet wine, birds caught in traps, and roaring lions.

---

[24] Hayes (*Amos*, pp. 230-31) gives some reasons for thinking that the narrative about Amaziah was inserted into the oral message of Amos. Hayes' arguments do not preclude that Amos himself could have arranged the book that way (though Hayes thinks it unlikely that Amos wrote down his own preaching).

[25] Cf. Douglas K. Stuart, *Studies in Early Hebrew Meter* (HSM 13; Missoula, Mont.: Scholars, 1976), pp. 197-213. Most versions and many recent commentaries display much more than one-fourth of the book as poetry (*contra* Stuart, p. 197). Stuart's criteria of meter for Hebrew poetry seem overly restrictive.

Various geographical areas are fully represented – the verdant summit of Carmel, all the neighbors surrounding Israel, various cities with their massive citadels, the rich pastures of Bashan, the hill country of Samaria, and the Nile as it overflows its banks.

Amos employs a wide range of literary forms adapted for his purposes. He uses the numerical saying, "X and X+1," to stress completeness of iniquity (1:3, 6, 9, etc.). In one beautifully crafted section, he gains full effect from rhetorical questions (3:3-8), and he can also use imperatives for rhetorical effect (3:9). Amos uses irony (4:4-5), humor (5:19-20), personification (5:2-3), climactic tension (1:3-2:6), hyperbole (5:21-23), and many other figures of speech.[26] Also to be noted are a courtroom-type scene (chap. 4), repetitive phrases, and strong sermonic exhortations. Parts of a powerful hymn describing the majesty and awe of the Creator appear in several strategic places (4:13; 5:7-9; 9:5-6; cf. Excursus on the Hymnic Passages in Amos). These are but a few from the vast array of literary devices the prophet from Tekoa displays in his repertory.

The Message Of The Book Of Amos

Amos brought the northern kingdom of Israel face to face with the news that God was about to bring it to an end. Yet such an announcement had reverberating theological implications for the covenant between Israel and her God. How could God abandon His people? What had they done to deserve this punishment, especially when they were so zealous in their religious habits?

Amos carefully develops Israel's lack of covenant loyalty, showing that her outward displays of worship failed to compensate for her lack of compassion and humanity that the covenant with Moses demanded. He also teaches the accountability of those who have been chosen by God. Divine election cannot be used as an excuse; if anything, the Lord must deal more severely with those whose disobedience is willful rather than out of ignorance. The stubbornness of the people appears from their consistent rejection of the prophetic word. Thus, throughout the book Amos defends his authority as God's spokesman to proclaim a message of judgment.

But will God abandon His eternal covenant with His people? Absolutely *not*, says Amos. The Lord has shown Himself full of compassion and mercy throughout the history of His dealings with Israel. Even past judgments were intended to bring the people back to their God. The future will mean complete destruction of the northern kingdom; there can be no escape from that awful sentence. But Amos holds out hope for a restoration of God's people in a new Davidic era. A righteous remnant will always exist to inherit the promises of the glorious Messianic Kingdom of the end times.

To summarize, Amos examines the covenant between Israel and her God and finds the nation guilty of rejecting it. Even though their apostasy will bring

---

[26] See also A. S. Super, "Figures of Comparison in the Book of Amos," *Semitics* 3 (1973): 67-80.

unprecedented judgment, the covenant will continue because of the faithfulness of the Lord.[27]

Outline Of Amos

I. Amos and His Message (chaps. 1-2)
- A. Heading (1:1)
- B. Theme (1:2)
- C. Israel's Guilt and Judgment (1:3-2:16)
  1. Israel's Neighbors (1:1-2:5)
     - a) Damascus (1:3-5)
     - b) Gaza (1:6-8)
     - c) Tyre (1:9-10)
     - d) Edom (1:11-12)
     - e) The Sons of Ammon (1:13-15)
     - f) Moab (2:1-3)
     - g) Judah (2:4-5)
  2. Israel (2:6-16)
     - a) Indictment of Israel (2:6-12)
       1) Oppression of the Powerless (2:6-8)
       2) Rejection of the Lord (2:9-12)
     - b) Sentencing of Israel (2:13-16)

II. Words of Warning (chaps. 3-6)
- A. Breach of the Covenant (chap. 3)
  1. Opening Statement (3:1-8)
  2. Summoning of Witnesses (3:9-10)
  3. Announcement of Judgment (3:11-15)
- B. Failure to Repent (chap. 4)
  1. The Carefree Attitude of Israel (4:1-3)
  2. The Ineffective Religion of Israel (4:4-5)
  3. The Unresponsive Position of Israel (4:6-11)
  4. The Awesome Judgment for Israel (4:12-13)
- C. Choice of Life or Death (chaps. 5-6)
  1. A Dirge for Fallen Israel (5:1-3)
  2. A Call to Seek Yahweh – on the Basis of Judgment (5:4-9)
  3. A Rebuke for Israel's Oppression of the Poor (5:10-13)
  4. A Call to Seek Righteousness – on the Basis of Grace (5:14-15)
  5. A Call for Lamentation (5:6-17)
  6. A Rebuke for Misplaced Zeal (5:18-27)
  7. A Rebuke for Misplaced Confidence (6:1-11)
  8. A Rebuke for Injustice and Pride (6:12-14)

---

[27] This understanding is directly opposed to that of Hayes: "There is no evidence in the book that the relationship between Yahweh and Israel was understood in terms of covenant theology at the time" (*Amos*, p. 38). The exegesis will argue that Amos frequently alluded to the Law of Moses (cf. 2:3-8) and that passages such as 3:1-2 presuppose the covenant relationship.

III. Visions of Judgment and Salvation (chaps. 7-9)
    A. The Lord Has Spared (7:1-6)
    B. The Lord Will Spare No Longer (7:7-8:14)
       1. The Vision of the Plumb Line (7:7-17)
         a) Presentation (7:1-9)
         b) Official Response (7:10-13)
         c) The Lord's Reply (7:14-17)
       2. The Vision of the Basket of Summer Fruit (8:1-10)
         a) Presentation (8:1-3)
         b) Popular Response (8:4-6)
         c) The Lord's Reply (8:7-10)
       3. Those Who Refuse to Listen (8:11-14)
    C. The Lord Will Spare None (9:1-6)
    D. The Lord Will Restore His People (9:7-15)

The Flow Of The Argument

I. Amos and His Message (chaps. 1-2). The book of Amos divides into three main parts. The first of these includes the initial two chapters and teaches that the weight of Israel's sins against the covenant demands judgment. The nation cannot expect to escape because of any special treatment it deserves beyond that of any other nation.

    A. Heading (1:1). Amos 1:1 gives information that introduces the prophet, sets the book in history (mid-seventh century B.C.), and strikes an initial note of doom in the mention of an earthquake. Amos spoke often of a shaking, using the motif of an earthquake to predict the overthrow of the foundations of Israel's national existence (cf. 2:13; 3:14, 15; 6:1; 8:8; 9:1, 5, 9). The earthquake that occurred shortly after he spoke confirmed his message.

    B. Theme (1:2). The second verse presents the theme: Yahweh, the God of the entire nation of Israel and Judah, is to be feared. Like a lion His roar will devastate the land, especially the northern kingdom as symbolized by Carmel. That kingdom cannot continue to exist; no comfort is to be had in the thought that the Lord is merciful. He is also the Judge who must act against a sinful kingdom.

    C. Israel's Guilt and Judgment (1:3-2:16). Amos begins his discussion of the coming judgment of God with Damascus (1:3-5), Philistia (1:6-8), Tyre (1:9-10), Edom (1:11-12), the Ammonites (1:13-15), Moab (2:1-3), and even Judah (2:4-5). Yet the book is not really concerned with these nations (except for Judah which does have an important role). Rather, they appear only to confront the northern kingdom with the truth that she herself is ripe for God's wrath. Israel could agree heartily with the fate of these nations, but in so doing she only condemned herself. Her own guilt was far greater.

    General charges against Israel are raised initially in 2:6-12. First, the people have ignored the provisions in the Mosaic covenant for kind and generous treatment of the poor and downtrodden among them (2:6-8). Through the laws concerning land distribution and the need to care for the helpless and the hungry, God revealed His own compassionate and merciful nature. When His people neglect or even violate such laws, how can they claim to serve the God of the covenant?

The second part of Amos's opening charges contrasts the Lord's gracious actions for His people with their rejection of His attempts to turn them to righteousness through the ministry of prophets and Nazirites (2:9-12). If the Lord's messengers arise and preach judgment, it does not do any good to try to silence them. That would only invoke even more anger from the Lord.

II. Words of Warning. Amos continues his message by calling the people to listen to three words of warning (chaps. 3-6; cf. 3:1; 4:1; 5:1).[28]

A. Breach of the Covenant (chap. 3). The problem of God's covenant with Israel dominates chapter 3. Amos points out that the divine election implicit in the covenant works against Israel rather than for her (3:1-2). Of "all the families of the earth" she has the greatest responsibility; therefore her sins pile up greater condemnation for her.

In 3:2-8 Amos uses the framework of a series of questions to defend his own prophetic ministry. He concludes, "The Lord Yahweh has spoken! Who can but prophesy?" That is, Amos has the divine right as God's spokesman to announce judgment to Israel.

When the Lord calls other nations to witness against Israel (3:9-10), one is reminded of the "covenant lawsuit" (רִיב, *rîb*) that is found in other prophets (e.g., Mic. 1:2-7). The witnesses, themselves nations which do not stand under the covenant, are summoned to observe oppression in Israel. When the Gentiles are called to testify against the elect by God Himself, the situation must be bleak indeed!

As with each of the major sections of Amos (except the conclusion to the book), this first "word" terminates with an announcement of judgment (3:11-15). The Lord may be Israel's shepherd, but her infidelity will cause action against the people and their system of worship.

B. Failure to Repent (chap. 4). The second "word" is also connected closely with the covenant, but now the accusations are more explicit, highlighting Israel's failure to respond to the Lord in the proper way. She relied on useless ritual and refused to repent. The people are repressing the poor (4:1-3) and have rejected the Lord through their lack of true commitment to Him. The ironic commands in 4:4-5 convey the idea that Israel's religion was outward, not inward (cf. 2:7b-8). Then 4:6-11 points out that God's continual overtures to win Israel back to himself were all rebuffed, even as the prophets were rejected (cf. 2:11-12).

The judgment with which the second "word" closes very subtly fits Israel's guilt. The people refused to "return" to God; therefore God would meet them, but as their Judge (4:12-13), not their Savior.

---

[28] Adri van der Wal, "The Structure of Amos," *JSOT* 26 (1983): 107-13, thinks various patterns of inclusio work better to structure the book than this formula that announces the Lord's word to Israel. He has some valuable insights about connections that tie 1-6 together as a tight unit, but his examples of inclusion are not entirely convincing for three reasons: 1) at one point (4:3) an unlikely textual emendation is necessary; 2) it is possible to think of other ways to structure the text around the concept of inclusion; and 3) his divisions do not work as well as a straightforward appeal to the context. "Hear this word" seems like a more obvious structuring device.

The description of God in 4:13 stresses his sovereign role as the Creator. The ~is one of three passages in Amos that are often described as "hymnic" or as uoxoiogies" because of the language of praise in them (see also 5:8-9; 9:5-6). Each contains the refrain, "Yahweh (the God of hosts) is His name." How awesome is Israel's God!

C. *Choice of Life or Death (chaps. 5-6).* The third "word" (chaps. 5-6) contains the only direct calls to repentance in the book.[29] An aura of death permeates the unit (5:1-3, 16-17; 6:9-10) and contrasts with exhortations to find life as a result of seeking the Lord (cf. 5:4, 6, 14). The cry of "Alas!" at a funeral (5:16) also rings against those who smugly think the Lord is with them (5:18) or who feel secure in their own accomplishments (6:1-3). Judgment is so certain that Israel is already as good as dead. Yet here Amos at last pleads for his listeners to repent. The Lord always holds out the possibility of grace. Even when a general judgment is certain, there may be a remnant that will respond and find life.

Two other motifs from chap. 4 are taken up in chap. 5: oppression of the poor and inward versus outward religion. One section (5:10-13) speaks of an appropriate punishment for oppression – the oppressors will not be able to enjoy the fruit of their efforts. The theme that God desires obedience more than sacrifice is summed up eloquently in 5:21-24.

In addition to the "dirge" language, the prophecy of the "day of Yahweh" (5:18-20) and the prediction of exile "beyond Damascus" (5:25-27) reinforce the severity and finality of God's judgment. More accurately, the additional elements of judgment are also part of the "dirge" form. Israel will not rejoice when the day of the Lord comes because she will herself be judged.

The theme of self-sufficient pride and complacency pervades chap. 6, and it forms a fitting conclusion to the larger unit of chaps. 3-6, with a block of material dealing mostly with judgment. Thus, the section that opened with accusation closes with punishment. Not until chap. 7 does the subject matter change significantly with the introduction of Amos's visions.

III. *Visions of Judgment and Salvation.* With chap. 7 Amos begins to unfold a series of five visions. They serve as a vehicle by which he grapples with the finality of Israel's punishment over against the covenant mercy of the Lord. Also, they tie together the differing perspectives about Israel's condition held by God, His true prophets, the leadership, and the citizenry.

A. *The Lord Has Spared (7:1-6).* First the Lord shows Amos a locust swarm about to devour the land. The prophet intercedes, praying for pardon. When the Lord answers, we realize God's desire to show mercy to sinners.

The second vision concerns drought under the figure of a fire that consumes all the ground water that supplies the springs and wells. Once again Amos intercedes and God listens.

These visions focus attention on the issues of sin, judgment, and mercy. In them we see the prophet as one who intercedes for the people, trying to obtain mercy from the Lord. We see then that God is willing to hold back judgment so

---

[29] The chapter occurs at the center of the book. For a discussion of the chiastic pattern of 5:1-17 see the exegetical comments.

there will be time for the people to repent. The prophets preach woe not out of perversity but out of compassion and love.

B. The Lord Will Spare No Longer (7:7-8:14). The next two visions speak rather of a judgment which will not be turned back (7:7-9; 8:1-3). The Lord will destroy the places of worship in the northern kingdom as well as the dynasty of Jeroboam II. Wailing and mass burial will overwhelm the people. Thus, Amos repeats in a new way the threat of 2:6: "For three transgressions of Israel and for four/ I will not revoke its punishment."

1. The Vision of the Plumb Line (7:7-17). In the third vision the Lord tests Israel with a plumb line, but she cannot pass the test. The time for mercy has gone; God can no longer spare the kingdom of Jeroboam II.

How quickly Amos stirred up controversy when he began to speak about the king! Amaziah, the priest of Bethel, first complained to the crown that Amos was guilty of conspiracy and then confronted the prophet, ordering him to go to Judah and there earn his living by prophesying.

This official negative response to Amos plays an important role in the book. Amos has pointed out continually that the Lord is displeased with the standard religion of the day, especially because it does not provide a context for the Israelites to fulfill the demands of the Law of love for their neighbors. Typically the leaders strive to maintain the status quo and to downplay the authority of those who challenge it. Amos, however, stands apart from the official religious institutions, challenging them from the standpoint of the very God who supposedly justifies their existence.

Amos replied to Amaziah both with a defense of his prophetic authority and with a further prophecy of doom. Essentially Amos claims that his role as a prophet does not derive from traditional means but from the direct call of the Lord. His aim is not to make a living but to deliver a message. The nation's official rejection of the prophet means that they have rejected their covenant relationship with the Lord and are ready for judgment.

2. The Vision of the Basket of Summer Fruit (8:1-10). The message concerning judgment is the same in both the vision of the plumb line and in the vision of the basket of summer fruit: "I will spare them no longer." The advance in thought here is the stress upon the end for Israel, an emphasis made through a word play (see exegesis). The ripeness of the fruit probably also points to the ripeness of the nation for judgment.

There is also a broad structural similarity between 8:4-10 and 7:10-17. In both cases Israel responds to the vision, and the Lord makes a rejoinder. In chap. 7 the response represented an official position. Now it is more popular in nature, though it comes from the merchants. The complaints of the merchants tie together the two emphases in the book on social injustice and an ineffective religious formalism. The people lament that they cannot take advantage of the poor in the marketplace while they keep the new moon and sabbath! Obviously they care neither for their religion nor for their fellow Israelites. They themselves utter the last words in the book about their specific crimes.

Amos has depicted a situation so bad that we expect the Lord to respond immediately. In fact, the Lord feels so strongly He begins His reply with an oath that He makes by Himself, affirming that He is the true God of Jacob. Because of who He is He has the authority to determine the destiny of His people. That destiny will be complete destruction, accompanied by bitter mourning and reversal of fortune.

3. Those Who Refuse to Listen (8:11-14). As a conclusion to the series of two visions which announce the end in light of the people's own evaluation of the Lord, Amos speaks of a time when there will be no prophetic word to assure the people. Amaziah had commanded Amos to cease his preaching; the wealthy merchants had expressed their inner feelings about even external efforts to worship the Lord. In the future a deep spiritual hunger and thirst, which cannot be satisfied, will engulf the nation.

C. The Lord Will Spare None (9:1-6). A final vision of judgment finds the Lord Himself standing beside the altar at Bethel and ordering the complete destruction of the temple and all the people in it. He will pursue the guilty ones to any place they may think to hide from His wrath. The awesome God who has created the universe will thus meet with the sinful nation.

D. The Lord Will Restore His People (9:7-15). The closing section of Amos discusses the status of Israel as a chosen people. In light of the "end" that the Lord will bring to her, will there be any hope for the future? The answer has three parts. First, God asserts His sovereignty over the affairs of all the nations and His intention to destroy the "sinful kingdom" (9:7-8a). Second, He declares that the judgment with reference to individuals will be a sifting process (9:8b-10). A righteous remnant will be saved. Third, salvation is announced through the renewal of "the fallen booth of David" (9:11-15). This will be a joyous time of restoration and rebuilding. Also, the new condition of Israel will be permanent: "They will not again be rooted out from their land" (v. 15).

The promise of restoration divides neatly into two parts at 9:13. "Behold, days are coming" introduces a new section, and the topic changes from Israel and the nations to Israel and her land. Interestingly this twofold sequence completes a nice chiastic or inverted structure to the book, displayed as follows:

A Judgment of the Land (Amos 1:2)
    B Judgment of the Nations (Amos 1:3-2:3)
        C Judgment of Judah and Israel (Amos 2:4-9:10)
        C′ Restoration of Judah and Israel (Amos 9:11)
    B′ Restoration of the Nations (Amos 9:12)
A′ Restoration of the Land (Amos 9:13-15)

Contemporary Context

For many Christians the OT prophets are valuable only as they contribute to knowledge of God's future plans or as they teach about Israel's Messianic expectations. The book of Amos sheds some light on these issues (cf. 5:18-20; 9:11-15), but its major value lies elsewhere. As Amos strikes out at injustice and oppression, he hits on themes that are not unknown in the pages of the New Testament or in the preaching of Jesus Christ (e.g., Luke 1:52-53; 4:16-21; 18:22; 19:8-9; Jas. 5:1-6). Also, when Amos condemns worship that considers only outward form and not acts of love and compassion in the life of the worshiper, he once again anticipates the teaching of our Lord (cf. Matt. 5:23; John 15). In these two areas Amos has much to say to the Christian who will be patient enough to

discern carefully the meaning of the book in the setting of eighth century B.C.
Israel, extracting the principles and teachings that are universally valid.

Perhaps we can press Amos a bit further for modern applications. Amos and
Micah figure prominently in current criticism of oppressive governments, '
especially through what is termed "liberation theology." Missionaries have
reported conditions in some countries that have nearly exact parallels with what
Amos describes. Certainly Amos at least evokes questions about the relationship
between private morality and public morality. That is, as will become clear from
the exegesis, Amos reacts against not merely hard-hearted individuals but also
against social structures that work contrary to systems divinely appointed for Israel
through the covenant. Again, the reader should seek general principles that could
be applied to any governmental system, regardless of the specifics of how it applied
to ancient Israel. Amos very plainly shows, for example, that God is concerned that
a government make channels available for addressing the issues of justice for all its
citizens.

It should also be stressed that while Amos raises the issue of government's
responsibility before God, the book does not give explicit direction as to how
Christians should be involved in government. Much less does it decide the issue of
the participation of the Church as an institution versus Christians as individuals. In
any case, Amos should certainly serve as a warning to both individual believers and
the Church to beware lest they become part of the problem rather than the solution
to social ills. (For more details, see Excursus on Social Justice in Amos).

The problem of how to apply Amos especially needs to be approached
theologically. The book reveals the Lord and various aspects of his covenant with
his people, Israel. Two theological motifs figure prominently in Amos's sermons.

First, the prophet sees the Lord as sovereign over the nations of the earth,
expecting righteousness from all peoples, especially Israel and Judah. That
perspective is possible for Amos because the Lord is the Creator of all the earth and
its inhabitants. Creation theology permeates the book and will have decided
consequences for the Christian who seeks to understand his or her relationship to
the world.[30]

Secondly, Amos relies heavily on the covenant relationship between the Lord
and Israel/Judah for his strong words against his generation. While there are
differences of opinion, the Church should not be equated with ancient Israel,[31] but
certainly all could agree that Amos's words about God's requirements for His
people ought to stir the heart of any believer in any dispensation. Moreover, the
Lord's expectations of Israel are not so foreign to his expectations of the Church
that we should not glean from them those issues that are relevant. Amos has much
to say to the Church about requirements for justice among Christians, as well as for
a sense of compassion and generosity in one's dealings with society in general. It is
our hope that this commentary will serve not merely as a source of information but

---

[30] Cf. Christopher J. H. Wright, *An Eye for an Eye: The Place of Old Testament Ethics
Today* (Downers Grove, Ill.: InterVarsity, 1983), pp. 68-70. He discusses Biblical
perspectives on economics and private property from the standpoint of creation theology.

[31] Wright, *An Eye for an Eye*, pp. 40-44; Kenneth L. Barker, "False Dichotomies
Between the Testaments," *JETS* 25 (1982): 10-15.

as a call for response to one of the most forceful preachers of Scripture, Amos of Tekoa.[32]

---

[32] See also Thomas Finley, "An Evangelical Response to the Preaching of Amos," *JETS* 28 (1985): 411-20. See more recently Mark Daniel Carroll, *Contexts for Amos: Prophetic Poetics in Latin American Perspective* (JSOTSup 132; Sheffield, England: JSOT Press, 1992).

1
Amos and His Message
(1:1-2)

The first two verses of Amos introduce the reader to the prophet, describe the historical setting, and focus attention on the message of judgment to Israel.

A. Heading (1:1)

Translation

*The words of Amos,
  who was among the sheep breeders from Tekoa,
  which he received by revelation concerning Israel
  in the days of Uzziah king of Judah
  in the days of Jeroboam son of Joash king of Israel,
  two years before the earthquake.

Note: The translation will normally display the text as poetry or prose. Here, in order to make the discussion which follows clearer, the grammatical relations are stressed by the arrangement of the text.

Exegesis and Exposition

The heading as it stands stresses the prophetic inspiration of Amos and points to his central concern with the nation of Israel. It also highlights his lay background and thereby the immediacy and directness of his experience with the Lord. The time references indicate the political situation under Jeroboam II and focus on the brief period of Amos's oral proclamation.

The tie-in with Uzziah of Judah is more than a mere chronological indicator; it points up the closely intertwined destinies of Israel and the southern kingdom. Though Amos preached to Israel, God's dealings with Judah were vital to the north. Originally north and south were a unity (3:1), and they will again find their oneness in the figure of David. Also, Amos's hometown of Tekoa hints at his own southern roots. He views the Israelite system of worship through the eyes of a Judean, a point reiterated several times throughout the book (2:4-5; 3:1; 6:1; 9:11).[1]

The initial verse of the book does not stand alone as a complete sentence; the rest of the book finishes its thought. That is, the heading, "words of Amos," lacking any main verb or predicate of its own, applies to the written work in front of the reader.

---

[1] Cf. G. Hinton Davies, "Amos—The Prophet of Re-Union: An Essay in Honour of the Eightieth Birthday of Professor Aubrey R. Johnson, F.B.A.," *ExpTim* 92 (1981): 196-200.

As indicated in the introduction, Amos's name should be taken as a shortened form for "sustained by the Lord." An ancient seal from Amman bears the name עמסאל ('ms'l), attesting to the combination with the divine name El.[2]

The term חָזָה (ḥāzâ) is literally "he saw," but it frequently implies prophetic revelation (cf. Isa. 30:10; Ezek. 12:27). When the text says Amos "saw" his "words" (cf. Isa. 2:1; Mic. 1:1), it means by any mode of revelation, whether visual or not. In noun form the same root means a "seer" (cf. Amos 7:12), and the verb used in the heading to a prophetic book would be a technical term to make the fact of divine inspiration clear.

The Targum applied this second relative clause to Amos himself rather than to his words: "The words of Amos ... who prophesied concerning Israel." The usage elsewhere of ḥāzâ argues against this interpretation.

Because of בַּנֹּקְדִים (bannōqĕdîm, "among the sheep breeders"), many have thought of Amos as a rustic shepherd of rather poor and simple background. For example, Keil says Amos "lived with the shepherds who fed their sheep in the steppe to the east of Tekoah; of course not as a rich owner of flocks, but simply as a shepherd."[3] However, it appears that his occupation as a "sheep breeder" gave him a position of importance and possibly even wealth. His insight into the corrupt practices of Israelite merchants may have come from frequent business trips to the north.

The NASB translated the rare word nōqēd as "sheepherder," whereas NIV used simply "shepherd." Yet the term could indicate a more important occupation. It occurs elsewhere only in 2 Kings 3:4, where Mesha, king of Moab, is also called a nōqēd ("sheep breeder," NASB). The context mentions "100,000 lambs and the wool of 100,000 rams" that Mesha "paid" to the king of Israel. A related form in the Akkadian language, nāqidu, translates as "herdsman"; the person who bears the title can be in charge of either sheep or cattle or both (see also Additional Notes).[4]

Consideration of the terms that Amos used to describe himself in his encounter with Amaziah (7:10-17) confirms the impression that the prophet once had a socially important position. He was a "livestock dealer" (בּוֹקֵר, bôqēr; or "herdsman," see exegesis of 7:14) and a "grower of sycamore figs" (בוֹלֵס שִׁקְמִים, bôlēs šiqmîm; see on 7:14). Evidently the latter position was also a significant occupation. One of David's officials "had charge of the olive and sycamore trees in the shephelah" (1 Chron. 27:28). Today sycamore fruit is eaten by poor people

---

[2] N. Avigad, "A Group of Hebrew Seals," *Eretz-Israel* 9 (1969): 8, seal numb. 18 (in Hebrew; English summary on p. 134 of English section). Giovanni Garbini, "Ammonite Inscriptions," *JSS* 19 (1974): 162, classifies the name *'ms'l* in this seal as "one of the typical Ammonite names."

[3] C. F. Keil, *Minor Prophets*, COTTV 10; Grand Rapids: Eerdmans, 1973), p. 233. The Arabic etymology he cites from Bochart as evidence that *n_q_d* "signifies only a rearer of sheep, *i.e.* not merely the owner, but the shepherd of choice sheep" is not as pertinent as the contextual usage.

[4] *CAD*, "N," 1:333-35; see also S. Segert, "Zur Bedeutung des Wortes Noqed," *Hebr+ische Wortforschung: Festschrift zum 80. Geburtstag von Walter Baumgartner* (VTSup 16; Leiden: E. J. Brill, 1967), pp. 279-83.

because figs are more desirable, but in Bible times sycamores were an important commodity (Ps. 78:47; Isa. 9:10).[5]

The geography of Amos's two occupations is interesting. Sycamores grow in the lowlands (1 Kings 10:27; 2 Chron. 1:15; 9:27) and coastal plains. Tekoa, on the other hand, is situated high in the hill country of Judah, about ten miles south of Jerusalem. Either Amos lived in Tekoa and owned land in the lower elevations, or possibly he was from Tekoa but not living there at the time he received his call.[6] The possibility of a more northern location for Tekoa has been advanced but does not seem likely.[7]

Amos prophesied during the reigns of two great kings. The Chronicler notes that Uzziah, also known as Azariah, "did right in the sight of the Yahweh" (2 Chron. 26:4) but later became proud and tried to burn incense on the altar. For this the Lord struck him with leprosy (2 Chron. 26:16-21). For the chronology of his reign see Additional Notes.

The Bible does not show much interest in Jeroboam II, devoting a mere handful of verses to one of the most influential kings of Israel. The writer'of Kings notes that he "did evil in the eyes of Yahweh" (2 Kings 14:24). Nevertheless, in his days God did send the prophet Jonah to proclaim the recovery of much Israelite territory, "for Yahweh saw the affliction of Israel" (2 Kings 14:24).

The contrast between the book of Kings and Amos is striking. Jeroboam was used by the Lord, according to the author of Kings, to deliver Israel, for "Yahweh did not say that He would blot out the name of Israel from under heaven" (2 Kings 14:27). Yet a short time later Amos comes and discerns a situation so evil that he must proclaim judgment on the house of Jeroboam (Amos 7:9). God would still preserve the name of Israel, according to Amos, but under the banner of David (9:11).

The second chronological note, שְׁנָתַיִם לִפְנֵי הָרָעַשׁ (šĕnātayim lipnê hārāʿaš, "two years before the earthquake"), helps to pinpoint the date more precisely, assuming that Yigael Yadin has correctly placed the destruction of Hazor by an earthquake about 765-760 B.C.[8] The statement probably means that the prophet ministered about a year. However, if it introduces v. 2 rather than the book as a whole, then some of the prophecy could have been delivered later than the earthquake.

In any case, the notice probably served more than a chronological function. Amos speaks several times of a shaking that will occur in the land (2:13; 8:8; 9:5). There is some controversy about whether he means to imply a literal earthquake, but certainly the destructive earthquake that s truck the entire land from north to

---

[5] Hans Walter Wolff, *Joel and Amos* (Hermeneia; trans. Waldemar Janzen, et al.; Philadelphia: Fortress, 1977), pp. 306-7; J. C. Trever, "Sycamore," *IDB* 4:470-71. Soggin also prefers the view of Amos's occupation presented here in *The Prophet Amos: A Translation and Commentary*, trans. John Bowden (London: SCM, 1987), pp. 10-12.

[6] S. R. Driver, *The Books of Joel and Amos* (Cambridge Bible for Schools and Colleges; Cambridge: University, 1907), p. 208.

[7] Most recently Klaus Koch, *The Prophets, Volume One: The Assyrian Period* (Fortress: Philadelphia, 1983), p. 70.

[8] See Introduction to Amos, n. 3.

south two years after Amos delivered his message served as a warning that the Lord was indeed serious about the coming judgment. Unfortunately, that warning went unheeded in Israel.

Additional Notes

1:1 אֲשֶׁר חָזָה ... אֲשֶׁר הָיָה: Some commentators have found difficulty with the heading. Wolff, for example, refers to "tensions and overloading" in support of his theory that an original title was expanded long after the period of Amos. He notes with regard to the descriptions of Amos and his words, "Two relative clauses with such different antecedents hardly flowed from the same pen."[9] That is, the first relative clause, "who was among the sheep breeders," refers to Amos, while the second relative clause, "which he saw concerning Israel," refers instead to the words of Amos.

The unusual grammar Wolff notices would be irregular for ordinary narrative, but it is not without precedent for biblical titles or headings. Nearly all the titles of prophetic books describe the prophet in some way, usually by a phrase of the type "son of X" which stands next to the prophet's name. In a structural sense Isaiah 1:1 is parallel to Amos 1:1, even though a relative clause is not used to qualify the prophet:

> The vision of Isaiah son of Amoz
> > which he saw [חָזָה] concerning Judah and Jerusalem in the days
> > of Uzziah...
> The words of Amos who was among the sheep breeders...
> > which he saw [חָזָה] concerning Israel...

The verb חָזָה in Amos also links his heading with the early prophecies of Isaiah (2:1) and Micah (1:1).

The LXX translates "the words of Amos which were among the *nakkarim* from Tekoa," possibly highlighting a problem with the preposition מִן (*from* Tekoa). The construct state might have been expected for "the sheep breeders from Tekoa."[10] With an already complex construction, the מִן could be for clarification (cf. Judges 17:7). Rosenbaum relates it to his view that Amos was actually a northerner who came to Tekoa only when he was exiled to Judah.[11]

בַּנֹּקְדִים: Ugaritic *nqd* may be cognate, but its precise meaning is unclear. Some have tried to give the Hebrew term a religious connotation because *rb nqdm* ("chief of the herdsmen [?]") occurs in apposition with *rb khnm* ("chief of the priests") in a colophon to a mythic text about Baal.[12] However, P. C. Craigie has argued that the term *nqdm* in this passage is not associated with the following *rb*

---

[9] Wolff, *Joel and Amos*, 117-18.

[10] Stanley N. Rosenbaum, עָמוֹס הַיִּשְׂרְאֵלִי *Amos of Israel: A New Interpretation* (Macon, GA: Mercer University, 1990), p. 31.

[11] Rosenbaum, *Amos of Israel*, p. 31.

[12] M. Dietrich, O. Loretz, and J. Sanmartin, eds., *Die keilalphabetischen Texte aus Ugarit* (Neukirchen-Vluyn: Neukirchener Verlag, 1976), 1.6:VI:56; cf. S. Segert, who discusses cognates from various other Semitic languages as well ("Zur Bedeutung des Wortes Noqed," p. 281).

khnm but only with the preceding word.[13] Amos's position was probably strictly secular.

מִתְּקוֹעַ: Wolff feels that the translation "from Tekoa" is an "impermissible smoothing" of a difficulty in the Hebrew.[14] Yet a noun modified by a prepositional phrase with no relative pronoun is not uncommon (Gen. 2:6; Lev. 2:3). Moreover, it occurs elsewhere in Amos: "his fruit above" (lit. "from above") and "his root below" (lit. "from below") in 2:9. Close grammatical parallels to Amos 1:1 also appear in 2 Kings 21:19; 22:1; 23:31, 36; 24:8, 18; 2 Chron. 13:2.

עֻזִּיָּה: Uzziah is also known as Azariah, which is apparently a phonetic variant.[15] The chronology of his reign is a more thorny issue. Typically he is said to have had a lengthy coregency with his father, Amaziah. Archer lists this period as 790-767 B.C.[16] The proposed overlap of reigns helps to solve various chronological problems, but it also runs into difficulty in the face of 2 Kings 14:18-21. The simplest reading of the text makes it appear that the people made Azariah (Uzziah) king at the age of sixteen immediately after his father, Amaziah, was killed in a palace revolt.

On the other hand, 2 Chron. 25:27 indicates that the conspiracy against Amaziah began "from the time when Amaziah turned away from Yahweh." The Chronicler further pinpoints that time as when the king worshiped Edomite idols after defeating Edom and just prior to challenging Jehoash of Israel to battle (2 Chron. 25:14-17). This lends credence to the view that Amaziah was forced out of Jerusalem long prior to his death.[17]

Turning to the narration in 2 Kings, the passage 14:17-20 apparently deals directly with Amaziah, while v. 21 turns back to the issue of how the Judeans handled the lack of a king in Jerusalem. They elevated Azariah, who at that time was only sixteen. The verse begins with a *waw*-consecutive with "imperfect" (וַיִּקְחוּ), but structurally the passage is similar to Gen. 2:18-19. There the expression "*and* Yahweh God *formed*" (וַיִּצֶר) indicates a change of subject rather than a different sequence of creation from that of Gen. 1.

Another possible objection to a coregency is that Amaziah is said to have reigned twenty-nine years "in Jerusalem" (2 Kings 14:2). This may imply no more, though, than a statement that Amaziah was Judah's king for that period of time, Jerusalem simply being the capital that stood for the nation.

---

[13] P. C. Craigie, "Amos the *noqed* in the light of Ugaritic," *SR* 11 (1982): 29-33. Cf. his conclusion with regard to Amos (p. 33): "Amos was not a simple shepherd. He was in the sheep business, a manager of herds, contributing both wool and meat to the economy."

[14] Wolff, *Joel and Amos*, p. 117.

[15] Hayim Tadmor, "Azriyau of Yaudi," in *Studies in the Bible* (Scripta Hierosolymitana 8; ed. Chaim Rabin; Jerusalem: Magnes, 1961), p. 232 n. 1.

[16] Archer, "Chronology of the Old Testament," p. 370.

[17] For more details about the coregency, see Edwin R. Thiele, *The Mysterious Numbers of the Hebrew Kings*, new rev. ed. (Grand Rapids: Eerdmans, 1983), pp. 118-20.

B. Theme (1:2)

Translation

> *Yahweh roars from Zion,
> and from Jerusalem He utters His voice.
> Then the shepherds' pastures wilt,
> and the summit of Carmel dries up. (1:2)

Exegesis and Exposition

The second verse stands as an appropriate summary of the theme of the book. The Lord, whose true dwelling place on earth is the Temple in Jerusalem, will break out in judgment that will sweep through to the north and devastate everything in between. In the rest of the book, the specifics of this general theme of judgment are filled in. John H. Hayes makes the verse an introduction only to the oracles against the nations (1:3-2:16),[18] but if so it is hard to see the reason for the separate introductory formulas ("thus says Yahweh") of the latter passage.

The loud "roar" (יִשְׁאָג, *yiš'āg*, "he roars") evokes the thought of a lion (cf. Job 4:10; Jer. 2:15; Zech. 11:3). Amos makes a similar comparison later in the book (3:8). The prophet was no doubt familiar with lions, and the analogy came naturally. The symbolism refers to judgment, as is made clear by the second half of the verse.

For the meaning "wilt" for אָבַל (*'ābal*) see the Exegesis and Exposition on Joel 1:10. The LXX took the more common meaning, "and the pastures of the shepherds lamented [ἐπένθησαν, *epenthēsan*]" (similarly the Syriac Peshitta). The Targum interpreted the figure, "the dwellings of kings will be made desolate" (cf. its treatment of Zech. 11:3, 8, 15, 16; 13:7).

Mt. Carmel was famous for its luxurious and abundant growth (Song of Sol. 7:6). Amos predicts that the most verdant area in the land of Israel will completely dry up from the searing judgment of the Lord (cf. 9:3). The mountain also figured prominently as a religious center in the days of Elijah and Elisha (1 Kings 18:19-20, 42; 2 Kings 2:25; 4:25). Perhaps a certain feeling of sanctity that was attached to it lingered after those days, with the result that Amos's words also pronounce judgment on the Israelite system of worship.

According to Hayes, כַּרְמֶל (*karmel*) has its more general sense of "woodlands" here, the wooded heights forming a "polar opposite" to the low pastures (Hayes translates "oases") of the shepherds.[19] The phrase רֹאשׁ הַכַּרְמֶל (*rō'š hakkarmel*), however, more likely refers to the geographical location.

"Wilting" and "drying up" are not meant to refer to an actual drought, for that is still part of the figure. When this Lion roars, all of nature dries up from the heat of His breath. The figure itself contains hyperbole, but the application to God's judgment is not to be understated. Amos depicts the total devastation of the land

---

[18] Hayes, *Amos, The Eighth-Century Prophet; His Times and His Preaching* (Nashville: Abingdon, 1988), pp. 55-56.

[19] Hayes, *Amos*, p. 65.

and people. The Assyrian armies will be the major divine instrument of destruction.

Additional Notes

1:2 The first line of Joel 3:16 (MT 4:16) reads almost exactly the same as the first line of Amos 1:2 (Joel has "and Yahweh"; cf. also Jer. 25:30). The possibilities are that Amos quoted Joel, that Joel quoted Amos, or that both prophets independently used a traditional saying associated with the awesome presence of the Lord. Joel refers only to Zion/Jerusalem, but since Amos mentions territory from both kingdoms ("the summit of Carmel" was Israelite territory), it is at least possible that he preserves a traditional saying handed down from the united kingdom period.[20]

---

[20] Cf. Georges Farr, "The Language of Amos, Popular or Cultic?" *VT* 16 (1966): 313-14. Farr thinks Amos quoted the first line from a traditional source and composed the second.

2
Judgment on Israel's Neighbors
(1:3-2:5)

After announcing the general theme of judgment against Israel, the book continues with brief words of punishment for seven of Israel's neighbors, followed by a longer pronouncement against Israel. Amos slips into his main topic – Israel's punishment – almost unnoticed, and he forces the audience into the uncomfortable position of having to apply his words directly to themselves. They could readily agree that hated enemies such as Aram and Philistia richly deserved divine wrath, but as Amos logically circumscribed Israel, the tension must have mounted, especially when the topic turned to Judah, their sister nation.

Once Amos' sermon touches Israel (2:6-16), he brings out themes of sin and judgment, which will be amplified by the rest of the book. The sins consist of mistreatment of the poor and disadvantaged in Israelite society (2:6-8), as well as rejection of the mercy God had shown to the people in the past (2:9-12). Because of these sins, God Himself will bring retribution and Israel will find no escape (2:13-16).

Along these same lines, the crimes of the nations consist of a lack of compassion toward other people as well. Damascus "threshed Gilead with implements of sharp iron"; Philistia "deported an entire population"; Tyre "did not remember the covenant of brotherhood"; the Ammonites "ripped open the pregnant women of Gilead"; and Moab "burned the bones of the king of Edom to lime." Each case represents an atrocity, a transgression of the boundaries guarding against behaviors that would not be expected even among the Gentile nations. The force is explosive when applied to Israel. She, like her sister Judah, is governed by the covenant Law and is therefore more reprehensible in the sight of God (cf. 3:1). [1]

Seven nations, which are near neighbors of Israel, receive a brief word of condemnation. Prophecies against all or most of these nations also occur in Isaiah (11:14-16; 13-24), Jeremiah (46-51), Ezekiel (25-32), and Zechariah (9:1-7). For these other prophets, the oracles are meant to encourage Israel, whereas in Amos they are meant as a warning.

Why did Amos arrange his predictions about the nations beginning with Damascus and ending with Judah? The problem cannot be solved completely, but three suggestions have been offered. A geographical arrangement is inviting but complicated. The series Damascus – Philistia – Tyre – Edom would form a crisscrossing pattern; then Ammon – Moab – Judah would fill in the design on the

---

[1] Cf. John Barton, *Amos's Oracles against the Nations: A Study of Amos 1.3-2.5* (SOTSMS 6; Cambridge: Cambridge Univ., 1980), pp. 42-44; and Samuel Amsler, "Amos et les droits de l'homme," in *De la Tôrah au Messie: Mélanges Henri Cazelles*, ed. Maurice Carrez, et. al. (Paris: Desclee, 1981), pp. 184-85.

eastern and southern sides from north to south to west. Note that a four plus three pattern would result.

Shalom Paul proposes a connection by association of words, phrases, or thoughts in the successive oracles.[2] His results are as follows:

Damascus-Philistia	link	"and I will cut off the one seated"
Philistia-Tyre	link	"because they delivered up/deported an entire population"
Tyre-Edom	link	"brothers"
Edom-Ammon	link	crimes committed with a sword
Ammon-Moab	link	"with war cries" and "his/her princes"

Following the same pattern it might be said that the issue of covenant violations links the Judah and Israel units (not discussed by Paul).

Wilhelm Rudolph groups the prophecies in a three plus four scheme, with the first three (Damascus, Philistia, and Tyre) concerned with nations genetically unrelated to Israel and the last four (Edom, Ammon, Moab, and Judah) with nations related to Israel by blood ties.[3] This view does not explain the arrangement within the two groups.

---

[2] Shalom M. Paul, "Amos 1:3-2:3: A Concatenous Literary Pattern," *JBL* 90 (1971): 397-403.

[3] Wilhelm Rudolph, *Joel--Amos--Obadja--Jona* (KAT 13:2; Gütersloh: Gütersloher Verlagshaus Gerd Mohn, 1971), p. 123.

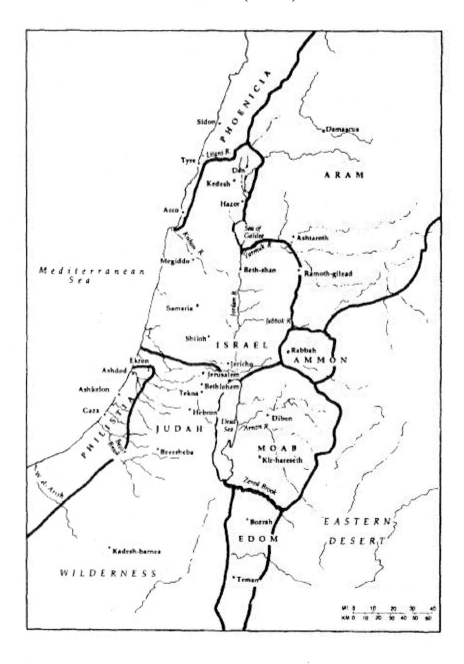

Rudolph's three-four pattern is interesting in light of the "three ... four" numerical saying within each judgment oracle (see exegesis of 1:3 below). Perhaps for Amos the number of seven nations, as completing the sequence of 3+4, points to the significance of the eighth, Israel.[4] Or it might be possible to consider Judah and Israel together to make up the seventh in the series, since the crimes of both sister nations involve a breach of covenant.[5]

In light of the purpose of these seven prophecies, a principle that stresses an increase in tension as the series progresses would seem best. Rudolph's idea coupled with the linking of key phrases or thoughts (Paul) would account for the facts well. Rudolph also stresses the climactic nature of the Israel oracle by comparing it with the parable of Nathan to David (2 Sam. 12:1-15) and Isaiah's parable of the vineyard (Isa. 5:1-7).[6] In all three cases the audience is expected to agree with the necessity of punishment in a seemingly unrelated case, only to suddenly have the point turned against them.

Andrew E. Steinmann found a pattern that alternated between a neighbor of Israel and a neighbor of Judah, with the neighbors getting progressively closer until Judah and Israel were themselves juxtaposed in chap. 2.[7] This has the effect of unifying the oracles as well as the two kingdoms of Judah and Israel, with both parts of God's people at the climax of the oracle.

A. Damascus (1:3-5)

Translation

> Thus says Yahweh:
> "For three transgressions of Damascus,
> even for four I will not *turn back (its punishment),
> because they threshed *Gilead with iron threshing sledges.
> [4]So I will cast fire on the house of Hazael,
> and it will consume the citadels of Ben-hadad.
> [5]I will also break the gate bar of Damascus
> and cut off him who sits (on the throne) from Aven Valley,
> and him who holds the scepter from Beth-eden.
> And the people of Aram will go exiled to Kir,"
> *says Yahweh.

Exegesis and Exposition

Damascus, the capital of Aram, had been a bitter foe within the recent memory of Amos's audience. At the beginning of the Jehu dynasty, of which

---

[4] Cf. Shalom Paul, "A Literary Reinvestigation of the Authenticity of the Oracles against the Nations of Amos," in *De la Tôrah au Messie: Mélanges Henri Cazelles*, ed. Maurice Carrez, et al. (Paris: Desclee, 1981), pp. 196-97.

[5] Gleason Archer includes both together in his outline of Amos in *A Survey of Old Testament Introduction*, rev. ed. (Chicago: Moody, 1975), p. 316.

[6] Rudolph, *Amos*, p. 123.

[7] Andrew E. Steinmann, "The Order of Amos's Oracles against the Nations: 1:3-2:16," *JBL* 111:4 (1992), pp. 683-689.

Jeroboam II was the fourth representative, Hazael of Damascus waged effective campaigns against Israel and took much of their territory, including sections of Gilead (2 Kings 10:32-33). War between Aram and Israel continued into the days of Jehoahaz, the son of Jehu, and Ben-hadad, the son of Hazael (2 Kings 13:3). Jeroboam II restored much of the lost territory (2 Kings 14:25-28).[8]

Amos either refers to a time when the Arameans had literally forced prisoners of war to lie down while an iron threshing sledge was drawn over their backs, or he refers figuratively to the ruthless slaughter of whole populations in Gilead (cf. 2 Kings 13:7).[9] Defenseless prisoners thus form the first link in the chain of cruel actions against those who cannot defend themselves.

1:3 The opening statement in v. 3, which is repeated at the beginning of each of the eight oracles, follows the pattern of a numerical sequence that can be described as X ... X + 1. This general pattern occurs elsewhere in the Bible (e.g., Job 5:19-21; Ps. 62:11-12 [MT 12-13]; Prov. 6:16-19; 30:15b-16, 18-19, 21-23, 29-31) and is also known in Ugaritic literature (ca. 1400-1200 B.C.) and in the Aramaic sayings of Ahiqar (composed sometime between the seventh and fifth centuries B.C.).[10]

Amos uses the numerical saying in two unique ways. First, he lists only one crime (or possibly two in some cases, 1:9, 11; 2:4). Contrast this with Prov. 30:29-31 where the four enumerated items are the lion, the strutting cock, the male goat, and "a king when his army is with him." Second, when Amos applies the statement to Israel, he lists seven sins (2:6-8), in effect adding the two numbers.[11]

Wolff argues that the final item listed in a numerical sequence contains the emphasis and also differs in some way from the others.[12] This does not always seem obvious, however (cf. Prov. 30:15b-16). We would conclude that the significance of the 3+4 pattern in Amos is cumulative, stressing the completeness of sin and

---

[8] V. Fritz ("Die Fremdvölkersprüche des Amos," *VT* 37 [1987]: 30-31) argues that the oracle cannot be genuine because Aram was no longer a threat to Israel. But surely Amos could have played to the bitter memories of his audience, or perhaps some instances of Aramean hostility during this period were not recorded in Scripture.

[9] Thomas Edward McComiskey, "Amos," in *EBC*, ed. Frank E. Gaebelein (Grand Rapids: Zondervan, 1985), 7:283, takes a figurative view, while Barton (*Amos's Oracles*, p. 19) takes the literal view.

[10] *ANET*, 3d ed., p. 134, part 7, lines 9-12; p. 428, part 6. Cf. Hans Walter Wolff, *Joel and Amos* (Hermeneia; trans. Waldemar Janzen, et al.; Philadelphia: Fortress, 1977), p. 137; and James Luther Mays, *Amos* (OTL; Philadelphia: Westminster, 1969), pp. 23-24. Note also W. M. W. Roth, "The Numerical Sequence X/X + 1 in the OT," *VT* 12 (1962): 301-11, as well as his larger work, *Numerical Sayings in the Old Testament: A Form-Critical Study* (VTSup 13; Leiden: E. J. Brill, 1965). Roth thinks the sayings in Amos are not "numerical sayings proper since they do not actually list the transgressions committed, but only refer to one crime" (*Numerical Sayings*, p. 63 n. 3).

[11] Cf. Mark Weiss, "The Pattern of Numerical Sequence in Amos 1-2; A Re-Examination," *JBL* 86 (1967): 416-23. Amos could have drawn on a standard formula but adapted it to his own uses.

[12] Wolff, *Joel and Amos*, p. 138.

thereby the necessity for judgment. Transgression after transgression has led to a situation that can be tolerated no longer.[13]

Another way to look at the numbers is to say that if three sins tried the Lord's patience, then surely the fourth was too much.[14] Perhaps the overall result will not differ significantly under this view. In either case the Lord can no longer tolerate the situation. Amos uses many patterns based on seven in his book, so the cumulative interpretation seems preferable.

The term "transgression" (פֶּשַׁע, *pešaʿ*), referring to a rebellion against or a violation of some accepted norm or law, occurs in a context of judgment from the Lord; God cannot turn it back because the "transgressions" are too weighty. Therefore, Amos's understanding of the term began with God. Wolff proposes the translation "crimes," because all the specific actions to which Amos applies the term "involve infractions of property and personal rights, deeds which deliberately violate community standards."[15] However, "transgressions" stresses the theological context of Amos's use of the term better.

Barton attempts to root the term more in human experience than theology, classifying the wrongs into violations of "international law proper," "agreed international conventions not legally ratified," and "unilaterally accepted norms of international conduct."[16] He feels it would have been "irrational" for Amos to base his accusations on divine law, because "we still run the risk of suggesting that [the nations] are condemned for breaking an edict they were unaware of: for what reason was there to think that God's will had been revealed to them?"[17]

Barton fails to consider the creation theology of Amos. In the first of the three majestic passages that describe God's power as the Creator, Amos says the Lord "declares to man what are His thoughts" (4:13). Amos may have viewed the transgressions as crimes against universally accepted human norms, but he considered all men responsible to the same God that Israel worshiped precisely because they had imbibed deeply of natural revelation.

S. Amsler discusses five views as to why the nations should be held responsible according to Amos. He concludes that the prophet believed the law revealed to Israel had a universal aspect in that it manifests the character of Yawheh Himself. Charles L. Feinberg has an appropriate comment: "What a refutation is a chapter like [Amos 1] to the contention that Israel's God was considered a tribal or national God. He is Lord of all the earth as the Scriptures maintain throughout."[18]

The mention of Damascus was calculated to arouse strong feelings of bitterness. The oracle against the city forms an appropriate introduction to a series that builds an atmosphere of tension, ultimately spilling over onto the audience itself.

---

[13] Cf. Douglas Stuart, *Hosea-Jonah* (WBC 31; Waco, Tex.: Word, 1987), p. 310.

[14] See Michael L. Barre, "The Meaning of *lʾ ʿšybnw* in Amos 1:3-2:6," *JBL* 105 (1986): 621.

[15] Wolff, *Joel and Amos*, p. 153.

[16] Barton, *Amos's Oracles*, esp. pp. 52-59.

[17] Ibid., p. 43.

[18] Charles L. Feinberg, *The Minor Prophets* (Chicago: Moody, 1976), p. 89; S. Amsler, "Amos et les droits de l'homme," pp. 184-86.

For the clause, אֲשִׁיבֶנּוּ לֹא (*lōʾ ʿăšîbennû*, "I will not turn it back"), commentators are divided over precisely what "it" (or "him") refers to. The judgment mentioned in v. 2 points specifically to Judah and Israel, whereas the present section begins with Damascus. Wolff lists four major interpretations and rightly draws attention to the necessity of finding something that will fit each of the eight oracles in which the expression occurs. Wolff himself prefers to connect it closely to the visions of chaps. 7 and 8, of which the first two show God relenting from the punishment, while the burden of the remaining visions is "I will spare them no longer" (7:8; 8:2).[19] Similarly, the Targum translates, "I will not forgive them."

The vision reports do strengthen the idea expressed in the oracles of chaps. 1 and 2, but it is not necessary to appeal to them to discover the context for the Lord's statement. Each of the prophecies against the nations describes a judgment from the Lord, and it is this threat of which the Lord says, "I will not turn it back." In a similar vein, Rolf Knierem argues that the reference is to the Lord's anger, expressed in each instance by the fire sent forth against the cities.[20] Hayes's idea that the judgment of v. 2 is the proper antecedent gives a similar result,[21] though that verse appears to be more introductory to the entire book of Amos (see comments on 1:2).

Michael Barre proposes that the pronoun refers in each case to the nation mentioned in the first half of the line. The verb would then mean "allow to return" or "take back." In other words, the Lord is saying He will no longer accept back these nations as His "vassals." Consequently, He must attack and overthrow them. That these nations were the Lord's vassals can be explained by reference to the earlier control exercised by the united kingdom over the broader territory implied in Amos's oracles. Also, one must not think that the Lord's relationship with these nations would in any way alter the status of Israel as His chosen people. Rather, "We might say that in the eyes of Yahweh Israel occupies the position of 'chief vassal,' a position that implies sovereignty over the other nations."[22]

Barre's view has the advantage of giving the pronoun a referent to a previous noun rather than to the punishment that has not yet been mentioned. Also, Barre strives to place the oracles in a broader political context of international relations in the eighth century B.C. However, his explanation for the vassal status of the nations to Yahweh as the sovereign seems forced, and it would introduce too early in Amos's ministry a concept that might not be so obvious to his audience. Would the Israelites have thought of these nations as, like themselves, vassals of Yahweh? Ultimately Amos does put Israel on a par with the other nations, but only at the close of his sermons (9:7). For now it was enough for him to show how God would overthrow the nations who had committed transgressions against divine standards.

---

[19] Wolff, *Joel and Amos*, p. 128 n. b.

[20] Rolf P. Knierem, "'I Will Not Cause It to Return' in Amos 1 and 2," in *Canon and Authority: Essays in Old Testament Religion and Theology*, ed. George W. Coats and Burke O. Long (Philadelphia: Fortress, 1977), pp. 163-75.

[21] John H. Hayes, *Amos, The Eighth-Century Prophet: His Times and His Preaching* (Nashville: Abingdon, 1988), pp. 70-71.

[22] Barre, "The meaning of *lʾ ʿšybnw* in Amos 1:3-2:6," pp. 611-31.

The Targum has "threshing sledges of iron" בַּחֲרֻצוֹת הַבַּרְזֶל (bahăruṣôt
habbarzel), and the Peshitta reads "spikes of iron" or "ploughshares of iron."[23]
Isaiah 41:15 uses a more explicit term for "threshing sledge" (מוֹרַג, môrāg), which
is "sharp" (ḥārûṣ).

David used "sharp iron instruments" (ḥărîṣê habbarzel) against the
Ammonites (2 Sam. 12:31). In fact, a number of military techniques described here
were not unknown among the Israelites. When Amos mentioned practices like
these, the audience possibly felt vaguely uneasy, further increasing the tension.
Wolff describes the ancient technique of threshing grain:

> Grain was threshed by drawing over it a heavy sledge, the boards of
> which were curved upward at the front and the underside of which
> was studded with prongs; the use of iron knives, rather than
> flintstones, for these prongs in the iron age significantly increased the
> efficiency of the sledge.[24]

Gilead belonged to the northern kingdom at this time, and Amos's audience
must have remembered this atrocity of the threshing sledges with shocked horror.
Surely it would be unnecessarily cruel to use such implements against an innocent
population.

1:4 Judgment by fire refers to military action, the burning of cities being a
part of the practice of war at the time (cf. 2 Kings 8:12; 25:9).[25]

The various kings of Aram are notoriously difficult to sort out, though both
biblical and extra-biblical evidence is available.[26] The "house of Hazael" refers to a
dynasty, so in all likelihood the king that Elisha anointed is meant (1 Kings 19:15-
17; 2 Kings 8:7-15). Hazael himself usurped a certain Ben-hadad (2 Kings 8:14-
15), and another Ben-hadad who was the son of Hazael is also known (2 Kings
13:3). Evidently Ben-hadad was a throne name meaning "the son of (the god)
Hadad." The reference in Amos, then, may indicate simply the dynasty of Hazael
and any king of Aram in that dynasty. This interpretation would be supported
further by the occurrence of each name in parallel lines, Ben-hadad balancing
Hazael in the same way that "I will cast fire" balances "and it will devour."

1:5 The people would feel secure if their city gates had a strong bar of bronze
or iron to hold it in place against an enemy. Even this, says Amos in v. 5, the Lord
will snap in two, allowing the enemy to stream into the city.

יוֹשֵׁב (yôšēb) would normally be translated "inhabitant," as in NASB.
However, the term may also imply a king who "sits" or is "enthroned," as in Ps.
22:3 (MT 22:4): "O Thou who art *enthroned* upon the praises of Israel." The
principle of poetic parallelis m argues for the latter interpretation, especially in light

---

[23] במורגי ברזלא (bĕmôrĕgê barzĕlā', Tg. Neb.) and bsk' dprzl' (Peshitta), respectively.
[24] Wolff, Joel and Amos, p. 154.
[25] Cf. ibid., pp. 154-55.
[26] See Merrill F. Unger, Israel and the Aramaeans of Damascus (Grand Rapids: Baker,
1980); Emile Puech, "L'ivoire inscrit d'Arslan-Tash et les rois de Damas," RB 88 (1981):
544-62.

of the similar line in the Gaza oracle.[27] Notice NIV, "I will destroy the king who is in the Valley of Aven." Admittedly, the more traditional rendering is possible if we think of an intensification in the second half of the line: not only the population but especially the king will be destroyed.

Two possible interpretations can be given to the place names. If the references to Aven Valley and to Beth-Eden are taken as literal geographic names, then kings other than the ruler of Damascus must be implied by the phrases "who sits (on the throne)" and "who holds the scepter." It would seem strange to describe one king as having three separate capitals. On the other hand, if the references further describe the dynasty reigning in Damascus, it would seem better to take the additional geographical references as symbolic, reading "valley of wickedness" and "house of pleasure," respectively. The Vulg., for example, read the names as "Plain of idols" (*Campo idoli*) and "House of pleasure" (*Domo voluptatis*).

If one compares the oracle of Damascus with that of Gaza (1:6-8), an important clue emerges. There, after describing the destruction of Gaza, Amos continues by predicting the fall of rulers in Ashdod and Ashkelon, using terms nearly identical with those for "valley of Aven" and Beth-Eden. A further parallel lies in the expression "remnant of the Philistines" at the end of the unit on Gaza, just as "people of Aram" occurs at the end of the section about Damascus. Evidently the controlling principles are Aram (Syria) for the first prophecy and Philistia for the second. Damascus and Gaza are simply the major cities that can be subsumed under each of these more general concepts. Therefore, "valley of Aven" and Beth-Eden should also be localities with separate rulers.

LXX reads "the plain of On" instead of Aven, lending some support to the suggestion to identify it with Baalbek, a city north of Damascus. The city of On mentioned in Genesis (41:45, 50; 46:20) is most likely Heliopolis in Egypt, and in the Seleucid period Baalbek also received the name Heliopolis. Baalbek means "Baal of the Bekaa," or "Baal of the valley" (cf. בִּקְעָה, *biqʿâ*, "valley"). It was a center of sun worship.[28]

Hayes proposes the rather novel idea that the ruler of Aven Valley is Pekah, the son of Remaliah and next-to-last king of Israel.[29] While Pekah was closely allied with the king of Damascus and most likely had either a rival rule or some degree of military control of the Gilead area from the time of Zechariah and Menahem,[30] Hayes's suggestion has some important improbabilities. First, the Beth-Aven discussed by Hayes would be located on the west of the Jordan, not in Gilead. Second, if the general topic of the first oracle is the Arameans, one would not expect it to include Pekah the Israelite, even if he was closely allied with Damascus. Third, the whole hypothesis stands or falls with Hayes's chronology,

[27] Cf. D. T. Tsumura, "'Inserted Bicolon,' The AXYB Pattern, In Amos I 5 and Psalm IX 7," *VT* 38 (1988): 234-35.

[28] Mays, *Amos*, pp. 30-31; A. Haldar, "Baalbek," *IDB* 1:330; T. O. Lambdin, "Heliopolis," *IDB* 2:579.

[29] Hayes, *Amos*, pp. 76-77.

[30] See Thiele, *Mysterious Numbers*, pp. 61, 63, 129-30; M. S. Seale, "Pekah," *ISBE*, rev. ed., 3:735.

which has Pekah's reign begin during Jeroboam II's final year (see also The Date of the Book of Amos in the Introduction).

Beth-Eden has been identified with an Aramean state (Bit-adini) east of the Euphrates in the area known in the Bible as Aram-naharaim (often translated "Mesopotamia" but northwest of Assyria and Babylonia; Gen. 24:10; Deut. 23:5 [MT 23:4]; Judg. 3:8; title of Ps. 60 [MT 60:2]).[31] M. C. Astour objects to this identification because Bit-adini had ceased to be an independent state more than a hundred years before Amos's prophecy.[32] However, the land of Aram-naharaim was ruled at the time of Amos by an Assyrian governor named Shamshi-ilu. The general weakness of the Assyrian kings helped him to exert great influence throughout his realm. Abraham Malamat describes his power:

> It is logical to assume that the prophet [Amos] would refer to an aggressive personality of Shamshi-ilu's stature. The mighty Assyrian autocrat, who attained a high degree of autonomy, was undoubtedly famous throughout the Near East, and his name must have been familiar, even in Palestine. The title, "He who holds the scepter," is a fitting appellation for him, and he is indeed worthy to appear with Hazael and Ben-Hadad, kings of Damascus.[33]

Perhaps Amos brings out the completeness of God's judgment when he deals with entire regions (Aram, Philistia, Phoenicia, Edom, Ammon, Moab, Judah and Israel). None of the Arameans will escape; nor can Israel hope to be saved.

The Aramean peoples came out of Kir, according to Amos 9:7. Also 2 Kings 16:9 identifies Kir as the place to which the Assyrian king Tiglath-pileser III (744-727 B.C.) later exiled the people of Damascus. Isaiah used the term alongside Elam (22:6), indicating that Kir was probably a region rather than a city. The location has not been identified conclusively,[34] but the meaning is clear. The Arameans would be completely destroyed through deportation to the land from which they came.

Additional Notes

1:3 אֲשִׁיבֶנּוּ: LXX uses three different pronouns to translate the suffix on the constant Hebrew form: αὐτόν (1:3, 13; 2:1, 4, 6); αὐτούς (1:6, 11); and αὐτήν (1:9).

אֵת־הַגִּלְעָד: LXX has "because they were sawing with iron saws the pregnant women of Gilead," a reading supported by a Hebrew fragment from Qumran (5QAm).[35] As Stuart points out, MT seems too short, leading to the suspicion that something is missing, and the particle אֵת is not common in poetry.[36] However, it would be easier to explain the Qumran reading as assimilation to 1:13.

---

[31] C. H. Gordon, "Beth-Eden," *IDB* 1:389.

[32] M. C. Astour, "Eden," in *IDBSup*, p. 251.

[33] Abraham Malamat, "Amos 1:5 in the Light of the Til Barsip Inscriptions, *BASOR* 129 (1953): 26; cf. Hayes, *Amos*, pp. 77-78.

[34] M. C. Astour, "Kir," in *IDBSup*, p. 524; cf. Gray, *I & II Kings*, p. 633.

[35] *DJD* 3, pl. 36.

[36] Stuart, *Hosea-Jonah*, p. 307 n. 3.d.

1:5 אָמַר יהוה: The concluding formula occurs only for the oracles about Damascus, Gaza (1:8), Ammon (1:15), and Moab (2:3). Wolff used this fact to support his contention that the oracles against Tyre, Edom, and Judah are secondary.[37] If the oracle with the concluding "says Yahweh" is labeled A and the variant types are labeled B, the pattern that results is A-A-B-B-A-A-B-C, where C stands for the Israel oracle because it is so drastically different from the others in length and detail.[38] Recently James Limburg argued that the total number of "says Yahweh" formulas in Amos is 14, contributing to a marked use of the number seven for patterning in Amos.[39] One might also note that the seven oracles against the nations have the further pattern of 4 + 3, similar to the numerical saying that introduces each pericope.

B. Gaza (1:6-8)

Translation

> Thus says Yahweh:
> "For three transgressions of Gaza,
> even for four I will not turn back (its punishment),
> because they deported an entire population
> to deliver it up to *Edom.
> [7]So I will cast fire on the wall of Gaza,
> and it will consume her citadels.
> [8]I will also cut off him who sits (on the throne) from Ashdod
> and him who holds the scepter from Ashkelon.
> Then I will turn my hand against Ekron,
> and the rest of the Philistines will perish,"
> says *the Lord Yahweh.

Exegesis and Exposition

When Amos turned from Damascus to Gaza, he again stirred up hostile feelings in his audience, this time of the long-standing enmity with the Philistines. Joshua and the invading Israelites encountered "the five lords of the Philistines," including "the Gazite, the Ashdodite, the Ashkelonite, the Gittite, [and] the Ekronite" (Josh. 13:3). Philistine territory consisted of the rich coastal plain extending between the base of the Shephelah (low hill country) to the Mediterranean Sea and lengthwise between the Brook of Egypt on the south and Ekron in the north.

Even though David and Solomon incorporated Philistia into the united kingdom, the Philistines often skirmished with Israel in later times and acted independently. Thus, we find Nadab, son of Jeroboam I (who founded the northern kingdom of Israel) warring against Gibbethon, a Philistine city. Here Baasha

---

[37] Wolff, *Joel and Amos*, pp. 139-40.

[38] Cf. Robert Gordis, "The Composition and Structure of Amos," *HTR* 33 (1940): 240 n. 10.

[39] James Limburg, "Sevenfold Structures in the Book of Amos," *JBL* 106 (1987): 217-22.

conspired against Nadab and became king of Israel (1 Kings 15:27). Under similar circumstances Omri became king when he left an Israelite siege against Gibbethon (1 Kings 16:15-18).

Later still the Philistines paid tribute to Jehoshaphat king of Judah (2 Chron. 17:11), but relations between the two countries were reversed under Jehoram when a coalition of Arabs and Philistines made a raid on Judah. According to the Chronicler, they carried away "all the possessions found in the king's house together with his sons and his wives, so that no son was left to him except Jehoahaz, the youngest of his sons" (2 Chron. 21:16-17, NASB). Another turnabout occurred around the time of Amos's prophecy when Judah's king, Uzziah, destroyed the walls of Gath and Ashdod (2 Chron. 26:6).

The Philistines were guilty of unnecessary cruelty when they captured entire towns and sold the populations into slavery. War and prisoners of war were a fact of life in Amos's time, even as now. Yet there seems to be a greedy motivation by which the people of Gaza conducted raids on the defenseless in order to increase the royal treasury. Thus, Amos anticipates the heartless actions of the powerful in Israel who were governed by the profit motive in their dealings with people.

1:6 Gaza, the southernmost of the five Philistine cities, is mentioned in the inscriptions of two Assyrian kings who ruled shortly after the period of Amos's prophecy. Tiglath-pileser III (744-727 B.C.) describes a campaign that included Judah, Edom, Muzri, and "Hanno of Gaza." In another inscription the Assyrian ruler claims to have conquered Gaza and imposed tribute upon it. Later Sargon II says he captured a certain Hanno, "the king of Gaza."[40]

In light of the biblical evidence, as well as the Assyrian inscriptions, it may be concluded that Gaza was the chief town of the Philistines in the days of Amos. This would account for its placement at the head of the word concerning the Philistines.

Gaza's transgression consisted not so much in the taking of prisoners of war as in the capture of an entire population followed by its deportation. The purpose was "to deliver it to Edom." The verb for "deliver" (לְהַסְגִּיר, *lĕhasgîr*; a hiphil pattern) can relate to turning over an escaped slave to his master (cf. Deut. 23:15 [MT 23:16]; 1 Sam. 30:15) or to turning over a fugitive to his pursuers (Josh. 20:5). When God performs the action, he delivers people to their enemies or to natural calamities (Deut. 32:30; Ps. 78:48; Amos 6:8). The element of "turning over" to the control of another is the common semantic thread, and Amos means the selling of captured people into slavery. That would help explain why the Philistines would be turning the people over to the Edomites as well as why the action seemed so reprehensible. It is not possible to pinpoint the precise event (cf. 2 Chron. 21:16; 28:18).

1:8 In v. 8 the poetic balance between "him who sits (on the throne)" and "him who holds the scepter" argues for the interpretation of Hebrew *yôšēb* as "sitter (upon the throne)" rather than as "inhabitant" (see above on v. 5). Ashdod and Ashkelon are coastal cities located north of Gaza.

---

[40] *ANET*, 3d ed., pp. 282, 283, 286-87.

Even though Gaza was the principal city, the other Philistine towns maintained a certain amount of sovereignty. Both Tiglath-pileser III and Sargon II make reference to a ruler of Ashkelon, and Sargon refers additionally to the king of Ashdod and to the rulers of *Pi-liš-te*. His inscription also groups Gath together with Ashdod. Perhaps Amos failed to mention Gath because it lacked the same independent status as the other cities, though none of the biblical prophecies against the Philistines includes all five of their cities. Also, Gath had earlier been captured by Hazael of Aram (2 Kings 12:17 [MT 12:18]), and Uzziah of Judah "broke down the wall of Gath" during a campaign against the Philistines (2 Chron. 26:6). Sargon claims that he conquered Ashdod and its territories and settled people there from other parts of his empire. Later, Ashdod played a role in the rebellion against Sennacherib led by Hezekiah of Judah.[41]

Ekron, the northernmost of the Philistine cities, also participated in the later Hezekiah rebellion. Sennacherib, the king of Assyria, stated: "I assaulted Ekron and killed the officials and patricians who had committed the crime [of non-payment of tribute] and hung their bodies on poles surrounding the city. The (common) citizens who were guilty of minor crimes, I considered prisoners of war."[42]

"Turn the hand against" (עַל יָד הֵשִׁיב, *hēšîb yād ʿal*) is an idiom for coming against with power; hence, NASB: "I will even unleash My power upon Ekron."

Additional Notes

1:6 לֶאֱדוֹם: M. Haran thinks Edom in vv. 6 and 9 needs to be changed to Aram in order to make sense of the passage.[43] This could have arisen through scribal confusion of *daleth* and *resh*, though there is no independent textual witness for it. However, it does not seem necessary to assume with Haran that "deliver up" means that the Philistines and Phoenicians returned escaped prisoners to a nation that had defeated Israel in battle. Anyone who purchases slaves will naturally be in a superior position to the ones being sold, so Edomites could be serving as middlemen. Edom was evidently under Judean control at this time (2 Kings 14:22), but that need not have stopped them from purchasing and reselling Israelite slaves.

1:8 אֲדֹנָי יהוה: LXX has simply κύριος, apparently reflecting omission of אֲדֹנָי, as at 4:2; 7:1, 4 [*bis*], 6; 8:1, 3, 11). At each place some of the LXX witnesses support MT (Lucianic for 4:6). Targum consistently agrees with MT, while Peshitta has a variant only at 7:6 and 8:11. In the former passage, אָמַר אֲדֹנָי יהוה is omitted altogether, while the latter seems to support LXX.

A survey of the formula אָמַר אֲדֹנָי יהוה in the prophets made on the basis of the Even-Shoshan concordance demonstrates that LXX frequently has only κύριος in these situations. In fact, in Isaiah (five instances, cf. 28:16) and Ezekiel that equivalent is practically the only one given. Ezekiel also has κύριος κύριος thirty

---

[41] *ANET*, 3d ed., pp. 282, 283, 286-88; M. Avi-Yonah and Y. Eph'al, "Ashkelon," in *Encyclopedia of Archaeological Excavations in the Holy Land* (Englewood Cliffs, N. J.: Prentice-Hall, 1975), 1:122; cf. also Paul, "The Oracles against the Nations," pp. 189-91.

[42] *ANET*, 3d ed., p. 288.

[43] Haran, "Historical Background of Amos 1:2-2:6," pp. 203-7.

times (e.g., Ezek 12:10), mostly in chapters 26-37, over against κύριος alone some 76 times. Also, κύριος (ὁ) θεός occurs exclusively in Ezek. 43-47. Unless a systematic revision of MT in Isaiah and Ezekiel be posited,[44] one can only assume that κύριος alone can represent either יהוה or יהוה אֲדֹנָי.

C. Tyre (1:9-10)

Translation

Thus says Yahweh:
"For three transgressions of Tyre,
even for four I will not turn back (its punishment),
because they delivered up an entire population to *Edom,
and did not remember an agreement between brothers.
[10]So I will cast fire on the wall of Tyre,
and it will consume her citadels."

Exegesis and Exposition

The city of Tyre controlled Sidon and surrounding areas in the period of Amos.[45] He probably has the whole Phoenician realm in mind, just as he spoke of the Arameans under the heading of Damascus and the Philistines under Gaza.

Tyre's sin was much like Gaza's, but the element of treachery against an ally adds to its repugnance. Here again Amos prepares his audience for their own guilt. Israelites were oppressing their fellow Israelites, surely no less reprehensible than a nation betraying its own friends for the sake of financial gain.

1:9 The participation of Phoenicia, well known for her mercantile interests, increases the likelihood that the reference is to selling slaves captured through war. Tyre and Philistia sometimes occur together in biblical references (Ps. 83:7 [MT 83:8]; Jer. 47:4; Ezek. 27:13), and Joel 3:4-8 (MT 4:4-8) pictures them cooperating in the sale of Judeans into slavery.[46] Edom probably served as an intermediary with distant southern nations that were interested in slaves.

Several suggestions have been made about בְּרִית אַחִים (běrît 'aḥîm), the "covenant between brothers" (lit. "a covenant of brothers"). Wolff proposes a reference to Deut. 23:7a (MT 23:8a) where Israel is told, "You shall not detest an Edomite, for he is your brother."[47] It would seem strange, however, for Amos to refer to a relationship between Israel and Edom when the focus is on Tyre.

King Solomon and Hiram of Tyre made an agreement for the sale of cedars and other materials for the Temple (1 Kings 5:1-12 [MT 5:15-26]; 9:11-14), and

---

[44] Walther Eichrodt does propose this for Ezekiel in Ezekiel; A Commentary (OTL; Philadelphia: Westminster, 1970), p. 12.

[45] H. Jacob Katzenstein, The History of Tyre from the Beginning of the Second Millennium B.C.E. until the Fall of the Neo-Babylonian Empire in 538 B.C.E. (Jerusalem: Schocken Institute for Jewish Research of the Jewish Theological Seminary of America, 1973), p. 132.

[46] See M. Haran, "Observations On the Historical Background of Amos 1:2-2:6," IEJ 18 (1968): 201-2.

[47] Wolff, Joel and Amos, pp. 159-60.

later Ahab's marriage to Jezebel cemented an alliance between Phoenicia and the northern kingdom of Israel. Feinberg notes that "no king of Israel or Judah ever made war upon Phoenicia."[48] Though the precise details are uncertain, the passage speaks out against nations that break treaties with other nations, especially when a lack of mercy or compassion is involved.

Additional Notes

1:9 לֶאֱדוֹם: See Additional Notes to 1:6 above.

D. *Edom (1:11-12)

Translation

Thus says Yahweh:
"For three transgressions of Edom,
even for four I will not turn back (its punishment),
because he pursued his brother with the sword
and destroyed his allies.
His anger also tore continually,
and his fury stormed perpetually.
[12]So I will cast fire on Teman,
and it will consume the citadels of Bozrah.''

Exegesis and Exposition

Scripture informs us that Esau was called Edom, a name meaning "red," when he sold his birthright to Jacob for the "red stuff" that Jacob had prepared (Gen. 25:30). Therefore, the people of Edom traced their ancestry back to the brother of Jacob. Bitter hostility runs through the entire history of relations between Israel and Edom, starting with the struggles between the two brothers for the rights of the firstborn.

Amos continues here the theme of treachery against allies. The background to the passage is obscure, but the general sense is that the Edomites murderously exterminated those they should have treated as friends.

1:11 Modern versions generally treat וְשִׁחֵת רַחֲמָיו (wĕšiḥēt raḥămāyw) something like "stifled his compassion" (NASB). "Stifle" departs widely from the normal usage of Hebrew šiḥēt, but since raḥămîm has the common meaning "compassion" the adjustment appears necessary. A more recent suggestion takes the latter term as "allies," based on usage in ancient Near Eastern treaties and a root meaning of "love" or "womb." Michael Barré has demonstrated that " 'pursue … destroy' is not a random series of terms but part of a well-established sequence that derives largely from the language of combat."[49] Observe also how a better poetic

---

[48] Feinberg, *The Minor Prophets*, p. 89.
[49] Michael Barré, "Amos 1:11 Reconsidered," *CBQ* 47 (1985): 420-27. He also discusses the important article by Michael Fishbane: "The Treaty Background of Amos 1 11 and Related Matters," *JBL* 89 (1970): 313-18.

balance is obtained: (a) pursued his brother // destroyed his allies; (b) his anger tore // his fury stormed.

"Allies" seems too mild as a parallel to "brother," but possibly *raḥămāyw* might indicate something like "his mother's sons," with an abstract noun meaning "brotherly feeling" standing for a concrete noun.[50] This would help to explain why a plural noun parallels a singular. That is, the plural indicates the abstract meaning. The Lord's admonition to His people not to "abhor an Edomite, for he is your brother" (Deut. 23:7) strengthens the sense of outrage against Edom, given that the language of the verse refers to the literal kinship relation.

Barré also translates "treaty-partner" rather than "brother."[51] In that case it is not necessary to think that either Judah or Israel is actually meant. Yet even if Amos does make reference to the well-known relationship between Jacob and Esau, he is still vague as to whether the specific application should be to Israel or to Judah as Edom's ally. This vagueness should be kept in mind when trying to find an underlying historical background.

The Edomites showed no mercy (וַיִּטְרֹף לָעַד אַפּוֹ, *wayyiṭrōp lā'ad 'appô*, "and his anger tore continually") with those who deserved their friendship rather than their wrath. Whether treachery or the suppression of family responsibilities is meant, Edom is condemned for an act contrary to normal human feelings.

The grammar of the passage calls for "his fury" (עֶבְרָתוֹ, *'ebrātô*; a feminine noun in Hebrew) to serve as the subject of שְׁמָרָה (*šĕmārâ*), something that also maintains the strict parallelism of the verse. The only problem with this interpretation is that *šāmar* normally means "keep" and requires an object. Wolff proposes, "his wrath is ever alert,"[52] but this would be more naturally expressed with the niphal pattern of the verb. However, an Akkadian cognate provides the necessary background for the rare sense of "storm" (cf. Jer. 3:5).[53] NIV seems to have the right idea: "and his fury flamed unchecked." Another possibility is to repoint the verb to שְׁמָרָהּ (*šĕmārāh*, "he kept it"), with "his wrath" as anticipatory emphasis: "As for his fury, he kept it perpetually."

1:12 Teman and Bozrah can refer to Edom itself (Isa. 34:6; Jer. 49:20; Ezek. 25:13). Teman is possibly located at modern Tuwilan, about 50 miles due south of the southern tip of the Dead Sea, although there is also evidence for taking it as a general region in Edom. Bozrah has been more clearly identified with Buseirah, a little over 10 miles south of the Zered Brook, which flows westward into the Dead Sea. Excavations there have revealed extensive fortifications and a major period of occupation from the eighth century B.C.[54]

---

[50] See Mitchell Dahood, *Psalms III* (AB 17A; Garden City, N.Y.: Doubleday, 1970), pp. 411-12, for abstract nouns in a concrete sense in the Psalms.

[51] Cf. the observations of Nelson Glueck, *Ḥesed in the Bible*, trans. Alfred Gottschalk, ed. Elias L. Epstein (n.p.: KTAV, 1975), p. 46: "Allies had the same rights and obligations as those who were blood relations. Allies, for all practical purposes, were אַחִים, 'brothers.'"

[52] Wolff, *Joel and Amos*, pp. 130-31 n. v.

[53] Moshe Held, "Studies in Biblical Homonyms in the Light of Akkadian," *JANESCU* 3 (1970/71): 47-55.

[54] J. B. Hennessy, "Bozrah (in Edom)," in *IDBSup*, p. 119; C.-M. Bennett, "Edom," in *IDBSup*, p. 252.

Additional Notes

Many have felt that the Edom segment must have been added to the book of Amos at a much later period, because it is thought to refer to Edom's betrayal of Judah during the Babylonian capture of Jerusalem (see comments on Obad. 10-14). But surely many opportunities could have arisen for the kind of event described by Amos.[55] Also, Ps. 83 includes the Edomites among those who are enemies of God, because "they make shrewd plans against Your people" (v. 3 [MT v. 4]). Later the psalmist states, "Assyria also has joined with them" (v. 8 [MT v. 9]). Assyria was Israel's enemy only in pre-exilic times, and the passage probably does not date to any later than the reign of Hezekiah of Judah (ca. 729-686 B.C.).[56]

E. The Sons Of Ammon (1:13-15)

Translation

Thus says Yahweh:
"For three transgressions of the sons of Ammon,
even for four I will not turn back (its punishment),
because they ripped open the pregnant women of Gilead
in order to enlarge their territory.
[14]So I will *kindle a fire on the wall of Rabbah,
and it will consume her citadels
amid tumultuous shouts in a time of battle,
amid a raging wind on a stormy day.
[15]Then *their king will go into exile,
*he and his royal officials together,"
says Yahweh. (1:13-15)

Exegesis and Exposition

Israel had a distant genetic relationship with the Ammonites as well as with the Edomites. The book of Genesis traces the ancestry of the Ammonites to one of Lot's two sons by incest with his daughters (19:38). Yet relations were frequently hostile between the two nations (1 Sam. 14:47; 2 Sam. 8:12; 11:1; 12:26, 30). In addition, Ammonite religion had been a temptation for Israel. Solomon built a high place for Molech (1 Kings 11:7; 2 Kings 23:13), and the Israelites were tempted to offer their children to this god from the time of Moses (Lev. 18:21) until the era of Jeremiah and of Josiah's reforms (2 Kings 23:10; Jer 32:35).

1:13 The Ammonites transgressed the boundaries of human feeling when they went to the extent of ripping out the helpless babies still in the wombs of the Gileadite women. This is the point Amos desires to make – those with power have a responsibility to protect the rights of the helpless, not to lash out against them by

---

[55] Wolff argues for its lateness (*Joel and Amos*, p. 160), but Shalom Paul presents good arguments for its genuineness ("The Oracles against the Nations," p. 193).

[56] For the chronological problems surrounding Hezekiah's reign see Archer, "Chronology of the Old Testament," in *EBC*, 1:369-71; Gray, *I & II Kings*, pp. 74-75.

murder and exploitation. Moreover, the Ammonites did this not because of revenge for a previous act of war but out of a greedy desire to expand their own territory.

The designation "sons of Ammon" is normally used in the OT for the Ammonites (sometimes merely עַמּוֹנִי, 'ammônî, "Ammonite[s]," Deut. 2:20; 23:3), a phrase also found in two Ammonite inscriptions that date to about 600 B.C.[57] The Assyrian king Shalmaneser III (858-824 B.C.) mentions a contingent of soldiers of "Ba'sa, son of Ruhubi, from Ammon" as part of the twelve kings who met him in battle at Qarqar in Aram on the Orontes River. Ahab of Israel also formed part of this anti-Assyrian coalition.[58]

The OT attests several instances of the wartime atrocity of ripping unborn children out of pregnant women (2 Kings 8:12; 15:16; Hos 13:16), as well as the practice of dashing children to pieces (2 Kings 8:12; Ps 137:9; Isa 13:16; Hos 10:14; 13:16; Nah 3:10). Wolff cites an Assyrian text that praises Tiglath-pileser I (ca. 1100 B.C.) because "he shredded to pieces the bellies of the pregnant" and an excerpt from Homer's *Iliad*, which urges that not even "the man-child whom his mother bears in her womb" be allowed to escape the battle.[59] Amos describes a practice that was common among the peoples of the ancient Near East, but it would be hard to choose a more poignant example of harsh action against the weak and powerless.

G. M. Landes suggests that the Ammonites took advantage of the strife between Israel and Aram to extend their territory.[60] Moses recognized the sovereignty of God in establishing the boundaries of nations (Deut. 32:8), and Joshua devoted much energy to the limits of the various tribes (Josh. 13-22). Borders could be changed or enlarged by decree of the Lord (Ex. 34:24; Josh. 22:25), but people are not permitted of their own will to tamper with them (Job 24:1; Prov. 22:28; 23:10).

1:14a The stereotyped expression אֵשׁ וְשִׁלַּחְתִּי (wĕšillaḥtî 'ēš, "I will cast fire"), which occurs in all the other prophecies against the nations in Amos, becomes "I will kindle [וְהִצַּתִּי, wĕhiṣṣattî] a fire" (v. 14) only in the oracle against Ammon. The reason for the variation is unclear (but see also Additional Notes). Possibly it indicates a more direct involvement by the Lord in the punishment.

Rabbah, modern-day Amman, was the capital of Ammonite territory. In the Greek period it was known as Philadelphia, one of the cities of the Decapolis. Archaeological investigation of the ancient site has shown evidence of destruction by fire in the eighth century B.C., probably as a result of an Assyrian invasion.[61]

1:14b Battles were often accompanied by shouts, as in v. 14, either by the attackers (Josh. 6:5, 20) or by the defenders of a city (Jer. 20:16). Several passages stressing the Lord's direct participation in battle use the terms for "storm" (סַעַר, sa'ar) and "tempest" (סוּפָה, sûpâ) together. For example, the author of Ps. 83 says, "So pursue them with your storm,/ and terrify them with your tempest" (v. 15 [MT

---

[57] S. H. Horn, "Ammon, Ammonites," in *IDBSup*, p. 20.

[58] *ANET*, 3d ed., p. 279.

[59] Wolff, *Joel and Amos*, p. 161.

[60] G. M. Landes, "Ammon," *IDB* 1:111.

[61] G. M. Landes, "Rabbah," in *IDBSup*, p. 724.

v. 16]; cf. also Isa. 29:6; Nah. 1:3). The directness of the Lord's judgment on Ammon seems prominent here, though it is not impossible that the terminology is figurative for the "storm of battle."[62]

1:15 A change of the vowels on "their king" (מַלְכָּם, *malkām*) could yield the reading "Milcom," the god of the Ammonites. Some of the ancient versions have this reading (see Additional Notes), but it should be rejected because of the phrase, "he and his royal officials [וְשָׂרָיו, *wĕśārāyw*]." Also, none of the other sections describes an action of the Lord against foreign gods.[63] The Ammonite rulers, like the Arameans, will go into exile.

Additional Notes

1:14a וְהִצַּתִּי: Wolff emends the text on the basis of a scribal assimilation to the phrase in Jer. 49:2, 27.[64] Yet the ancient versions (LXX, Targum, Peshitta) all use a different word in v. 14 than in the other passages. Stanislav Segert suggests that synonymous variations of this type may have been used in ancient times as a form of "error checking." The checker could quickly tell whether a scribe was being careless in a repetitious passage of this sort.[65] Perhaps Segert's explanation could also be applied to the high frequency in many OT passages of free grammatical or orthographic variants in close proximity (cf. לְמִינוֹ and לְמִינֵהוּ in Gen. 1:11-12). Or the variants in such cases could be due to a desire to preserve known textual variants.

1:15 מַלְכָּם: The Lucianic recension has μελχομ (*melchom*), a reading followed by the Syrohexapla, Aquila, Symmachus, Theodotian, Peshitta (*mlkwm*), and Vulg. (*Melchom*).[66] George Charles Heider explains thinks that this reading is probably best explained by scribal assimilation to Jer. 49:1, 3 [LXX 30:17, 19], where the original reading was most likely Milcom. Heider compares the Jeremiah passage with Jer. 48:7 where it is clear that it is the god Chemosh who goes into exile. The context of Amos, on the other hand, speaks of people, not gods, going into exile.[67] That the main text of LXX does not have the variant is significant in that for Amos this translation is characterized by an unusually large number of transliterations and misreadings. For chap. 1, cf. also νακκαριυ for נֹקְדִים (v. 1),

[62] Cf. Mays, *Amos*, pp. 37-38; Wolff, *Joel and Amos*, p. 161.

[63] Cf. Wolff, *Joel and Amos*, pp. 161-62.

[64] Ibid., p. 161.

[65] Stanislav Segert, "A Controlling Device for Copying Stereotype Passages? (Amos I 3-II 8, VI 1-6)," *VT* 34 (1984): 481-82.

[66] Variants in Greek traditions as listed in Joseph Ziegler's edition, *Septuaginta*, 2d ed. (Göttingen: Vandenhoeck & Ruprecht, 1967), vol. 13, "Duodecim prophetae." The Peshitta text is from the edition issued by The Peshitta Institute: *Vetus Testamentum Syriace* (Leiden: E. J. Brill, 1980), pt. 3, fasc. 4, "Dodekapropheton--Daniel--Bel--Draco." For Vulg. see *Biblia Sacra Iuxta Vulgatam Versionem*, ed. Bonifatio Fischer, et al., 2 vols. (Stuttgart: Württembergische Bibelanstalt, 1969).

[67] George Charles Heider III, *The Cult of Molek: A New Examination of the Biblical and Extra-Biblical Evidence*, diss. for Yale Univ. (Ann Arbor: University Microfilms, 1984), pp. 302-4; Charles L. Feinberg, "Jeremiah," in *EBC*, 6:665. For a different view, see C. F. Keil, *Jeremiah, Lamentations* (COTTV 8; Grand Rapids: Eerdmans, 1973), 8:237-38.

Αδερ for הֲדַד (v. 4), χαρραν for עֵדֶן (v. 5), and Σαλθμθν for שָׁלְמָה (vv. 6, 9).
Evidently the translator had a difficult time reading the *Vorlage*.

הִוא; LXX has "their priests" in this position. Could this be influenced by the variant "Milcom" in the previous line?

F. Moab (2:1-3)

Translation

Thus says Yahweh:
"For three transgressions of Moab,
even for four I will not turn back (its punishment),
*because he burned the bones
of the king of Edom to lime.
²So I will cast fire on Moab,
and it will consume the citadels of Kerioth.
And Moab will perish amid tumult,
with war cries and the sound of a trumpet.
³I will also cut off the ruler from *her midst,
and all *her royal officials I will slay with him,"
says Yahweh.

Exegesis and Exposition

In the case of Moab, Amos condemns a sin that clearly was against Edom, not Israel. This emphasizes that the Lord is sovereign over all the nations, not restricting His activities to Israel and Judah alone. For Amos it is not so important whether Israel, Judah, or some other nation was wronged as that the offenders had acted against the weakened or helpless. After the king of Edom was dead, he was unable to do anything to prevent the desecration of his body. Common morality should dictate that more respect be shown for a dead body. But beyond the desecration itself was the motive for it. The Moabites desired to use the ashes in their own building materials.

Like Ammon, Moab was conceived through the incestuous union of Lot with his daughters (Gen. 19:30-38). The Israelites and the Moabites mostly treated each other as bitter enemies. Their first encounter recorded in the Bible finds Balak, king of Moab, hiring Balaam son of Beor to curse Israel (Num. 22-24). When Balak's plan failed, the Moabite women seduced the Israelite men into sexual immorality and idolatry (Num. 25). Later the Israelites served Eglon, king of Moab, for eighteen years until deliverance came through Ehud (Judg. 3:12-30).

Saul fought with Moab (1 Sam. 14:47) and David forced the Moabites to become his servants (2 Sam. 8:2). In a continuation of the theme of religious seduction, King Solomon built a high place for Chemosh, the god of Moab, which was later destroyed by Josiah (2 Kings 23:13). Moab rebelled against Israelite rule after the death of Ahab (2 Kings 1:1; 3), and at the time of Elisha's death the Moabites were conducting regular spring raids into Israel (2 Kings 13:20).

Moab is important to biblical history for another reason. We are fortunate to have an account by the Moabite king, Mesha, of his rebellion against Israel.[68] This inscription gives the additional information that Omri of Israel subdued Moab, a condition that lasted forty years.

Jehoshaphat of Judah joined with the king of Edom and Jehoram of Israel against Mesha (2 Kings 3). They devastated Moab in this military action, though Mesha was able to spare himself from complete defeat by sacrificing his own son on the wall of Kir-hareseth. Mesha's boast in his inscription was obviously premature: "I have triumphed ... while Israel hath perished for ever!"

2:1 The nature of Moab's offense in v. 1 is difficult to determine, both because the language is obscure and because it is otherwise unknown in history. The Targum interprets in this way: "because he burned the bones of the king of Edom and used them [וסדינון, wĕsādînûn] in the plaster on his house." This probably gives a good clue. The body was burned to gain lime for building materials. Undoubtedly a spirit of revenge and an act of desecration of a dead body lie behind the action, but for the ashes to be put to a useful purpose makes it even more culpable.

The enjambment of עַצְמוֹת מֶלֶךְ־אֱדוֹם (ʿaṣmôt melek-ʾĕdôm, "the bones of the king of Edom") between two poetic half-lines is unusual but necessary for the proper balance. The other oracles all have a two-part line in this position.

2:2 In the Moabite inscription, Kerioth is singled out as the place where Mesha displayed a cult object before the god Chemosh (lines 12-13). Comparison with the other oracles against the nations in Amos 1 and 2 shows that the city must have been important to the Moabites, perhaps either as a capital or as a center of worship.

The description in this verse of Moab's downfall amid the noise and tumult of battle ties it closely with the depiction of Ammon's destruction (1:14).

2:3 The participle in v. 3 normally translated "judge" (שׁוֹפֵט, šôpēṭ) can be used in the sense of "rule" (cf. 2 Kings 15:5; Dan. 9:12). Moab had a monarchy during the time of Amos and for at least another century. It is likely, therefore, that Amos is here using another synonym for "king" or "ruler" rather than the more specific "judge," as given in NASB (also LXX and Targum). Note Amos's variety of expressions for political leaders: "house of" (i.e., dynasty, 1:4); "one who sits (on a throne)" (1:5, 8); "scepter-bearer" (1:5, 8); "king" (1:15); "princes" (1:15); and "ruler" (2:3).

The historical situation that fulfills the prophecy is difficult to pinpoint. The Assyrians forced Moab into submission under Tiglath-pileser III, Sennacherib, Esarhaddon, and Ashurbanipal,[69] but the Assyrian monarchs do not mention that they killed the rulers of Moab. Martin Noth infers from the "Wadi Brisa" inscription of Nebuchadnezzar that the Babylonian king "made war on and subjugated the Ammonites and Moabites" while on a campaign to Lebanon,[70] but the information in the inscription is quite sketchy. According to E. D. Grohman,

---

[68] See *ANET*, 3d ed., pp. 320-21.

[69] *ANET*, 3d ed., pp. 282, 287, 291, 298, 301.

[70] Martin Noth, *The History of Israel*, 2d ed. (New York: Harper & Row, 1960), p. 293.

"archaeological exploration has shown that Moab was largely depopulated from *ca.* the beginning of the sixth century [B.C.], and in many sites from *ca.* the eighth century [B.C.]." Several centuries later the Nabateans settled in Moab and Edom.[71] The fulfillment of Amos's prophecy could be seen either in the Arab raid under Ashurbanipal or in events following the fall of Jerusalem in 586 B.C.

Additional Notes

2:1 עַל־שָׂרְפוֹ עַצְמוֹת מֶלֶךְ־אֱדוֹם לַשִּׂיד: Duane Christensen followed Albright in emending the text to *'al-śorpô molk 'ādām laśśēd* ("because he burned a human sacrifice to a demon").[72] Not many others have followed this suggestion. It requires the assumption that the root מלך can be used of a sacrifice (cf. HALOT and Lev. 20:5), in addition to revocalizing several words. Christensen dropped עַצְמוֹת for metrical reasons, though it would not be necessary in order to maintain Albright's reading. Does it seem likely, however, that a very clear meaning (offering a human sacrifice) would be changed into something obscure? MT should be retained as the more difficult reading.[73]

2:3 מִקִּרְבָּהּ and שָׂרֶיהָ: In the first two verses of the oracle Amos refers to Moab with a masculine pronoun, but feminine forms are used in the present verse. Some propose a textual change (cf. *BHS*), but it would be more likely for a difficult change of suffixes to be smoothed (as in the Lucianic Recension of LXX) than for an originally harmonious text to be made grammatically difficult. The masculine reference is possibly used to refer to the inhabitants, whereas the feminine refers to the country itself. Or the referent of the feminine pronouns may be to Kerioth rather than to Moab in general.[74]

G. *Judah (2:4-5)

Translation

> Thus says Yahweh:
> "For three transgressions of Judah,
> even for four I will not turn back (its punishment),
> because they rejected the law of Yahweh,
> and His statutes they have not kept.
> Their false gods also have led them astray,
> those after which their fathers walked.
> [5]So I will cast fire on Judah,
> and it will consume the citadels of Jerusalem."

---

[71] E. D. Grohman, "Moab," *IDB* 3: 418; cf. S. Cohen, "Nabateans," *IDB* 3:491-92.

[72] Duane Christensen, "The Prosodic Structure of Amos 1-2," *HTR* 67 (1974): 432, 434, esp. nn. 22, 23.

[73] Heider also rejects the proposal (*The Cult of Molek*, pp. 304-305).

[74] Cf. Wolff, *Joel and Amos*, pp. 132-33 n. e.

Exegesis and Exposition

The sins of the first six nations consist of instances of cruel and inhuman conduct. They have committed atrocities against the weak or powerless. However, when Amos turns to Judah, he stresses instead how the people broke their covenant with the Lord and followed idols. This news must have astonished the Israelites, but it was the climax in preparation for Amos's application of his preaching to the northern kingdom. Israel, like the foreign nations, is guilty of inhuman conduct against the poor and afflicted, but the behavior of its people proves that they have rejected God's covenant law. Thus, Israel is just as guilty of idolatry as Judah. Both nations may claim to serve Yahweh outwardly, but their actions betray the true condition of their heart.

2:4 At the time of Amos, Uzziah was the king of Judah. According to the author of Kings, "he did right in the sight of Yahweh, according to all that his father Amaziah had done" (2 Kings 15:3). However, he did not remove the "high places," and "when he became strong," as the Chronicler puts it, his pride led him to usurp the authority of the priests by entering the Temple to burn incense on the altar (2 Chron. 26:16).

Uzziah was followed by Jotham, another king who "did what was right in the sight of Yahweh," but who also did not remove the high places where the people sacrificed and burned incense (2 Kings 15:34-35). Ahaz, a king who "did not do what was right in the sight of Yahweh his God" (2 Kings 16:2), succeeded Jotham, and Ahaz in turn was followed by Hezekiah.

Hezekiah finally did remove the high places, break down the "sacred pillars," and break in pieces "the bronze serpent that Moses had made" and to which the Judeans had been burning incense (2 Kings 18:1-4). Hezekiah's reforms were short-lived, for his son, Manasseh, "did evil in the sight of Yahweh, according to the abominations of the nations whom Yahweh dispossessed before the sons of Israel" (2 Kings 21:2). Josiah later effected another reform that was even more far-reaching than Hezekiah's (2 Kings 22-23; 2 Chron. 34-35), but even Josiah's work did not have a deep and lasting effect on the people. Amos properly foresaw in v. 4 Judah's stubborn bent toward rebellion against the Lord.

The term חֻקִּים (ḥuqqîm, "statutes") occurs elsewhere in conjunction with תּוֹרָה (tôrâ, "law"; Deut. 17:19; Ps. 105:45). In the present context, tôrâ is the more general term, while ḥuqqîm refers to specific rules or regulations the people have not kept or obeyed.[75]

The term כִּזְבֵיהֶם (kizĕbêhem) is literally "their lies," but since the people are said to have "walked after" them, it is evident that idols are in view, even though kĕzābîm means "idols" only here. LXX has "their vain things which they made," the additional phrase making the concept of idolatry clear. The idea of "walking after" false gods is presented in Deuteronomy (8:19; 11:28; 28:14), Judges (2:12, 19), and 1 Kings (11:10; 13:2; 18:18; 21:26). Elijah complained to the king of Israel, "I have not troubled Israel, but you ... because you have left the

---

[75] Cf. Jack P. Lewis, *TWOT* 1:317, entry 728.

commandments of Yahweh, and you have *walked after* the Baals" (1 Kings 18:18). Hosea (2:13 [MT 2:15]) also applies the phrase figuratively to idolatry.

2:5 The Babylonian destruction of Jerusalem in 586 B.C. clearly fulfilled Amos's prediction in v. 5. After Josiah died the Judeans turned back to their idolatrous ways, making the Lord's judgment of Jerusalem just as inevitable as His judgment of Samaria and Bethel. For a discussion of the genuineness of the pericope about Judah, see Additional Notes.

Additional Notes

2:4 Of all the passages in Amos, the oracle against Judah (2:4-5) has been attacked the most in regard to its authenticity. Its language or terminology is said to be late, and its content supposedly differs from the other oracles in that it deals with "religious" sins as opposed to international crimes.[76]

The lateness of the language is said to reflect the work of a "Deuteronomistic" editor (or editors) who supposedly was responsible for a unified work that included Deuteronomy, Joshua, Judges, and both books of Kings.[77] Our own study has shown that while the language of Amos 2:4-5 contains some terms or concepts common to Deuteronomy and/or Joshua-Kings, it also has some distinctive language that is at least rare in that corpus (כָּזָב, "idol" and הִתְעָה, "lead astray"). Moreover, some other shared forms are also found in passages that are nearly unanimously dated prior to the "Deuteronomistic History" (מָאַס in 1 Sam. 15:23; חֻקָּיו in Ps. 18:22 [MT 18:23]; הָ[מְאַהֲבֶיהָ] אַחֲרֵי וַתֵּלֶךְ of idolatry in Hos. 2:13 [MT 2:15]). The linguistic basis for late-dating the oracle against Judah is weak.

As for the religious perspective of the passage, all of the crimes committed by the various nations have an ultimate foundation in divine law. Moreover, the Israel oracle gives specific instances of transgressions of the Mosaic Law. It is also hard to imagine that the oracle against Moab (2:1-3) does not involve some more specifically "religious" violation. Besides, modern distinctions between "religious" and "social" violations may not have been so strongly felt in ancient times.[78]

---

[76] For the main issues, see Wolff (*Joel and Amos*, pp. 112, 139-40, 163-64). A recent writer who accepts the passage as genuinely from Amos is Shalom Paul ("The Oracles against the Nations," pp. 194-97). See also Hayes, *Amos*, pp. 101-4.

[77] Cf. Martin Noth, *The Deuteronomistic History* (JSOT 15; Sheffield: JSOT, 1981).

[78] Recently V. Fritz attacked all of the oracles against the nations as "*vaticinium ex eventu*" added to the book some time after 722 B.C. ("Die Fremdvölkersprüche des Amos," p. 38). A rebuttal was given by G. Pfeifer, "Die Fremdvölkersprüche des Amos -- spätere *vaticinia ex eventu?*" *VT* 38 (1988): 230-33.

3
Those Who Trample the Poor
(Amos 2:6-16)

Amos boldly places Israel on the same level as the other nations by using the stereotyped phrase, "for three transgressions of ... even for four." One can imagine the pained expressions among the audience when Amos got to this point. Throughout the remainder of the book, the prophet seldom departs from his direct condemnation of Israel, though he will often include Judah since it too is part of the covenant people.

A. Indictment Of Israel (2:6-12)

The first major declaration against Israel can be divided by the interjection "behold" in 2:13. It introduces the announcement of punishment to Israel (2:13-16) as a response to a two-pronged accusation. First, Amos charges the Israelites with oppressing their less fortunate neighbors (2:6-8). Second, he contrasts the Lord's gracious actions for His people with their rejection of His leadership through prophets and Nazirites (2:9-12). Because of these sins the Lord will bring a great shaking which will completely upset the comfortable life the people currently enjoy.

1. Oppression Of The Powerless (2:6-8)

Translation

Thus says Yahweh:
"For three transgressions of Israel,
even for four I will not turn back (its) punishment,
because they sell the innocent for money
and the needy for a pair of sandals.
7They trample *the dust of the earth
on the head of the helpless,
and they turn aside the way (to justice) for the afflicted.
Both a man and his father resort to the (same) girl,
thereby profaning My holy name.
8And *on garments taken as pledges they stretch out
beside every altar.
Even wine purchased from those fined they drink
in the house of their God."

Exegesis and Exposition

Amos condemns, by the authority of the Lord, debt slavery (v. 6), gouging of the poor (v. 7a), the denial of legal redress to the afflicted (v. 7b), improper

147

treatment of a maidservant (v. 7c), depriving debtors of their only clothes (v. 8a), and using the legal system to extort money (v. 8b). The Mosaic law gave explicit regulations or prohibitions for each of these crimes [1]

Amos accuses the people of practicing oppression while simultaneously participating in religious ritual, anticipating a theme to be developed later (esp. 4:4-5; 5:21-24). First, the Lord's "holy name" is profaned (v. 7b); then the improperly seized garments are stretched out "beside every altar." Finally, the wine purchased with extorted funds is drunk "in the house of their God." Despite the interpretation of the Targum, "And upon couches taken in pledge they recline beside their heathen altars, and the wine of robbery they drink in the house of their idols," the stress is not so much on idolatry as on the separation of religious rites from righteous living. This idea also forms a smooth transition to Amos's next topic: the way the people have rejected the gracious actions of the Lord.

"Their god" (spelled in lowercase) might get across Amos's desire to disassociate himself from these practices, but "their gods" (also possible from the Hebrew) would press the issue beyond the vagueness that Amos intends at this point in his argument.

2:6 The term "righteous" or "innocent" (צַדִּיק, ṣaddîq) in v. 6 describes the legal status of the poor. They are innocent of wrongdoing; they have not done anything to deserve the treatment of their oppressors. The word occurs only twice in Amos (2:6; 5:12) and puts stress on the poor as victims of injustice. A victim is an innocent party. The oppressor is guilty, not the victim.

NASB and NIV translate both instances of ṣaddîq in Amos as "righteous," though they do use "innocent" at 2 Kings 10:9. The NEB renders "innocent" for Amos 2:6 and "guiltless" for 5:12. "Righteous" may stress too much the victim's relationship to God, which is not of great concern in the context. The legal connotations of "innocent" or "guiltless" point to the victimization of the poor by their oppressors.

The specific situation that Amos condemns is not entirely certain. The money represents either a debt owed to a creditor (Mays), the purchase price of a slave (Fendler), or a bribe paid to a judge in a civil case (Feinberg). [2] The verb for "sell" elsewhere refers to debt slavery but never to bribery (Ex. 21:7-8; Lev. 25:39; Deut. 15:12). Moreover, Amos mentions in other places, using different terminology, the "acceptance of bribes" and "turning aside" the poor from the courts (5:12; cf. 2:7). [3] The amount owed and the amount paid to a purchaser may have been the same, especially if self-enslavement is in view.

---

[1] Cf. Frank H. Seilhamer, "The Role of Covenant in the Mission and Message of Amos," *A Light unto My Path: Old Testament Studies in Honor of Jacob M. Myers* (Gettysburg Theological Studies 4; ed. Howard N. Bream, et al.; Philadelphia: Temple Univ., 1974), pp. 438-39.

[2] James Luther Mays, *Amos* (OTL Philadelphia: Westminster, 1969), p. 45; Marlene Fendler, "Zur Sozialkritik des Amos," *EvT* 33 (1973): 38; Charles L. Feinberg, *The Minor Prophets* (Chicago: Moody, 1976), p. 91.

[3] Cf. Hans Walter Wolff, *Joel and Amos* (Hermeneia; trans. Waldemar Janzen, et al.; Philadelphia: Fortress, 1977), p. 165.

In what sense were these individuals "innocent"? If they went into slavery because of a debt, wouldn't they be liable? Several possibilities suggest themselves. First, the person might have been kidnapped and sold into slavery (cf. Ex. 21:16; Deut. 24:7).[4] If Amos had meant kidnapping, he could perhaps have used more explicit language to that effect. Second, the victim might be a child of a debtor who died. Elisha dealt with a widow who complained that a creditor had come to seize her two children for her husband's debt (2 Kings 4:1). Elisha then performed a miracle so the woman could get the money she needed to pay the debt. Apparently the children were liable.

Actually, Amos would probably tell us not to focus so much on the technicality of liability. Rather, the enslaved individuals are "innocent" because the debts they incurred were extorted out of them by their creditors. Perhaps they were forced to buy basic necessities and were unable to pay, or possibly exorbitant interest was charged on the loan. In some cases the creditor may have had a technical right to force his claim, but in a moral sense he was wrong and the debtor was right.

In a parallel case, some Israelites complained to Nehemiah that they had to mortgage their fields, vineyards, and houses in order to get grain during a famine, while others needed to borrow money to pay the king's tax (Neh. 5). The debts were in the strictest sense legally owed, but Nehemiah's reply to the creditors was, "The thing which you are doing is not good" (v. 9). Moreover, he set an example by refusing to eat "the governor's food allowance" to which he was entitled.

Famine did not threaten Israel during the reign of Jeroboam II, but the wealth accumulated by a few resulted from the impoverishment of many, often through illegal or ruthless tactics (cf. Amos 4:1; 5:11; 8:4-6). Not only does this view of the situation agree with the general tenor of the compassion demanded by God through the Mosaic law, it also is supported by the parallel clause at the end of the verse (see below). Of course, the situation of 2 Kings 4:1 also fits when viewed from this perspective.

Debt slavery was permitted in the Law of Moses, but only as a temporary condition (Ex. 21:7-11; Lev. 25:39-43; Deut. 15:12-15). The master needed to treat the indebted person as a fellow-Israelite and to give him or her some compensation. While *ṣaddîq* is used of a "victim," אֶבְיוֹן (*'ebyôn*) is a term of "need." The *'ebyônîm* needed money, power, and legal recourse in the courts. Lacking these things, they were merely a means for others to get rich.[5]

The pair of sandals apparently represents the debt in this case, though some think it stands for the ownership of property, citing the ceremony of exchanging a sandal to seal the transfer or redemption of property (Ruth 4:7). The parallel with money would then be strengthened, but some problems arise with this view. In the

---

[4] Cf. Bernhard Lang, who thinks the individuals were sold to foreigners and consequently would never be able to obtain their freedom, "Sklaven und Unfreie im Buch Amos (II 6, VIII 6)," *VT* 31 (1981): 484-85.

[5] For a full discussion of *'ebyôn* in terms of etymology and usage, see J. David Pleins, *Biblical Ethics and the Poor: The Language and Structures of Poverty in the Writings of the Hebrew Prophets*, diss. for the University of Michigan (Ann Arbor: Univ. Microfilms, 1986), pp. 92-109.

case of Boaz only one sandal is mentioned, and it is unclear whether it stands for the property itself or simply as a seal of the transaction.[6]

More likely, therefore, the sandals represent a very small debt owed by the individual. The compassion demanded by God of those who love Him should have motivated the creditor to forgive such a paltry sum (cf. Matt. 5:7). Instead he demands that the poor person sell himself into slavery in order to pay it off.

2:7a A third term for the poor is דָּל (dal), found in v. 7, and like 'ebyôn it also expresses need. Perhaps its frequent use in contrasts between "rich" and "poor" will help to clarify the difference. For example, Boaz praised Ruth because she did not go after "young men, whether rich or poor" (3:10). One may also note the "lean cows" (dallôt) versus the "fat cows" of Pharaoh's dream (Gen. 41:19). The dallîm in Amos's time were the "have nots," while the 'ebyônîm lacked some basic necessity. Whether a person is considered rich or poor may be a relative matter, but usually the poor are also needy. The word "poor," then, is a term of comparative need, implying a standard of wealth or abundance against which to compare the lack of wealth. One may thus concur with the following definition by J. David Pleins: "The term dal, therefore, may simply be defined as poverty in its concrete and socially debilitating form."[7] That is, in the social structure the dal stand out for their poverty.

For the present verse dal is placed in parallel with "afflicted" (עֲנָוִים, 'ănāwîm) in the next line ("humble" in NASB, "oppressed" in NIV, see below). This would indicate that power is a point of comparison between the rich and the poor. The powerful trample on the powerless or helpless.

The verb שָׁאַף (šā'ap) may be translated either "pant after" or "trample upon." The same term also occurs at Amos 8:4 (cf. Ps. 56:1, 2 [MT 56:2, 3]; 57:3 [MT 57:4]; Ezek. 36:3). NIV has consistently rendered "trample" in both places in Amos, while NASB has "pant after" for the first ("trample" in the margin) and "trample" for the second. The ancient versions lend support to the idea of trampling or treading.[8] Note especially the Vulg., "who grind [conterunt] upon the dust of the ground the heads of the poor."

LXX splits the phrase into two parts: "(the sandals) which tread upon the dust of the ground, and they strike at [ἐκονδύλιζον, ekondulizon] the head of beggars." LXX thus takes the first part to refer back to the sandals of v. 6 (the article with "the treaders" is neuter plural). This interpretation reflects an understanding of the

---

[6] For further information about Boaz's action, see Roland de Vaux, *Ancient Israel*, 2 vols. (New York: McGraw-Hill, 1965), 1:169; Donald A. Leggett, *The Levirate and Goel Institutions in the Old Testament: With Special Attention to the Book of Ruth* (Cherry Hill, N.J.: Mack, 1974), pp. 249-53; and Edward F. Campbell, Jr., *Ruth* (AB 7; Garden City, N.Y.: Doubleday, 1975), p. 150. Mays, *Amos*, p. 45, and more recently John Andrew Dearman in *Property Rights in the Eighth-Century Prophets: The Conflict and its Background* (SBLDS 106; Atlanta: Scholars, 1988), p. 21, think that Amos speaks of property.

[7] Pleins, *Biblical Ethics and the Poor*, p. 124. Pleins arrived at similar conclusions to my own concerning the terms for poverty.

[8] LXX, τὰ πατοῦντα (ta patounta, "those who tread"); Peshitta, ddyšyn ("who trample"); Targum, דשיטין (dešāyĕṭîn, "who despise," or "who wander about").

Hebrew consonants *š̆p* as both "tread" and "strike at" (cf. Gen. 3:15). The Peshitta also divides the section through a dual interpretation of the single Hebrew verb, "who trample upon the dust of the earth and buffet the poor."

Feinberg lists three views, the first of which he prefers: (1) the wicked bring the poor so low that they cast dust on their heads in mourning; (2) the ungodly tread the poor in the dust of the earth under their feet; and (3) creditors begrudge the poor even the dust that they, as mourners, cast on their heads.[9] The thought of mourning seems strange to the context, and in light of Amos 8:4 and the ancient versions the verb is better translated "tread on" than "pant after." Therefore we prefer Feinberg's second view. The literal sense of the Hebrew as it stands is, "Who trample upon dust of the ground on the head of the poor." A. Szabó proposes that the awkwardness of the Hebrew may be due to the use of a traditional or stereotyped phrase, "dust of the ground."[10] The general sense is that some in Israel are unrelenting in their cruelty toward the poor.

2:7b *'ănāwîm* sometimes implies the positive virtue of humility or meekness (see esp. Num. 12:3 and Prov. 3:34). This helps to explain why some versions have "the humble" (NASB) or "the meek" (KJV) for its two occurrences in Amos (2:7 and 8:4 [*ketib*]). The contexts demand a concept parallel to "poor" (*dallîm* in Amos 2:7) or "needy" (*'ebyôn* in Amos 8:4). Therefore, the NIV has more correctly used "the oppressed" in Amos 2:7, though it used "the poor" in 8:4 (perhaps suggested by its parallel association with "needy"; see below).

Etymological connection with the verbal root *'ānâ*, "be afflicted," suggests the translation "afflicted" or "distressed" (see also Additional Notes). A study of the usage reveals that the term is connected most often with *'ebyôn* ("needy"). In fact, the two together form almost a stereotyped expression (e.g., Deut. 15:11; Job 24:4; Ps. 12:5 [MT 12:6]; Prov. 31:20; Isa. 41:17; Jer. 22:16; Ezek. 16:49). The afflicted are also connected with the "brokenhearted ... captives ... prisoners ... all who mourn" (Isa. 61:1-2), the orphan (Job 29:12), the stranger or sojourner (Lev. 19:10), widows (Isa. 10:2), the thirsty (Isa. 41:17), and the hungry (Isa. 58:7). Additionally, Scripture views them as robbed of their rights (Isa. 10:2), homeless (Isa. 58:7), oppressed (Ezek. 18:12), pursued (Ps. 10:2, 9), devastated (Ps. 12:5 [MT 12:6]), pushed aside (Job 24:4), and killed (Job 24:14). Probably *'ănāwîm* can be described best as a term of "suffering." The poverty-stricken suffer because they are helpless and vulnerable.

The "way" (דֶּרֶךְ, *derek*) of the "afflicted" refers to their attempt to get relief from their suffering through the courts. A similar expression occurs in Isa. 10:2, "to deprive the needy of justice," which uses the same verb translated here "turn aside" (יַטּוּ, *yaṭṭû*). The Mosaic Law affirms the right of all to legal redress before God (Deut. 10:17-18).

2:7c In the context Amos speaks of oppression and those it hurts. Therefore, the "man and his father" of v. 7c are most likely in a position to afflict, while "the girl" is somehow suffering. This would eliminate immediately those views that see

---

[9] Feinberg, *The Minor Prophets*, p. 91.
[10] A. Szabó, "Textual Problems in Amos and Hosea," *VT* 25 (1975): 502-3; see also Additional Notes for a discussion of textual issues.

her as a temple prostitute. It is true that v. 8 refers to an altar and a temple, but the wrongs cited still concern acts of oppression.[11]

Wolff explains: "The elder, already married, father has intruded upon his son's love affair, and by so doing has turned a young woman into an object for the gratification of forbidden lusts."[12] Although Wolff rejects the more specific connotation of "maidservant" for נַעֲרָה (na'ărâ), in the same context with "innocent," "needy," "poor," and "afflicted," it should stand for a special status of oppressed person.

Moreover, since the other sins that Amos describes are based on a specific Mosaic commandment, the same might be expected for the present case. In fact, Ex. 21:7-11 gives a pertinent legal background. The master of a female slave may "designate her for his son," but if so, "he shall deal with her according to the custom of daughters" (vv. 8-9). Evidently, as Marlene Fendler argues, Amos thinks of a father and his son who both pervert this proper family situation degrading the girl and depriving her of her rights.[13]

The rendering above takes לְמַעַן (lĕma'an) as expressing result, a rare usage according to Williams.[14] As a purpose conjunction it would place more blame on Israel ("you do this in order to profane My holy name," cf. NASB). However, that seems to take the willfulness of the Israelites to an extreme. At this stage of the argument it would make more sense for Amos to say, "When you violate this girl, you thereby pollute My holy name as well."

2:8a The translation "stretch out" for yaṭṭû in v. 8 is a problem, because the verb in the hiphil stem elsewhere always has a transitive meaning (e.g., "stretch out My hand," Jer. 6:12). In fact, the form is exactly the same as that used in v. 7, but there it means "turn aside." Yet the general sense is clear. Some Israelites are keeping the only garments of their poverty-stricken neighbors to recline on at religious ceremonies near the altar. The evil of this practice is heightened when one considers the Mosaic prohibition against keeping a garment taken in pledge after the sun goes down (Ex. 22:26 [MT 22:25]).

2:8b The passive participle of עֲנוּשׁ ('ānaš) in v. 8b is unique, but the verb is used elsewhere of exacting fines as punitive damages (Ex. 21:22; Deut. 22:19). Prov. 17:26 warns in a similar vein, "It is also not good to fine the innocent." That is, an innocent person might unjustly receive a fine in court, and Amos probably has such a situation in mind. Those in power unjustly extort money in legal cases and use it to purchase wine to drink in temples. Such fines, in fact, should go to the victim as restitution (Ex. 21:22; Deut. 22:19).[15] Or, the money might represent

---

[11] A view found in Feinberg (*The Minor Prophets*, p. 91) and in S. R. Driver, *The Books of Joel and Amos* (CBSC; Cambridge: University, 1907), pp. 149-50. Perhaps the most exhaustive treatment in favor of the view is given by Hans M. Barstad, *The Religious Polemics of Amos* (VTSup 34; Leiden: E. J. Brill, 1984), pp. 17-36.

[12] Wolff, *Joel and Amos*, p. 167.

[13] Fendler, "Zur Sozialkritik des Amos," pp. 42-43.

[14] Ronald J. Williams, *Hebrew Syntax; An Outline*, 2d ed. (Toronto: Univ. of Toronto, 1976), p. 62, par. 368.

[15] John H. Hayes, *Amos, The Eighth-Century Prophet: His Times and His Preaching* (Nashville: Abingdon, 1988), pp. 113-14.

payment on a debt or a tax. [16] The Targum's "wine of robbery" (אונסא חמר, *ḥămar ʾûnsāʾ*) and LXX's "wine of dishonest prosecutions" (οἶνον ἐκ συκοφαντιῶν, *oinon ek sukophantiōn*) bring out the underlying meaning.

Additional Notes

2:7 עַל־עֲפַר־אֶרֶץ: Some commentators think "upon (the) dust of (the) earth" is a gloss to make sure the meaning "trample" rather than "pant after" is given to the verb.[17] LXX and Peshitta give some slight evidence for this. This would give a smoother reading, "who trample on the head of the poor," but it does not seem necessary. In any case, it would not change the general sense of the Hebrew.

הַשֹּׁאֲפִים: It is not necessary to emend to a form from שׁוּף. Both forms can mean "trample." They are either biforms (cf. BDB) of each other or possibly the *aleph* has been inserted through the linguistic process of paradigm mixing (cf. וְשַׁבְתִּי in Ps. 23:6, where the expected form is וְיָשַׁבְתִּי)[18] or as a vowel letter.

עֲנָוִים: BDB lists two forms, a noun עָנָו and an adjective עָנִי, both with the meanings "poor, afflicted, humble," but with the added meaning "meek" for the former term. While the historical origins of these two forms may be distinct, the following should be noted: (1) the only occurrence of עָנָו in the singular is in Num. 12:3, and even there the *qere* is עניו (this compares with 20 instances of the term in the plural); and (2) out of 75 occurrences of עָנִי only 19 are singular, and even two of these are עניום in the *ketib* (Ps. 9:18 [MT 9:19]; Amos 8:4). The singular, then, tended to used *yod* instead of *waw*, whereas the *waw* was normally preserved in the plural.[19] Only the plural occurs in Amos.

2:8 וְעַל־בְּגָדִים ... יַטּוּ: Wolff removes the preposition עַל on the basis of LXX, yielding "garments taken in pledge they spread out."[20] The other versions retain the preposition but give an intransitive meaning. The Peshitta renders the verb by something like "they gird themselves" (*ḥzqyn hww*). Possibly the translator of LXX omitted the preposition because of the same difficulty felt by modern interpreters.

2. Rejection Of The Lord (2:9-12)

Translation

"Yet it was I who destroyed the Amorites before them,
who were as tall as cedar trees
and strong as oaks.

---

[16] Dearman, *Property Rights in the Eighth-Century Prophets*, p. 24.

[17] E.g., Wolff, *Joel and Amos*, p. 133 n. 1.

[18] For examples in English and other languages see Raimo Anttila, *An Introduction to Historical and Comparative Linguistics* (New York: Macmillan, 1972), p. 76.

[19] For a detailed discussion of the etymology and usage of עָנָו/עָנִי, see Pleins, *Biblical Ethics and the Poor*, pp. 124-53. He prefers to see two forms that are etymologically distinct. Two separate historical origins are posited by Kjell Aartun, "*Hebräisch ʿāni und ʿānāw*," *BO* 28 (1971): 125-26.

[20] Wolff, *Joel and Amos*, p. 134.

Yes, I destroyed their fruit above
and their roots below.
[10]It is I who brought *you up from the land of Egypt
and led *you in the wilderness forty years
that you might inherit the land of the Amorites.
[11]Then I raised up some of your sons to be prophets
and some of your young men to be Nazirites.
Is this not so, house of Israel?"
(This is) Yahweh's solemn declaration.
[12]But you made the Nazirites drink wine
and commanded the prophets, saying,
"You must not prophesy."

Exegesis and Exposition

The section beginning with v. 9 contrasts the people's outward devotion to the Lord, and simultaneous ruthless behavior, with the compassion and graciousness of the Lord Himself. The Lord, speaking through Amos, starts by declaring how He destroyed the Amorites before Israel. Then the scene shifts back in time to the Exodus and the wilderness wanderings, culminating in a restatement or closure: "That you might take possession of the land of the Amorite." Mays gives a plausible reason for the sequence of vv. 9 and 10:

> This unusual order has its own logic; it emphasizes that Israel's existence in the land of the Amorites is the result of Yahweh's work. Because this is uppermost in Amos's mind the conquest is listed first, and then emphasized again at the end of v. 10 as the goal of the acts of Yahweh.[21]

Later the people strayed from their covenant obligations, but the Lord attempted to woo them back through the work of prophets and Nazirites. Yet Israel had only contempt for divine grace, forcing the Nazirites to drink wine and commanding the prophets not to prophesy. It would be hard not to see a close connection with Amos's own confrontation with Amaziah (7:12-17). Thus, another strand of the book is prefigured – Amos's defense of his prophetic message. Refusal to hear God also accounts for the famine for the word of God that will come (8:11-12). When God's people flaunt His grace in this manner, judgment is inevitable.

2:9 The language of v. 9 follows Deut. 1:27 closely. When the people rebelled against God they said, "Because Yahweh hates us, He has brought us out of the land of Egypt to deliver us to the Amorites *to destroy* us." Amos turns the phrase around: "Yet it was I who *destroyed* the Amorites before them." The translation takes הָאֱמֹרִי (*hā'ĕmōrî*, "the Amorite") as a collective singular.

"Amorite" in the OT means either a particular Canaanite tribe (Gen. 10:16; Ex. 3:8) or, as in the present passage, the population of the whole area of Canaan (Gen. 15:16; Josh. 24:15). This two-fold usage is explained by Huffmon as "apparently using a self-designation in an expanded sense." Some Mesopotamian

---

[21] Mays, *Amos*, p. 50.

sources have a similar dual use of the term.[22] Amos uses hyperbole to describe the height and might of these giants, paralleling the report of the unbelieving spies (Num. 13:32-33). Despite the way the Israelites feared these people, the Lord was able to overthrow them.

The picturesque language of פִּרְיוֹ ... וְשָׁרָשָׁיו (*piryô ... wĕšorāšāyw*, "his fruit ... and his roots") stresses complete removal. Wolff cites a fifth century Phoenician inscription from Sidon that contains a curse formula, "May they have no root down below and no fruit up on top."[23] See also 2 Kings 19:30 and Isa. 37:31.

2:10*a* Verse 10 has a close relationship to the report of the spies (Num. 13:30-31). Caleb said, "We should by all means *go up*," using the basic (qal) pattern of the root עלה (*'lh*). But the others who "*went up*" with him countered, "We are not able to *go up*." Moses (Deut. 1:26) rephrased what happened to highlight the rebellion of the people, "Yet you were not willing *to go up*, but rebelled against the command of Yahweh your God." Therefore the use of the causative (hiphil) stem lends more force to Amos's accusation. To paraphrase, "Even though you refused to go up to destroy the Amorites and accused Me of bringing you out to let them destroy you, yet it was I who both destroyed the Amorites and *brought you up* from the land of Egypt." For the change of personal reference from "they" or "them" to "you," see Additional Notes.

2:10*b* The Hebrew wording is virtually the same as in Deut. 29:5 (MT 29:4; the position of בַּמִּדְבָּר [*bammidbār*] is reversed), further evidence of the traditional nature of the language and a reflection of Amos's knowledge of the Law of Moses. The tradition of 40 years in the wilderness occurs again at Amos 5:25.

2:11 Amos uniquely places the Nazirites alongside prophets as those whom the Lord had specially raised up. The Targum reads "teachers" (מלפין, *mallĕpîn*), an interpretation which emphasizes a parallel function for both offices.[24] Numbers 6 contains the laws that govern the "Nazirite vow": that is, a temporary vow to dedicate oneself to the Lord by abstaining from any product of the vine, by letting the hair grow long, and by avoiding contact with a dead body. God commanded Samson's parents to dedicate their boy as a Nazirite "from the womb to the day of his death" (Judg. 13:7).

Also Hannah, Samuel's mother, vowed that if the Lord would give her a son she would dedicate him "all the days of his life, and a razor shall never come on his head" (1 Sam. 1:11). LXX adds that the child would be a Nazirite and not drink any wine.[25] Samuel was also a prophet (1 Sam 3:19-21), and he was the first to stress the major prophetic theme implied in his rebuke of Saul, "to obey is better than sacrifice" (1 Sam 15:22). Amos apparently intends to bring out the dedication of the prophets to Yahweh, who commissioned them with a message for the people.

---

[22] Huffmon, "Amorites," in *IDBSup*, p. 21.

[23] Wolff, *Joel and Amos*, p. 169.

[24] Cf. Leivy Smolar and Moses Aberbach, *Studies in Targum Jonathan to the Prophets* (New York: KTAV, 1983), p. 11. They comment, "This novel interpretation manages to ignore the Nazirites altogether, while placing teachers virtually on a level with the prophets."

[25] Cf. P. Kyle McCarter, Jr., *I Samuel* (AB 8; Garden City, N.Y.: 1980), pp. 53-54.

נְאָם יהוה (nĕ'um YHWH, "declaration of Yahweh") is virtually synonymous with אָמַר יהוה ('āmar YHWH, "says Yahweh"), but the term nĕ'um occurs only with reference to divine speech, though sometimes the subject is a prophet when he delivers a word of revelation (Num. 24:3, 15; 2 Sam. 23:1; Prov. 30:1 is problematic). Therefore, it lends greater solemnity to the words that precede it.

2:12 It seems incredible that the Israelites would have forced the Nazirites to drink wine, though one can well imagine them ordering prophets to cease their negative warnings and threats, even as Amaziah did with Amos (7:12-13; cf. 1 Kings 22:6-27; Jer. 20:1-6; 26:1-24; 36:1-26). Perhaps the Targum gives a clue to the issue of the Nazirites: "And you led astray your teachers with wine" (ואטעיתון ית מלפיכון בחמרא, wĕ'aṭ'îtûn yāt mallĕpêkôn bĕḥamrā'). Evidently the Israelites encouraged the Nazirites to break their vow of abstinence by offering them wine in a situation where it would be difficult to refuse.

Additional Notes

2:10 אֶתְכֶם: The pronoun "you" in v. 10 contrasts with the reference to "them" in v. 9. This change of person is maintained through v. 13. Mays explains that "the third-person pronoun 'them' of v. 9 for Israel continues the third-person plurals of vv. 6-8 and furnishes a transition to the second-person pronouns of vv. 10ff."[26] Apparently the traditional nature of the language led to the change of personal reference. That is, Amos cited from memory and did not change the pronoun references. The effect of the shift is to bring the audience into personal participation with the Lord's grace to them in the past. Fluctuations in personal reference are not uncommon in prophetic material.

B. Sentencing Of Israel (2:13-16)

Translation

"Look! I will soon *make the ground tremble beneath you,
just as a wagon makes (the ground) tremble
    when filled with sheaves.
[14]Then flight will be impossible (even) for the swift,
and a strong man will not be able to maintain his might.
[15]The warrior will not be able to save his (own) life,
and the bowman will not be able to stand.
The swift of foot will not *escape;
even one riding a horse will not save his (own) life.
[16]Even the *bravest among the warriors
will flee naked in that day."
(This is) Yahweh's solemn declaration.

Exegesis and Exposition

The judgment for the surrounding nations consisted of a fire sent by the Lord to devour the citadels of various cities. The Lord will intervene with direct

---

[26] *Amos*, p. 49.

judgment against Israel also. When it comes no one will have any power at all to resist. The Lord had fought for His people many times before (cf. Judg. 5:20; 7:22; 2 Kings 3:22); now He will send such terror among them that even the bravest of warriors will flee. Neither speed, nor might, nor weapons, nor bravery will be of any use.

2:13 The root עוּק ('wq), translated "tremble" ("totter" in the KB lexicon) is unique to v. 13 (two occurrences), and its meaning must be guessed from the context. The ancient and modern versions offer a wide variety of renderings. NASB's "I am weighted down beneath you" should be rejected for reasons of context, etymology, and theology. Feinberg calls this interpretation "an inelegant picture of the Lord."[27] "Crush you" of the NIV fails to account explicitly for the preposition "under," apparently understanding it as governing a verbal complement. Wolff gives a strong etymological basis for his proposal, "I break open beneath you," meaning the Lord will break open the ground under Israel in an earthquake.[28]

The earthquake imagery suggested by the translation might relate the passage to allusions to a temblor elsewhere in Amos (1:1; 8:8; 9:1, 5). In fact, the various reactions described in the rest of the passage fit well with the panic incited by an earthquake. When the ground shakes violently, how can speed or strength or bravery or a weapon or a horse help?

It is also significant that much of the imagery Amos uses here applies to an army. An enemy army marching through the land might cause the ground to shake. If so, the passage would agree with other references to military disaster in Amos (3:11; 4:2-3; 5:27; 9:4, 10). Apparently the earthquake in the days of Jeroboam foreshadowed the Lord's judgment in the form of the overwhelming might of Assyria and of the resultant internal strife that would strike the "house of Jeroboam" with the sword (see 7:11). But perhaps the vagueness of the passage before us leaves open the details and merely points to the general judgment of God that would bring an end to the kingdom of Israel.

The same verb for "trembling" is also used of the wagon. As it is heavily laden with sheaves, the ground shakes beneath it. Alternatively, Wolff suggests a heavy cart that makes deep furrows or tracks in the ground.[29]

2:14-15 The text of v. 14 actually says that flight will "perish" (אָבַד, 'ābad) from the swift. That is, the fast runner will not be able to make use of speed. In an earthquake he would be thrown to the ground, and even if he could run he might not find a place of safety. Similarly, the strong man "will not make firm [לֹא־יְאַמֵּץ, lō'-yě'ammēṣ] his might [כֹּחוֹ, kōḥô]." No power he might exert would be strong enough to overcome the disaster.

Finally, even the seasoned warrior (גִּבּוֹר, gibbôr) will not even be able to save his own life, let alone deliver anyone else. BHS rightly arranges the text so that the line about the warrior finds its balanced partner in the following verse about the

---

[27] Feinberg, *Minor Prophets*, p. 93. The view that "Amos did not hesitate to employ even a gross anthropomorphism to indicate God's disgust with the people" is defended by A. S. Super in "Figures of Comparison in the Book of Amos," *Semitics* 3 (1973): 79.

[28] Wolff, *Joel and Amos*, pp. 134, 170.

[29] Ibid., p. 171.

bowman. In an earthquake it is difficult to stand. How, then, would a bowman be able to take aim? Or, if he is suddenly overwhelmed by the invaders, of what use will he be to the defending army?

2:16 The final image in brings to a climax the scene of panic in an unexpected calamity. The naked warrior (sleeping or bathing?) has no time to dress, and even though he is the bravest in the army he flees in terror. The Targum glosses "naked" by "without weapons," but that lessens the tension of the situation.

Quite often "in that day" points to the day of the Lord or the end times (cf. Joel 3:18; Amos 9:11; Zech. 12:9), but here it refers merely to the imminent judgment against the northern kingdom. *Nĕ'um YHWH* at the end of this verse (cf. v. 11) marks the end of the extended oracle about Israel in Amos's first cycle of messages. The change in form from "says Yahweh" to "declaration of Yahweh" adds to the severity of the conclusion.

Additional Notes

2:13 מֵעִיק: H. Neil Richardson takes the verb as "bring distress."[30] Yet he then assumes the next line is an explanatory gloss. Also, the preposition "under" is awkward if the verb is translated "bring distress."

2:15 יְמַלֵּט: Ordinarily the verb occurs in the niphal pattern for the intransitive (reflexive) use, whereas the piel pattern, which occurs here, has the transitive idea of "save" or "deliver." The ancient and modern versions give an intransitive form because it fits the context and no object is included. The older versions might give evidence for a tradition of different vowels with the same consonants as MT (*yimmālēt*), but this is by no means certain. Possibly the term "life" (נֶפֶשׁ, *nepeš*) carries over from v. 14: "Nor the mighty man *save his life* ... The swift of foot will not save (his life)." Another suggestion is that on rare occasions the piel form can be used intransitively,[31] but that does not seem likely for the root מלט.

2:16 וְאַמִּיץ: The LXX has "and he shall find [εὑρήσει] his heart," presupposing a metathesis to וּמָצָא.

[30] H. Neil Richardson, "Amos 2:13-16: Its Structure and Function in the Book," in *Society of Biblical Literature 1978 Seminar Papers*, ed. Paul J. Achtemeier (Missoula, Mont.: Scholars, 1978), p. 362.

[31] Robert Gordis, *The Book of Job* (*Moreshet* Series 2; New York: Jewish Theological Seminary of America, 1978), p. 218.

4
Breach of the Covenant
(3:1-15)

The "words" that Amos calls the people to hear (chaps. 3-6) have at their heart a plea for repentance (chap. 5). All three units remind Israel that the Lord must judge them despite their confident trust in the covenant as a magical charm that will ward off all harm. Yahweh cannot be manipulated in this way. The ancient covenant brings with it responsibilities, and it is just as much in God's character to judge sin as it is to graciously allow time and opportunity for repentance. Neither thoughtless reliance on the Lord's continued good will nor trust in empty rituals will substitute for a new era of seeking life in Yahweh.

Addressing Himself to "the entire family" that He "brought up from the land of Egypt," the Lord calls for the punishment of Israel on the basis of her unique election to covenant relationship with Him (3:1-2). One can get a good overall view of the chapter by imagining a courtroom scene where a "lawsuit" is brought against Israel by the Lord.[1] The opening statement (3:1-8) includes a summons for Israel to "hear" the proceedings (v. 1), the initial call for Israel's punishment (v. 2), and a justification of the charges based on the authority of the Lord and of the prophet as His representative (vv. 3-8). Amos then summons foreign nations as witnesses to Israel's crimes (3:9-10) and concludes with an announcement of judgment against the land, the people, the altars at Bethel, and the luxurious houses (3:11-15).

A. Opening Statement (3:1-8)

Translation

Hear this word which Yahweh speaks against you, sons of Israel, against "the entire family which I brought up from the land of Egypt." *He says:

---

[1] See Marjorie O'Rourke Boyle, "The Covenant Lawsuit of the Prophet Amos: III 1-- IV 13," *VT* 21 (1971): 338-62. She carries the imagery over into chap. 4. George Snyder modifies some of her conclusions in "The Law and Covenant in Amos," *Restoration Quarterly* 25 (1982): 158-66. Gary V. Smith, *Amos: A Commentary* (Library of Biblical Interpretation; Grand Rapids: Zondervan, 1989), p. 98, feels that the covenant interpretation is "suspect," because the passage does not contain the term רִיב (*rîb*, "lawsuit") or some of the structural parts of covenant lawsuits found in Hos. 4 and Mic. 6. Norman K. Gottwald, *The Hebrew Bible: A Socio-Literary Introduction* (Philadelphia: Fortress, 1985), p. 305, challenges the validity of the idea of "covenant lawsuit" in general, because "it is difficult to reconstruct a plausible institutional origin" for it. We still find it a useful "general metaphor," to use Gottwald's term, for conceptualizing the chapter. It would be hard to press the details into a "covenant lawsuit" in the more precise sense of a literary genre.

²"You only have I chosen
from all the families of the earth.
Therefore, I must punish you
for all your iniquities."
³*Do two people walk together
unless they have made an appointment?
⁴Does a lion roar in the thicket
when he has no prey?
Does a young lion let out a sound from his den
unless he has captured something?
⁵Does a bird fall into a *trap on the ground
when there is no bait in it?
Does a trap spring up from the ground
and capture nothing at all?
⁶Or will a trumpet be blown in a city
and the people not tremble?
Or will calamity occur in a city
and Yahweh has not done it?
⁷For the Lord Yahweh does not do anything
except He has (first) revealed His *secret counsel
to His servants the prophets.
⁸A lion has roared.
Who would not be afraid?
The Lord Yahweh has spoken!
Who would not prophesy?

Exegesis and Exposition

The translation should make the general threefold structure of the section clear. Amos first calls upon Israel to listen. Then the Lord makes a statement about the choice of Israel and why that choice makes punishment inevitable. Finally, Amos defends his authority as a prophet to announce the word of judgment to the people. It is a very natural thing for him to do, since the Lord Himself has already revealed His intentions.

Taking up the language of the promise to Abraham ("all the families of the earth") and of the Exodus from Egypt, Amos challenges the people to listen to what the Lord has to say. In His opening statement the Lord stresses Israel's divine election and privileged position. Special privilege entails great responsibility, however, and Israel failed to keep the requirements of the covenant.

There follows a unit that finds its coherence through the device of rhetorical questions. Amos places side by side a series of paired events, demanding that the listener draw a relationship between them. [2] The verses can be divided into three sections.

---

[2] James Luther Mays, *Amos: A Commentary* (OTL; Philadelphia: Westminster, 1969), pp. 59-60, calls the passage a "dispute-saying," in which the prophet responds to hostile objections to the message of judgment given in v. 2. Cf. Hans Walter Wolff, *Joel and Amos* (Hermeneia; trans. Waldemar Janzen, et al.; Philadelphia: Fortress, 1977), p. 183.

First, seven ques tions focus on the improbability or impossibility of a certain event if some other happening had not preceded it. The relationship between the two events is not so much cause and effect as action-result, though the Lord's control over them (v. 6*b*) is more than incidental. In v. 3 Amos raises a common situation: two men are walking together. Would they do that unless they had previously arranged to meet? Questions two through five form two pairs dealing with lions and their prey, (v. 4) and traps and the birds caught in them (v. 5). Two additional questions (v. 6) have a slightly different form in the Hebrew (see Additional Notes) and also relate more directly to the sphere of human catastrophes.

Second, a statement (v. 7) makes the connection explicit: when the Lord plans to act in the affairs of Israel, He reveals his secret counsels to prophets. Because of the unique position and form of this declaration, it communicates the central idea of the section.

Finally two statements, each followed by an additional rhetorical question, force the listeners to apply what has been heard to themselves.[3] Have they heard a lion roar? Then they must tremble with fear. Has the Lord spoken a message? Then the prophet must deliver it.

The entire portion from vv. 1-8 is framed by the fact that the Lord has spoken His word. It is a frightening word; it ought to make any person tremble or any prophet sound a warning. But this word also contains a seed of hope: it is heard only within the context of a relationship. Because the Lord has chosen His people, He must judge them for their iniquities, but not without a warning. The two who walk together are God and Amos, or any who agree to walk along with them on the Lord's terms. The lion and the bird trap are God; and the warning trumpet is Amos's message. The Lord must be the ultimate source of any calamity, according to v. 6; but v. 7 shows His mercy. He may bring calamity but His revelation to the prophets gives a warning. It is up to the people to respond appropriately. Will they heed the warning?

3:1 Amos calls Israel to listen to God's word three times in this section (3:1, 4:1, 5:1; cf. also 8:4). The phrase makes a convenient division between the parts. Similar expressions mark major divisions in other prophetic books (cf. Isa. 28:14; Hos. 4:1; Mic. 6:1).

The Lord speaks directly of delivering Israel from Egypt, though Amos began the sentence by speaking about God. The verb "bring up" is the same one used in 2:10, and the traditional nature of the language probably explains the abrupt shift from "(He) has spoken" to "I brought up."[4]

Israel and Judah were psychologically distant at the time of Amos. Yet the basis for the indictment of both was the same covenant between united Israel and Yahweh made in the wilderness. The northern kingdom needed to realize that its covenant relationship included its southern neighbor – in fact, in the Lord's mind there was only one Israel. Therefore, it was necessary to remind the "sons of Israel" that when God established His covenant with them, they were a single family.

---

[3] Smith, *Amos*, p. 111.
[4] Cf. Mays, *Amos*, p. 55. See also the discussion at 2:10 above.

3:2*a* Israel was not the only nation established by God. Later in his book, Amos points out that the Lord also "brought up" the Cushites, Philistines, and Arameans (9:7). The unique event with respect to Israel is expressed by the verb יָדַע (*yāda‘*), translated "choose" in v. 2 but in other passages more commonly rendered "know." It refers to the covenant God made with Israel on the basis of divine election. H. B. Huffmon has demonstrated the use of a cognate of *yāda‘* in international treaties, giving the sense of "recognize by covenant."[5]

Many interpreters currently hold that the covenant, as expressed especially in the book of Deuteronomy, was theologically analogous to treaties between a more powerful nation and a lesser nation.[6] With God as the initiator of the condition expressed by *yāda‘*, completely apart from any factor other than His divine love and mysterious election (Deut. 7:6-8), the term could well be translated "have I chosen" as in NASB, NIV, and the Targum (cf. Gen. 18:19; Jer. 1:5).[7]

Amos apparently derives "all the families of the earth" (כֹּל מִשְׁפְּחוֹת הָאֲדָמָה, *kōl mišpĕḥôt ha’ădāmâ*) from the Abrahamic covenant as stated in Genesis (12:3; 28:14). Notice the rare sense of "earth" for *’ădāmâ* in both passages; more commonly it means "ground."

3:2*b* The verb פָּקַד (*pāqad*), in the second part of v. 2, is notorious for its wide range of meanings. Often it means "visit," either for good or for inflicting harm or punishment. Here the context indicates the negative connotation of "visit with punishment or judgment."

Such a direct connection between divine election and divine punishment for sin is a striking feature of Amos's prophecy. He knows Israel's privileged status, but her special standing before God in no way excuses her from the consequences of sin. Rather, she is more prone to judgment precisely because God has chosen her and she has spurned that choice (cf. 2:9-16).

Amos's words should serve as a warning especially to those who have a strong belief in divine election. Amos believed it too, but he speaks against what might be called an "election syndrome." The believer (or one who thinks he is a believer) who suffers from this syndrome begins to assume that what he or she does makes no difference and that because salvation is "once and for all," God will overlook disobedience. The NT contains many warnings against this very attitude (e.g., Rom. 6:1-7; Heb. 6:4-8; James 2:14-26). Even for the one whose faith is genuine, God's chastisement can be severe.

3:3 Who are the two walking together? In one respect, it may not be necessary to decide; this initial rhetorical question simply invites the reader to apply some reasoning to a specific situation in life. Then the additional questions will delve more into the main issue of the Lord's authority to judge.

Since the previous verse has just dealt with the relationship between the Lord and Israel, one could think that they correspond to the two parties that have agreed

---

[5] Herbert B. Huffmon, "The Treaty Background of Hebrew *YADA‘*," *BASOR* 181 (1966): 34-35.
    [6] Cf. Gleason L. Archer, Jr., *A Survey of Old Testament Introduction*, rev. ed. (Chicago: Moody, 1975), pp. 253-55.
    [7] "You only have me" in older editions of *NASB*.

to walk on the same road.[8] On the other hand, the way the passage concentrates on the role of the prophet in bringing a warning might make us think that the two walking together must be the Lord and Amos.[9] Even though there is nothing in the first question to suggest a meeting between the Lord and His prophet, the passage as a whole moves in that direction, reaching its climax in vv. 6-8. Could it be that the one who agrees to walk with the Lord is whoever gives a correct response to the rhetorical questions of v. 8? That person, whether prophet or individual Israelite, recognizes that the Lord has indeed roared with a warning for His people.

The meaning of the verb נוֹעָד (nôʻad) is not clear. The Targum renders "unless they have made an appointment to meet together" (אלהין אם אזדמנו, 'ălāhên 'im 'izdāmanû). Some other passages that use the term imply a meeting at an appointed place (e.g., Ex. 25:22; 29:42, 43; Num. 17:4 [MT 17:19]) or an agreement to meet (e.g., Josh. 11:5).

Shalom Paul denies the element of prior arrangement, translating simply, "without having met."[10] They could have met by chance, he argues. Admittedly such chance meetings would have been commonplace, but perhaps the speakers of biblical Hebrew would not have worried so much about the fine details. If two people met by chance, they still had to agree to walk together. Or two walking together could have started their journey that way.

3:4 Lions do not roar before a prey is captured but only afterward. Otherwise the animal would be frightened away by the roar.[11] Therefore, if a lion roars, it must have captured an animal and killed it. This connection between an event and the logical conclusion drawn from it is the point Amos wishes to make.

Why are there two references to the roar of a lion? From a purely aesthetic point of view, v. 4 is part of one of Amos's sequences of seven things (the travelers, two lions, two traps, and two questions about danger to a city). Then Amos returns to the roar of the lion in v. 8 and makes the connection with the Lord's speaking explicit.

Each of the paired actions represents a disaster in process. The lions are ready to devour their prey; the birds are trapped; the city is in the middle of a calamity. By bringing together pairs in this way, Amos leads his listeners to picture a terrifying scene in different ways. In the first half of v. 4 an older lion is in a thickly wooded area. The lion roars just prior to devouring an animal. In the second half we see a young lion, possibly a cub, in its den, growling over that which has been captured.[12] The roar in each case will have a different sound, and the settings have enough variations in detail to force a new image into the mind.

---

[8] Charles L. Feinberg, *The Minor Prophets* (Chicago: Moody, 1976), p. 95; Smith, *Amos*, p. 107.

[9] C. F. Keil, *Minor Prophets* (COTTV 10; Grand Rapids: Eerdmans, 1973), p. 260.

[10] Shalom Paul, "Amos 3:3-8: The Irresistible Sequence of Cause and Effect," *Hebrew Annual Review* 7 (1983): 210-11.

[11] Wolff, *Joel and Amos*, p. 185.

[12] For the suggestion of a lion cub, see Philip J. King, *Amos, Hosea, Micah – An Archaeological Commentary* (Philadelphia: Westminster, 1988), p. 129. Smith, *Amos*, p. 108, presents a different picture, assuming that the lion roars at the moment of attack and that the second half of v. 4 repeats the same point as that found in the first half.

3:5 The movement is downward in the first scene of v. 5, whereas the second concerns the upward movement of a springing trap. Aside from the general facts of two hunting scenes (probably with a bird understood also for the second) and of downward versus upward movement, the details are not clear. The expression "trap of the ground" (פַּח הָאָרֶץ, *paḥ hā'āreṣ*) must somehow contrast with the simple "trap" (*paḥ*) that springs up from the ground. Yet the bird descends, and the Hebrew word for "ground" (*'ereṣ*) is not the expected *'ădāmâ*.

Also מוֹקֵשׁ (*môqēš*) presents difficulties. LXX and the Targum interpret it as a "fowler." However, the vowels do not seem to be appropriate for this meaning. The two major proposals are that it refers to bait in the trap (BDB) or to part of a trap (G. R. Driver). Probably the best explanation is that the bird flies down to the trap when it sees the bait (Paul). Mays views it as a throw-net, while Wolff assumes that the first occurrence of *paḥ* is a scribal addition and explains *môqēš* as a boomerang (see Additional Notes).[13]

3:6 אִם (*'im*) normally means "if," but it may be used to coordinate questions (GKC, par. 150g). The change in structure from *he*-interrogative to coordinating *'im* marks the change in focus from lions and fowling to distress in a city.[14] Now the danger to the people as a whole becomes more apparent. (For the blowing of the trumpet in danger, see the comments on Joel 2:1.)

The previous two pairs depicted two separate incidents, whereas here the calamity befalling only one city is examined two different ways. The trumpet blast alerts the city to the danger according to the first half, but the second half gives the underlying cause. The Lord must have brought it. Thus, the second half brings this part of the passage to a climax, at the same time making a transition into the underlying thought behind the entire section.

While רָעָה (*rā'â*) can be used of moral evil (e.g., Jer. 2:19), the context often specifies the sense of calamity or distress (cf. Jer. 5:12; Joel 2:13). Here the alarm given by the sounding trumpet indicates some kind of physical disaster (cf. Hos 5:8; Joel 2:1). Shalom Paul observes how Amos speaks against the popular belief that the divine election of Israel means that harm cannot come to the nation (cf. 9:10; Mic. 3:11).[15]

Recently Mulder proposed the translation, "Does evil occur in the city, and should YHWH not react?"[16] NEB has a similar interpretation. The main problem with this view is the form of the verb, which would indicate a past reference. It is true that the Hebrew perfect can sometimes indicate a future action, but here Amos maintains a strict distinction between the imperfect for a present or future action and the perfect for a past event.[17]

---

[13] G. R. Driver, "Reflections on Recent Articles," *JBL* 73 (1954): 131-36; Paul, "Amos 3:3-8," pp. 212-13; Mays, *Amos*, p. 59; Wolff, *Joel and Amos*, p. 185.

[14] Cf. Paul, "Amos 3:3-8," pp. 206-7.

[15] Paul, "Amos 3:3-8," p. 214.

[16] Martin Jan Mulder, "Ein Vorschlag zur Übersetzung von Amos III 6B," *VT* 34 (1984): 106-8 ("Geschieht Schlechtes in der Stadt, und sollte JWHW [*sic*] nicht reagieren?").

[17] For a discussion of verb tense in Amos, see Thomas J. Finley, "The *WAW*-Consecutive with 'Imperfect' in Biblical Hebrew: Theoretical Studies and Its Use in Amos,"

3:7 The term "anything" (דָּבָר, *dābār*) in v. 7 should not be absolutized too much. Amos does not intend to limit God, saying that He *must* reveal His plan before He can do anything. Rather, the statement points to the importance of the prophetic office. When God is ready to bring a complete disaster on His people, the prophets will learn of it and therefore proclaim it as a warning. If that is so, why should the people try to stop prophets from preaching judgment? If it is Yahweh's plan, nothing can stop it, and in His grace He reveals it to selected individuals.

The noun סוֹד (*sôd*, "secret counsel") refers either to a gathering of individuals, or to advice or plans. In the former sense it can be used of people (Gen. 49:6) or of the heavenly council, which includes God and the angels (Ps. 89:7 [MT 89:8]). When it means advice or counsel, it often has the associated sense of a secret (Prov. 11:13; 25:9), hence the translation "secret" or "mystery" in the Targum (רז, *raz*).

Feinberg mentions Noah (Gen. 6-9), Abraham (Gen. 18), and Joseph (Gen. 41) as examples of men prior to Amos to whom God revealed plans of destruction.[18] Of course, there were many non-writing prophets prior to Amos who received revelations of importance to the history of Israel, such as Samuel (1 Sam. 3) and Elisha (2 Kings 8:7-15; cf. also 2 Kings 9:7; 17:13, 23; 21:10; 24:2; Jer. 7:25; 25:4; 26:5, 19; 35:15; 44:4; Dan. 9:10; Zech. 1:6). Some would include Joel and Obadiah among Amos's predecessors, but for chronological reasons this seems unlikely for Obadiah and debatable for Joel (see introductory chapters to Joel and Obadiah). Certainly Hosea did not precede Amos, though his book is first in the order of the canon of the Minor Prophets.

3:8 Again in v. 8, Amos explains the perfect logic of his role as Israel's accuser. If Yahweh Himself has spoken the word of judgment, what prophet could possibly hear it and not speak out? Basically Amos says, "I speak because God has spoken!" Silence is hardly an option. Amos may bear bad news, but it is necessary for Israel to listen if she has any hope of averting the disaster. Having thus established his right to be the Lord's spokesman, Amos can continue with the specific charges in the next section.

Additional Notes

3:1 לֵאמֹר: This word (lit. "to say") introduces direct speech. It is often best left untranslated or given an equivalent expression, as in the translation above.

3:3-8 Many have been struck by the intricate structure of this passage. The first five lines in *BHS* begin with *he*; the last four, if v. 7 is left out of consideration, each begin with *aleph*. The poetic lines consist of two parts, some of them forming synonymous couplets. A sense of closure comes from the way the last line, with its intimate connection between the Lord and the prophets, returns to the thought of two who walk together.[19]

---

in *Tradition and Testament: Essays in Honor of Charles Lee Feinberg*, ed. John Feinberg and Paul Feinberg (Chicago: Moody, 1981), pp. 241-62.

[18] Feinberg, *The Minor Prophets*, p. 96.

[19] See Gerhard Pfeiffer, "Unausweichliche Konsequenzen; Denkformenanalyse von Amos III 3-8," *VT* 33 (1983): 341-47.

The different form of v. 7 intrudes into the tight poetic structure, so much so that many have conjectured that it must be a gloss to serve as commentary to v. 6*b* (cf. the note in JB).[20] In principle this is not impossible; marginal notes sometimes found their way into the text itself. The KJV of Rom. 8:1, compared with a modern version such as NASB, contains a classic NT illustration. Yet the situation is different when no external evidence for a gloss exists. Perhaps the conjecture is correct, but the interpreter must first try to exhaust all possible means of explaining the text as it is before resorting to speculation.

As a matter of principle, does an interruption in form have to mean a secondary intrusion? As a literary device, might it not also indicate climax? In fact, v. 7 does form the climax to vv. 3-6 and sets them off from v. 8. Verse 7 makes a direct statement, and the final verse of the section gives the application.

BHS does not display v. 7 as poetry, and many consider it to be prose. On the other hand, RSV, NASB, and NIV make it a tricolon, and JB makes it a bicolon. There are other places in Amos where the versions and *BHS* disagree on poetic form (e.g., NASB of 3:9-10 is prose). Whether the passage is prose or poetry, its form differs markedly from its surroundings. Such a difference need not point to different authors, however.[21]

3:5 פַּח: LXX omits "trap" in v. 5, yielding, "Does a bird fall upon the ground?" Some have followed this reading, noting that the term could be a gloss that disturbs the poetic meter. Wolff calls it a "scribal dittography."[22]

3:7 סוֹד: C. E. B. Cranfield argues that the Hebrew term underlies the NT sense of μυστήριον (*mystērion*).[23] The translators of LXX did not use μυστήριον for סוֹד in any OT passage (παιδείαν, "chastisement," "discipline," was used instead in Amos 3:7), but the Greek term often occurs in the Apocrypha for secrets, whether human (Tobit 12:7, 11) or divine (Wisd. of Sol. 2:22). Symmachus and Theodotion both use *mystērion* for סוֹד at Job 15:8. Also of interest is the way the book of Revelation reflects closely the language of Amos 3:7, "then the *mystery* of God is finished, as He preached to His servants the prophets" (10:7). Cranfield explains: "It seems as if the earlier translators purposely avoided μυστήριον on account of its pagan religious associations, but that after it had passed into common usage in a neutral sense the later translators came to use it quite freely."[24]

---

[20] Pfeiffer, "Unausweichliche Konsequenzen," pp. 345-46; Wolff, *Joel and Amos*, p. 181.

[21] A detailed defense of the verse is given by Paul ("Amos 3:3-8," pp. 215-16) and by Smith (*Amos*, p. 102). Also John H. Hayes reasons that the verse must be genuine, *Amos, The Eighth-Century Prophet: His Times and His Preaching* (Nashville: Abingdon, 1988), pp. 126-27.

[22] Wolff, *Joel and Amos*, p. 180 n. d.; cf. Mays, *Amos*, p. 59.

[23] C. E. B. Cranfield, *The Gospel According to Saint Mark* (CGTC; New York: Cambridge Univ., 1979), pp. 152-53.

[24] Ibid., p. 153.

B. Summoning Of Witnesses (3:9-10)

Translation

Make a proclamation on the citadels in *Ashdod
and on the citadels in the land of Egypt.
Say (this):
"Gather on the *mountains around Samaria,
and see the great tumults within her,
and the extortions among her."
[10]"They do not know how to do what is honest,"
declares Yahweh,
"those who hoard plunder and loot in their citadels."

Exegesis and Exposition

Amos now summons Ashdod and Egypt as witnesses against Samaria. Ashdod represented the uncircumcised Philistines, while Egypt stood for the slavery from which the Lord had delivered Israel. Both nations were thus completely outside the scope of the covenant. Moreover, the Israelites were probably tempted to rely for aid on these countries. Not very many years later Hoshea, the last king of Israel, "sent messengers to So king of Egypt and had offered no tribute to the king of Assyria, as he had done year by year" (2 Kings 17:4). As John H. Hayes notes, "Legal procedures in Israel required two witnesses to provide evidence in a capital case (see Num. 35:30; Deut. 17:6; 19:5)."[25]

An appeal to send envoys to these lands with a message commanding them to gather and observe sin within Samaria heightens the sense of irony. Gentile nations, which have no covenant with the Lord, are to participate in the condemnation of Israel. Not only will they observe violence and oppression occurring in the center of Samaria, they will also notice that the people of God's own covenant do not even know how to do what is honest. The sense of guilt could hardly be stated in any stronger way.

3:9 Amos views the "citadels" (v. 9) as symbols of human might in opposition to God (1:4, 6, 10, 12, 14; 2:2, 5; 3:10, 11; 6:8). Israel also has her citadels, but they are storehouses of plunder taken by murderous violence (3:10). Once again the effect is to heighten the irony. The messengers are to stand on the tops of heathen citadels and proclaim a message of the guilt stored up in the strongholds of God's own covenant people.

Incidentally, the commands are rhetorical and not meant to be carried out literally. The effect lends much more vividness to the scene than a simple statement that even the Gentile nations would know Israel was guilty of inhumane actions.

The city of Samaria itself is located on a large hill, which Amos calls "the mountain of Samaria" (4:1; 6:1; see also Additional Notes). There are also hills all around the city, with those to the east higher than Samaria's mound. The prophet envisions the nations gathering on these hills to observe what happens in Samaria.

---

[25] Hayes, *Amos*, pp. 127-28.

The "tumults" (מְהוּמֹת, *mĕhûmōt*) indicate confusion and disorder. Sometimes the Lord sent confusion on an enemy army as a means of fighting for Israel (Zech 14:13). Here the reference is to the tumult caused among the poor because of their oppressors. Violence and extortion leaves the community in an uproar. Wolff has a forceful translation, "the boundless terror," giving as parallels Prov. 15:16 and Ezek. 22:5.[26] The Proverbs passage evidently means it is better to have only a little while living a righteous life before the Lord than to get rich through means that create terror among the people.[27] Many commentators interpret the proverb with F. Delitzsch, "[*mĕhûmâ*] is restless, covetous care and trouble,"[28] but everywhere else the term occurs in a context of violence.

עֲשׁוּקִים (*'ăšûqîm*) is often taken as "oppressions" (NASB and NIV), but it means more specifically extortion or the gain of money or property through unjust or dishonest practices. NASB translates the related verb *'āšaq* as "extorted" in Lev. 6:2 (MT 5:21) and the derived noun *'āšaq* as "extortion" in Lev. 6:4 (MT 5:23). The root is also associated with robbery (Deut. 28:29; 1 Sam. 12:3; Jer. 21:12; Ezek. 18:18; 22:29), bribery (Eccles. 7:7; Ezek. 22:12), false balances (Hos. 12:7 [MT 12:8]), and unfair wages (Mal. 3:5).

3:10 חָמָס (*ḥāmās*, "violence") sometimes has a more general meaning of unrighteousness or lawlessness (e.g., Gen. 6:11; 16:5; Mal. 2:15).[29] Amos normally refers to specific instances of unrighteousness, however, and the same Hebrew term can occur in conjunction with "bloodshed" (Jer. 51:35; Ezek. 7:23; 9:9; Hab. 2:8). Possibly "violence and devastation [שֹׁד, *šōd*]" should be considered a joined pair (hendiadys) meaning the plundering of other people's possessions through violent or unlawful methods. The translation above follows NIV, which seems to express the general idea, "who hoard plunder and loot in their fortresses." However, the "plunder and loot" was not gained through warfare but through violence against the poor. Some irony may be involved as well. The fortresses will themselves be violently devastated as punishment for injustice, so the people hoard in them the seeds of their own destruction.

Additional Notes

3:9 בְּאַשְׁדּוֹד: LXX has "Assyria" (adopted by JB). The scribes could easily have confused *daleth* and *resh*. Assyria makes a better parallel with Egypt in that both were major powers. Also, Assyria accomplished much of what Amos predicted. Therefore it is easier to explain how a scribe might have unconsciously

---

[26] Wolff, *Joel and Amos*, pp. 190, 193.

[27] Cf. A. Cohen, *Proverbs*, Soncino Books of the Bible (London: Soncino, 1980), p. 98.

[28] F. Delitzsch, *Proverbs, Ecclesiastes, Song of Solomon* (COTTV 6, pt. 1; Grand Rapids: Eerdmans, 1973), p. 325; cf. William McKane, *Proverbs* (OTL; Philadelphia: Westminster, 1970), pp. 486-87.

[29] Cf. U. Cassuto, *A Commentary on the Book of Genesis*, trans. Israel Abrahams (Jerusalem: Magnes, 1972), 2:52-53.

altered the reading "Ashdod" into "Assyria." Intrinsic probability, therefore, supports the MT.[30]

הָרֵי שֹׁמְרוֹן: Wolff objects that the surrounding mountains are not close enough to see from them what is going on in the city. Therefore he adopts the reading "mountain of Samaria" found in the LXX.[31] Amos is hardly concerned with the practicalities of the situation, however. Surely many foreign merchants had observed the oppressed poor in Samaria, and he merely calls on them in a figurative sense to surround the city and witness its crimes. LXX was probably influenced by the singular elsewhere in Amos (4:1; 6:1).

C. Announcement Of Judgment (3:11-15)

Translation

> Therefore, thus says the Lord Yahweh:
> "An enemy *will surround the land
> and pull down from you your strength.
> Then your citadels will be plundered."
> [12]Thus says Yahweh:
> "Just as the shepherd snatches from the lion's mouth
>   two legs or a piece of an ear,
> so the sons of Israel shall be delivered,
>   who sit in Samaria
>   at the side of a bed
>   and at the corner of a *couch."
> [13]"Listen! Then testify against the house of Jacob."
> (This is) the solemn declaration of the *Lord Yahweh, God of the hosts.
> [14]"For in the day when I punish
> the transgressions of Israel,
> then I will punish the altars of Bethel.
> So the horns of the altar will be cut off
> and fall to the ground.
> [15]Also I will strike down the winter house
> together with the summer house.
> Indeed the houses decorated with ivory will perish,
> and the mansions will come to an end."
> (This is) the solemn declaration of Yahweh.

Exegesis and Exposition

In common with other major sections of Amos, the present "word" (3:1) ends with a statement of judgment. After establishing Israel's guilt, the various pronouncements in the remainder of the chapter include threats against the land (3:11), the people (3:12), the altars at Bethel (3:13-14), and the luxurious houses built by the rich (3:15). This prophecy of complete devastation fits well the charges of injustice against Israel. Even as the citadels and temples of Israel were filled

---

[30] Cf. Wolff, *Joel and Amos*, p. 189 n. c.

[31] Ibid., p. 190 n. d.

with evidence of violence and robbery, so would those same structures be plundered by an enemy. Moreover the people would die a violent death, their fine houses perishing with them.

3:11 The Hebrew reads literally, "an enemy and the surrounding of the land." The translation gives the general sense (cf. NIV, Peshitta, and Targum). NASB attempts a more literal translation, "An enemy, even one surrounding the land," but "one surrounding" would require a participle. Technically, "surrounding" can be viewed as a nominalization (an action expressed as a noun). The expression evidently gives the announcement more of a shocking sense: "An enemy! And a surrounding of the land!"[32]

Even the term enemy is not without some difficulty. A homonym in Hebrew means "distress," and the Peshitta and Targum followed this sense. The remainder of the verse, however, makes the theme of enemy invasion plain enough. The enemy will do away with all the defenses of Israel, permitting her citadels to be plundered. How useless it was for the nation to trust in outward defenses when her inward condition was of greater importance.

3:12a Amos's tone is sarcastic in v. 12. Perhaps some wondered whether the Lord would not deliver His people in battle as He had done so often in the past. "Yes, He will," says Amos, "but not in the way you expect. A shepherd might be able to snatch a couple of legs or a piece of an ear out of a lion's mouth, but what good is that? The animal is already dead. In the same way shall you Israelites be delivered!" Compare the evidence required of a shepherd to prove that an animal had fallen prey to a wild beast (Ex. 22:10-13).

3:12b The concluding phrase of v. 12 is one of the most difficult in the book. All the words are fairly clear except that translated here as "corner" (דְמֶשֶׁק, dĕmešeq). Superficially it resembles the word for Damascus, and many of the ancient versions translated it that way (LXX, Targum, Peshitta, and Vulg.). The KJV has, "in the corner of a bed, and in Damascus on a couch" (cf. also NIV). Though the passage is difficult, three factors lead us to reject a reference to the city of Damascus.

First, the Jewish scholars who provided the texts with vowels according to traditional synagogue pronunciation (Masoretes) used different vowels and indicated that the consonant śin used in "Damascus" should really be a šin. The same written sign had more than one pronunciation and really represented two different letters or phonemes. Also, Hebrew otherwise doubles the mem for Damascus. Thus, Damascus should be dammeśeq, whereas the text has dĕmešeq. This means that Amos's term is unique in the OT (a hapax legomenon), at least in the MT tradition.[33]

Second, the phrase in question has a parallel structure, which reads as follows (with "X" standing for the term in question): "at the corner of a bed, and at the X

---

[32] Gerhard Pfeifer came to a similar conclusion in "Die Denkform des Propheten Amos (III 9-11)," VT 34 (1984): 481 n. 7.

[33] Though Ebenezer Henderson, The Twelve Minor Prophets: Translated from the original Hebrew with a critical and exegetical commentary (Thornapple Commentaries; Grand Rapids: Baker, 1980), p. 144, points out that some Hebrew manuscripts do have דְמֶשֶׁק (dammeśeq).

of a couch." An alternate parallel structure is suggested in the NIV (cf. KJV): "in Samaria on the edge of their beds, and in Damascus on their couches."[34] In this case, the preposition *b* ("on") would govern the noun in both halves of the line. Diagrammatically, the two suggestions are as follows:

A.   *hayyôšĕbîm bĕšōmĕrôn*   A - B
        bipĕ'at miṭṭâ   C - D
        ubidĕmešeq 'āreś   C' – D'
B.   *hayyôšĕbîm bĕšōmĕrôn bipĕ'at miṭṭâ*   A - B - C - D
        ubidĕmešeq 'āreś   B' – D'

The pattern given by "A" seems more balanced. Also, some have noted that the two phrases about beds may parallel the two phrases about "rescued" body parts.[35]

Finally, Amos speaks about the inhabitants of Samaria in chap. 3. It would seem strange for him to mention the people of Damascus without any apparent motivation, even if there were some Israelites living there (cf. 1 Kings 20:34). In the prophecies against the nations, Amos kept Damascus and Israel quite distinct. Possibly Amos could be referring to some Israelite merchants who lived in Damascus (cf. 1 Kings 20:34; 2 Kings 14:28)[36] or to Damascus as a place of exile,[37] but still the passage as a whole seems to have its focus on Samaria.

Many modern commentaries take *dĕmešeq* to mean a type of material. From the context something associated with a bed, such as a cover or some part of a bed, must be meant. Many etymologies or textual emendations have been proposed, none of which is completely convincing.[38] Some think of the material known as damask (Keil). However, for historical and etymological reasons we must reject this view, as well as Mays's idea that the bed comes from Damascus.[39]

Aside from the controversy about the unique term, it is still important to ask what the phrase means in its setting. In light of the criticisms Amos makes of the luxurious lifestyle of the people (esp. 6:1-7), he probably intends to show them perishing suddenly while living lavishly, sprawled on beds and couches (cf. 6:4). Others suggest that all that remains of the luxuries of the Israelites is a small piece of a bed or couch.[40]

3:13 The prophet once again summons the witnesses (of v. 9) to give their testimony. Mays gives a good explanation of the connection: The role of the witnesses "is not to bring evidence, but to hear and be the guarantors of the court's verdict."[41]

---

[34] Cf. also ibid.; Hayes, *Amos*, pp. 134-35.

[35] Smith, *Amos*, p. 123. But see also Hayes, *Amos*, p. 135, for contrary arguments.

[36] Henderson, *The Twelve Minor Prophets*, p. 144; Thomas Edward McComiskey, "Amos," in *EBC*, ed. Frank E. Gaebelein (Grand Rapids: Zondervan, 1985), 7:301.

[37] Hayes, *Amos*, p. 135.

[38] Wolff has a long note on the subject (*Joel and Amos*, pp. 196-97 n. b.).

[39] Keil, *Minor Prophets*, p. 264. Mays has to reverse the order of the Hebrew words (*Amos*, p. 66).

[40] Henderson, *The Twelve Minor Prophets*, p. 144; Smith, *Amos*, p. 123.

[41] Mays, *Amos*, pp. 68-69.

When Amos addresses Israel as "the sons of Jacob," he emphasizes the covenant relationship of the whole people of God, even as he had done previously by calling them "the entire family which I brought up" (3:1).

Amos loves to use a variety of names for God. Verse 13 contains one of them: הַצְּבָאוֹת אֱלֹהֵי יהוה אֲדֹנָי (*'ădōnāy YHWH 'elōhê haṣṣĕbā'ôt*, "the Lord Yahweh, God of the hosts"). Others are Yahweh (1:2), the Lord (i.e., *'ădōnāy*; 7:7), the Lord Yahweh (1:8), Yahweh the God of hosts (4:13), Yahweh the God of hosts, the Lord (5:16), Yahweh whose name is the God of hosts (5:27), the Lord Yahweh of hosts (9:5), and Yahweh your God (9:15).

Every instance of "the Lord God" or of "the LORD God" in NASB represents Hebrew *'ădōnāy YHWH* (Lord Yahweh), regardless of whether it is noted in the margin. The Masoretic tradition follows the synagogue reading of *YHWH* as *'ădōnāy* ("Lord"), except in the combination *'ădōnāy YHWH*, which was read as *'ădōnāy 'ĕlōhîm* ("Lord GOD" in mo st English versions).

The precise significance of "hosts" is uncertain. In the divine epithet it might signify either the angelic armies of heaven or possibly everything that fills heaven and earth (cf. Gen. 2:1). The translators of the NIV render *YHWH Ṣĕbā'ôt* as "the LORD Almighty," in that they take the Hebrew to mean "he who is sovereign over all the 'hosts' (powers) in heaven and on earth, especially over the 'hosts' (armies) of Israel" (Preface). This seems to be a helpful way to bring out the general sense of the Hebrew in English translation.[42]

3:14 Perhaps it seems strange in v. 14 for Amos to introduce Bethel into a judgment dealing with the city of Samaria.[43] As Amaziah the priest of Bethel declared, however, the city was closely associated with the kingdom of Samaria as "a sanctuary of the king and a royal residence" (Amos 7:13). It was one of the two cities where Jeroboam I placed a golden calf (1 Kings 12:26-29). It is instructive that Amos uses the word "house," contained in Bethel as "house of God" (*bêt-'ēl*), to structure his prediction of judgment. Disaster will befall the "house of God" (Bethel), the "winter house together with the summer house" (v. 15), the "houses of ivory," and the "great houses."[44]

The combination of Samaria and Bethel also serves to focus on a major theme of the book of Amos. In Samaria the witnesses saw violence and oppression, whereas at Bethel there were altars. Amos proclaims that religious observance alone cannot please the Lord; it must be accompanied by justice. Bethel symbolized how the people relied on their religion, which could not save them from divine wrath.

A fine example of a horned altar (הַמִּזְבֵּחַ קַרְנוֹת, *qarnôt hammizbēaḥ*, "the horns of the altar") was discovered in excavations at Beersheba.[45] The horns were large enough for a person to grasp when he needed sanctuary (1 Kings 1:50; 2:28).

---

[42] Kenneth L. Barker, "YHWH Sabaoth: '*The Lord Almighty*'," in *The NIV: The Making of a Contemporary Translation*, ed. Kenneth L. Barker (Grand Rapids: Zondervan, 1986), pp. 109-10.

[43] Cf. Wolff, *Joel and Amos*, p. 199 n. b.

[44] Cf. Mays, *Amos*, p. 69.

[45] A picture is given in B. Boyd, "Beer-sheba," in *IDBSup*, p. 94.

Moses designated the altar as a place of asylum but not for sheltering a murderer (Ex. 21:13-14). Amos singles out the altar not only because it was a place of false and ineffective worship, but also because it was the only place where the people could hope for any refuge.[46]

3:15 As implied by v. 15, Israel has two seasons. The summer (קָיִץ, *qayiṣ*) runs from about mid-May to mid-September and is warm and mostly dry. The winter (חֹרֶף, *ḥōrep*) is cool and rainy, though there can also be periods of sunny and warm weather.[47] Snow sometimes occurs in the higher elevations, such as at Bethel, but this would be unlikely in the city of Samaria itself. Ahab had a palace at Jezreel (1 Kings 21:1), in the warmer plain, as well as at Samaria (1 Kings 21:18). The use of two residences shows the great wealth in Israel.[48]

Numerous ivory plaques and fragments, some of them probably dating from the eighth century B.C., have been discovered through archaeological investigation at Samaria. N. Avigad explains their presence: "the ivories are considered as products of Phoenician art, and they were probably used as inlays in the palace furniture of the Israelite kings."[49] "Houses of ivory" (בָּתֵּי הַשֵּׁן, *bāttê haššēn*) then, most likely means houses containing such furniture. The Targum interpreted the houses themselves to be "inlaid with ivory" (מכבשין בשין דפיל, *mĕkabbĕšîn bĕšēn dĕpîl*). As an imported product ivory would have been quite expensive.

Hebrew רַב (*rab*) can mean "many," but the translation "great houses" or "mansions" is preferred because of the parallel with "houses of ivory." Amos does not mean that beautiful and fine houses are inherently evil. But the Israelites obtained the money for them, as he makes plain more than once (e.g., 2:6-8; 3:9-10), through oppression, unfair practices, and even violence. The lavish houses stand as monuments to injustice and selfishness.

Additional Notes

3:11 וּסְבִיב: Because the Targum and Peshitta translate "will surround," some have emended the text to יְסוֹבֵב.[50] This would involve the interchange of *waw* and *yod*, a common scribal error in Hebrew. However, the LXX read the text as is, even though an awkward sense resulted: "Tyre and from all around your land shall be laid waste." The reading "Tyre" (צֹר) results from reading צָר ("enemy") with a different vowel.

3:12 עָרֶשׂ: It might seem at first glance that LXX, with ἱερεῖς ("priests"), must represent a different text. However, as Wolff shows, it is probably simply an inner-Greek corruption from a transliteration of the Hebrew.[51]

---

[46] Cf. Wolff, *Joel and Amos*, p. 201.

[47] Cf. D. Baly, "Season," *ISBE*, rev. ed., 4:375-76.

[48] See also King, *Archaeological Commentary*, pp. 64-65.

[49] Avigad, "Samaria," in *Encyclopedia of Archaeological Excavations in the Holy Land*, 4 vols., ed. Michael Avi-Yonah (Englewood Cliffs, N.J.: Prentice-Hall, 1975-1978), 4:1046; cf. also King, *Archaeological Commentary*, p. 139.

[50] Cf. Wolff, *Joel and Amos*, p. 191 n. l.

[51] Ibid., pp. 196-97 n. b.

3:13 אֲדֹנָי יהוה אֱלֹהֵי הַצְּבָאוֹת: When Amos inserts "God" between "Yahweh" and "hosts" he deviates from the more usual title "Yahweh of hosts." Besides the eight instances in Amos of the longer form (3:13; 4:13; 5:14, 15, 16, 27; 6:8, 14) it occurs only in 2 Samuel (5:10), 1 Kings (19:10, 14), Psalms (e.g., 89:9), Jeremiah (e.g. 5:14), and Hosea (12:6).

"Yahweh God of hosts" may represent a more original form that eventually gave way to the shortened "Yahweh of hosts," thus explaining the syntactical connection between יהוה and צְבָאוֹת. Note that Amos, Hosea, and Elijah (quoted in 1 Kings 19:10, 14) are all relatively early prophets. Jeremiah is later, but he may have used the older phrase in an archaizing type of language. The passage from 2 Samuel may also be quite early. The shorter form may have already been in vogue before these prophets, who preferred the older name (cf. Samuel's use of "Yahweh of hosts," 1 Sam. 15:2). The Psalms that use the longer form are variously ascribed to David (59), Asaph (80), the sons of Korah (84), and Heman the Ezrahite (88).

The LXX lacks an equivalent for אֲדֹנָי. See Additional Notes on 1:8.

5
Failure to Repent
(4:1-13)

The theme of the rich living carefree on the money obtained unfairly from the oppressed continues into the second "word" (4:1-3). Then Amos picks up the idea that sacrifice or religious worship is fruitless in the face of such living (4:4-5), and he concludes his accusations against Israel by recounting their repeated failure to respond despite God's gracious attempts to bring them to repentance (4:6-11). In the end, according to Amos, Israel must prepare to meet her Creator (4:12-13), not as a merciful God but as an awesome Judge.

The threefold pattern of accusations in chap. 4 repeats that of chap. 2. There also Amos dealt first with social injustice and how it was combined with religious practices that were offensive to the Lord (2:6-8), and he finished with how the Israelites spurned God's gracious dealings with them (2:9-12).

A. The Carefree Attitude Of Israel (4:1-3)

Translation

> Hear this word,
> you cows of Bashan who are on the mountain of Samaria,
> who oppress the poor,
> who crush the needy,
> who say *to their husbands,
>   "Bring now something for us to drink!"
> [2]The Lord Yahweh has sworn by His holiness:
> "*Behold! Days will come upon you
> when they *will take you away with meat hooks,
>   even the last of you with fish hooks.
> [3]Each of you will exit straightway through the breaches,
>   and *you will be cast to *Harmon."
> (This is) the *solemn declaration of Yahweh.

Exegesis and Exposition

In this section Amos first condemns the Israelite women for the high living that has been made possible by their oppression of the poor. A vivid picture of well-fed cows occurs alongside a scene where women ask their husbands to bring them something to drink. The image is therefore one of complete satisfaction, yet Amos's accusation rings out: "who oppress the poor, who crush the needy." Consequently he predicts that these women will be led away into exile in complete disgrace.

4:1a The threefold repetition of "hear this word" (3:1; 4:1; 5:1) signals, each time, the start of a new section. There does not seem to be any good explanation for the lack of the Hebrew object marker (אֵת, 'et) in v. 1, since it does occur with the other two instances of the command. It can be omitted in poetic texts, and 4:1 is more characteristically poetic than the other two passages (note format in *BHS*).

Bashan, the northernmost part of Israel, east of the Jordan River and north of the Yarmuk River, consists of a fertile tableland and a mountain range known as Mount Hauran (Ezek. 47:16, 18) or Mount Bashan (Ps. 68:15 [MT 68:16]). The well-watered mountains, which rise more than 5,000 feet, protect the tableland from the desert. The Mount Hermon range forms the northern border.[1]

The Biblical writers sometimes compare Bashan and Carmel for their fertility (Isa. 33:9; Jer. 50:19; Nah. 1:4), and Bashan is also noted for its oak trees (Isa. 2:13; Ezek. 27:6; Zech. 11:2). The pastures are so lush that various types of cattle and sheep can grow fat and strong there (Ps. 22:12 [MT 22:13]; Jer. 50:19; Ezek. 39:18; Micah 7:14).

When Amos addresses the women of Samaria as "cows of Bashan," then, he refers to their luxurious and comfortable living. Interpreters mostly understand Amos to be singling out the wealthy women in Samaria, but the female element may also be figurative, making it the wealthy of Israel who were trampling the poor and, therefore, included in the condemnation. According to this interpretation, the subsequent reference to "husbands" would be part of the image. Under Jeroboam II Israel was enjoying its most prosperous times ever. However, as Amos is quick to point out, the prosperity did not reach everyone.

Some have preferred to see a figure for idolatrous worship behind the phrase "cows of Bashan." That is, the Israelites are depicted as worshipers of a cow, possibly as a female counterpart to the worship of the Lord as a bull (or as enthroned upon a bull; cf. the golden calves set up by Jeroboam I [1 Kings 12:28-29]).[2] This view is somewhat speculative, but more importantly it does not fit well with Amos's clear pronouncements against those who oppress the poor. The scene is one of luxury, not worship.

In OT times Samaria was a city situated on a high hill overlooking the valley below. Only later does "Samaria" mean a province, as in the NT. Previously Amos referred to the hills that surround the valley (3:9). Twice he refers to the city itself as "the mountain of Samaria" (also 6:1).

4:1b-c The series of four descriptions following the reference to "cows of Bashan" (v. 1) culminates with a request made to their husbands, "Bring now, that we may drink!" The juxtaposition with the two previous lines about oppression and the crushing of the poor and needy makes it clear that the final scene represents a morally evil situation. What might be taken to be an innocent domestic scene becomes deplorable, because it stems from horrible crimes against helpless people.

---

[1] Cf. Yohanan Aharoni, *The Land of the Bible: A Historical Geography*, rev. ed., trans. A. F. Rainey (Philadelphia: Westminster, 1979), pp. 37-38.

[2] See Hans M. Barstad, *The Religious Polemics of Amos* (VTSup 34; Leiden: E. J. brill, 1984) 37-44; A. J. Williams, "A Further Suggestion about Amos IV 1-3," *VT* 29 (1979): 209-11; Paul F. Jacobs, " 'Cows of Bashan'--A Note on the Interpretation of Amos 4:1," *JBL* 104 (1985): 109-10.

In fact, even the domestic situation itself flaunts societal norms; the women order their husbands about, even though the unusual word used for "husband" (אָדֹן, 'ādōn, "lord") would seem to belie the facts.[3] The women and their husbands live well only because poor people have been crushed to the ground.

"Oppress" (עָשַׁק, 'āšaq) and "crush" (רָצַץ, rāṣaṣ) often occur together in reference to social injustice (Deut. 28:33; 1 Sam 12:3). Through various forms of extortion and unfair tactics the women were able to live like well-fed cows. The poor and the needy thus formed a class of oppressed people in Samaria, and their distress is the real cause for the prosperity of the city.

'ādōn can mean "lord," "master," "owner," but also "husband," as here (cf. Gen 18:12). It is at least suggestive that the rare word for husband is also applied to the Lord in the next verse. Does Amos mean to imply that the rich Israelites have made themselves wealthy by plundering their less fortunate neighbors and now call to the Lord to provide them with even more luxury? Such a thought seems too gross even for Amos's bold accusations, but compare the incredible words of the merchants who cannot wait for the Sabbath to be over so they can extort more money (8:4-6).

4:2 God, who cannot swear by anyone or anything greater than Himself, swears by "My holiness" (v. 2). Writers other than Amos say He swears "by Myself" (Gen. 22:16), "by His right hand and by His strong arm" (Isa. 62:8), and "by My great name" (Jer. 44:26). Amos uses three expressions for God's oath, "by My holiness," "by Himself" (6:8), and "by the pride of Jacob" (8:7).

The holiness of God demands purity of life, a key element of which is compassion and generous treatment of others (cf. esp. Lev. 25). The aristocratic citizens of Samaria presented quite an opposite picture. Their hands were stained with blood and oppression, but they glibly continued to live in selfish disregard for the plight of others.

Wolff takes the conjunction כִּי (kî) in v. 2 as emphatic.[4] However, it may simply mark the content of the Lord's oath; if so, it is best left untranslated. הִנֵּה (hinnēh, usually translated "behold," often serves before a participle to give the sense of the imminent future.[5]

Since the verb וְנִשָּׂא (wĕniśśā) is singular, the translation "they will take away" is not immediately obvious. "He will take away" is possible but does not seem likely. The only person to which it could refer is the Lord, but then the direct speech would be mixed with the introductory statement. LXX, Targum, Peshitta, and the modern versions have a plural verb. The grammatical justification is a rule that a singular verb can be used for an "impersonal" construction, that is, a sentence with an indefinite or unspecified subject.[6] The English equivalent can be framed

---

[3] Cf. Gary V. Smith, *Amos: A Commentary* (Library of Biblical Interpretation; Grand Rapids: Zondervan, 1989), pp. 128-29.

[4] Hans Walter Wolff, *Joel and Amos* (Hermeneia; trans. Waldemar Janzen, et al. (Philadelphia: Fortress, 1977), p. 203 n. e.

[5] Cf. GKC, par. 116p.

[6] Ibid., par. 144b.

either with a plural "they" or in the passive (cf. JB, "when you will be dragged out"; see also Additional Notes).

The meaning of צִנּוֹת (ṣinnôt) is problematic. The versions relied on the fairly well-attested meaning of "shields." Consider the Targum, noting how the translator made the subject explicit, "And the nations shall carry you on their shields" (cf. NEB).[7] This, however, does not give a probable meaning in the context.

The principle of parallelism in Hebrew poetry leads us to the next phrase for clues. The last word is fairly clear; דּוּגָה (dûgâ) means "fish." Moreover, the term סִיר (sîr), in the form sîrîm (masculine plural) sometimes means "thorns" (Eccles. 7:6; Isa. 34:13; Hos. 2:8; Nah. 1:10), as apparently does ṣinnîm, a masculine plural form related to ṣinnôt. The BDB lexicon then arrives at the meaning "hooks" for both sîrôt and ṣinnôt by comparison with a third word, חוֹח (ḥôaḥ), which can mean either "bramble" or "hook."

This line of reasoning has some validity but does not inspire confidence that certainty has been attained.[8] At any rate, according to this view, the captives are taken away with hooks, probably in their noses. As J. Alberto Soggin says, "the women, accustomed always to being served and doing little or nothing, are now led off as though they were cattle, with rings in their noses."[9] Another idea is that the corpses of the women will be lifted up with hooks,[10] though v. 3 seems to imply that the women exit the city alive.

The meaning of אַחֲרִיתְכֶן ('aḥărîtĕken) is also difficult. Suggestions include "your posterity" (BDB lexicon), "the last of you" (NIV, NASB, cf. JB), or "your backside" (KB lexicon). Wolff rejects the rare sense of "backside" because it would require emendation of 'etĕkem ("you") to אַפְּכֶן ('appĕken, "your face"; cf. note in BHS) to make a better parallel and would be contrary to Amos's usage of the term elsewhere (8:10; 9:1).[11] Perhaps these are not insurmountable objections, but the only other parallel usage cited in the KB lexicon is Ps. 139:9 ("the remotest part of the sea"). NEB has, "when men shall carry you away on their shields and your children in fish-baskets." However, the instances of 'aḥărît listed under the meaning "posterity" in the BDB lexicon imply more the concept of descendants than children (Ps. 37:37, 38; 109:13; Dan. 11:4).

As was mentioned above, the term סִירוֹת (sîrôt) probably means "fish hooks," though others have suggested gaffs or harpoons to prod the women as they march to Assyria.[12] This view could support taking 'aḥărît as "backside," but Wolff has, "and your remnant (prodded) with harpoons."[13] The difficulties of the passage can be

---

[7] ויטלון יתכון עממיא על תריסיהון (wĕyiṭṭĕlûn yātĕkôn 'amĕmayyā' 'al tārîsêhôn).

[8] Cf. A. J. Williams, "Amos IV 1-3," pp. 208-9.

[9] Soggin, The Prophet Amos; A Translation and Commentary, trans. John Bowden (London: SCM, 1987), p. 68.

[10] John H. Hayes, Amos, The Eighth-Century Prophet: His Times and His Preaching (Nashville: Abingdon, 1988), p. 141.

[11] Wolff, Joel and Amos, p. 204 n. i.

[12] Soggin, The Prophet Amos, p. 68; Douglas Stuart, Hosea-Jonah (WBC 31; Waco, Tex.: Word, 1987), p. 328. Stuart takes אַחֲרִית ('aḥărît) as "remains," that is, the corpses.

[13] Wolff, Joel and Amos, p. 204.

appreciated by comparing the translation given in LXX: "They shall take you with weapons, and fiery destroyers shall cast those who are with you into kettles heated from below."[14]

4:3 When Amos says "you will go out," he implies that the people are alive when they exit the city. As Wolff points out, "each one straight before her" (נֶגְדָּהּ אִשָּׁה, 'iššâ negdāh) corresponds to the situation at the fall of Jericho (Josh. 6:5, 20): "Just as in that story, after the collapse of the city walls of Jericho every Israelite could enter 'straight ahead,' directly into the city, so now every woman of Samaria must leave by the shortest and fastest route."[15] The "breaches" (פְּרָצִים, pĕrāsîm) would evidently be those made by a battering ram.[16] According to Hayes the pĕrāsîm are bloated corpses, but the noun is masculine.[17]

Modern translators normally follow renderings of וְהִשְׁלַכְתֶּנָה הַהַרְמוֹנָה (wĕhišlaktena haharmônâ, "and you will be cast to Harmon") found in the ancient versions. The text has some difficulties (see Additional Notes) that make it hard to determine the precise meaning. If we assume that MT has the correct reading, Harmon is some unknown geographic location. James Mays sums up what is most certain from the passage: "The women whose present is enriched by the suffering of the poor have a future more terrible than the agony of the needy."[18]

Additional Notes

4:1 לַאֲדֹנֵיהֶם: The masculine suffix refers obliquely to the women. Many parallels to the use of masculine plural forms for either gender exist, however, so there is no need to emend the text (cf. GKC, par. 135o). The masculine form is also used for the initial imperative verb (cf. GKC, par. 145p) and for two phrases with pronouns in v. 2 (עֲלֵיכֶם and אֶתְכֶם). The third person is used despite the vocative sense of the noun ("cows of Bashan") because the additional phrases simply modify it. Presumably the NASB and the NIV have altered one or more pronouns to the second person ("your husbands") to make the translation conform more with English usage (a practice referred to in the Preface to the NIV). The ancient versions all support the Hebrew text.

4:2 בְּקָדְשׁוֹ: Examples of the Lord swearing by His own attributes are rare. An additional instance of swearing by His holiness occurs in Ps. 89:35 [MT 89:36], a psalm that also indicates the attribute of faithfulness in connection with the oath made to David (v. 49 [MT v. 50]). In Ps. 95:11 wrath accompanies God's oath, but

---

[14] λήμψονται ὑμᾶς ἐν ὅπλοις, καὶ τοὺς μεθ᾽ ὑμῶν εἰς λέβητας ὑποκαιομένους ἐμβαλοῦσιν ἔμπυροι λοιμοί (lēmpsontai hymas en hoplois, kai tou meth᾽ hymōn eis lebētas hypokaiomenous embalousin empyroi loimoi).

[15] Wolff, *Joel and Amos*, p. 207.

[16] Philip J. King, *Amos, Hosea, Micah – An Archaeological Commentary* (Philadelphia: Westminster, 1988), p. 73.

[17] Hayes, *Amos*, p. 141. Hayes notes that masculine forms interchange with feminine forms in the passage, but the lack of gender agreement still adds to the semantic difficulty (elsewhere *pĕrāṣîm* are normally "breaches" or "outbursts," never bloated corpses).

[18] James Luther Mays, *Amos: A Commentary* (OTL; Philadelphia: Westminster, 1969), p. 73.

there the prepositional phrase with *beth* is temporal because it describes historical events (Num. 14:23, 28-30; Deut. 1:34-35). Hence the common translation gives the correct sense, "I swore in My wrath" (i.e., "when I was angry").

כִּי הִנֵּה: Two other combinations with הִנֵּה are גַּם הִנֵּה and עַתָּה הִנֵּה. The former tends to occur in a sentence that has no verb (with a form of "to be" as understood; Gen. 32:21), while the latter occurs in a past context with a verb in the perfect. A paradigm could then be set up as follows:

1. immediate future – כִּי הִנֵּה + participle;
2. present or descriptive – גַּם הִנֵּה + noun phrase;
3. past – עַתָּה הִנֵּה + perfect.

An exception occurs in Amos 4:13, where כִּי הִנֵּה introduces a participle used as a noun ("He who forms," etc.). In Ex. 4:14 גַּם הִנֵּה occurs before a participle, but the action is present progressive ("he is coming") rather than future. The use of גַּם rather than כִּי may help to stress this.

וְנִשָּׂא: The piel pattern for this term with the meaning "take away" would be unique (2 Sam. 19:43 is also problematic), but with other roots the piel can be used for a "privative" ("away") sense (cf. also שָׁלַח, "send away").[19] The vowel *qamets* in נִשָּׂא is probably due to assimilation to the pattern of *lamedh-he* verbs (GKC, par. 75 nn). Wolff prefers to take the verb as niphal (a possibility also raised in GKC).[20] The form overlaps the active, and the presence of the object marker is not an overwhelming objection.[21] However, the disagreement between subject and verb then becomes very difficult to explain.

4:3 וְהִשְׁלַכְתֶּנָה: The verb has a unique feminine ending for the perfect, though the subject pronoun אַתֶּנָה is similar in form.[22] More difficult is that an active form (hiphil) occurs instead of an expected passive, as in the LXX and the Peshitta. It hardly seems possible that the women will cast something away. Therefore, it is probably best to take the reading as a *hophal* passive by changing one vowel (resulting in *wĕhošlaktena* or *wĕhušlaktena*).

הַהַרְמוֹנָה: Suggested textual emendations include reading it as Mt. Hermon (חֶרְמוֹן; Wolff), "on a dunghill" (NEB, Hayes), or "from the palace" (Henderson).[23] The Targum read "from the mountains of Armenia [חוּרְמִינִי]." This is impossible for historical reasons, but it lends some support to the proposed "Hermon." On the other hand, τὸ ὄρος τὸ Ρεμμαν supports the MT, in that both the article and "mountain" presuppose *he* rather than *heth*. The two best views are to either accept "Harmon" as an unknown place or to emend the text to Mt. Hermon.

---

[19] Ronald J. Williams, *Hebrew Syntax: An Outline*, 2d ed. (Toronto: Univ. of Toronto, 1976), 146.

[20] Wolff, *Joel and Amos*, p. 203 n. g.

[21] See Williams, *Hebrew Syntax*, pp. 13-14, par. 59.

[22] Cf. GKC, par. 44k.

[23] Wolff, *Joel and Amos*, p. 204 n. o.; Hayes, *Amos*, p. 142; Ebenezer Henderson, *The Twelve Minor Prophets*, (Thornapple Commentaries; Grand Rapids: Baker, 1980), p. 147.

נְאָם־יהוה: Rahlf's edition of the LXX has λέγει κύριος ὁ θεός, but the Göttingen edition (ed. J. Ziegler) rejects ὁ θεός, found only in part of the Greek tradition.

B. The Ineffective Religion Of Israel (4:4-5)

Translation

"*Come to Bethel and transgress,
to Gilgal (and) transgress even more!
Yes, bring your sacrifices every morning,
your tithes every three years.
⁵Also *offer up in smoke a thank offering with leaven,
and proclaim freewill offerings, make them known.
For so you love (to do), you sons of Israel,"
declares the Lord Yahweh.

Exegesis and Exposition

At this point Amos once again proclaims how ineffective religion is when based on sacrifice or ritual alone (cf. 2:7-8). He uses irony in a stunning way, giving the Lord's command for the people to enter various cult sanctuaries and thereby "transgress."

Do these verses speak mainly against idolatry and false worship, or do they have a different theme? Of course, Amos as a Judean and true worshiper of Yahweh knew that Jeroboam I had led the northern kingdom astray by setting up golden calves at Bethel and Dan. At first the people evidently thought they were worshiping Yahweh at Bethel under the figure of the calf. It seems unlikely that Jeroboam I would have tried to unify his country by getting the people to abandon the worship of Yahweh entirely. Also, many of the Israelite kings have names compounded with a form of "Yahweh" (Joram/Jehoram, Jehu, Jehoahaz, Jehoash, Zechariah, Pekahiah, Hoshea). Many Israelites failed to understand the finer distinction, however, and the author of Kings and the prophet Hosea rightly regarded worship of these calves as idolatry (2 Kings 17:16; Hos. 8:5-6; 10:5).

Amos also knew that Jerusalem was the correct place to sacrifice (cf. 1:2). The thrust of his book, however, treats violations of laws concerning human relationships. Amos goes deeper than the level of outward form of worship. Amos's point is that any worship is false when the participants are oppressing the poor and helpless. His attitude might be compared with Jesus' teaching in Matt. 6:22-24. The people who worshiped at Bethel considered themselves tied to Yahweh by the covenant. "No," says Amos, "you have severed yourselves from the covenant because you do not keep its provisions."

In another sense Amos does attack idolatry in 4:4-5. Because the inner essence of the covenant was missed, the people were not really worshiping Yahweh; rather, they were sacrificing to a god of their own making, both physically and theologically. Hosea stresses the physical problem, while Amos emphasizes the theological issue.[24]

John Hayes makes some pertinent observations about the passage. First, only voluntary sacrifices are dealt with, not those required for sin and repentance. Second, the meat would be consumed by the worshipers, and the poor were probably unable to participate.[25]

4:4 When the kingdom divided and Jeroboam I became ruler of the northern kingdom, Bethel already had a history as a religious center. Abraham pitched his tent between Bethel and Ai, built an altar, and "called upon the name of Yahweh" (Gen. 12:8). Jacob set up a stone pillar at Bethel, anointed it with oil, and gave the site its name, "House of God" (בֵּית־אֵל, bêt-'ēl; Gen. 28:19). Later, God appeared to Jacob in a dream and said, "I am the God of Bethel, where you anointed a pillar, where you made a vow to Me" (Gen. 31:13). Later still, the prophet Samuel visited Bethel as part of his yearly circuit (1 Sam. 7:16).

The incongruity of the two commands in v. 4 must have greatly impressed Amos's listeners. Since Bethel was a major center of worship for the northern kingdom, the Israelites would have taken the command, "come to Bethel," as an invitation to meet God and seek His favor. If the people had sinned, would it not be possible to appease Him through sacrifices and vows? Amos seems to summon them to this, until the next sound creates a horrible dissonance, "and transgress!" These words denote rebellion against God and His commandments. Bethel, then, is changed from a place of worship to a place to show contempt for God. The irony lies not in the fact that God commands sin, but that an action supposedly aimed to please Him has the opposite effect. When two commands are coordinated in Hebrew, the second often indicates result (compare another well known statement of Amos: "Seek Yahweh and live" (5:6), meaning "seek Yahweh that you may live"). That is, Amos's words have the sense, "Come to Bethel in order to transgress."

The above translation "come to" for בֹּאוּ (bō'û) rather than "enter" (NASB) is designed to obtain a better parallel with the next phrase. Amos uses a common poetic device whereby a verb in one clause carries over in thought to the next. Compare the NIV: "Go to Bethel and sin;/ go to Gilgal and sin yet more."

Gilgal's location has not been pinpointed, but from the early days of Israel's entry into the land it was an important center of worship. The people camped there while preparing to take Jericho. There they set up twelve stones that they had taken from the Jordan (Josh. 4:19-20). Also at Gilgal, Joshua circumcised all the males who had been born during the wilderness wanderings (Josh. 5:2-9), and the people celebrated Passover (Josh. 5:10-12). Gilgal continued to serve as a base of operations during the conquest (Josh. 10:6, 7, 9, 15, 43; 14:6). The site later

---

[24] Cf. Lewis B. Paton, "Did Amos Approve the Calf-Worship at Bethel?" *JBL* 13 (1894): 80-90. For a different view, see Charles L. Feinberg, *The Minor Prophets* (Chicago: Moody, 1976), p. 100.

[25] Hayes, *Amos*, p. 145. Hayes also thinks Bethel and Gilgal were "cult centers for rival political groups," but that involves a number of assumptions that do not seem very likely.

became part of the prophet Samuel's annual circuit (1 Sam. 7:16), and Saul was reaffirmed as king there (1 Sam. 11:14-15).

The translation "transgress even more" follows Wolff, who gives a very forceful rendering. The hiphil of the root רבה (*rbh*) usually has an adverbial sense of increasing an action, and the main verb often follows it as an infinitive.[26]

Hebrew grammar permits several interpretations of the time references in v. 4. One possibility is that Amos depicts worshipers who have just arrived at one of the holy cities. They then follow traditional procedures for carrying out their worship. According to this view, translate: "Bring your sacrifices in the morning [לַבֹּקֶר, *labbōqer*], your tithes on the third day [לִשְׁלֹשֶׁת יָמִים, *lišəlōšet yāmîm*]."[27]

Or Amos may simply indicate the general situation in Israel. That is, "Bring your sacrifices every morning, your tithes every three years." The Law required daily sacrifice (Num. 28:3-4) and a tithe every three years. The Israelites were scrupulous with the details, though they had forgotten the "weightier" aspects of the Law.[28] Strengths of this view are that it agrees with Amos's emphasis on covenant law and that the concluding statement, "for so you love to do," gives the same feeling of a general situation.

Just as לַיּוֹם (*layyôm*, lit. "for the day") can mean "every day" or "daily" (Ex. 29:36, 38; Jer. 37:21), so *labbōqer* ("for the morning") can mean "every morning." The BDB lexicon (p. 517) likewise lists this passage with some others for the rare use of the preposition *lamedh* "to denote the *close* of a period" (Gen. 7:4, 10; Ex. 19:15; 2 Sam. 13:33; 2 Chr. 21:19; Ezra 10:8, 9; Neh. 6:15; Dan. 12:7). The most difficult linguistic issue for the view taken here is the meaning "year" for *yāmîm* (lit., "days"). Probably the closest parallel is the "yearly sacrifice" (זֶבַח הַיָּמִים, *zebaḥ hayyāmîm*) that Samuel's parents brought "from year to year" (*miyyāmîm yāmîmâ*; 1 Sam. 2:19; cf. Lev. 25:29; Judg. 17:10). Perhaps in these instances *yāmîm* stresses the completion of a particular period of time as measured in so many days.

A third interpretation sees the irony in commanding the Israelites to go beyond the requirements of the Law for tithes every third year (Deut. 14:28; 26:12): "Bring your sacrifices every morning,/ Your tithes every three days" (NASB). This view avoids the problem of the rare sense of "year" for "days," but the exaggeration thereby attributed to Amos seems, as S. R. Driver stated it, "somewhat extreme."[29]

4:5 Many commentators think that the command to make a burnt offering from unleavened bread (v. 5) was against the Mosaic Law. Mays, for example, explains that "In later [than Amos] Israelite practice leavened bread could be used in sacred meals except at Passover, but was forbidden as an offering by fire (Lev.

---

[26] Wolff, *Joel and Amos*, p. 208; GKC, par. 114n.

[27] Cf. Wolff, *Joel and Amos*, p. 219.

[28] Cf. Feinberg, *The Minor Prophets*, p. 100.

[29] S. R. Driver, *The Books of Joel and Amos* (CBSC; Cambridge: University, 1907), p. 166. For further discussion in favor of "every three days," see Thomas Edward McComiskey, "Amos," *EBC*, ed. Frank E. Gaebelein (Grand Rapids: Zondervan, 1985), 7:305; and Smith, *Amos*, pp. 142-43.

2.11; 7.11-14)."[30] Mays assumes, incorrectly we believe, that the passage cited from Leviticus represents a later (and therefore non-Mosaic) writing than Amos.

The prohibition against using leaven in a burnt offering applies to the cereal offering (Lev. 2), not to the peace offering (Lev. 7:11-36). Leavened bread was required as part of a thanksgiving offering, a subdivision of the peace offering (Lev. 7:11-15). Leavened bread thus seems to be a distinguishing feature of this offering. The Mosaic commandment does not mention burning of the leavened bread, but a portion of each segment of the offering goes toward a "contribution to Yahweh."[31] The thank offering may be exceptional, then, in that leavened bread could be part of a burnt offering.

As another possibility, "that which is leavened" may have been a technical expression to identify this special offering, and the leavened portion itself was not actually burned (Feinberg). C. F. Keil thinks that leaven in a burnt offering was contrary to the Law, but the people were simply overzealous in their attempt to please the Lord.[32] It would seem strange, though, for Amos to mention something directly prohibited by the laws governing sacrifice as an example of religious zeal.

The term קִטֵּר (qiṭṭēr) occurs most often in Kings and Jeremiah, where the people are condemned either for offering incense on the high places or for sacrificing to foreign gods (e.g., 2 Kings 14:4; Jer. 1:16).[33] In fact, the piel pattern of this verb always, with one exception (1 Sam. 2:16), occurs outside of Amos for illegitimate worship. The hiphil pattern of the same Hebrew root, on the other hand, occurs regularly in the Pentateuch and in Kings and Chronicles for offering incense or burnt sacrifice to the Lord (e.g., Lev. 1:9). Even the hiphil, though, may be used when the verb refers to worshiping foreign gods (cf. 1 Kings 3:3; Hos. 2:15).

A possible grammatical difference emerges from the fact that the piel forms occur in contexts that speak of general situations (cf. 2 Kings 14:4), whereas the hiphil is used for specific occasions (cf. 1 Kings 13:1).[34] Thus, Amos chose the piel, not to stress that the worship was illegitimate, but to give an ironical invitation that applies to the general practice of the Israelites. The alternate explanation, that Amos used the piel because it applied to idolatrous worship, would be against the context, destroying the irony of the situation.[35]

---

[30] Mays, *Amos*, p. 75.

[31] See Gordon J. Wenham, *The Book of Leviticus* (NICOT; Grand Rapids: Eerdmans, 1979), pp. 123-24.

[32] C. F. Keil, *Minor Prophets* (COTTV 10; Grand Rapids: Eerdmans, 1973), p. 272; Feinberg, *The Minor Prophets*, p. 100.

[33] Kjeld Nielsen, *Incense in Ancient Israel* (VTSup 38; Leiden: E. J. Brill, 1986), pp. 57-59, concluded that *qiṭṭēr* and *hiqṭîr* (the hiphil) can mean either "burn incense" or more generally "offer," though the former sense is more common for *hiqṭîr* than for *qiṭṭēr*.

[34] This explanation follows Ernst Jenni, *Das hebräische Pi'el: Syntaktisch-semasiologische Untersuchung einer Verbalform im Alten Testament* (Zurich: EVZ, 1968), pp. 271-72). He mentions some exceptions (1 Kings 3:3; 11:8; 2 Chron. 28:3) where the piel might be expected rather than the hiphil.

[35] But cf. Leonard J. Coppes, *TDOT* 2:796.

The freewill offering (נְדָבָה, *nĕdābâ*) is also a special kind of peace offering. Gordon Wenham describes it as "a spontaneous act of generosity by the worshipper, prompted by God's goodness, e.g., at harvest time (Deut. 16:10)."[36] When an Israelite offered a freewill offering, then, it should have been an outpouring of love for God. Yet as the apostle John taught, centuries later, "the one who does not love his brother whom he has seen, cannot love God whom he has not seen" (1 John 4:20). Amos makes the same point but more indirectly.

Additional Notes

4:4 The LXX interprets the actions as past tense rather than commands, though in the second person (Εἰσήλθατε, ἠνομήσατε, ἐπληθύνατε, ἠνέγκατε). Evidently the translators had difficulty with the extreme irony. As for the change in personal reference, see v. 5, where the LXX took הַשְׁמִיעוּ with אֲהַבְתֶּם but reversed the pronominal elements: ἀπαγγείλατε ὅτι ταῦτα ἠγάπησαν.

4:5 וְקַטֵּר: It is rare for the infinitive absolute to be embedded in a series of imperative forms. *BHS* proposes emending the form to a plural imperative, but Wolff refers to the standard grammars as support for MT.[37] The LXX's ἀνέγνωσαν apparently presupposes a form of קְרָא. With all the unusual drastic departures from MT in these verses, perhaps the *Vorlage* of LXX was damaged or difficult to read.

C. The Unresponsive Position Of Israel (4:6-11)

Translation

"Now I for my part have given to you
teeth with nothing to chew in all your cities
and lack of bread in all your districts,
but still you have not returned to Me,"
declares Yahweh.
[7]"Moreover I withheld the rain from you
while three months remained until the harvest.
Then I would send rain on one city,
while on another city I would not send rain.
One portion would receive rain,
but a portion without rain would dry up.
[8]Thus, (the people of) two or three cities would stagger
to another city to drink water,
but they would not get enough.
Still you have not returned to Me,"
declares Yahweh.
[9]"I struck you with *blight and mildew.
The *increase of your gardens, your vineyards,
your fig and olive trees the locust would devour.

---

[36] Wenham, *Leviticus*, p. 79.
[37] Wolff, *Joel and Amos*, p. 290 n. a.

Still you have not returned to Me,"
declares Yahweh.
[10]"I sent out among you a plague after the manner of Egypt.
I slew with the sword your young men,
along with your *captured horses,
making the stench of your camps go into your nostrils.
Still you have not returned to Me,"
declares Yahweh.
[11]"I overthrew some of you
as God overthrew Sodom and Gomorrah,
so that you were like a log snatched from a blaze.
Still you have not returned to Me,"
declares Yahweh.

Exegesis and Exposition

After describing the sins of the elite of Israel against the poor and oppressed, Amos pointed out with biting sarcasm the ineffectiveness of ritual worship as a substitute for justice and compassion: "Come to Bethel and transgress!" Now he turns to God's graciousness in the situation.

Actually, the grace of God in this case consists of a series of seven minor judgments, grouped into five pericopes, against portions of Israel. These were calculated to move the people to repentance so as to avoid the overwhelming disaster that would destroy the nation. That final judgment will consist of a direct encounter with God (4:12-13). The consistent refusal of Israel to repent made the threat of that fateful meeting inevitable.

The five sections of the passage are divided from each other by the refrain, " 'Still you have not returned to Me,' declares Yahweh." The punishments include famine, drought, blight, locusts, plague, war, and complete destruction. Blight and locusts are grouped together (4:9), as are plague and war (4:10). Much of the material in this section parallels various penalties for disobedience promised in the books of Leviticus (26:14-39) and Deuteronomy (28). Note especially the Lord's threat: "I, even I, will strike you seven times for your sins" (Lev. 26:24).[38]

Apparently some of the verses in this section are prose rather than poetry, or at best a loosely structured verse. Repetition of phrases and the similar themes of the larger segments lend to the sense of patterned regularity.

4:6 Amos sometimes uses stunning word pictures: נִקְיוֹן שִׁנַּיִם (niqyôn šinnayim, "cleanness of teeth"). The teeth are clean, of course, when there is nothing to eat. The parallel with "lack of bread" shows that famine is meant, though it is unusual for the more picturesque and concrete phrase to occur first. The translator of the LXX apparently misunderstood the figure, rendering "gnashing of teeth" (or, "a toothache"; γομφιασμὸν ὀδόντων, gomphiasmon

---

[38] Cf. the detailed analysis in Wolff, *Joel and Amos*, pp. 212-14, though we would not agree with Wolff that the passage in Amos is a late addition.

odontōn). Notice also the Targum: "bluntness of teeth" (שְׁנִין אַקְהָיוּת, *'aqhāyût šinnîn*).[39]

In the book of Leviticus, the Lord makes a promise after giving threats for disobedience to the covenant: "If they confess their iniquity…, then I will remember My covenant" (Lev. 26:40-42). Since Israel had not responded to chastisement (וְלֹא־שַׁבְתֶּם עָדַי, *wĕlō' šabtem ʿāday*, "but still you have not returned to Me"), the people cannot expect mercy from the Lord.

The preposition *ʿad* is rare with the verb "return," and nearly all of the examples indicate repentance (cf. Deut. 30:2; Job 22:23; Ps. 94:15; Isa. 19:22; Lam. 3:40; Hos. 14:2; Joel 2:12).

4:7 The Lord speaks in v. 7 of drought, which hurt some cities but not others, in contrast to the famine, which touched all the cities. According to Feinberg, "This was purposeful to show that the giving or withholding was not by chance, but by the sovereign act and choice of God."[40]

The timing of the drought, three months before the harvest, would of course be disastrous for the crops. The spring months of March or April are meant. Crops of wheat and barley were usually harvested in May or June.[41]

4:9 The words for blight (שִׁדָּפוֹן, *šiddāpôn*) and mildew (יֵרָקוֹן, *yērāqôn*) always occur together with reference to plants (Deut. 28:22; 1 Kings 8:37; 2 Chron. 6:28; Hag. 2:17). A dry hot wind from the east first dries out the crops, which are then attacked by parasitic worms.[42] The Scripture uniformly views blight and mildew as the result of divine judgment for sin.

Of the many Hebrew words for "locust" (cf. on Joel 1:4), גָּזָם (*gāzām*) implies a "cutter," possibly in the caterpillar stage (cf. NASB). Together with the blight and mildew, the locust plague would devastate all the crops, ruin of the crops being the central idea that ties together v. 9.

Note the KJV, "When your gardens … increased, the palmer worm devoured them," a translation close to the one proposed here. Our proposal takes הַרְבּוֹת (*harbôt*) as a substantive with the meaning of "increase," or "fruit."[43] Certainly a problem for this rendering is that there are no parallel examples, but the semantic development seems clear enough (see also Additional Notes).

4:10 The Lord had sent plagues upon the Egyptians, but "after the manner of [בְּדֶרֶךְ, *bĕderek*] Egypt" means simply a plague that is known or common in Egypt. This was an "Egyptian plague" (cf. Deut. 28:27, 60). The same construction occurs with reference to Egypt's enslavement of Israel (Isa. 10:24).[44]

The reference to war is literally "I killed with the sword" (הָרַגְתִּי בַחֶרֶב, *hāragtî beḥereb*). The "sword" wielded by the Lord often stands for war that is

[39] LXX and Targum do not necessarily reflect a different text, despite Wolff's idea that they may have read קָהוּי (*Joel and Amos*, p. 209 n. g.).

[40] Feinberg, *The Minor Prophets*, p. 101.

[41] Wolff, *Joel and Amos*, pp. 220-21.

[42] Ibid., p. 221.

[43] Cf. Keil, *Minor Prophets*, p. 274, though his translation is "many of your gardens."

[44] Richard S. Cripps, *A Critical & Exegetical Commentary on the Book of Amos*, 2d ed. (n.p.: S.P.C.K., 1960), p. 174.

directed by Him (e.g., Deut. 32:42; Judges 7:20; Jer. 12:12). Or it may be that the parallel with "plague" (דֶּבֶר, *deber*) indicates only one punishment, though comparison with similar expressions in the Pentateuch (see below) would argue for war and plague.

War and plagues were promised punishments for not keeping the covenant (Lev. 26:25; Deut. 28:21, 25). Scripture records numerous occasions when enemies invaded the land. The book of Judges mentions periods when Israel was dominated by foreign powers. Pharaoh Shishak made a devastating raid against the southern kingdom of Judah (2 Chron. 12), and prior to the reign of Jeroboam II the Syrians had harassed the northern kingdom of Israel continually (cf. 1 Kings 20; 2 Kings 6:8-7:20; 12:17-18). The "young men" would be the choice young soldiers of Israel's army.

Were the horses captured (עִם שְׁבִי סוּסֵכֶם, '*im šĕbî sûsĕkem*, "with the captivity of your horses") by the Israelites and subsequently slain in battle with them? Or did the enemy capture the horses after they killed the Israelite warriors? LXX, Targum, and Peshitta all imply the latter, and they are followed by KJV, "and have taken away your horses." However, Cripps notes a grammatical difficulty. The preposition '*im* "couples two *like words*... In the present passage, however, there is no word in the preceding clause to which 'captivity' is strictly *parallel*."[45] The pronoun "your" in the Hebrew phrase can be attached to the word "capture," yielding "along with your capture of horses," that is, "the horses you have captured." The parallel is then between the young fighting men and the horses they have managed to capture, both of which fell in battle.

The grammar of וָאַעֲלֶה בְאֹשׁ מַחֲנֵיכֶם וּבְאַפְּכֶם (*wā'a'ăleh bĕ'ōš maḥănêkem ûbĕ'appĕkem*) is unusual: "And I made the stench of your camps rise, even into your nostrils."[46] By it Amos emphasizes the effect of the catastrophe. Repentance should have resulted, but even after such visible evidence of judgment Israel remained stubborn.

Also the *waw*-consecutive in *wā'a'ăleh* ("and I made go up") connects the thought closely with the main verb הָרַגְתִּי (*hāragtî*, "I slew"). The smell comes from the decaying carcasses of the dead soldiers and horses.

4:11 Only in v. 11 does the preposition *beth* precede the object of the verb "overthrow" (הָפַךְ, *hāpak*). The BDB lexicon (p. 88) classifies the passage with those where *beth* is used "when the action refers to only part of the object." In other words, the judgment was limited in scope. There was an overthrowing, but only of parts of the nation. This agrees with the general context: various disasters of limited scope were sent in hopes of bringing repentance. Failing that, a major catastrophe that would affect the whole nation would be necessary.

The precise type of judgment meant for this final pericope in the series is difficult to determine. "Sodom and Gomorrah" provides the major clue, but as Harper observes, "the point of comparis on is not the manner of the overthrow, but its thoroughness."[47] Therefore, the text does not allow us to specify whether an

---

[45] Ibid., p. 174.
[46] Cf. GKC, par. 154a n. 16.
[47] Harper, *Amos and Hosea*, p. 101.

earthquake or some other specific type of catastrophe is meant.[48] God destroyed these cities so completely they became a sign of what happens to those who refuse to repent (see Deut. 29:22-24 [MT 29:21-23]; Jer. 20:16; Matt. 10:15; 11:23-24). Amos argues that the similar complete destruction of other cities in Israel should have served as examples for the rest.

The Israelites who survived various disasters (כְּאוּד מֻצָּל מִשְּׂרֵפָה, *kĕ'ûd muṣṣāl miśśĕrēpâ*, "like a log snatched from a blaze") should have recognized that only God's grace had spared them. A piece of firewood in a blaze cannot survive unless someone yanks it out. Zechariah later applied the phrase to the rescue of Judah from the Babylonian captivity (Zech. 3:2).

Additional Notes

4:9 שִׁדָּפוֹן: Once again the LXX shows the propensity of its translator or of its *Vorlage* to misread letters, πυρώσει presupposing derivation from the root שׂרף.

הַרְבּוֹת: The word is apparently an infinitive construct from the root רבה, but its grammatical relationship with the rest of the sentence is unclear. Literally the expression is something like "the multiplying of your gardens." The NASB has "your *many* gardens,"[49] but for the adjectival meaning *harbôt* might be expected to follow rather than precede the modified noun (cf. Prov. 25:27). The NIV takes the term in an adverbial sense: "*Many times* I struck your gardens and vineyards." This idiom normally requires a finite form of רבה in the hiphil and the infinitive or finite form of the modified action (cf. Ps. 78:38; Amos 4:4).

Some other modern versions (e.g., JB, NEB, RSV) rely on a widely accepted emendation first proposed by Wellhausen.[50] According to this view, the original reading was הֶחֱרַבְתִּי ("I withered"), but the *cheth* fell out by haplography because of its similarity with *he*. The resulting impossible word then generated the vowels of the present form.

The emendation is tempting because it fits the context so well and has a plausible textual explanation. Still, the ancient versions support the MT even though they had difficulty with it.

4:10 שְׁבִי סוּסֵכֶם: Some have felt that the meaning "your captured horses" does not fit the context well enough, proposing that the phrase be deleted as a gloss or emended to "your well-trapped horses," reading צבי for שבי. Possibly the term in the MT could be taken simply as a dialectal variant of צבי, even as יִשְׂחָק is a variant of יִצְחָק (Isaac). The meaning would suit the context, but a *hapax legomenon* would also be created.

D. The Awesome Judgment For Israel (4:12-13)

Translation

Therefore I will treat you the same way, Israel.

---

[48] Against S. M. Lehrman, *The Twelve Prophets* (Soncino Books of the Bible; ed. A. Cohen; London: Soncino, 1969), p. 101.

[49] See Keil, *Minor Prophets*, p. 274.

[50] Cf. Wolff, *Joel and Amos*, p. 210 n. m.

Since I will treat you this way,
prepare to meet your God, Israel.
[13]For here (is what He is like):
He formed the mountains
and created the wind,
yet reveals His thoughts to mankind.
He turns the dawn into darkness
and treads on the high places of the earth.
His name is Yahweh, God of the hosts. (4:12-13)

Exegesis and Exposition

Amos has a strong sense of God's control of history. The Lord called Israel out of Egypt and established His covenant with her. When she proved incapable of fulfilling her covenant obligations, He was gracious and sought to draw her back to Himself, both through the preaching of prophets and through chastisement. As Amos surveys this panorama of Israelite history, he sees the prophets scorned and punishments ignored. Under divine direction, he can come to only one conclusion. Israel must face a new judgment from the Lord, which will be more destructive and final than all the rest. Amos sees the future as consisting of a face-to-face encounter between Israel and her Maker.

A beautifully crafted hymn to the Lord follows the summons, "Prepare to meet your God!" Similar passages occur two other places in Amos (5:8-9; 9:5-6), and it may be that portions of a single hymn have been used at appropriate spots (see Excursus on the Hymnic Passages in Amos at the end of the commentary). Each contains the refrain, "Yahweh (God of the hosts) is His name." The hymns dwell on the essential character or nature of the Lord, especially His creative power. Thus, they lend a certain universal aspect to Amos's message. Will not He who created mankind and their world be concerned about justice? Will any man or woman be able to stand before the wrath of the God who made them?

4:12*a* In v. 12 the prophet points back with כֹּה (*kōh*, "thus" or "in the same way") to the previous punishment to show what the Lord will do to Israel in the future (a similar use of *kōh* with עָשָׂה ['*āśâ*, "do"] can be found in Ezek. 23:39; Neh. 13:18; 2 Chron. 19:9, 10; 24:11). That is, He will overthrow all of Israel, not merely part of her, just as He overthrew Sodom and Gomorrah. The reason (לָכֵן, *lākēn*, "therefore") is based on the refrain repeated so often in the chapter: "Yet you have not returned to Me." As Thomas McComiskey notes, a certain vagueness comes across from Amos's style, lending to the ominous effect he desires to make.[51]

The second half of the line both strengthens the previous thought and sets up the frightful command to Israel in the next line. עֵקֶב כִּי (*ēqeb kî*) makes the causal connection as strong as possible, "*because of* this." That is, because the Lord is ready to overthrow all Israel as He overthrew Sodom and Gomorrah, therefore the people need to prepare themselves.

---

[51] McComiskey, "Amos," 7:307.

4:12*b* Mays shows how the terms "prepare" and "meet God" in the second part of v. 12 are also used of the covenant made with the Lord at Sinai (Ex. 19:11 [NASB="be ready"], 17). The insight Mays derives from this observation is worth quoting: "They will not return to him, so he will come to them in a terrifying historical theophany so inexorable that no Israelite can avoid it (9.1-4) and so awesome that none can mistake it (2.13-16) – not in a sanctuary, but in history – not for covenant-making, but for judgment."[52] Undoubtedly at least part of that historical fulfillment came in the Assyrian invasion; when the Israelites encountered the Assyrians, they were actually meeting God – in judgment (cf. Isa. 10:5).

4:13 In v. 13 the connection with the previous thought is indicated by כִּי הִנֵּה (*kî hinnēh*), literally "for behold." The terse style rivets attention immediately on the God who will encounter Israel. No one will be able to stand before Him when He appears.

The passage consists of a series of participial phrases that describe who Yahweh is. The climax comes at the end of the verse with His full name: "Yahweh, God of the hosts." LXX makes a different connection between vv. 12 and 13 by making "I" the subject of the participles ("Behold, I make firm the thunder and create wind..."), yet "His name" at the end marks the section as description rather than declaration.

God as Creator is one of the most persistent and deeply imbedded images in the OT. The terms יָצַר (*yāṣar*, "form") and בָּרָא (*bārā'*, "create") often occur either together or in closely associated contexts. For example, the Scriptures open with the statement that "in the beginning God created the heavens and the earth" (Gen. 1:1), while the detailed account of the creation of man says that Yahweh God "formed" man from dust (Gen. 2:7). Isaiah uses the two terms as virtual synonyms (Isa. 43:1, 7; 45:7, 18). *Bārā'* stresses an action that uniquely manifests divine power, while *yāṣar* calls to mind the analogy of a potter.

The verbs for God's creative activity are actually participles ("Former" and "Creator"), forms that lend to the poetry of the passage a feeling of compactness and balance. Since they refer to creation, the time is past, though Hebrew participles are neutral with respect to time. One may think of the participles as vivid descriptions of God. He is the "mountain-Former" and the "wind-Creator."

The Hebrews stood in awe of the mountains with their strength and height. That God created them shows His boundless power (Ps. 65:6 [MT 65:7]). Mountains appear often in Amos's imagery. The Lord roars from Zion with the effects reaching to Carmel's summit (1:2; cf. 9:3). The mountains surrounding Samaria become a theater for the violence and injustice in Samaria (3:9). Samaria itself is located on a mountain, a place where the "cows of Bashan" live in luxury (4:1; cf. 6:1). At the end of the book Amos sees a glorious future for an Israel restored under the banner of David. At that time "the mountains will drip sweet wine,/ and all the hills will be dissolved." That the Lord formed the mountains means that He is the ultimate source of all the blessings enjoyed by Israel. Yet the people have refused to turn back to Him.

---

[52] Mays, *Amos*, p. 82.

רוּחַ (*rûaḥ*), like its Greek counterpart, can mean either "wind" or "spirit."
The parallel with mountains makes the reader think immediately of wind, but the
following phrase, which speaks of God's revelation to mankind evokes, the human
spirit. Either one required the miraculous power of God for its creation. In light of
the association with "mountains," the "wind" is primarily in view, though the
ambiguity of the Hebrew term makes for a smooth transition into the following
phrase. "Wind" probably focuses on the Lord's power over the storm (Mays
translates "and creates storm").[53]

Klaus Koch thinks of the divine Spirit in prophecy, especially as this connects
back to the "word" of 4:1.[54] However, it would be theologically problematic to refer
to the creation of the Spirit of God. If we think of the human spirit, it is still
possible to make a connection with prophetic revelation. God, who created the
spiritual capacity in mankind, also reveals His spiritual thoughts to people.

A marginal reading in a Targum manuscript (Reuchlinianus) gives an
interesting paraphrase: "God reveals Himself – He who formed the embryo in the
womb of its mother [based on הָרָה, *hārâ*, "become pregnant"?] and created in it the
spirit of the soul, and brought it forth to the world to make known His wondrous
deeds to the sons of men."

Amos gave us a glimpse of God as a roaring lion who reveals His secret
counsels to the prophets (3:7). Now he shows us the powerful Creator who reveals
His own musings (שֵׂחוֹ, *śēḥô*, "His thoughts") to man. That the Lord would be so
gracious to His creatures brings into relief even more the culpability of Israel in
rejecting the prophetic word.

Some think that *śēḥô* should be referred to man instead. That is, God declares
to people even the words they think and say. The image would be consonant with
Jer. 11:20 and Ps. 94:11.[55] However, מַגִּיד (*maggîd*) specifies more the idea of
revelation or telling than of knowing or ordaining. A similar connection between
creation and true revelation also occurs in Isa. 44:24-28. Amos's words contain a
progression: 1) God creates man's environment (for Israel the "mountains" and the
storm); 2) God reveals His plans to man; and 3) God carries out His judgment on
His creation (see exegesis of the following phrases).

The theme changes subtly from creation to judgment. In isolation the phrase
containing "darkness" (עֵיפָה, *'êpâ*) need mean nothing more than that the Lord
changes day into night. Perhaps the reference is even to creation, when each day
had an "evening" and a "morning." But darkness stands for judgment as well as for
the night (cf. Amos 5:18), and *'êpâ* refers to death the only other place it occurs
(Job 10:22). Even the dawn is often associated with death or darkness (Ps. 139:8-9;
Hos. 10:15; Joel 2:2). The day of enjoyment and luxury will soon be the night
where God is encountered.

---

[53] Cf. Wolff, *Joel and Amos*, p. 223; Mays, *Amos*, p. 77.
[54] Klaus Koch, "Die Rolle der hymnischen Abschnitte in der Komposition des Amos-
Buches," *ZAW* 86 (1974): 513-14.
[55] Cf. Cripps, *Amos*, p. 177; Feinberg, *The Minor Prophets*, p. 102.

Keil argues for the translation, "He who makes dawn (and) darkness," taking the second noun as an asyndeton.[56] The grammatical explanation he gives seems strained, however, and the reverse process of changing night into day occurs in the second hymnic portion in Amos (5:8).

The passage (4:12-13) began with the Lord forming the mountains, and it closes with Him treading on them. בָּמוֹת (bāmôt, "high places") often signifies places of worship, even in Amos (7:9). Other times it is simply a synonym for mountains or hills (cf. Deut. 32:13; 2 Sam. 1:19, 25; M ic. 1:3, 4). Once again the phrase indicates the Lord's might and power, but it also stresses His presence and sovereignty throughout the world. From the heights he gains access to the farthest reaches of the earth so that none can escape His judgment.

Micah 1:3 also depicts the Lord coming "from His place" to "tread on the high places of the earth." As a result, "the mountains will melt under Him, and the valleys will be split open, like wax before the fire, like water poured down a slope." The treading may then be compared with the one who tramples grapes to press out the juice (Amos 9:13). The very mountains the Lord created for the benefit of mankind will be destroyed at His sudden appearance on the earth.[57] The hymn probably signifies the catastrophic changes that will accompany the day of the Lord at the end of the age, but Amos applies it here to the earthquake and the Assyrian captivity, which spell the end for Israel. The literal "high places" used for false worship will suffer judgment, but Amos's words are more universal in scope.

All of the participial phrases used so far should be taken as part of the name "Yahweh, God of the hosts." Each portion of the name defines a characteristic of the God the Israelites must prepare to face: He has created the world by His power; He has revealed His own thoughts to man; He superintends the natural forces; He ranges over the whole world; He is the covenant God of Israel. The solemnity of the cadence, "Yahweh the God of hosts is His name," contrasts with the bare mention of "Israel" in the previous verse.

---

[56] Keil, *Minor Prophets*, p. 277.
[57] Cf. Koch, "Die Rolle der hymnischen Abschnitte," pp. 509-11.

6
Choice of Life or Death
(5:1-17)

Certain phrases show dividing points in the book of Amos. Such is the case with the summons to "Hear this word" (3:1; 4:1; 5:1). The final portion that opens with this admonition continues until the visions of chaps. 7-9 (but cf. 8:4). Within chaps. 5 and 6 the topics change frequently, but various key phrases and the overall structure give further clues to a valid analysis.

Four rhetorical units can be discerned within chaps. 5 and 6. A chiastic structure, with a section calling for lamentation at the beginning and end, mark off the first unit (5:1-17). The interjection "woe!" (הוֹי, *hôy*) shows us where the next two units start (5:18-27; 6:1-14). Each of these has a four-part structure, and the remaining verses, 6:12-14, make up the final unit. This last pericope is introduced by a rhetorical question (6:12a), and implications are drawn from it (cf. 3:3-8).

Three issues – accusation, judgment, and appeal – govern the content of these units, and Amos employs a variety of forms to focus on them. Calls for lamentation (5:1-3, 16-17) treat the nation as though it has already died, pointing out both the inevitability of the judgment as well as dramatically appealing to the people to consider their spiritual condition. Diagnosing a fatal disease can cause the sufferer to evaluate his or her life. Twice Amos appeals directly to his listeners to repent (5:4-6, 14-15). These calls to "seek the Lord" are the only times the prophet makes explicit the need to repent. More commonly, he prefers a more subtle approach by which he draws the listener into the message, as in the two woe oracles (5:18-27; 6:1-14).

In these, he appeals to the people to evaluate their view of reality. They may think their religion is adequate or that their wealth guarantees security, but they need to reexamine their situation from the Lord's point of view. Amos also includes two strongly worded statements in which the Lord even expresses hatred or loathing for the objects of Israel's trust: their sacrificial system (5:21-25) and their pride (6:8). A second hymnic passage (5:8-9) occurs in the center of the first rhetorical unit, and it combines all three elements of accusation, judgment, and appeal by emphasizing the power of the Lord as Creator to execute His wrath. These are only some of the many ways by which Amos intricately varies his presentation of the word of the Lord for Israel.

Jan de Ward and William Smalley noted a chiastic structure for Amos 5:1-17, later extending it to cover the entire book.[1] The general picture seems obvious:

---

[1] J. de Waard, "The Chiastic Structure of Amos 5:1-17," *VT* 27 (1977): 170-07; Jan de Waard and William Smalley, *A Translator's Handbook on the Book of Amos* (Helps for Translators; n.p.: United Bible Societies, 1979), pp. 189-92. "Yahweh is His name" (5:8)

A Lament for Fallen Israel (5:1-3)
   B Appeal to Seek the Lord and Live (5:4-6)
      C Accusations Against Israel (5:7)
         D Hymn to Yahweh (5:8-9)
      C' Accusations Against Israel (5:10-13)
   B' Appeal to Seek Good and Live (5:14-15)
A' Lamentation in the Streets (5:16-17)

This analysis in terms of broader units results in seven sections, and it is also possible to discern structure within the indiv idual parts.[2] Such additional structures will be discussed in the sections that treat those units.

A chiastic structure focuses attention on the center, drawing the reader into a key idea and then gradually moving away from it by retracing the same path. However, different things are noted on the way out than on the way in.

From a funeral, then, Amos moves to a "what if" question: What if the people would seek the Lord and live instead of die? But then reality intrudes and he sees their wickedness, which leads inexorably to the presence of the Lord. The God who creates is also the God who destroys. He is the center of Israel's existence, whether the people wish to admit it or not.

On the way back to his starting point Amos looks again at the evil around him, but this time he sees specific instances of how the people have perverted justice and destroyed righteousness. Again he contemplates the possibility of repentance; only now he urges Israel to turn to that which is good, to make true their claim that the Lord is with them. Finally, he comes back to where he started. But whereas before he gave the dirge himself, now he envisions the chaos of crowds wildly calling for lamentation in the streets, marketplaces, and fields of the land.[3]

A. A Dirge For Fallen Israel (5:1-3)

Translation

Listen to this word that I take up against you. (It is) a dirge (about) the house of Israel:

---

occurs at the center of the book, according to their analysis. The larger chiastic structure for the entire book of Amos seems less coherent than that for 5:1-17, but it is suggestive and worthy of careful consideration.

   [2] A more complicated structure is given by John H. Stek, "When the Spirit Was Poetic," in *The NIV: The Making of a Contemporary Translation*, ed. Kenneth L. Barker (Grand Rapids: Zondervan, 1986), pp. 82-83. He sees a pattern of A (vv. 2-3), B (vv. 4-6), B' (vv. 14-15), A' (vv. 16-17). Since the syntax of v. 7 seems to be continued by v. 10, he views the central element as a "stanza of implicit indictment" ("those who ... who ... who," vv. 7, 10, 12b,13), but it is interrupted by two sections: the hymn (vv. 8-9) and a "stanza of explicit indictment" ("you ... you ... you," vv. 11, 12a). This analysis has the advantage of dealing more precisely with the Hebrew syntax, though the thematic analysis of J. de Waard seems more useful for understanding the overall message.

   [3] Cf. Gary V. Smith, *Amos: A Commentary* (Library of Biblical Interpretation; Grand Rapids: Zondervan, 1989), p. 159. He thinks that the first half of 5:1-17 gives "a greater emphasis on death and destruction," while the second half focuses more "on the reason for destruction."

[2]"She has fallen! She will not rise again,
the virgin Israel.
She lies forsaken on her land;
no one lifts her up."
[3]For thus says the *Lord Yahweh:
"The city that goes out a thousand strong
shall have left (only) a hundred,
and that which goes out a hundred
shall have left (only) ten."
(This shall be what is left) for the house of Israel.

Exegesis and Exposition

The announcement of a funeral dirge for Israel forcefully proclaims the inevitability of judgment for the people. It also sets the tone for the entire "word" to Israel in this section, which turns again and again to the contrasting themes of life and death. The announcement is in two parts. The first, the dirge itself (5:2), personifies Israel as a young woman who has died. A reason for the dirge is given in the second part (5:3). Israel will send many troops into battle, but only a handful will return.

Structurally the section consists of three prose phrases with two poetic couplets. The prose statements identify the Lord as the source of the prophet's inspiration and make the application to Israel. Amos probably used traditional sayings for both couplets, the second (v. 3) perhaps consisting of a proverb appropriate for a somber occasion.

5:1 During a funeral procession the mourners would chant a "dirge" (קִינָה, qînâ), which would refer to the deceased and the circumstances of the death (cf. 2 Sam. 3:31-34). Often women were called on to participate (cf. Judg. 11:39-40; Jer. 9:17 [MT 9:16]; Ezek. 32:16). The prophet Ezekiel "took up" a number of such dirges for the rulers of nations (Ezek. 19:1; 26:17; 27:2, 32; 28:12; 32:2), and Jeremiah lamented for the land of Israel (Jer. 9:10, 19-20 [MT 9:9, 18-19]).

The qînâ consists typically of two half lines with a shorter second half (3+2). The following diagram featuring a woodenly literal translation should make the structure clear for the reader unfamiliar with this form:[4]

Fallen	not-she-adds	to-rise	(3 units)
	virgin-of	Israel.	(2 units)
Forsaken	Upon	her-land	(3 units)
	None	raising-her.	(2 units)
The-city	going-forth	a-thousand	(3 units)
	she-will-remain	a-hundred.	(2 units)
[The city]	going-forth	a-hundred	(3 units)
	she-will-remain	ten.	(2 units)

---

[4] For more details about the form, see Anders Jørgen Bjørndalen, *Untersuchungen zur allegorischen Rede der propheten Amos und Jesaja* (BZAW 165; New York: Walter de Gruyter, 1986), pp. 161-74.

The entire nation ("house of Israel") must listen to a lament to be recited at their own funeral. The effect must have been quite shocking.[5] Judging by the tone of the book of Amos, however, the shock was not enough to persuade the people to repent.

5:2 The dirge applies to the northern kingdom as seen in v. 2. After the Assyrian captivity, Jeroboam II's Israel will never be restored. God does have a future plan for national Israel, but it is through the tribe of Judah and the line of David (cf. Amos 9:11; Jer. 31:4-6).

As far as is known, Amos was the first prophet to address Israel as "virgin" (בְּתוּלַת יִשְׂרָאֵל, bĕtûlat yiśrā'ēl). Later, Jeremiah used the expression in promising future restoration for Israel, noting that her watchmen shall call out "on the hills of Ephraim" for the people to "go up to Zion,/ to Yahweh our God" (Jer. 31:6). He thereby takes the prophecy of Amos and shows how there is still hope if the people will seek the Lord at Zion. Amos apparently addressed Israel this way to emphasize the tragedy of the situation. A young woman has been cut down in the prime of her life (cf. also Isa. 23:12; 47:1; Jer. 31:21; 46:11; Lam. 1:15; 2:13).

The term bĕtûlâ can be used of a woman betrothed to her husband. Amos probably stresses more the youth and vitality of the woman than her sexual purity as such. Israel would be destroyed as a nation when she should have been enjoying the rich physical and spiritual blessings available through the Lord.

The KJV reads "the virgin of Israel," evidently because bĕtûlâ occurs in the "construct" form. The construct form can be used for expressing appositional relationships,[6] however, and that seems to be the significance here. This is the "virgin" *who is* Israel.

John H. Hayes says "virgin of Israel" should not be taken as an apposition ("the virgin which is Israel") but as a reference to Samaria, the capital city.[7] However, the usage of the phrase elsewhere argues for its application to the whole nation (cf. Jer. 18:13; 31:4, 21). Even if we accept Hayes's view, the capital city would still stand by extension for the entire nation. Bĕtûlâ also occurs in the appositional construct in the expression "virgin daughter of Zion" (2 Kings 19:21; Isa. 37:22; cf. Isa 47:1; Jer. 14:17; 46:11; Lam. 1:15).

The Lord can "raise up" even the dead (1 Sam. 2:6), but Israel's guilt is too great for divine intervention (אֵין מְקִימָהּ, 'ên mĕqîmāh, "no one lifts her up"). The Lord restores life to the righteous, not the wicked.[8]

5:3 A coming military disaster of catastrophic proportions serves as the reason for the lamentation over Israel. About forty years later, the nation was overwhelmed by the Assyrian might. Only an insignificant portion of the people survived; the national existence of Israel came to an end. The military context of

[5] For a detailed discussion of the rhetorical effect of Amos's words, see N. J. Tromp, "Amos V 1-17: Towards a Stylistic and Rhetorical Analysis," *OTS* 23 (1984): 74.

[6] Ronald J. Williams, *Hebrew Syntax; An Outline*, 2d ed. (Toronto: Univ. of Toronto, 1980), p. 11, par. 42.

[7] John H. Hayes, *Amos, The Eighth-Century Prophet: His Times and His Preaching* (Nashville: Abingdon, 1988), pp. 154-55.

[8] Cf. James Luther Mays, *Amos; A Commentary* (OTL; Philadelphia: Westminster, 1969), p. 85.

the verse is shown by the terms "thousand" (אֶלֶף, 'elep) and "which goes out" (הַיֹּצֵאת, hayyōṣē't), indicating a troop that goes out for war (cf. 2 Sam 18:4).[9]

Hayes proposes that תַּשְׁאִיר (taš'îr), usually translated "she shall have left," be taken instead to mean that the city of Samaria (see above), normally able to provide large contingents of troops in battle, will only be able to "spare" a small number. Since the verb š'r expresses a condition ("be left"), the hiphil can have the intransitive sense "have left," "be remaining," admittedly a unique sense for this root. The causative translation would require the thought that the land/city caused only a few to remain, whereas Hayes thinks of the city being unable to supply the troops, also a unique sense. Since the context has such a strong atmosphere of death about it, the traditional interpretation is best.

The phrase לְבֵית יִשְׂרָאֵל (lĕbêt yiśrā'ēl, "to the house of Israel") does not seem to enter into the poetic structure, which is already complete (see diagram above). It probably takes the second saying and applies it to the whole nation, although it may complete the prose statement at the beginning of the verse: that is, "Thus says the Lord Yahweh ... to the house of Israel." Syntactically that would be awkward. Therefore, some have suggested that the phrase may have originally been next to the formula for divine speech or that it may have been simply a gloss.[10] The ancient versions contain the phrase in the same position as found in MT.

Additional Notes

5:3 אֲדֹנָי יהוה: The LXX tradition is not uniform, with the Lucianic recension having simply κύριος, while κύριος ὁ θεός and κύριος κύριος are also attested.[11]

B. A Call To Seek Yahweh – On The Basis Of Judgment (5:4-6)

Translation

For thus says Yahweh to the house of Israel:
"Seek after Me that you may live,
⁵but do not seek (advice) at Bethel.
Also do not enter Gilgal,
nor cross over to Beersheba.
For Gilgal will certainly go into captivity,
and Bethel will become an empty place."
⁶Seek after Yahweh that you may live,
lest He burst upon the house of Joseph like a fire,
and it consumes with none to extinguish it *for Bethel.

---

[9] Hans Walter Wolff, *Joel and Amos*, trans. Waldemar Janzen, et al. (Philadelphia: Fortress, 1977), p. 237; Gerhard F. Hasel, *The Remnant: The History and Theology of the Remnant Idea from Genesis to Isaiah* (Andrews Univ. Monographs; Studies in Religion 5; 3d ed.; Berrien Springs, Mich.: Andrews Univ., 1980), pp. 188-89.

[10] See Wolff, *Joel and Amos*, p. 227 n. g.

[11] For details, see the Göttingen edition.

Exegesis and Exposition

Since Israel was not resorting to the Lord but to her own forms of worship, Amos calls her to seek her God afresh. This is the first time in his book that Amos leaves open the possibility that some might obtain life by heeding his message. Yet the location of this exhortation, along with others in the same chapter, is at the heart of the message. The fact that Amos sees the situation in Israel as hopeless does not mean he cannot continue to plead for repentance. In fact, continued graciousness on the Lord's part agrees entirely with the mercy He had shown throughout the history of Israel.

5:4-5c Hebrew שָׁרַד (*dāraš*) became a technical term for resorting to or seeking out a deity to worship. It can be used for either worship of the Lord (Ps. 9:10 [MT 9:11]) or of idols (Jer. 8:2). Additionally it can be used for consulting a deity or spirit for information or guidance, again either from the Lord (1 Kings 22:5-7) or from false gods or spirits (2 Kings 1:2-16; Isa. 8:19). Since Amos so often stresses the importance of prophetic revelation (cf. 2:12; 3:7-8; 4:13), his meaning is that the Lord, through His prophet, instructs the people to seek Him by paying attention to the prophetic revelation. That was the only way to life.[12]

Amos was a master at startling his audience. Bethel was the main sanctuary for the capital city, Samaria. Yet he tells the people that life is to be found in Yahweh, not at Bethel. (For Bethel as an important cult center, see the exegesis on 4:4.) Note that the Hebrew verb for "resort to" is the same as that used of "seeking" the Lord. The use of a place directly with this verb ("to" being implied) is unusual but deliberate. The contrast is very vivid: "Seek Yahweh and live! But do not seek (advice at) Bethel."

The view of some that Bethel is a god is both unnecessary and contrary to the context.[13] The religion practiced at Bethel was in fact syncretistic and not in line with what the Lord required. Beyond the issue of mere religious practices, however, Amos probes a deeper question. Can it really be the Lord who is sought at Bethel if the people do not practice the demands He has made on them for justice and mercy?

Gilgal was located in Israelite territory, and the citizens of the northern kingdom evidently made many pilgrimages there. (See the exegesis on 4:4 for its religious significance.)

Beersheba, located in the biblical Negeb in the extreme south of Judah, seems at first glance out of place. Yet Amos forbids the people to "cross over" (לֹא תַעֲבֹרוּ, *lo' taʿăbōrû*), implying that they crossed over the border into Judah in order to seek religious guidance. Possibly the pilgrims took a route along the coastal highway, which eventually turned eastward toward the Negeb.

Beersheba, along with Bethel and Gilgal, had an illustrious history and would be the sort of place to inspire religious attachments. Here God appeared to Hagar and promised her a great nation through her son (Gen. 21:14-19). Later, Abraham

---

[12] Cf. Wolff, *Joel and Amos*, p. 238. Hayes's attempt to make the entire passage political rather than religious in nature is based on his rather tenuous historical reconstruction (*Amos*, pp. 158-60).

[13] Cf. J. P. Hyatt, "Bethel (Deity)," *IDB* 1:390-91.

planted a tamarisk tree there and "called upon the name of Yahweh, the Eternal God" (Gen. 21:33), and Isaac built an altar there (Gen. 26:23-25). Then Samuel's sons judged the people at Beersheba (1 Sam. 8:1-3), and even Elijah encountered an angel "a day's journey into the desert" from Beersheba (1 Kings 19:3-7). Long after the time of Amos, Josiah desecrated the high places "from Geba to Beersheba" (2 Kings 23:8), completing the reforms begun under Hezekiah.

    5:5d-e The name "Gilgal" in v. 5 forms a pun on the term "go into captivity" (גָּלֹה יִגְלֶה, gālōh yigleh), and possibly when Amos says Bethel will become אָוֶן ('āwen, "empty place"), he also imitates another name for Bethel as "Beth-Aven" (Hos. 4:15; 5:8; 10:5).[14] Many, however, think Hosea derived his use of "Beth-Aven" for Bethel from Amos.[15] The construction of the first line with the infinitive absolute (gālōh) stresses either the certainty or the completeness of the captivity. The former idea seems more likely in a context where Amos seeks to dissuade the people from going to Gilgal. "Their doom is certain," Amos says.

    What exactly does 'āwen mean? The NASB has "trouble," a possible meaning but not as suitable a parallel for exile as "an empty place" or "nothing" (NIV). The LXX gives "as though it did not exist" (ὡς οὐχ ὑπάρχουσα, hōs ouch hyparchousa), a reading which may be influenced by אַיִן ('ên, "not"; Wolff), though 'āwen itself can move in that direction semantically.[16]

    5:6 The Hebrew in v. 6 is difficult; parallels to יִצְלַח (yiṣlaḥ, "burst upon") are found only in the sense of an army rushing to the Jordan River (2 Sam. 19:17 [MT v. 18]) and of the Spirit rushing upon individuals (Judg. 14:6, 19; 15:14; 1 Sam. 10:6, 10; 11:6; 18:10). In light of these other passages, though, it would seem that the verb requires a goal, in this case the "house of Joseph." Therefore, it is better to take the name as the goal of the verb (2 Sam. 19:17 [MT v. 18] also lacks the preposition) than as a vocative (but cf. NASB and LXX). "Joseph" stands for the northern kingdom, since Ephraim and Manasseh, progenitors of the largest and most influential northern tribes, were his sons.

    Amos often speaks of divine judgment in terms of fire (e.g., in the "oracles against the nations" of 1:3-2:5). Here he sees an unquenchable fire that will totally consume Bethel.

C. A Rebuke For Israel's Perversion of Justice (5:7)

Translation

    *(They are) those who turn justice *to wormwood,
    and they have thrust righteousness to the ground.

---

[14] Cf. Ernst A. Knauf, "Beth Aven," *Bib* 65 (1984): 251-53. The name occurs also for a place near Ai and east of Bethel (Josh. 7:2; 18:12; 1 Sam. 13:5; 14:23), and one need not follow Knauf in thinking that the Joshua passages are historically inaccurate. See also W. L. Reed, "Beth-Aven," *IDB* 1:388-89; and Yohanan Aharoni, *The Land of the Bible; A Historical Geography*, rev. ed., trans. A. F. Rainey (Philadelphia: Westminster, 1979), p. 250.

[15] See C. F. Keil, *Minor Prophets* (COTTV 10; Grand Rapids: Eerdmans, 1973), p. 82.

[16] Wolff, *Joel and Amos*, p. 228 n. 1.; G. Herbert Livingston, *TWOT* 1:23 (entry no. 48). See also Smith, *Amos*, p. 157 n. f., who argues for "Bethel will have sorrow."

Exegesis and Exposition

God will judge all false forms of worship; His fury will come like fire that consumes everything in its path. It will come against all those who have pretended to seek after the Lord through religious actions but who show their true heart condition by perverting justice and that which is right. Justice and righteousness were the only ingredients in Israel that could have quenched the burning heat of God's wrath, but instead the Israelites converted them into evil.

5:7 The flow of the context in Amos seems to be broken rather abruptly at v. 7. KJV connects it with what follows: "Ye who turn judgment to wormwood…, Seek him who maketh the seven stars." Of course, it was necessary to supply the words "seek him." Compare the Targum: "They have ceased to fear Him who makes Pleiades and Orion." Keil, on the other hand, connects it with "the house of Joseph" in the previous verse.[17] The NASB ties it more closely with "Bethel" by supplying the word "for" at the beginning of the verse. The NIV connects it with v. 10 by making vv. 8-9 parenthetical,[18] and JB rearranges it to follow vv. 8-9, also supplying "trouble" as an equivalent for an allegedly omitted *hôy*.[19] Keil's view has the advantage of applying the verse to Israel in general, the object elsewhere of Amos's condemnation for injustice. The chiastic structure of the entire passage discussed above indicates that the verse is in its proper position and that the central focus of the entire pericope is on the hymnic passage. Verse 7 itself also has its own chiastic structure (abc-a'b'c').

The people have so perverted justice that it is like deadly poison. Wormwood (לַעֲנָה, *laʿănâ*) is an aromatic herb noted for its bitter taste.[20] Also the Israelites have hurled righteousness violently (הִנִּיחוּ, *hinnîḥû*) to the ground.[21] The two lines together state most emphatically how perverted and contemptuous of truth the people are. Notice also the close juxtaposition of injustice and false worship in the context; in Amos's mind they were not separate.

Additional Notes

5:7 הַהֹפְכִים לְלַעֲנָה: LXX renders κύριος ὁ ποιῶν εἰς ὕψος, apparently picking up אֵל from the previous verse by dittography and making the noun the subject of the verb: "The Lord who does (justice) to the haughty." κύριος as an equivalent for אֵל is rare (see Josh. 3:10; Pss. 16:1; 74:8; 85:8 [MT 85:9]; 136:26; 139:23; Isa. 40:18; 42:5; 43:12) except in Job (8:5 and over 30 others), and it is not impossible that the translator inserted it according to what was felt to be the required meaning. Possibly the *Vorlage* did differ from the MT's לְלַעֲנָה, since the same term at 6:12 was more correctly rendered with πικρίαν ("bitterness"). The

---

[17] Keil, *Minor Prophets*, p. 280. Cf. Smith, *Amos*, p. 165.
[18] Cf. n. 2 above.
[19] Cf. Mays, *Amos*, p. 91.
[20] Philip J. King, *Amos, Hosea, Micah – An Archaeological Commentary* (Philadelphia: Westminster, 1988), p. 124.
[21] See Mays, *Amos*, p. 92, for a detailed study of the terms מִשְׁפָּט and צְדָקָה as they are used for the judicial process in Amos.

apparatus to *BHS* suggests reconstructing לְמַעְלָה, though not necessarily as the better text. On the other hand, dittography of אֵל could have forced the translator to make drastic changes (e.g., the verbs are plural in MT) in order to derive sense from the passage. MT fits much better in the context.

לַעֲנָה: Rev. 8:10-11 refers to a star called "Wormwood" that "fell from heaven" and polluted the water on earth. The Greek term, Ἄψινθος, has a related form (ἀψίνθιον) used in Aquila's version for לַעֲנָה in Prov. 5:4 and Jer. 9:15 (MT 9:14) and 23:15.[22] In light of the hymnic references to stars and flooding in the next verse, some support may exist for Koch's idea that the stars were believed to correlate with social relationships (see below on v. 8).

D. A Hymn To Yahweh Who Will Judge (5:8-9)

Translation   ·

> He who made the Pleiades and Orion,
> who turned the deep darkness to morning
> and darkened day to night,
> who called for the waters of the sea
> and poured them over the face of the earth –
> Yahweh is His name.
> [9]He causes destruction to flash upon the *mighty.
> Yes, destruction will come upon the stronghold.

Exegesis and Exposition

The second of Amos's three hymns to the Lord once again brings the Israelites into direct contact with Him whom they have refused to seek. If they had repented and sought Him, they would have found life. Instead, their obstinate reliance on a false form of worship and their distortion of justice will lead to an unwanted encounter with Yahweh Himself.

5:8a כִּימָה (*kîmâ*) and כְּסִיל (*kĕsîl*) are generally identified with the constellations Pleiades and Orion, respectively. These connections are naturally difficult to make, but they have their basis in etymology, parallel passages (Job 9:9; 38:31), and translations in the ancient versions. The Hebrew for Pleiades seems to refer to a "heap" or "cluster," while the equivalent for Orion is evidently "foolishness." Klaus Koch prefers Sirius or the Dog Star for *kĕsîl*.[23]

Why should Amos mention the stars? The Israelites also worshiped the stars (5:26). Hence, there can be some polemical value to a passage that says the Lord made them.[24] Koch presents evidence that the ancients connected these stars with the weather and the change of seasons. He then joins this idea to the statement that

---

[22] Edwin Hatch and Henry A. Redpath, *A Concordance to the Septuagint*, 3 vols. (Grand Rapids: Baker, 1983) 1:188.

[23] For details, see W. Brueggemann, "Orion," *IDB* 3:609; "Pleiades," *IDB* 3:826; Klaus Koch, "Die Rolle der hymnischen Abschnitte in der Komposition des Amos-Buches," *ZAW* 86 (1974): 518-19.

[24] Cf. Kenneth L. Barker, "The Value of Ugaritic for Old Testament Studies," *BSac* 133 (1976): 122-23.

the Lord poured out water over the earth. Koch's conclusion is, "It appears as if our section alludes to a mutual action of the water [Pleiades] and heat [Sirius] stars which accompanied the deluge."[25] Especially pertinent is a quotation from the Talmud, "When the Holy One, praised be he, wanted to bring the deluge over the world, he removed two stars from the Kima and thereby brought the deluge over the world" *(Ber. 59a).*[26] Additional evidence comes from the close association between the stars and the storm in Job 38:31-35.

Koch assumes that ancient traditions persisted into the Talmudic period. Also, one wonders whether the Talmud passage gives independent evidence. Perhaps a deduction was made on the basis of Amos. It might be objected as well that Koch's view seems too mythological for scriptural revelation. Perhaps, though, his theory is helpful to understand why the creation of the stars and the sending of the flood are collocated in the hymn. As a matter of observation the ancients connected the stars with weather and seasonal patterns (cf. Gen. 1:14). Deborah's song refers to a great rainstorm the Lord sent to bog down the chariots of Sisera's army. She also associates the stars with this event: "From heaven the stars fought; from their courses they fought against Sisera" (Judg. 5:20-21).[27] The prophetic word affirms that all natural phenomena stand under the Lord's control.

Koch also presents Babylonian and Assyrian evidence for a connection made by the ancients between the stars and social relationships. This, according to Koch, helps to explain the association between vv. 7 and 8.[28] It would be incorrect to attribute such an explicit teaching to the text of Amos. Yet if such ideas were popular then, Amos argues that the lack of justice in Israel is incongruent with the natural order established by God.

5:8*b* Another chiastic structure (abc-a'b'c') occurs in v. 8b:

וְהֹפֵךְ לַבֹּקֶר צַלְמָוֶת וְיוֹם לַיְלָה הֶחְשִׁיךְ (*wĕhōpēk labbōqer ṣalmāwet wĕyôm laylâ heḥšîk,* lit. "and turns to the morning deep darkness, and day to night he darkens"). The language is similar to that in v. 7. The Israelites *changed* justice to wormwood, but the Lord *changed* deep darkness to morning (forms of *hapak* are used both times). A principle of joining passages with similar language ("catchwords") may be partly in operation, but the contextual relations are deeper.

After the participle, the perfect form of the verb הֶחְשִׁיךְ (*heḥšîk*) could well represent a general situation viewed as a whole. The Lord characteristically is the

---

[25] "Es scheint, als ob unser Abschnitt auf ein Zusammenwirken des Wasser-und Hitzegestirns anspielt, das die Sintflut begleitet hat" ("Die Rolle der hymnischen Abschnitte," p. 520). His discussion includes pp. 517-20.

[26] Translation from Koch: "Als nämlich der heilige, gepriesen sei er, die Sintflut über die Welt bringen wollte, nahm er zwei Sterne aus der Kima fort und brachte hierdurch die Sintflut über die Welt."

[27] J. Alberto Soggin, *Judges: A Commentary* (OTL; trans. John Bowden; Philadelphia: Westminster, 1981), points out for this passage that in Ugaritic writings the stars "are one of the sources of rain" (p. 91). See also Richard Patterson, "The Song of Deborah," in *Tradition and Testament: Essays in Honor of Charles Lee Feinberg*, ed. John S. Feinberg and Paul D. Feinberg (Chicago: Moody, 1981), p. 138.

[28] Koch, "Die Rolle der hymnischen Abschnitte," pp. 523-25.

one who darkens the day so that it becomes night.[29] On the other hand, the passage may reflect the original establishment of night and day as detailed in Gen. 1. This possibility is strengthened by the word for darkness (צַלְמָוֶת, ṣalmāwet; cf. Job 38:17; Ps. 23:4; 107:14; Isa. 9:1; Jer. 2:6; 13:16), perhaps indicating the pervasive darkness before God organized the world into its habitable form.[30] Koch compares it with the darkness accompanying the storm that brought the flood, though he finds his parallel in the Gilgamesh Epic rather than in the biblical account.[31]

Ṣalmāwet probably represents a compound noun (a rare situation in Hebrew), "shadow of death," where death is used as a superlative for the deepest kind of darkness imaginable.[32] Alternatively, the word may be related to the Semitic root ṣlm, attested in Akkadian, Arabic, Ethiopic (Geez). Then the original abstract noun ṣalmût ("darkness") would have changed to ṣalmāwet by a process of "folk etymology." That is, because the word reminded the Hebrews of "shadow" and "death," it changed its form.[33] In either case, the interpretation "shadow of death" is attested by σκιὰν θανάτου (skian thanatou) in the LXX. The NASB and the NIV use a number of forms for the sixteen occurrences of the term in the OT, including "dark," "darkness," "deep darkness," "shadow of death," "black gloom," "deep shadow," and "thick darkness."

5:8c Many think the general action of forming rain clouds is in view. While the grammar of the Hebrew can be interpreted this way, the use of וַיִּשְׁפְּכֵם (wayyišpĕkēm, "then He poured them out") points to a sudden and overwhelming action, probably the flood in the days of Noah.[34] This interpretation becomes even more likely if the previous line refers to creation. God brought the world into existence out of utter blackness, establishing a regular pattern of day and night. But He also plunged it beneath the waters of the flood, indicating His power as the sovereign Judge. As noted under 4:13, the use of participles does not preclude reference to a specific event, the participle being neutral with respect to time but chosen to describe the attributes of Yahweh. When the Lord is called "the Maker of [עֹשֶׂה, 'ōśēh] the Pleiades and Orion," a participle is used.

The refrain YHWH šĕmô ("Yahweh is His name") occurs within the hymn proper instead of at the end (cf. 4:13; 9:6). Two other observations are important to the structure of this hymn. First, in 4:13 a longer expression was used ("Yahweh, God of the hosts, is His name"), while in 9:6 the line omits "God of the hosts." Second, at 9:6 the statement also follows immediately upon the line, "Who

---

[29] W. Gross, Verbform und Funktion. wayyiqtol für die Gegenwart? (St. Ottilien: Eos, 1976), p. 101.

[30] Cf. John E. Hartley, TWOT 2:767 (entry 1921).

[31] Koch, "Die Rolle der hymnischen Abschnitte," p. 519.

[32] Hartley, TWOT 2:767.

[33] See Robert Gordis, The Book of Job (Moreshet Series, Studies in Jewish History, Literature and Thought New York: The Jewish Theological Seminary of America, 1978), p. 33; Kenneth L. Barker, "The Value of Ugaritic for Old Testament Studies": 122 n. 11.

[34] See Thomas J. Finley, "The WAW-Consecutive with 'Imperfect,' in Biblical Hebrew: Theoretical Studies and Its Use in Amos," in Tradition and Testament: Essays in Honor of Charles Lee Feinberg, ed. John S. and Paul D. Feinberg (Chicago: Moody, 1981), p. 256.

summoned the waters of the sea and poured them out on the surface of the earth."
Perhaps this would indicate that the two parts belonged together and thus were
repeated in both places.

5:9 No one knows for certain the meaning of מַבְלִיג (*mablîg*) in v. 9. The
verb occurs only four times, and in the other three passages it means "look
cheerful" (Job 9:27; 10:20; Ps. 39:13 [MT 39:14]), a sense that hardly fits the
present context.[35] "Flash upon" comes from comparison with an Arabic word.[36] The
Targum renders, "Who makes the weak stronger than the mighty"
(דמגבר חלשין על חקיפין, *dimĕgabber ḥallāšîn ʿal taqqîpîn*), but this is not of
much help. The LXX and the Syriac have similar translations. Wolff lists two
textual emendations which yield a meaning similar to the translation given here.[37]

Amos accused the rich in Samaria of hoarding up "plunder and loot in their
citadels" (3:10), which had been gained by oppression. How fitting that the
"destruction" the Lord will bring against the strong of the land is the same as the
"loot (gained by devastation)" found in their fortified places, the identical Hebrew
word (*šōd*) occurring in both passages.

The people not only oppressed the poor; they also tended to rely either on
religious actions or on their own military defenses. Appropriately, then, destruction
would reach both the people and their fortresses. The order of the Hebrew focuses
attention on the "destruction," a word repeated from the previous statement. This
makes it more likely that the second prediction speaks of an additional destruction
rather than a result of the first action (as in NASB). Thus, עָז (*ʿāz*) would mean the
powerful or mighty people (as in BDB), while מִבְצָר (*mibṣār*) would indicate the
fortified strongholds (or possibly the "fortified cities"; cf. NIV).

Additional Notes

5:9 עָז: The LXX has ἰσχὺν, possibly showing that the translator read the
word as עֹז. The latter term could be translated "stronghold," since an abstract
noun in a poetic passage can stand for a more concrete meaning.[38] This would also
yield a sense more parallel to "fortress" in the following clause, although semantic
parallelism is not a major characteristic of the hymnic passages in Amos. Note also
the NIV: "he flashes destruction on the stronghold."

E. A Rebuke For Israel's Oppression Of The Poor (5:10-13)

Translation

> They hate someone who points out the wrong in the gate,
> and whoever *speaks the truth they loathe.

---

[35] Against William Rainey Harper, who proposes "He that laughs at" in *A Critical and
Exegetical Commentary on Amos and Hosea* (ICC; Edinburgh: T. & T. Clark, 1979), p. 116.

[36] Cf. S. R. Driver, *The Books of Joel and Amos* (CBSC; Cambridge: University,
1907), p. 180.

[37] Wolff, *Joel and Amos*, pp. 229-30 n. v.

[38] Cf. Wolff, *Joel and Amos*, p. 230 n. v.

[11]Therefore, because you *impose heavy rent upon the poor
and even exact a payment of grain from them,
you may have built houses of hewn stone,
but you will not go on living in them.
You may have planted *lush vineyards,
but you will not go on drinking their wine.
[12]For I know your transgressions are many,
and your sins are numerous.
You harass the innocent, take bribes,
and turn aside the needy at the gate.
[13]Therefore, the prudent keeps silent at that time,
because it is an evil time.

Exegesis and Exposition

Amos rebukes Israel at this point for their mistreatment of the poor, aiming especially at dishonest business practices and the perversion of justice. These practices can be viewed as expansions on the previous general description of those who pervert justice (5:7).

Perhaps a man might seek the protection of the city elders. He has been forced to submit to a position as a tenant farmer with a rent so excessive that he cannot ever hope to escape his plight, and even the small amount of grain for his own subsistence is cruelly snatched away. Any who speak out in favor of the plaintiff are ignored. The poor man is harassed for even bringing his case to court. Bribes exchange hands secretly, and the rich land owner wins the case. The innocent party has found no justice here.

Amos's description is typical; the same thing happens over and over again. Only the names and minor details change. Because these practices are so prevalent the Lord, who is the real owner of the land anyway, threatens to turn everything over to foreigners. Since those who were entrusted with it have ignored the covenant law that governed its use, they have forfeited their right to it. The Lord Himself will apply the justice that is lacking from the courts.

A further chiastic structure may be found in this section:

A Hatred for the Truth (5:10)
   B Oppression of the Poor (5:11a)
      C Judgment (5:11b, c)
   B' Oppression of the Poor (5:12)
A' Silencing of the Truth (5:13)

Verse 12a is problematic for this analysis, because it speaks in more general terms of "transgressions" and "sins." However, v. 12b specifies that they are oppressions of the poor.

5:10 Much of the important business of a city took place in an area just inside the city gates. The elders and judges would conduct official business there (Deut. 21:19; Ruth 4:1-12).[39] Amos sets the scene for what happens at such a gathering of

---

[39] King has a picture and plan of the Solomonic gate at Gezer. Stone benches in several alcoves where the elders would sit for judgment are clearly visible (*Archaeological Commentary*, pp. 76, 77).

officials who have come together to hear the case of a poor man bringing his complaint.

The מוֹכִיחַ (môkîaḥ, "reprover") is the man who would recognize the injustice and dare to point it out (see translation above), but it would only add to the contempt the others felt for him. The elders were interested in maintaining their own interests, not justice (cf. Isa. 29:21).

In the small cities and towns, many in the community would undoubtedly be aware of the dishonest actions of their fellow-citizens. But if any would dare to stand up and tell the truth (דֹבֵר תָּמִים (dōbēr tāmîm, "speaker of truth") about what they knew, the elders sitting in judgment would abhor that witness. The term tāmîm sometimes has the idea of "complete" (Job 36:4) or "whole" (Ezek. 15:5) or having integrity (Ps. 18:30 [MT 18:31]). Here, as the BDB lexicon indicates, it means "what is complete, entirely in accord with truth and fact."

5:11a If the Israelites hate and abhor those who speak the truth, it is only because they fear that they might lose the material rewards of their unjust practices (v. 11). It is for these practices that judgment will fall. The conjunction "therefore" looks ahead to the punishment: failure to enjoy accumulated wealth. The reason for the punishment is given by the two clauses following the conjunction "because" (יַעַן, yaʿan; a stronger term than the more usual כִּי, kî).

Some form of tenant farming is in view. Evidently a rich class of nobles had acquired much of the land and were renting it out to the poor who needed to pay off a debt or get enough food to survive. As Mays indicates, "The small farmer no longer owns his own land; he is a tenant of an urban class to whom he must pay a rental for the use of the land, a rental that was often a lion's share of the grain which the land had produced."[40]

Mays's use of "own" should not be thought of in the same way as the modern Western concept of private property, however. The Mosaic law made provision for extended families to receive the right to derive a livelihood from certain portions (נַחֲלָה, naḥălâ, often translated "inheritance") of the land (Num. 33:50-54). The Lord owns the land, but various families actually control the different plots. It was also intended that these tracts of land should remain within the families perpetually; they were not to be bought and sold permanently. The year of Jubilee was intended to restore the land to its rightful condition whenever individuals did get displaced (Lev. 25:23-28). Yet the rich were in fact taking land for themselves, forcing the poor into a status as tenant farmers. This is the situation which Amos condemns.[41]

The verb translated "impose heavy rent" (בּוֹשֵׁס, bôšēs) occurs only here. An older opinion related it to בּוּס (bûs), "trample," with the šin arising through the phonetic process of dissimilation (BDB, p. 143b). NASB gives the alternate

---

[40] Mays, Amos, p. 94; cf. John Andrew Dearman, Property Rights in the Eighth-Century Prophets: The Conflict and its Background (SBLDS 106; Atlanta: Scholars, 1988), pp. 28-31.

[41] See Jon Lee Dybdahl, Israelite Village Land Tenure: Settlement to Exile (Diss., Fuller Theological Seminary, School of Theology; Ann Arbor, Mich.: University Microfilms, 1981), pp. 164-65. Cf. also Marlene Fendler, "Zur Sozialkritik des Amos," EvT 33 (1973): 37-38; Cristopher J. H. Wright, An Eye for an Eye: The Place of Old Testament Ethics Today (Downers Grove, Ill.: InterVarsity, 1983), pp. 38-39, 57-59.

reading "trample upon" in the margin. LXX has "oppress," using κατακονδυλίζω (*katakondylizō*), an intensified form of κονδυλίζω (*kondylizō*), the latter occurring at 2:7 as one of two Greek words used to translate *haššō'āpîm*. More recently a view which relates the form to an Akkadian word meaning "levy taxes" (*šabāšu*) has become widely accepted.[42] This would involve a metathesis or reversal of two Hebrew consonants, a standard phonetic process.[43] The fact that מַשְׂאַת־בַּר (*maś'at-bar*, "payment of grain") has a meaning parallel to "impose heavy rent" lends support to the Akkadian derivation.

5:11*b* Almost all references to "well-hewn stone" (גָּזִית, *gāzît*, or גָּזִית אַבְנֵי, *'abnê gāzît*) in the OT apply either to the Temple built by Solomon or to his palace (1 Kings 5:17 [MT 5:31]; 6:36; 7:9, 11, 12; cf. Ezek. 40:42). An altar could not be built of "hewn stone" (Ex. 20:25). Also, Isaiah quotes the "inhabitants of Samaria" as asserting proudly that they would replace ruined brick houses with hewn stone and fallen structures of sycamore wood with cedar (Isa. 9:9-10 [MT 9:8-9]). These stone houses were, therefore, quite costly, a sign of the great wealth accumulated through unjust gain. Fine examples of the Phoenician style of masonry with dressed stones fitted tightly together can be seen at the excavations in the city of Samaria.[44]

The Lord must judge the wealthy who have acquired such fine houses by oppression, and He will do this by taking the houses away from them. The prosperity of Israel was only temporary. The dynasty of Jeroboam II disintegrated soon after his death. Amos's prophecy concerning the houses and vineyards is patterned after the curses in Deuteronomy (28:30, 39), and the same pronouncement shows up later in Micah (6:15) and Zephaniah (1:13). Amos later predicts the reversal of the coming judgment when David's kingdom is reestablished (9:14).

כַּרְמֵי־חֶמֶד (*karmê-ḥemed*) is literally "vineyards of desire"; it signifies vineyards that are desirable because they produce high quality fruit in large quantity. But the lush abundance is due to the ability of the owner to apply his riches to tending it. Perhaps the nobleman who planted it acquired the land through treachery, even as Ahab, a predecessor of Jeroboam II, had secured the vineyard of Naboth (1 Kings 21).

5:12*a* The parallel structure in v. 12 (transgressions // sins; many // numerous) reinforces the thought that the transgressions are too numerous even to be counted. The Lord has not reacted to a few isolated instances. All Samaria and the whole country is filled with misdeeds. עֲצֻמִים (*'ăṣumîm*) may signify either strong or numerous, and it often occurs coupled with רַבִּים (*rabbîm*), which has a similar alternation between "mighty" and "many." In Prov. 7:26 both terms clearly refer to quantity rather than strength (see also the discussion of Joel 1:6).

---

[42] Harold R. (Chaim) Cohen, *Biblical Hapax Legomena in the Light of Akkadian and Ugaritic* (SBLDS 37; Missoula, Mont.: 1978), p. 49. Cf. Wolff, *Joel and Amos*, p. 230 n. aa; Dearman, *Property Rights in the Eighth-Century Prophets*, p. 28. Smith, *Amos*, p. 168, prefers the rendering "tread" or "trample."

[43] See GKC, par. 19n.

[44] N. Avigad, "Samaria," in *Encyclopedia of Archaeological Excavations in the Holy Land*, 4:1041; King, *Archaeological Commentary*, pp. 65-67.

The additional basis for judgment seems at first glance to disturb the flow of the passage in that the judgment has already been described.[45] Yet it serves a climactic function, with a pronouncement of punishment wedged between two accusations or rebukes (cf. the chiastic arrangement discussed above). The stress on the overwhelming number of Israel's transgressions increases through an enumeration of several characteristic examples and through the ironic observation that a wise man keeps silent in the face of such pervasive evil.

5:12b Amos sums up various ways the wealthy Israelites would harass or distress defenseless people who were innocent of any wrongdoing. By using the participle of צָרַר (ṣārar, "harass"), he shows how characteristically the wicked do these things. Perhaps the powerful were using the courts to give the appearance of legality to their crimes against the helpless. The term "innocent" (in a legal sense, cf. on 2:6) and the following references to bribery and obstruction of justice give the verse a judicial context.

כֹּפֶר (kōper) usually means "ransom," that is, the price paid as a substitute for a man's life (e.g., Ex. 21:30; Num. 35:31, 32). In Amos the term must have a more general sense of money accepted to influence a judge's decision – a bribe. In this usage it is similar to שֹׁחַד (šōḥad), "gift" or "bribe."

For the term "afflicted," see the comments on 2:6, and refer to the exegesis of 5:10 for "in the gate." The use of the verb הִטּוּ (hiṭṭû, "they turn aside") in the perfect tense, following participles that state general conditions, indicates a general situation viewed as a whole.[46] Also, the verb has the third person form ("they") because of the descriptive context. "You are," Amos says, "those who harass ... and (who) turn aside..."

5:13 In v. 13 Amos is not condoning silence in the face of evil. After all, he himself is speaking out very forcefully. He gives a description of the evil times, not a prescription for right behavior. If a person wants to look out for his own interests, he keeps silent. Speaking the truth could incur the wrath and hatred of those who prefer to pervert justice (cf. 5:10), with potentially grave consequences. Amos also had to face the consequences for his outspokenness when Amaziah the priest of Bethel confronted him (7:10-17).

Other suggestions are that even a wise man cannot find anything to say about such rampant evil or that the silence is to mourn the disaster that has come upon the nation.[47] The former view would seem to require more stress on the wise man (perhaps וְגַם, wĕgam, "and even the wise man"). The idea of mourning is not found in the immediate context, and if Amos meant silence in the face of disaster, it is not clear why he chose the term "wise man" (מַשְׂכִּיל, maśkîl). Rather the terminology raises a conflict in the reader's mind: wisdom but silence when men are evil.

---

[45] Cf. Mays, Amos, pp. 96-97.

[46] See Finley, "WAW-Consecutive," pp. 254-55.

[47] See N. J. Tromp, "Amos V 1-17; Towards a Stylistic and Rhetorical Analysis," OTS 23 (1984): 78 n. 90; Smith Amos, p. 170. Smith applies the term מַשְׂכִּיל (maśkîl, "wise man") to the wealthy who are "prosperous, successful, or clever."

Hatred of justice, milking the poor, transgressions and sins that cannot be counted, perversion of the courts, bribery of judges, denial of legal rights to those with legitimate complaints, an atmosphere where silence is the only prudent course – such are the conditions prevalent in what Amos sums up as "an evil time" (עֵת רָעָה, 'ēt rāʿâ). No wonder then that the Lord has to visit the land in judgment. Injustice goes against the very nature of God, who is personally concerned with the rights of the downtrodden of society (cf. Job 5:15-16; Ps. 140:12 [MT 140:13]; Prov. 14:31).

Additional Notes

5:10 דֹבֵר תָּמִים: It is difficult to decide whether the witness speaks "with integrity" (NASB) or speaks "the truth" (NIV). The latter seems better in that דבר normally takes an object. The participle (and once the infinitive construct, Ps. 51:6 [MT 51:4]) is the only form of the root that occurs in the *qal*. This may be because the *qal* is used for the general case, whereas the *piel* is used for specific occasions of speaking.[48]

5:11 בּוֹשַׁסְכֶם: Note that both the NIV and the JB (and the NJB) still have the rendering "trample upon," a translation first seen in the Syriac (*qphtwn*). The Targum, erroneously interpreting the *bet* as a preposition, has "despoil" (מיבז [for שסה?]).

כַּרְמֵי־חֶמֶד: The phrase apparently occurs also in Isa. 27:2, where the *BHS* has חֶמֶד, "desire," but many Hebrew manuscripts have חֶמֶר, "wine."[49]

F. A Call To Seek Righteousness – On The Basis Of Grace (5:14-15)

Translation

> Seek good and not evil
> that you may live.
> Thus let it be so! "Yahweh God of hosts be with you,"
> even as you have said.
> [15]Hate evil and love good,
> and establish justice in the gate.
> Perhaps the Lord God of hosts will be gracious
> to the remnant of Joseph.

Exegesis and Exposition

Amos repeats his call for the Israelites to repent, this time in the hope that they might receive grace from the Lord. If the times were evil, then the people should seek for the good. Previously Amos exhorted them to seek the Lord for counsel (5:4, 6); now they must follow after that which is pleasing to the Lord (cf. Prov.

---

[48] Ernst Jenni, *Das hebräische Piʾel: Syntaktisch-semasiologische Untersuchung einer Verbalform im Alten Testament* (Zurich: EVZ, 1968), pp. 164-70.
[49] See Otto Kaiser, *Isaiah 13-39: A Commentary* (OTL; trans. R. A. Wilson; Philadelphia: Westminster, 1974), p. 224 n. g.

11:27). The result will be life; perhaps they will even escape the searing judgment that cannot otherwise be stayed.

The leaders of the people already hate the person who wants to give the righteous verdict in a legal case or to present a true witness (5:10). Repentance will be evident if, instead, they hate evil. That is, they must abhor anything that stands in the way of bringing justice to the poor and oppressed. The Law of the Lord given through Moses demanded that the innocent should be acquitted, the needy fed, the poor respected, and the afflicted comforted.[50]

Amos hopes that some of his present audience might form part of "the remnant of Joseph" and escape the coming judgment. He has no illusions that the nation as a whole might turn around. The northern kingdom cannot continue, but some might repent and thereby leave a remnant for "Joseph" (cf. 5:7, "house of Joseph"). If the Lord wills to save a remnant to honor His promise to Joseph as one of the sons of Jacob, Amos tells his audience, perhaps they can be part of it by seeking the way of life that shows faith in God.[51]

5:14 As Gerhard Hasel points out, v. 14 serves as a commentary on the earlier exhortation to seek the Lord. He cannot be found in sanctuaries or holy places; only when a person seeks for righteousness will he or she find the Lord.[52]

The people evidently had a saying with which they would encourage each other in battle: "Yahweh God of hosts be with you!" Amos says, "Let it be so!" (כַּאֲשֶׁר אֲמַרְתֶּם, ka'ăšer 'ămartem, "even as you have said"). Thereby, he shows that the words are not true as long as evil prevails over good, but he also raises a hope. Things could be different; once again the Lord could be with Israel as her God.[53] NASB interprets the particle כֵּן (ken) differently: "and thus may the LORD … be with you," but the word order argues rather for "may it be so."[54]

5:15 In speaking of "the remnant of Joseph" Amos already recognizes that the threat to the nation is certain (cf. 5:6). A remnant cannot be left unless the nation is first decimated. Perhaps Amos referred to the northern kingdom as descendants of Joseph because he realized that the patriarch stood under the blessing of the Lord and preserved alive a remnant (שְׁאֵרִית, šĕ'ērît) of Israel during a crucial threat to their existence (Gen 45:7).[55]

Verses 14a and 15a, as many have noted, contain an additional chiasmus: "Seek good and not evil… Hate evil and love good."

---

[50] Cf. Thomas J. Finley, "An Evangelical Response to the preaching of Amos," *JETS* 28 (1985): 411-20.

[51] After my own study of the passage, I noticed that Gerhard Hasel came to a similar conclusion (*The Remnant*, pp. 196-205).

[52] Hasel, *The Remnant*, pp. 196-97.

[53] Wolff, *Joel and Amos*, p. 250. Wolff speculates that the passage derives from a disciple of Amos but admits "the majority of scholars" regard it as from Amos (p. 234).

[54] See Thomas J. Finley, "The Sheep Merchants of Zechariah 11," *GTJ* 3 (1982): 56-58.

[55] Hasel, *The Remnant*, p. 201.

G. A Call For Lamentation (5:16-17)

Translation

> Therefore, thus says Yahweh God of hosts, *the Lord:
> "In all the plazas there shall be wailing,
> and in all the streets they will say, 'Alas! Alas!'
> They will summon the farmer to mourning,
> and *professional lamenters to wailing.
> [17]And in all the vineyards there will be wailing,
> for I will pass through your midst,"
> says Yahweh.

Exegesis and Exposition

At this point Amos returns to the theme of mourning for the dead. The immediately preceding call to seek good did interrupt the sequence, but it also formed a backdrop to highlight God's grace. Perhaps some might repent and receive grace from the Lord, but the fact that it would apply only to a remnant already showed that the judgment to which Amos devotes full attention now could not be turned back.

Previously Amos recited a dirge for the nation's funeral (5:1-3); now he calls for a general lamentation throughout the land. It will be a public demonstration of mourning that involves the entire community, and it will take place after a great calamity (cf. Jer. 6:26).

The judgment will fall most heavily on the nobles who have become rich by placing burdens on the tenant farmers (5:11). Some of these farmers who remain will be summoned to mourn the loss of their countrymen. The lush vineyards whose owners will not be able to enjoy them (5:11) are now singled out as special sites of lamentation.

Amos closes the section by further reference to God as the awesome Judge of Israel. The Lord will pass through the land and leave behind Him wailing and lamentation. The Lord's visitation also sets the scene for the next section in which Amos discusses the popular hope that the "day of Yahweh" will arrive soon.

5:16 The conjunction לָכֵן (*lākēn*, "therefore") in v. 16 connects the passage with vv. 10-13.[56] Inexcusable injustices throughout the land fully justify what the Lord will do.

The plazas and streets are places where the mourning would be highly visible. מִסְפֵּד (*mispēd*) and its related verb סָפַד (*sāpad*) are sometimes associated with sorrow because of death (cf. Gen. 50:10; 2 Sam. 1:12), but they can also be connected to repentance (Joel 2:12; cf. Zech. 12:10 where both ideas are present).

The phrase יוֹדְעֵי נֶהִי (*yôdĕ'ê nehî*) is literally "knowers of a mourning song," evidently indicating professional mourners (cf. 2 Chron. 35:25; Jer. 9:17 [MT 9:16]). One problem with this view is understanding why professional mourners should be mentioned in the same context with the farmer. The translation given is

---

[56] Cf. Ebenezer Henderson, *The Twelve Minor Prophets* (Thornapple Commentaries; Grand Rapids: Baker, 1980), p. 156.

AMOS

based on a textual change, and it is not impossible that the true meaning of the line cannot now be discerned (see Additional Notes). In any case, some irony is conveyed when the farmer is called upon to mourn for those who had previously oppressed him.

5:17 Feinberg rightly compares v. 17 with the Lord's action in Egypt during the Israelite captivity: "For I will pass through [וְעָבַרְתִּי, *wěʿābartî*] the land of Egypt in that night, and will strike down all the first-born in the land of Egypt" (Ex. 12:12).[57] The Lord had previously threatened through Amos this visitation for iniquity (3:2).

The singular pronoun that occurs with בְּקִרְבֶּךָ (*běqirběkā*, "through your midst") is noteworthy. Most frequently the nation is addressed with a plural pronoun in the book of Amos, but singular forms occur also at 3:11; 4:12; and 5:23. A similar alternation occurs in other books (cf. Ex. 12:3-4 with vv. 5-10; Deut. 6:1 with vv. 2-3). In Amos the singular forms apparently stress the solidarity of the people as one unit.

Additional Notes

5:16 אֲדֹנָי: LXX has no equivalent for the word, having only κύριος ὁ θεὸς ὁ παντοκράτωρ. The Peshitta agrees, and it is not impossible that these versions have the better text. However, the poetry is more balanced in the MT if אֲדֹנָי אֱלֹהֵי צְבָאוֹת comprises a half-line in apposition to יהוה. Also, the title is unique, and Amos loved to vary the titles used for the Lord.

וּמִסְפֵּד אֶל־יוֹדְעֵי נֶהִי: Literally the line reads, "and wailing to knowers of a mourning song." Thus, the preposition "to" seems out of place. Lehrman, following the plan of the Soncino Books of the Bible series to abide consistently by the received text, translates, "And they shall call the husbandman to mourning,/ And proclaim lamentation to such as are skilful of wailing."[58] At first glance this seems to solve the problem, but note that the single Hebrew verb "call" (וְקָרְאוּ), which does indeed apply to both halves of the line, has to be given two different meanings.

According to Henderson, it is not necessary to change the Hebrew text in order to arrive at the meaning given here (cf. KJV, NIV, NASB, JB),[59] but this does not seem to be the case. It is true that מִסְפֵּד does not need a preposition for the meaning "(summon to) wailing," but "(summon to) wailing to the knowers of lamentation" is strained syntactically. It is best to assume that the preposition אֶל

---

[57] Charles L. Feinberg, *The Minor Prophets* (Chicago: Moody, 1976), p. 105. Michael James Hauan, "The Background and Meaning of Amos 5:17B," *HTR* 79 (1986): 337-48, rejects the connection with Ex. 12:12 because he assigns it to the "Priestly" code that he thinks was later than Amos. Instead he connects Amos's statement with a covenant ritual in which Yahweh "passes through" (*ʿābar*) the pieces of a sacrifice (as in Gen. 15). Feinberg's explanation seems simpler and less encumbered with speculation about ritual background.

[58] S. M. Lehrman, "Amos" in *The Twelve Prophets* (Soncino Books of the Bible; ed. A. Cohen; London: Soncino, 1969), p. 105.

[59] Henderson, *The Twelve Minor Prophets*, p. 157.

has been displaced by metathesis. Some slight support for this reading appears in the Perhitta, though the evidence is by no means clear.

The LXX solved the problem by adding the conjunction καί: "and to those knowing a dirge" (καὶ εἰς εἰδότας θρῆνον). Admittedly this gives evidence for the MT at least as early as the second century B.C.

7
Woe to Zion
(5:18-6:14)

Since the call for Israel to hear God's word serves as a major organizer for chaps. 3-6, it seems best to include chap. 6 of Amos with chap. 5. The summons to "hear" of 5:1 applies to both chapters, and the cry of "woe" in 6:1 is a further link between them (cf. v. 18). On the other hand, Amos 6 speaks mostly of coming judgment and makes an appropriate conclusion to the entire section of 3-6. For a discussion of the rhetorical divisions of chaps. 5-6, see the introductory remarks for chap. 6 of the commentary.

A. A Rebuke For Misplaced Zeal (5:18-27)

Both pronouncements of "woe" in Amos have a similar structure of four parts. The statement of woe itself (5:18a; 6:1a) is followed by a challenge to what the listeners thought about reality (5:18b-20; 6:1b-7). The Lord's perspective differs. The threat of judgment is implied within the first challenge, whereas in the second, it is both implicit and explicit (6:7). Third, Amos delivers strongly worded statements by the Lord that He has rejected their perspective on what pleases Him (5:21-25) or on what they are relying for their security (6:8a). In the fourth part, Amos predicts God's judgment on the nation. For the first pronouncement of woe, the threat of judgment is limited to a brief statement about exile (5:26-27), but for the second woe oracle, an extended pronouncement of judgement occurs as a separate unit attached to the main oracle itself (6:9-11).

Amos knew that the Israelites were deceiving themselves. They thought they were alive, but they were really dead. They could not receive life until they sought the Lord and the justice He demanded (5:1-17). In 5:18-27 Amos reveals the truth about three areas of false beliefs:

1. the truth about the day of the Lord (vv. 18-20);
2. the truth about what God requires from His people (vv. 21-26); and
3. the truth about what God will do to the people because of their sins (v. 27).

The third point makes explicit the threat contained in the first, giving a type of chiastic structure to the passage (judgment – requirements – judgment).

1. The Pronouncement Of Woe And Its Challenge (5:18-20)

Translation

*Woe, you who long for the day of Yahweh!
Why should the day of Yahweh mean anything to you?
It will be darkness and not light.
[19]It will be just like a man who escapes from a lion,
and a bear meets him.

217

Then he arrives home and leans his hand against the wall,
and a snake bites him.
[20]Is not the day of Yahweh darkness rather than light?
And oppressive darkness with no brightness to it?

Exegesis and Exposition

That the unrighteous in Israel would long for the day of the Lord shows the
extent of their self-deception. Various prophets uniformly treat "the day of
Yahweh" as a time of judgment against the wicked. Obadiah, for example, says it
will come for "all the nations" when they will be judged for their sins against Judah
(Obad. 15-16); and Isaiah sees it coming with such "fury and burning anger" that
sinners "will writhe like a woman in labor" (Isa. 13:6-16). Sometimes the prophet
stresses that the judgment falls especially on Israel (Joel 1:15; 2:1, 11; Zeph. 1:7,
14; Mal. 4:5 [MT 3:23]), but at other times the major force of the punishment is
against the nations who are enemies of Israel (Joel 3:4, 19 [MT 4:4, 19]).

The people of the northern kingdom were evidently familiar only with the
latter tradition. They could not imagine that the day of the Lord would mean
anything except vengeance on their enemies (cf. Amos's announcements of
judgment against Israel's neighbors in 1:3-2:5). Yet again Amos makes a bold
statement calculated to bring shock and consternation to those who hear it.

All attempts to escape from the Lord in His awesome day are futile. Some
might try to flee, even as a man runs in terror from a lion. But if he can outrun the
lion, a bear will meet him, and even if he should arrive at the security of his home, a
snakebite will seal his fate. None of the Lord's foes can hope to escape. One might
compare Judah's later foretaste of the terrible wrath God will pour out on the
judgment day: "He is to me a bear lying in wait,/ a lion in a hiding place" (Lam.
3:10).

5:18a The day of the Lord in the OT usually refers to a time of judgment at
the end of the age. Yet Amos speaks as though his own countrymen would go
through it. Does he view it, then, more in terms of an ordinary historical event?

Perhaps Amos only mentions the subject because the people were talking
about it.[1] He does not predict that the eschatological day of the Lord will overtake
them; he only points out that they cannot expect good to come from it for them.
Since they were hoping to escape its judgment, Amos corrects them.

In fact, he uses the term "day of Yahweh" to speak more precisely of the
judgment he has been predicting for them all along. For all he knows, it may even
be the eschatological judgment, but he is sure that devastation rather than prosperity
awaits Israel. Israel's conquest by Assyria turned out to be only a foreshadowing of
the ultimate day of the Lord, but the utter destruction brought by Assyria was really
a day of darkness and utter gloom. The northern kingdom's existence as a nation
came to an end, and many of her people were either killed or deported.

5:18b Amos challenges his audience to reflect on the true meaning of the day
of the Lord for them The particle (הֶז, zeh) is not the demonstrative pronoun

---

[1] K. A. D. Smelik, "The Meaning of Amos V 18-20," *VT* 36 (1986): 247, thinks Amos
has false prophets in mind as those who long for the day. It is difficult to accept that the
context limits the deluded ones so much.

("this"). Rather it brings out the amazement of the questioner: "Why, really, should the day of Yahweh mean anything to you?" How could the people be so ignorant of the Lord and His ways as to suppose they can become rich and powerful by crushing others to the ground, while at the same time they express a deep longing for the Lord to come and crush His (and their) enemies?[2]

5:19 Through the masterful irony and humor of v. 19 Amos paints a vivid picture of a hopeless situation. It is hard to know for sure if he thinks of two unrelated incidents or of a chain of four connected events. The latter is best because of the conjunction *waw* with "and he comes home." Also, Amos does not repeat the word אִישׁ (*'îš*, "man") with that part. So we should think of *one* poor soul who *twice* escaped from lethal danger, only to relax in the "safety" of his own home and be bitten by a poisonous snake.

5:20 Through the verbal and thought repetition of v. 20 Amos comes back to the theme of the utter darkness of the day of the Lord. He knows the Lord as the Controller of darkness and light (4:13; 5:8), and on the unique day when the Lord comes as the Judge, He will withdraw all light. Other prophets also recognized the element of darkness (Isa. 13:10; Joel 2:2, 31 [MT 3:4]; 3:15 [MT 4:15]; Zeph. 1:15); it is a characteristic feature of this future expectation. Probably, then, Amos's audience was aware of this aspect of the day of the Lord. Their mistake was in not recognizing that darkness would envelop them as well as the nations.

Additional Notes

5:18 הוֹי: One should not place too much emphasis on the different spelling of הוֹ in 5:16, even though they mean "woe" and "alas," respectively. First, the latter form is unique, but more importantly two or more variant spellings commonly occur in close contexts in OT Hebrew. Note, for example, לְמִינוֹ and לְמִינֵהוּ for "after its kind" in Gen. 1. Whether this practice stems from the original authors or from later scribal practice is uncertain.

2. The Lord's Rejection And His Judgment (5:21-27)

Translation

> I hate, I reject your festivals!
> And I take no pleasure in your religious assemblies.
> [22]*Even though you offer to Me burnt offerings
> with your grain offerings, I will not accept them;
> and I will not look favorably upon your fatlings brought as peace offerings.
> [23]Remove from Me the noise of your songs;
> I do not want to hear the music of your harps.

---

[2] For זֶה (*zeh*), see GKC, par. 136c; BDB, p. 261a. Hans Walter Wolff, *Joel and Amos*, trans. Waldemar Janzen, et al. (Philadelphia: Fortress, 1977), p. 255, notes that "The idiom למה ל [*lāmmâ lě*] inquires after the meaning, the usefulness or the disadvantage, of something for someone" and cites the additional case of Job 30:2.

^{24}But let justice roll down like water,
and righteousness like a continually flowing stream.
^{25}Did you bring sacrifices and grain offerings to Me
*in the wilderness for forty years, house of Israel?
^{26}(Granted,) but you will take up *Sikkuth *your king
and *Kiyyun, your *divine images,
   your star-gods, which you have made for yourselves,
^{27}when I send you into exile beyond Damascus,
says He whose name is Yahweh, God of hosts.

Exegesis and Exposition

Even though Amos described Israel as laden with evil and injustice, the people did maintain the outward appearance of devotion to the Lord. They longed expectantly for Him to come and bring revenge on all their enemies. They celebrated special religious festivals, assembled the people for worship, offered various kinds of sacrifices, and even devoted their musical talent to worship.

Yet the Lord's startling language concerning the very offerings He required of Israel through the Mosaic Law is designed to make the people realize that they have perverted the intent of the sacrifices. They have come to view them as a magical way of manipulating God to bless them even though their lives show a neglect of the inner requirements of the covenant.

This theme of misdirected religious zeal increases to a climax in the present portion of Amos. We were given a first glimpse of unrighteous religiosity when Amos described people stretched out on the garments of the destitute beside an altar and drinking wine obtained by extortion in a temple (2:8). Later Amos prophesied that the "altars of Bethel" will perish when the Lord judges the "house of Jacob" (3:14). Then he commanded Israel in ironic tones to worship God at Bethel and Gilgal, and thereby sin (4:4-5). Obviously Israel was a very religious nation.

But now Amos makes explicit the Lord's hatred for Israel's zeal, because it was not a zeal accompanied by righteous behavior. In one masterful stroke Amos summarizes the heart of what God requires. It is an abundance of justice and righteousness, which rushes through the land like an overflowing, life-giving stream.

Another side of the issue is pure devotion to the Lord alone. Israel mixed the worship of the Lord with the worship of idols. Of course, they were not really worshiping the Lord anyway when they failed to practice justice. Therefore, idolatry expressed the true nature of their adoration. They served false gods. These gods will condemn the people to exile from the land. The Lord rejects the people who have rejected Him: they will carry their false religion with them to a strange land.

5:21 On three occasions Amos speaks of hatred (5:10; 5:15; 5:21). The elders at a trial hate anyone who might render a just decision by reproving the one who is actually at fault (v. 10). In other words, they hate justice. Contrary to this practice, Amos gives the commandment of the Lord: "Hate evil and love good!" (v. 15). Now in v. 21 the prophet points out the Lord's own hatred: "I hate ... your festivals." The three hatreds are connected. Because the Israelites hate justice and refuse to hate evil, God holds in contempt their efforts to please Him through ceremony.

Strengthening the sense of rejection even more, the Lord says their religious assemblies will not be pleasing to Him, and He will not accept their offerings. The verb הֵרִיחַ (*hērîah*) refers to the action of smelling, deriving apparently from a noun that means "smell." From the more restricted context of "smelling the sweet aroma" of sacrifice, the more general "delight in" (cf. Isa. 11:3) developed. רָצָה (*rāṣâ*, "accept") also occurs often in the context of the sacrificial system, though in the niphal pattern ("be pleasing," "be acceptable"; Lev. 1:4; 7:18; 19:7; 22:23, 25, 27) or in the noun form רָצוֹן (*rāṣôn*, "acceptance"; Lev. 1:3; 19:5; 22:19, 20, 21, 29; 23:11).

5:22 The "burnt offering" (עוֹלָה, *'ôlâ*), the "grain offering" (מִנְחָה, *minḥâ*), and the "peace offering" (שֶׁלֶם, *šelem*) are each described in Leviticus as "a soothing aroma to Yahweh" (רֵיחַ נִיחֹחַ לַיהוה, *rêah nîḥōah leYHWH*; Lev. 1:13; 2:9; 3:16). Thus, the last part of v. 21, which uses the verb *hērîah*, suggests the very sacrifices that were commonly thought of as pleasing to God.

These sacrifices functioned to maintain the relationship between the Lord and His people. When conducted properly and with the devoted attitude of the worshiper, God would accept them to make atonement for sin (Lev. 1:4) and as a means to express their love and devotion to Him. [3] The Lord will vehemently refuse these offerings, says Amos, if the worshipers oppress their neighbors and refuse to seek justice.

Usually the two words כִּי אִם (*kî 'im*) or *kî* by itself are translated "but" after a negative statement (see Ps. 1:2), though sometimes *kî* will receive one of its more usual senses in this situation (cf. Ex. 22:22-23 [MT 22:21-22]; 2 Sam. 13:33; Jer 37:9-10). Here the context demands the concessive sense: "*Even though* you offer … I will not accept them."

5:23 Music (v. 23) was a regular means for the worshiper to express devotion to the Lord (cf. Ex. 15:1-18; Deut. 31:30-32:43; Judg. 5). Amos even makes the connection between music and David (6:5). Yet, as with David, music should be a spontaneous expression of love for the Lord. When the Israelites made music a part of their regular worship, they made their hypocris y even worse. The impression was of great zeal and devotion, but everyday behavior showed a lack of genuine commitment. As a result, their music, no matter how melodious and beautiful, was only "noise" in the Lord's ears.

The נֵבֶל (*nēbel*) was a stringed instrument (Pss. 33:2; 92:3 [MT 92:4]) of uncertain shape (no clear representations are known). It is found as an instrument of music in a variety of situations depicted in Scripture (cf. 2 Sam. 6:5; Neh. 12:26; Isa. 5:12), often in the company of a "lyre" (כִּנּוֹר, *kinnôr*; e.g., Ps. 57:8 [MT 57:9]; 1 Chron. 15:26). Representations of the latter stringed instrument are known from Assyrian reliefs, Mesopotamian paintings, and Jewish coins. [4]

---

[3] For details about these sacrifices, see Gordon J. Wenham, *The Book of Leviticus* (NICOT; Grand Rapids: Eerdmans, 1979), pp. 55-63, 69-72, 76-81; E. E. Carpenter, "Sacrifices and Offerings in the OT," *ISBE*, rev. ed., 4:260-73.

[4] E. Werner, "Musical Instruments," *IDB* 3:474.

The line that describes the music has a balanced yet reversed (chiastic) structure in Hebrew, as shown by the following diagram:

Remove	from-Me	noise-of	your-songs
And-music-of	your-harps	not	I-will-hear

The effect of the structure is to tie together the parts. More prosaically, the people should remove both the songs and the harps, for the Lord does not desire to hear either the music or the noise.

5:24 Amos, as a sheep dealer and a cultivator, was keenly interested in water and its importance for the land. He recognizes the devastation caused by drought (1:2; 4:7-8; 7:4) and the life-giving properties of hills that are saturated with water from springs and streams (9:13). In 5:24 justice and righteousness are made liquids that bring healing to the land.

"Justice" in the context of Amos encompasses reparation for the defrauded, fairness for the less fortunate, and dignity and compassion for the needy. "Righteousness" indicates the conditions that make justice possible: attitudes of mercy and generosity, and honest dealings that imitate the character of God[5] as He has revealed Himself in the Law of Moses. Here is what it means to "seek Yahweh" and to "seek good" and "hate evil."

We should be careful, however, not to make the statement overly absolute. Amos avoids broad generalizations in favor of rather specific pronouncements that apply directly to his audience. Justice and righteousness were the two missing ingredients for Israel in Amos's day, but that does not mean we have to assume either that "social justice" is the sum total of all that God requires or that we must somehow make this verse a summary of all of Scripture. On the other hand, the full implications of Amos's call for justice should not be blunted or ignored when application is made to modern societies (see also Excursus on Social Justice in Amos).

5:25 It is very difficult to determine the connection of vv. 25-27 with the rest of the chapter, especially because of the question with which the passage opens: "Did you bring sacrifices and grain offerings to Me in the wilderness for forty years, house of Israel?" The crucial issue is how to interpret the question. The grammar normally would expect a negative answer:[6] "No. You did not do this."

On the face of it, this would appear to make Amos contradict passages that clearly showing that sacrifices were offered during the period of wilderness wanderings (Ex. 24:4-8; Num. 7). In fact, some do think that Amos follows a tradition, known also from Jer. 7:21-23, that conflicts with the allegedly later traditions found in the Pentateuch about the Tabernacle and the sacrifices.[7] Such an extreme view is unwarranted, raising more problems than it solves, and most commentators seek a harmonizing solution. Of these, some base their explanation

---

[5] Cf. James Luther Mays, *Amos: A Commentary* (OTL; Philadelphia: Westminster, 1969), p. 92.

[6] See GKC, par. 150d.

[7] E.g., Mays, *Amos*, p. 111; Wolff, *Joel and Amos*, pp. 264-65. For a discussion of the issues in Jer. 7:21-23, see Charles L. Feinberg, "Jeremiah," in *EBC*, ed. Frank E. Gaebelien (Grand Rapids: Zondervan, 1986), 6:431.

on a negative answer to Amos' question, while others prefer to posit a positive answer.

If the answer to the question is "no," then it is necessary to make some qualifications. Perhaps Amos points out that Israel's relationship with the Lord was not sustained by the *frequent* offering of sacrifices and grain offerings. Rather, the Lord brought Israel into existence as a nation through His grace, proving that mere ritual is not the most important thing for a right relationship between God and man.[8]

A problem with this view is that Israel did offer at least some sacrifices in the wilderness, and the people could have pointed that out to Amos by way of response. Keil gets around this difficulty by restricting the statement to "the time during which the people were sentenced to die in the wilderness after the rebellion at Kadesh."[9] In order to do that, however, he has to claim that the cited forty years is a round number. Moreover, Scripture nowhere else indicates that the Israelites did not offer sacrifices in the wilderness, while the building and transport of the Tabernacle leads us to suspect that they did so frequently.

Hayes offers a variation on this view by suggesting that Amos only meant cereal offerings and "well-being" offerings but not other types of offerings.[10] Yet Amos did speak of "burnt offerings" (*'ōlôt*) in v. 22, and *zebāḥîm* with *minḥâ*, seems rather to imply the whole gamut of offerings (cf. Ps. 40:6 [MT 40:7]).

Others argue that Amos' stress was not *only* that sacrifices were necessary to sustain their relationship to the Lord. They were also required to walk obediently with God and to worship Him in sincerity of heart. This view would require a translation like that offered by Gary V. Smith: "Did you offer to me *only* sacrifices...?" (italics added).[11]

Some would place the main emphasis of the passage on לִי (*lî*, "to Me"), so that the answer is: "No. It was not *to Me* that you offered sacrifices."[12] This could stress two things: their idolatry even from the time of their wandering in the wilderness (as in Stephen's citation of the passage in Acts 7:39-43; cf. Excursus on the Citation of Amos 5:25-27 in Acts 7:42-44); or the insincerity in their worship in the wilderness. That is, they did not have lives that supported their profession of faith. This is possible, though from a grammatical point of view, the stress does not seem to occur on *lî* ("to Me").

---

[8] C. F. Keil, *Minor Prophets* (COTTV 10; Grand Rapids: Eerdmans, 1973), p. 290. Cf. S. R. Driver, *The Books of Joel and Amos* (CBSC; Cambridge: University, 1907), p. 188; Douglas Stuart, *Hosea-Jonah* (WBC 31; Waco, Tex.: Word, 1987), p. 355.

[9] Keil, *Minor Prophets*, p. 290.

[10] John H. Hayes, *Amos, The Eighth Century Prophet: His Times and His Preaching* (Nashville: Abingdon, 1988), p. 175. It is unclear why he refers to "well-being" offerings (*šelāmîm?*) when the Hebrew term is the more general זְבָחִים (*zĕbāḥîm*, "sacrifices").

[11] Gary V. Smith, *Amos: A Commentary* (The Library of Biblical Interpretation; Grand Rapids: Zondervan, 1989), p. 188.

[12] See Ebenezer Henderson, *The Twelve Minor Prophets: Translated from the Original Hebrew with a Critical and Exegetical Commentary* (Thornapple Commentaries; Grand Rapids: Baker), p. 159, who states but does not accept the view; and Robert B. Chisholm, Jr., "Amos," in *BKCOT*, ed. John F. Walvoord and Roy b. Zuck (Wheaton: Victor, 1985), p. 1442.

Perhaps, then, Amos expected the answer "yes" to his question. Possibly he answers an objection raised by the Israelites to his message that God requires obedience to the demands of the covenant and not mere ritual. The answer must be correlated closely with the thought of vv. 26-27: "Indeed you did offer sacrifices and grain offerings in the wilderness, but now you will take up your idols, since you have rejected me, and I will send you into exile."[13]

A. S. van der Woude presents an alternative grammatical explanation that results in a similar interpretation. He argues that vv. 25 and 26 represent a question coordinated with a second clause to which it is logically subordinate (GKC, par. 150m). The result is that the second clause, not the first, needs to be translated as a question (cf. Num. 16:22b, lit., "will one man sin? And You will be angry with the entire congregation?"). Van der Woude's translation is, "When you brought me sacrifice ... did you then carry around the Sakkut?"[14] In other words, in the wilderness the people offered sacrifice and served the Lord, but now they are serving foreign gods.

A problem arises from the small amount of space Amos devotes otherwise to idolatry, but certainly he was aware that the Israelites were practicing a syncretistic religion. Realizing that the nation still stands under the covenant promises and claims to include the Lord in her worship, albeit combined with the worship of false gods, Amos concentrates not on the idolatry but on her claim. Since she does not obey the demands of the covenant for justice and righteousness, she cannot sustain that claim. Therefore, there is nothing left for her but to take up her idols and carry them into captivity.

5:26 Amos's listeners apparently pointed back to the wilderness period when the Lord established Israel as a nation, yet the people had offered sacrifice. In v. 26 the Lord does not really offer a detailed rebuttal of this argument. Surely the people had offered sacrifice in the wilderness, but that does not lessen the guilt of the present generation. If anything, their guilt is greater because they have mixed in the worship of idols with their supposed worship of the Lord. Therefore, they will take up those idols to accompany them into captivity, demonstrating the totality of their rejection of the Lord. Even their reliance on the sacrificial system could not be called true worship, because it was polluted by contact with false religion.

The Lord was supposed to be Israel's king (Deut. 33:5; Ps. 10:16), and no image could represent Him (Ex. 20:4). When He sends the ten tribes into exile, their king will be Sikkuth and their divine image Kiyyun. The latter god has been

---

[13] P. Paul Joüon, *Grammaire de l'hébreu biblique* (Rome: Institut Biblique Pontifical, 1965), par. 161, lists the passage as an example of an interrogative sentence with an exclamatory nuance. Cf. also Henderson, *The Twelve Minor Prophets*, p. 159; and Charles L. Feinberg, *The Minor Prophets* (Chicago: Moody, 1976), p. 106.

[14] "Als Opfer ... ihr mir brachtet ... habt ihr da herumgetragen den Sakkut ... ?" A. S. van der Woude, "Bemerkungen zu einigen umstrittenen Stellen im Zwölfprophetenbuch," in *Mélanges bibliques et orientaux en l'honneur de M. Henri Cazelles* (AOAT 212; ed. A. Caquot and M. Delcor; Neukirchen-Vluyn: Neukirchener Verlag, 1981), pp. 485-88.

identified with a Babylonian name for Saturn.[15] The Hebrew forms of the names may represent a slight change in the original vowels based on a word-play with *šiqqûṣ*, "detested thing." For discussion of alternate readings and interpretations, see the Additional Notes.

There are various ways to construe the verb וּנְשָׂאתֶם (*ûnĕśā'tem*), and the decision is not an easy one. Some versions take it as reference to action in the past or else a present action that first began in the past.

    NIV: "You have lifted up the shrine of your king."
    NASB: "You also carried along Sikkuth your king."
    KJV: "But ye have borne the tabernacle of your Moloch."

    The translation for this commentary is in the future tense. This is based on the contextual arguments developed above. Also, a perfect with *waw* can be taken in a future sense even after another perfect (Judg. 13:3; 1 Sam. 15:28; 1 Kings 2:44). The JB (and NJB) has a rendering similar to that argued for here: "Now you must shoulder Sakkuth your king."[16]

5:27 Previous to v. 27 Amos promised exile for Samaria (4:3) and Gilgal (5:5); now the scope extends to all Israel. The expression "beyond Damascus" probably means something like "beyond your borders." Foreign conquerors from the East would certainly go through Damascus, as the city was a major crossroads for traffic in various directions. The city represented the fringe of Israelite control (2 Kings 14:28), and of course it had also warred against Israel constantly. The Assyrian empire conquered Damascus, making it an Assyrian province in 732 B.C., almost exactly a decade before Samaria fell. For a discussion of the citation of 5:25-27 by Stephen (Acts 7:42-43), see the excursus at the end of the chapter.

Additional Notes

5:22 In addition to the unusual usage of כִּי אִם in the verse, there is also a poetic structure that consists of a line divided into two parts of three metrical units each, with the Lord as the subject of each verb except, "you offer up." Thus, some feel the translation given here goes against both the poetic meter and Hebrew grammar. Wolff, for example, would delete "though you offer up to Me burnt offerings" as a gloss, while Mays supposes that a parallel clause has dropped out (cf. JB).[17] The MT is supported by the ancient versions. As for the metrical pattern, v. 22 could be taken as a tricolon with enjambment (carryover of thought) between

---

[15] *AHW* 1:420. Andersen and Freedman take both gods to represent Saturn (*Amos: A New Translation with Introduction and Commentary* [AB 24A; New York: Doubleday, 1989], p. 534.

[16] But cf. Jan de Waard and William A. Smalley, *A Translator's Handbook on the Book of Amos* (Helps for Translators; n.p.: United Bible Societies, 1979), p. 122. They argue that linguistic considerations favor the following translation and interpretation of v. 26: "'Did you then (that is, at that time) carry the images of your deities?' implying 'as you do now.'" They think it is less preferable to translate v. 26 as a future, because in the "overall discourse structure of Amos, ... action by the Lord is always mentioned before the consequences which it has for the people." Smith (*Amos*, p. 189) agrees with those who would take v. 26 as a continuation of the question in v. 25: "And will you now lift up Sakkuth?"

[17] Wolff, *Joel and Amos*, p. 259 n. c.; Mays, *Amos*, p. 105.

the first two cola. The tricolon would then emphasize the break in thought between the Lord's displeasure and what He actually demands of Israel (vv. 23-24). Other tricola appear in the book of Amos (4:13; 2:12, 13; 3:7; 5:6; 6:2).

5:25 בַּמִּדְבָּר אַרְבָּעִים שָׁנָה: Peshitta has "40 years in the wilderness," while some important manuscripts of the LXX omit "in the wilderness." Codex A includes it but reads "in the wilderness, house of Israel, 40 years," whereas the group C-68, 233', and Syh have "house of Israel, 40 years in the wilderness." The shorter form may have arisen through an interpretation of the passage as a question expecting a negative answer: "Did you offer ... for 40 years?" The answer would then be, "No, you did not offer sacrifice for 40 years, only for a small part of that time." The omission of "in the wilderness" makes the stress on the precise amount of time more obvious. Perhaps the hesitation in word order found in the other texts reflects a correction of the older LXX tradition on the basis of the text-form lying behind the MT, which should be retained.

5:26 סִכּוּת מַלְכְּכֶם וְאֵת כִּיּוּן צַלְמֵיכֶם: Possibly סִכּוּת should be read as "booth of" and כִּיּוּן as "pedestal of" (cf. NIV).[18] The Greek offers some support for interpreting the first term as a noun, though it ignores the suffix on מַלְכְּכֶם (τὴν σκηνὴν τοῦ Μολοχ).[19] Note that the KJV ("the tabernacle of your Moloch") followed the LXX but attached a pronoun to the proper noun, an impossibility for Hebrew. Thomas McComiskey implies that the MT should be taken as common nouns rather than divine names,[20] but the expected Hebrew forms would be סֻכַּה and כֵּן, respectively. The MT instead seems to have taken both words as proper nouns, and the plural צַלְמֵיכֶם is perhaps intended to apply to both gods. The correspondence between כִּיּוּן and the Babylonian name for Saturn is striking, and the "star of your gods" gives a clue that astral deities are meant. Some take the latter expression as a gloss, but "star" is attested in all the ancient versions.

The fact that the Babylonian and Assyrian evidence dates from a period later than Amos might be taken to argue against the interpretation given, but it is only an argument from silence to say that the idols mentioned could not have been worshiped in the eighth century B.C. Morton Cogan argues that the worship of Assyrian astral deities was due to Aramean influence in Israel.[21]

---

[18] Argued in detail by Hayes, *Amos*, pp. 176-78. He describes a royal procession during the "fall festival" in which the king was carried in a "temporary canopy," a litter bore religious objects, and a "star-standard" was carried "as a sign of divine presence or authority."

[19] For more detail on the reading in LXX, with additional suggestions and bibliography, see George Charles Heider III, *The Cult of Molek: A New Examination of the Biblical and Extra-Biblical Evidence* (diss. for Yale Univ.; Ann Arbor, Michigan: U.M.I., 1984), pp. 306-10.

[20] Thomas Edward McComiskey, "Amos," in *EBC*, 7:316-17.

[21] Morton Cogan, *Imperialism and Religion: Assyria, Judah and Israel in the Eighth and Seventh Centuries B.C.E.* (SBLMS 19; Missoula, Mont.: Scholars, 1974), p. 104. William Rainey Harper, *A Critical and Exegetical Commentary on Amos and Hosea* (ICC; Edinburgh: T. & T. Clark, 1979), p. 138, takes the passage as late. See also Heider, *The Cult of Molek*, pp. 306-10.

Excursus on the Citation of Amos 5:25-27 in Acts 7:42-44

According to Acts 7:42-43, Stephen referred to Amos 5:25-26 in his defense before the Sanhedrin. The text of Acts follows LXX closely, but with some significant differences. We would translate Luke's Greek (Nestle-Aland) as follows: "Did you bring offerings and sacrifices to Me for forty years in the wilderness, O house of Israel? And you took up the booth of Moloch and the star of [your] god, Raiphan, the images that you made to worship them, and I will exile you beyond Babylon." The question expects a negative answer, "No. We did not bring offerings and sacrifices to You for forty years in the wilderness."

Stephen cited the passage to support his argument that Israel had been disobedient to God from the period of wilderness wanderings. This disobedience started with the worship of the golden calf, after which "God turned away and delivered them up to serve the host of heaven." Stephen's interpretation of the passage apparently followed a Jewish tradition that supported his own argument but deviated some from the precise meaning in the context of Amos. It did not, however, give an interpretation contrary to actual historical fact. According to this view, the sacrifices and offerings Israel brought were not genuine because they were tainted by idolatry. Note that Stephen also changed "beyond Damascus" to "beyond Babylon." He views the whole sweep of history from the wilderness to the Babylonian captivity as under the sway of idolatry, and so it was.

That Stephen's citation of the passage was really interpretive rather than literal is also shown by the change of "Sakkuth your king" to "the tabernacle of Moloch," and by "Kiyyun your divine image, your star-gods" to "the star of the god Rompha." Both these changes are also found in the LXX. Molech, the national god of Ammon, was worshiped by the rebellious Judeans (1 Kings 11:7; 2 Kings 23:10; Jer. 32:35). "Rompha" is generally thought to be a form of Kiyyun that was altered through scribal confusion (in the older script reading *resh* for *kaph* and *pe* for *waw*). Stephen correctly showed how idolatry characterized the history of Israel down to the Babylonian captivity, drawing on an interpretation of the Amos passage that was undoubtedly familiar to his audience. If he had corrected that tradition to agree with a literal meaning of the passage, the necessity for detailed argumentation would have detracted him from his essential purpose.[22] There is no reason to think that Luke did not record accurately Stephen's speech before the Sanhedrin.

B. A Rebuke For Misplaced Confidence (6:1-11)

As noted previously, it is possible to see a four-part structure to each of the woe oracles. Each statement of "woe" with its accompanying challenge to reality is followed by the Lord announcing His rejection of the nation and the judgment that will inevitably follow.

---

[22] Cf. Gleason L. Archer and G. C. Chirichigno, *Old Testament Quotations in the New Testament: A Complete Survey* (Chicago: Moody, 1983), pp. 151-53.

1. The Pronouncement Of Woe And Its Challenge (6:1-7)

Translation

> *Woe,
> *you who are at ease in Zion,
>> and who are confident in the mountain of Samaria,
> (you who are) the nobles of the foremost of the nations,
>> and those to whom the house of Israel comes.
> [2]Go over to Calneh and look.
> Then go from there to Hamath the great,
> and go down to Gath of the Philistines.
> Are (you) *better than these kingdoms?
> Or was their territory greater than your territory?
> [3](Woe,)
> (you) who refuse to think of a day of calamity,
> yet you have brought closer a reign of violence,
> [4](you) who recline on beds of ivory
>> and are sprawled on your couches,
>> eating lambs from the flock
>> and calves from the midst of the stall,
> [5](you) who strum on the opening of the lyre,
>> like David composing (songs) for yourselves on musical instruments,
> [6](you) who drink wine from bowls
>> and anoint yourselves with the finest of oils.
> Yet they have not grieved over the ruin of Joseph.
> [7]Therefore now, they will go into exile at the front of the exiles,
> and the sprawlers' banqueting will pass away.

Exegesis and Exposition

The leaders of Israel have been smugly trusting in the greatness of their nation. Careless confidence and a false sense of security led to a refusal to even think about the possibility of national disaster. Amos objects that the nation may be powerful, but there is a deep-seated problem her leaders ought to worry about. The house of Joseph is destined for ruin – a violent overthrow by an enemy who will lead the people away into exile.

Instead of grieving over this coming destruction, the wealthy classes in the nation push aside all thought of the future and enjoy a life of ease. They have many banquets where they pass the time in luxurious debauchery. Yet as Amos has pointed out before, the riches that support such high living have come about through oppression, extortion, and violence against the poor and disadvantaged.

When judgment falls, those who so thoughtlessly ignored the warning to repent will lead the way into exile. All the good things they have enjoyed will pass away with the nation itself.

6:1a When Amos mentions Zion at this point in his book, he introduces some dissonance that clashes with the flow of his argument. Yet he balances it immediately with "and who are confident in the mountain of Samaria." The Judeans do play a role in the book, especially in the reference to "the fallen booth of

David" (9:11), but here Amos is continuing his rebuke of the leaders in Israel. Therefore, it seems strange that he should mention the southern kingdom.

Wolff, among others, prefers to treat the reference to Zion as an expansion after the time of Amo s,[23] but the finely balanced parallelism argues in favor of the unity of the first line. Other commentators think Amos treats both Israel and Judah throughout the section (6:1-7), with "these kingdoms" in v. 2 meaning the two parts of Israel (cf. NIV). However, it may be preferable to view "these kingdoms" and "their border" (גְּבוּלָם, gĕbûlām) as referring to Calneh, Hamath the great, and Philistia. In support of this, "house of Israel" (v. 1) and "ruin of Joseph" (v. 6) narrow the context to the northern kingdom. "House of Israel" *might* mean the entire twelve tribes, but elsewhere Amos has used "sons of Israel" to designate the whole nation (3:1).

Erling Hammershaimb thinks Amos speaks initially of both cities but then focuses only on Samaria.[24] A reason for this might be found through comparing the homiletical device used in the oracles against the nations (1:3-2:4). There, it will be recalled, Amos targeted others first in order to draw his audience into the denunciations he was making. That section dealt with Judah immediately prior to a more lengthy diatribe against Israel. Even so here Amos pronounces his woe initially against Zion before moving on to the "mountain of Samaria."

Both places were considered religious centers that lay under the protection of the Lord. A pronouncement of "woe" against either citadel would be shocking, but Amos starts with outsiders before turning more directly to his audience. The effect would be something like this: "Trouble is in store for those who are at ease in Zion. That should be shocking enough to you who think that the Lord protects this city, but here is something even more devastating. Trouble also awaits those of you who confidently trust in the hillside fortress of Samaria."

John Hayes goes a step farther when he says that Jerusalem was a "satellite to Samaria ... of one mind and policy with its northern partner."[25] Yet it still is necessary to explain why Amos would start with Zion and then focus exclusively on Samaria.

"Zion" referred initially to the hill between the Tyropoeon and Kidron valleys that was heavily fortified in Jebusite (pre-David) times and on which David built his city (cf. 2 Sam. 5:6-10).[26] In the Psalms, Zion is often the mountain where the Lord dwells (cf. Pss. 2:6; 9:11 [MT 9:12]). The only other time Amos mentioned Zion, he referred to it as the place where God would roar out His judgment (1:2).

שַׁאֲנָן (ša'anān) often has a negative sense of comfort and ease that amounts to arrogance or insensitivity to reality (cf. Ps. 123:4; Zech. 1:15). The combination with "who feel secure" indicates a state of confidence and security that refuses to be disturbed by the facts.

---

[23] Wolff, *Joel and Amos*, pp. 269 n. a. He also deals with various proposed emendations of בְּצִיּוֹן to something else (e.g., בעיר).

[24] Hammershaimb, *The Book of Amos: A Commentary*, trans. John Sturdy (New York: Schocken, 1970), p. 96.

[25] Hayes, *Amos*, pp. 182-83.

[26] See G. A. Barrois, "Zion," *IDB* 4:959.

6:1*b* Amos specifies in v. 1 those who "are at ease" and who "feel confident": they are Israel's most distinguished citizens. With a touch of irony he calls these leaders of society "distinguished men" or "nobles" (נְקֻבֵי, *nĕqûbê*), using a verb form (passive participle) that means, literally, "named" or "designated." These are men of "renown." An Arabic cognate means "leader" or "chief."

Israel herself is designated "the foremost of nations" (רֵאשִׁית הַגּוֹיִם, *rē'šît haggôyim*). Hebrew *rē'šît* also means "beginning" or "first." Here the nation is "first" in rank or importance. JB captures the meaning and ironic mood of the phrase nicely: "those famous men of this first of nations."

In the parallel line Amos further describes these noblemen: the common people of Israel look up to them for leadership. Apparently a judicial scene is once again in view. The recipients of the "woe" oracle are the elders responsible for judging a case; therefore the people go to them (cf. JB, "to whom the House of Israel goes as client").

6:2 Commentators are divided over how to connect v. 2 with v. 1. According to one view, it gives a further description of the greatness of the kingdoms of Israel and Judah. That is, the leaders of Israel and Judah are commanded to go to other kingdoms, which are not as great as these two kingdoms, to confirm in their own minds their national strength. When they do this, they reinforce the arrogance and complacency that Amos accused them of in v. 1. For example, as a representative of this school of thought, Gary Smith states:

> The comparative questions at the end of 6:2 ask whether Hamath,
> Calnah [*sic*], and Gath are better than "these kingdoms" of Judah and
> Israel. The obvious answer to this rhetorical question would be no.
> The Israelites would claim that they are better, stronger militarily,
> more affluent, and the leaders of nations. The parallel question
> compares the size of the nations. Again the Israelites would have
> claimed that the size of their territory was much greater than the
> territories of Calnah, Hamath or Gath. Their attitudes confirm that
> the people have become confident and lulled to sleep by their
> leaders.[27]

A second view takes the subject of the rhetorical question, הַטוֹבִים מִן־הַמַּמְלָכוֹת הָאֵלֶּה (*hăṭôbîm min-hammamlākôt hā'ēlleh*), as "you" (the leaders of Israel or possibly the leaders of Israel and Judah) and "these kingdoms" as a reference to Hamath, Calneh, and Gath: "Are you better than these kingdoms?"[28] The question expects a negative answer: "Of course you are not any

---

[27] Smith, *Amos*, p. 202. Cf. Keil, *Minor Prophets*, p. 298; Feinberg, *The Minor Prophets*, p. 108; Mays, *Amos*, p. 115; de Waard and Smalley, *A Translator's Handbook on the Book of Amos*, p. 127; McComiskey, "Amos," p. 318. Henderson, *The Twelve Minor Prophets*, p. 164, also takes this view, but he explains that Amos challenges Israel and Judah to consider the other nations "in order that they might become sensible of the superiority with which Jehovah had distinguished them, and the greater punishment to which they had exposed themselves by their ungrateful returns." Cf. Driver, *Joel and Amos*, pp. 191-92.

[28] Cf. Harper, *Amos and Hosea*, p. 144; S. M. Lehrman, "Amos," in *The Twelve Prophets: Hebrew Text & English Translation with Introductions and Commentary*

better than these kingdoms." Possibly the point of comparison is moral. That is, Amos wonders if Israel has behaved so much better than these other kingdoms that she does not deserve to be punished. Alternatively, he points out that Samaria is no better defended than these other cities that have fallen prey to disaster. The two thoughts are not necessarily mutually exclusive.

One major objection to this view is historical. It is pointed out that these nations were not destroyed until later than Amos. Therefore, one cannot accept the interpretation unless it is coupled with the view that the passage is a later addition (as Wolff). Yet it does not seem impossible to fit the interpretation with the known historical facts somewhere near the time of 760 B.C.

Calneh is the most problematic from an historical standpoint. It is probably the same as the capital of the North Syrian kingdom of Patin (also, Unqi). The same city is evidently called Calno by Isaiah (10:9). The Syrian town was located on a large mound in the Amuq Plain. It was conquered in 738 B.C. by the Assyrian Tiglath-pileser III, but Amos could have an earlier conquest in mind. Such an event is not presently known, but our information on ancient Syria is incomplete.[29]

Ancient Hamath is located on a large mound beside the Orontes River in Syria. It was the center of a powerful kingdom with a history dating back to at least the Amarna period (early fourteenth century B.C.). An Aramaic inscription of the early eighth century B.C. was found on a stele set up by "Zakir, king of Hamath and Lu'ath."[30] Shalmaneser III of Assyria conquered the city in the mid-ninth century, and later it was forced into submission by Tiglath-pileser III in 730 B.C., then by Sargon II in 720 B.C.[31] Perhaps Amos had in mind the earlier conquest or some other unknown event.

The location of Philistine Gath is uncertain, but some would place it at Tell es-Safi in northeast Philistia.[32] A number of towns by the name of Gath are known, but the designation "of the Philistines" singles out the strategic fortress city that served for many years as the major Philistine city (cf. Josh. 11:22; 1 Sam. 17:52; 21:12; 2 Sam. 1:20). Hazael, the king of Syria, captured Gath and was so enamored with his feat that he decided to lay siege to Jerusalem (2 Kings 12:17). Later, Uzziah of Judah "broke down the wall of Gath" during a campaign against the Philistines (2 Chron. 26:6). After Sargon II of Assyria captured it, the city drops out of known history.[33] Amos could be referring to any of these military defeats, given that Uzziah's campaign had already taken place.

Another objection to the translation, "Are (you) better than these kingdoms?" is that the second rhetorical question would then have to be emended to read: "Or is *your* territory greater than *their* territory?" (cf. JB and the apparatus to *BHS*).

(Soncino Books of the Bible; ed. A. Coohen; London: Soncino, 1969), p. 108; Wolff, *Joel and Amos*, p. 275 (though I do not agree that the passage is a late insertion; see below); Stuart, *Hosea-Jonah*, p. 359 (but he says the point is simply to indicate "the equality between those nations and Israel"); Donald R. Sunukjian, "Amos," in *BKCOT*, pp. 1442-43.

[29] Cf. M. C. Astour, "Calneh (Calno)," in *IDBSup*, pp. 124-25.

[30] *ANET* (3d ed.), p. 655. See also A. Haldar, "Hamath," *IDB* 2:516.

[31] *ANET* (3d ed.), pp. 279-80, 283-84; H. F. Vos, "Hamath," in *ISBE*, rev. ed., 2:603.

[32] Cf. A. F. Rainey, "Gath," in *IDBSup*, p. 353.

[33] *ANET* (3d ed.), p. 286; W. F. Stinespring, "Gath," *IDB* 2:356.

However, changing the text is not really necessary. As it stands, the question that is coordinated with אִם ('im), also expects a negative answer: "No, their territory is not greater than your territory." Wolff proposes that a small size would actually have been desirable in the face of the Assyrian threat. Perhaps Israel hoped it would not be bothered because of its smallness, but even smaller kingdoms had been devastated by the Assyrians.[34] Yet this view still assumes that the text was later than the conquests of Tiglath-pileser III and/or Sargon II.

Suppose, however, that Amos was not talking about size in a strategic sense. What if he meant that these cities once controlled larger territories that have now been greatly reduced? Then the two questions would make the following points:

1. Are you (Samaria) better than they? No, they were conquered, and so it will happen to you.
2. Are their territories bigger than yours? No, they were greatly reduced in size, and so it will happen to you.

This interpretation would presuppose all or most of the great expansion accomplished for Israel by Jeroboam II (2 Kings 14:25, 28). "Territory" (גְּבוּל, gĕbûl) would correspondingly mean area under some measure of control, though not necessarily complete governmental rule.

Since either translation of the first rhetorical question is possible from the Hebrew, contextual considerations will have to help determine which one to prefer.[35] For the following reasons, the interpretation that sees both questions as addressed to the leaders of Samaria would seem to be preferred.

First, the passage as a whole (vv. 1-7) seems to stress the northern kingdom, whereas the alternative view applies "these kingdoms" to both Israel and Judah. Even though Amos starts with the leaders of Zion, he seems to focus immediately on the northern nation.

Second, the first woe oracle (5:18-27) challenges the reality of Israelite thinking about the day of the Lord. Amos questioned why the people should long for it when it would be the time of their destruction. The view adopted in the above translation of 6:2 presents a similar structure. Amos tells the leaders to consider three well-fortified capitals that were unable to withstand assault and diminution of their territories. Once they too were strongholds like Zion or Samaria, but they experienced at some time in the past a great defeat. Israel cannot expect to escape because of her spiritual relationship to Judah or because of the strength of her capital city. It is false for a nation to hope in religion or in human fortifications and geographical impregnability when unrighteousness reigns within it. No nation is invulnerable; if the Lord wills, He can bring devastation to the strongest of fortresses. Even Zion is not immune to destruction.

Third, with the first translation ("are *they* better"), it is a bit awkward to make the connection between the rhetorical questions and the statement of woe unless one assumes that Amos is quoting the Israelites themselves. For example, Thomas

---

[34] Wolff, *Joel and Amos*, p. 275.

[35] Hayes, *Amos*, p. 185, combines elements of both views with his paraphrase: "Were not Calneh ... once greater kingdoms than Israel and Judah and was not their combined territory larger than the territory of Israel and Judah?" This gives essentially the same significance to Amos' words as is preferred here.

McComiskey explains: "It is as though he were echoing what the people of Israel were saying – 'Look at the other countries: there is none greater than we.'" [36] This would make for a rather complicated sequence, where Amos first addresses the leaders who in turn must be addressing themselves.

6:3 The first cry of "woe" apparently applies to all of the various attitudes or actions that demonstrate a lack of concern in vv. 1-6. The main line of thought extends from "at ease" and "trust" in v. 1 to "refuse," "bring near," "eat," etc. of vv. 3-6, following the prolonged exhortation in v. 2. After demonstrating in vv. 1-2 why the leaders in Samaria should be moved to action, Amos considers them in v. 3 as unresponsive, those who put any thought of disaster out of their minds. The irony throughout these verses (esp. vv. 1b, 3) gives both reasons for the coming judgment as well as implications of the judgment itself. Verse 7 concludes by making a specific reference to exile.

The NASB translators analyzed הַמְנַדִּים (haměnaddîm) as he-interrogative (a particle for forming a question from a statement) with the plural participle and an implied "you" for the subject ("Do you put off the day of calamity?"). In agreement with the ancient versions, however, it seems better to take the he as the article,[37] giving the term the sense of an additional recipient of the "woe" of v. 1: "(Woe), you who put off the day."

Not only do the leaders passively ignore Amos's warning, they also actively participate in the coming calamity by bringing closer a "reign of violence." "Reign" here translates שֶׁבֶת (šebet), more literally "seat" (cf. "throne sitter" for yōšēb in 1:4, 8). Some explain that the Israelites participated in violence,[38] but the thrust of the section is that despite the complacency of the people, judgment will still come (cf. "yet they have not grieved over the ruin of Joseph," v. 6). It is not impossible that Amos intends some ambiguity. Because the oppressors have been violent, violence will overtake them. Certainly they have hastened the onset of judgment by their evil deeds.

6:4 In v. 4 Amos begins to describe various acts of revelry that took place at a certain banquet, called a מַרְזֵחַ (marzēaḥ, the "absolute" form; the construct, mirzaḥ, occurs in v. 7). Philip King points out the significance of Amos's description in comparison with extra-biblical materials:

Amos 6:4-7 is a clear description of the marzeaḥ, although many commentators have failed to identify it as such. In denouncing those who indulged in the marzeaḥ, Amos enumerates five components of this revelry. His listing is not haphazard; it follows the traditional order of elements in an ancient banquet, as known from other sources. For example, the preparation of the meat always preceded the preparation of the wine. Also, the rite of anointing, musical

---

[36] McComiskey, "Amos," p. 318. Cf. Mays, *Amos*, pp. 115-16; de Waard and Smalley, *A Translator's Handbook on the Book of Amos*, pp. 127-28.

[37] For the lack of *dagesh forte* in the *mem* see GKC, par. 20m.

[38] Cf. Feinberg, *The Minor Prophets*, p. 108; Mays, *Amos*, p. 116.

accompaniment, and eating in a prostrate position were integral parts of the banquet scene.[39]

Sometimes a *marzēaḥ* was associated with religious rites that accompanied a funeral (cf. Jer. 16:5-9). The most well-known extra-biblical parallel is a text in alphabetic script from Ugarit which describes a *mrzḥ* established in the house of Shamuman.[40] Often a *marzēaḥ* could belong to a particular deity, demonstrating a religious character of the term (cf., "the *marzih* of the god Satran").[41] On another occasion the god El is depicted as belonging to a *mrzḥ*. While attending it he drinks too much wine (*yn*) and new wine (*trṯ*).[42]

Some similarities with the Amos text are evident. The context does not necessarily point to a meeting for religious purposes, however. Perhaps "banquet" is the best translation in that Amos seems to depict regular events that involve food, music, and wine.

At this banquet, then, the participants would lie down on "beds of ivory." The headboards or posts were apparently inlaid with ivory, a sign of great wealth. In the parallel line, Amos gives a more vivid picture of the revelers "sprawled on their couches." An ugly picture is presented by the term "sprawled" (סְרֻחִים, *sĕruḥîm*). The verb *sāraḥ* is used elsewhere of hanging textiles (Ex. 26:13) or of vine tendrils (Ezek. 17:6). The banqueters lying listlessly on their couches, a sign of careless leisure.

Complete grammatical and semantic parallelism occurs in this line. "Recline" // "sprawl" and "beds of ivory" // "their couches" are the parallel pairs, with the preposition "upon" repeated. (For "your couches" in the translation instead of "their couches," see Additional Notes.)

At the banquet, lambs and stall-fattened calves are served. Most Israelites would not be rich enough to eat meat very often. The participles used for the main actions imply their regular and frequent nature, showing once again the great wealth of the kingdom of Jeroboam II.

6:5 The rich and powerful among the Israelites had so much leisure time that they were able to spend long hours making music at their banquets (v. 5). פֹּרֵט (*pōrēṭ*) is unique to this passage, and the meaning "strum" (NIV) is based on the context.[43] "On the opening of the lyre" is literally "on the mouth of [עַל־פִּי, *'al-pî*]

---

[39] King, *Amos, Hosea, Micah--An Archaeological Commentary* (Philadelphia: Westminster, 1988), p. 138.

[40] Stanislav Segert, *A Basic Grammar of the Ugaritic Language: With Selected Texts and Glossary* (Berkeley: Univ. of California, 1984), p. 138. Segert gives a hand-copy of the Ugaritic, a transliteration, and extensive notes and glossary for this text. The official edition is found in L. R. Fisher, *The Claremont Ras Shamra Tablets* (AnOr 48; Rome: Biblical Institute, 1971), IV:1-3.

[41] RS 15.70 in Fisher, *Claremont Ras Shamra Tablets*, p. 44.

[42] Text 1.114, lines 15-16 in M. Dietrich, et al., *Die keilalphabetischen Texte aus Ugarit* (AOAT 24; Neukirchen-Vluyn: Neukirchener Verlag, 1976).

[43] According to Ernst Klein, *A Comprehensive Etymological Dictionary of the Hebrew Language for Readers of English* (New York: Macmillan, 1987), there is some cognate help from Arabic and Samaritan Hebrew, though it is not certain that the Samaritan evidence would be independent of the Amos passage.

the lyre." Perhaps this refers to the open space between the supports where the strings are touched. Alternatively, *'al-pî* could be given the rather common meaning of "according to," in which case the NASB rendering would be more appropriate: "Who improvise to the sound of the harp." The instrument, a נֵבֶל (*nēbel*), is not a "harp" but a type of lyre, larger than the כִּנּוֹר (*kinnôr*).[44]

The second half of the verse attests an ancient tradition that David composed many songs, as is also known from his numerous Psalms and other Scripture references (cf. 1 Sam. 16:14-23; 2 Sam. 23:1). The mention of David suggests a steady output of songs, indicating the leisure-filled days and nights of the composers. David Noel Freedman suggests that these songs may have been "scurrilous, obscene or blasphemous, and possibly all three."[45] Yet the context need not imply that the activity was in itself wrong, only that it was a sign of wealth and leisure that derived from oppression and that refused to consider the need to repent.

כְּלִי־שִׁיר (*kĕlê-šîr*) occurs often with the meaning "musical instruments" (e.g., 1 Chron. 15:16; 16:42; 2 Chron. 5:13; Neh. 12:36). The preposition "upon" is not in the Hebrew text, but it can be implied from the previous line.[46]

6:6a The Hebrew of v. 6 is literally, "who drink with bowls of wine." The stress is on the large quantity that a bowl can hold. The term מִזְרָק (*mizrāq*, "bowl") most often occurs in a sacrificial context (cf. Num. 7:13; 1 Kings 7:50). It indicates a "vessel for *throwing* or *tossing* a liquid" (BDB, 284b).

Hans Barstad maximizes the religious context of the passage. In his words, "the banquet is condemned for its connections with non-Yahwistic deities rather than for its immorality."[47] Barstad leans heavily on parallels from other Near Eastern cultures, especially with reference to the *marzēaḥ* ("banquet") mentioned in v. 7. It is not clear that the term *mrzḥ* of the Ugaritic texts, with its counterpart in Akkadian texts discovered at Ugarit, has as much religious significance as Barstad wants to give it (see above on v. 4).

Fine olive oil (רֵאשִׁית שְׁמָנִים [*rē'šît šĕmānîm*, "the finest of oils"]) was often used for rubbing into the skin and hair, sometimes mixed with various perfumes (Eccles. 9:8; Song of Sol. 1:3; Esther 2:12). The person who loves wine and oil too much, warns Solomon, "will not become rich" (Prov. 17:18). Yet these Israelites were so rich that even vast quantities of wine and the highest quality oils did not impoverish them.

6:6b The "ruin of Joseph" (v. 6) is parallel in thought to the "seat of violence" (v. 3). Amos knows that the judgment is already certain, and he is delivering the Lord's word faithfully. The leaders of Israel ought also to be aware of the coming

---

[44] King, *Amos, Hosea, Micah*, p. 155; David Noel Freedman, "But Did King David Invent Musical Instruments?" *Bible Review* 1:2 (Summer 1985), p. 50.

[45] Freedman, "But Did King David Invent Musical Instruments?" p. 51.

[46] Ibid., p. 51.

[47] Hans Barstad, *The Religious Polemics of Amos* (VTSup 34; Leiden: E. J. Brill, 1984), pp. 137-42. The quotation is found on p. 141. King is uncertain about the religious significance of *mizrāq* in this context, but he also mentions a "fluted bronze bowl" dating from the fourth century B.C. with a Phoenician inscription: "We offer two cups to the marzeah of Shamash" (*Amos, Hosea, Micah*, p. 158).

destruction and grieving for it; instead they lose themselves in debauchery and frivolous pleasures.

6:7 רֹאשׁ (rō's, "front") contains a wordplay that is difficult to translate. The same root occurs in the description of the leaders as nobles of "the *foremost* of nations" and as those who favor the "*finest* of oils." Now they will be the *first* of the captives.

Repetition ties together the description of those to whom the "woe" is directed and the announcement of their punishment. Those who are "sprawled [*sĕruḥîm*] upon their beds" (v. 4) are the "sprawlers" whose banquets will cease when the exile begins. Page Kelley puts it this way: "These who have made themselves conspicuous by their extravagance will soon be conspicuous by their absence."[48]

Additional Notes

6:1 הוֹי: Delbert Hillers presents a convincing case that "woe" oracles with a participle after the initial הוֹי should be construed as direct address or vocative. As with other vocative constructions, personal pronouns that later refer back to the persons addressed may be in the third person (cf. Zech. 3:8).[49] From an English perspective, it seems best to supply second person forms for the third person consistently throughout the section (cf. NIV).

הַשַּׁאֲנַנִּים בְּצִיּוֹן: The LXX has "those who despise Zion" (τοῖς ἐξουθενοῦσι Σιων), evidently based on a metathesis of *aleph* and *nun*. Thus, the translator solved the apparent historical problem by condemning the northern kingdom in both half-lines.

6:2 כַלְנֵה: Spellings in the Assyrian inscriptions show a variation between endings with "-*ia*" and "-*ua*," which corresponds to Hebrew *Kalnēh* and *Kalnô*. The location of Nimrod's "Calneh" in "the land of Shinar" (Gen. 10:10) is unknown. Some prefer to emend the Hebrew text of the latter passage to וְכֻלָּנָה, "and all of them."[50] Interestingly, the LXX reads πάντες ("all") in the Amos passage.

הַטּוֹבִים: The LXX and Peshitta took the *he* as the article. This seems to reflect the interpretation that the cities are mentioned to illustrate the greatness of the kingdoms of Israel and Judah. The Targum supports the MT.

6:5 כִּדָוִיד חָשְׁבוּ לָהֶם כְּלֵי־שִׁיר: The LXX is difficult to understand and to connect with the Hebrew: ὡς ἑστῶτα ἐλογίσαντο καὶ οὐχ ὡς φεύγοντα ("as standing they have considered [them] and not as fleeing"). Evidently the translator meant that the Israelites considered the sounds of the music (to which they clapped their hands, according to the first line of LXX) as things that ought to have been avoided rather than made a permanent part of life. Possibly a text close to the following was read: כדור חשבו ולא כשׁור, though דּוּר and שׁוּר are never

---

[48] Page Kelley, *The Book of Amos: A Study Manual* (Shield Bible Study Outlines; Grand Raids: Baker, 1966), p. 77.

[49] Delbert Hillers, "*Hoy* and *Hoy*-Oracles: A Neglected Syntactic Aspect," in *The Word of the Lord Shall Go Forth: Essays in Honor of David Noel Freedman* (ASOR Special Volume Series 1; Winona Lake, In.: Eisenbrauns, 1983), pp. 185-88.

[50] See Astour, "Calneh (Calno)," in *IDBSup*, pp. 124-25.

elsewhere equivalents for ἵστημι and φεύγω.[51] Either the text was difficult to read, or possibly there was some desire to avoid any hint of putting David in a bad light. The Syriac and the Targum support the MT in reading "like David."

2. The Lord's Rejection And His Judgment (6:8-11)

Translation

Yahweh has sworn by His own life;
*it is a declaration of Yahweh God of Hosts:
"How I *loathe the arrogant pride of Jacob,
and I hate his fortresses.
So I will deliver up the city and all it contains."
So it will happen:
[9]*If ten men be left in a single house, they will die. [10]Then one's uncle,
*who would prepare his body, will lift him up to carry the bones from
the house. And he will say to the one who is in the innermost part of the
house, "Is anyone else with you?" And he will say, "No one..." Then
he will say, "Hush! For we must not invoke the name of Yahweh."
[11]For consider this! Yahweh will give the command,
and He will smash the large house into pieces
and the small house into splinters.

Exegesis and Exposition

Amos has taken up the theme of a funeral for Israel on two previous occasions (5:1-3, 16-17). As a conclusion to the section that began with the second pronouncement of woe, he returns to the subject of death and to the reactions of those who might survive the catastrophe. God always desires to express His grace, but when His overtures are continually spurned, there comes a time when the judgment cannot be turned back. Amos presented his listeners with a choice between life and death. Since they have chosen death, the prophet is impelled by the Lord to present a scene of fear and destruction and the heavy odor of death that contrasts starkly with the joyous and carefree attitude of the Israelites who had lived so lavishly.

Structurally the passage has three parts, as the translation attempts to illustrate. Verse 8 gives the general declaration of punishment for Samaria in terms of a solemn oath of the Lord. Then vv. 9 and 10, in prose rather than poetry, describe in graphic and somewhat mysterious terms the aura of death that will grip the city. Finally, v. 11 discusses what the Lord has decreed for the destruction of the houses in the city.

6:8a The oath of v. 8a seals the solemnity and irreversibility of the coming judgment. It functions as a broad structural parallel to the Lord's declaration that He hates and rejects the Israelite's worship ceremonies (5:21-23). It is possible to translate בְּנַפְשׁוֹ (běnapšô) as "by His life" rather than "by Himself," as in most modern translations. Perhaps "by Himself" actually gives a better English

---

[51] See Wolff, *Joel and Amos*, p. 272 n. j., for a different retroversion.

rendering, but *nepeš* can have the meaning "life" in addition to "soul," "self," or "breath" (cf. Ex. 21:23; Judg. 12:3; 2 Sam. 14:7). Also, there is a certain parallel to the previous oath the Lord had sworn "by His holiness" (4:2). In the latter passage the punishment involves a humiliating march of captives into an unholy land. The Lord is the source and sustainer of life, and the oath He now makes by His own life concerns the taking away of life.

The second statement about the source of the coming pronouncement (נְאֻם־יהוה אֱלֹהֵי צְבָאוֹת, *nĕ'um-YHWH 'ĕlōhê ṣĕbā'ôt*, "declaration of Yahweh, God of Hosts") adds to its significance and authority. The two introductory declarations balance each other well (4+4). (For some textual issues see Additional Notes.)

6:8b All of the things in which "Jacob" (the people of the northern kingdom) has placed his trust fail to impress the Lord. Rather, he "loathes" and "hates" them, even as the unrighteous "hate" and "loathe" those who carry out true justice (5:10). Since the word order with the pronoun אָנֹכִי (*'ānōkî*, "I") following the verb (a participle) is rare, the translation above attempts to bring out the stress on the verb. Literally it is "loathe I the arrogant pride of Jacob."

גָּאוֹן (*gĕ'ôn*) can mean either "pride" or "arrogance," and the same Hebrew expression occurs later in the book as a divine title (8:7) where it is translated "Pride of Jacob." Jacob's pride should be the Lord Himself, but since the people have rejected Him, their "pride" is really "arrogance." It consists of false reliance on national strength and religious practices as a substitute for righteousness.

Because of the Lord's strong hatred for the prideful trust the people have in themselves and in their own defenses, He will deliver the city of Samaria over to its enemies, along with all its fortifications, people, and beautiful mansions (vv. 9-11). The verb הִסְגִּיר (*hisgîr*, "deliver up") is used in a similar way in the oracles against Gaza (1:6) and Tyre (1:9). Just as enemies sold some of the Israelites into slavery, so the Lord will send the entire city into exile.

6:9 Amos envisions the conquered city in v. 9 and paints a scene heavy with the blackness of death. If any survivors should be left in a house, they will die. Evidently the prophet foresees a plague that will follow the destruction of war.

The reference to "ten men" calls to mind the dirge for the city that, decimated by war, has only ten surviving warriors (Amos 5:3). Perhaps Amos also intends to evoke the memory of Abraham's bargain with the Lord on behalf of Lot. If only ten righteous people are found in Sodom, the Lord would spare it (Gen. 18:32). Or the ten tribes given to Jeroboam I, the first king of Israel (1 Kings 11:31) may be in view. Thus, the great catastrophe in the death of these ten highlights the totality of the destruction which the Lord will bring to Israel.

6:10 In v. 10 Amos depicts for us the aftermath of the ravages of disease and destruction when survivors have to haul bodies out of the houses for burial or disposal. The precise meaning of the details, however, remains obscure. In fact, the obscurity of the passage lends to the sense of mystery and fear that Amos hopes to arouse.

A paternal uncle (דּוֹד, *dôd*) had many family responsibilities, among them the burial of the dead. Aaron, for example, called on his uncle's sons to bury his own sons Nadab and Abihu (Lev. 10:1-5; cf. Ex. 6:18-22). Thus, the uncle of v. 10 has come to carry out his relative's "bones," that is, his body (cf. 2 Kings 13:21). Perhaps the sense "uncle" could be generalized more to "the nearest relative."[52]

The function of the individual designated מְסָרְף (mĕsārēp) cannot be determined with certainty. On the basis of the Peshitta (mn dqryb lh, "someone who is his relative") we might conjecture that another relative is meant. Some of the early Jewish commentaries take this view, but it has no solid etymological basis.[53] For the reading of the LXX, see under Additional Notes.

The KB lexicon lists the passage as the only case where the root סרף (srp) means "burn," as opposed to the more common spelling with sîn (שׂרף, śrp).[54] The Hebrews did not practice cremation of bodies, though there was at least one exception, as Feinberg points out (1 Sam. 31:12). According to S. R. Driver, not the body but spices were burned as a memorial.[55] The ceremony is attested only as an honor for a dead king (cf. 2 Chron. 16:14; 21:19; Jer. 34:5).

Yechezkel Kutscher, a well-known linguist who specialized in Hebrew and Aramaic, has suggested that the root is really srp and relates it to the practice of anointing a body or preparing it with spices for burial.[56] The term is often spelled with sîn in later Hebrew and Aramaic. Actually the meanings "burn," "anoint," and "prepare with spices" may go back to a common root, connected by the concept of burning spices (for which Kutscher gives some examples).

If Kutscher's suggestion is correct (cf. NASB, "undertaker"), the text probably means to describe the one who "lifts up" the body (וּנְשָׂאוֹ, ûnĕśāʾô) both as the deceased's uncle and as the one who will prepare him for burial.

The ensuing conversation remains a mystery to modern interpreters. In the Hebrew even the identity of the speakers is not very clear. Silence is commanded *because* it is not appropriate to mention the Lord's name, yet no one is said to have mentioned it yet. Perhaps the one who answers is a survivor who has been using the name in his groaning. Yet v. 9 speaks of the death of all ten men in the house. If the responder is one of the searchers, possibly he was about to use or had been using the Lord's name as he assessed the terrible extent of the tragedy.

The translation above reflects a conjecture that the one who commands silence interrupts the speaker who is on the verge of invoking the Lord's name. Thomas McComiskey has a pertinent observation:

> In the statement of the man in Amos's picture who cringes among the corpses in the house we find a Yahweh who acts, not on the basis of one's relationship to him, but on the basis of the superstitious pronouncement of his name. This is not the Yahweh of Moses, but the Yahweh of the pagan mind – a Yahweh who is little more than

---

[52] Andersen and Freedman, *Amos*, p. 569.

[53] Mays, *Amos*, p. 119; Eduard Yechezkel Kutscher, "Notes to the Biblical Lexicon (1957)," in *Hebrew and Aramaic Studies*, ed. Zeev Ben-Hayyim, et al. (Jerusalem: Magnes, 1977), no. 7, "*Mesārēp* (Amos 6, 10)," pp. 338-40 (in Hebrew).

[54] See GKC, par. 6k, for additional examples of שׂ (ś) being replaced with ס (s).

[55] Feinberg, *The Minor Prophets*, p. 110; Driver, "*Joel and Amos*," p. 197.

[56] Kutscher, "Notes to the Biblical Lexicon," pp. 338-39. Cf. also the HALOT lexicon.

the pagan gods whose activities were determined by what was done
to anger or placate them. Such was the religion of Amos's day.[57]

Also Douglas Stuart makes a helpful comment from another perspective:
"Yahweh will have become foe, not friend. Survivors will want him to stay away,
not come back."[58]

6:11 Amos returns to the announcement of judgment in v. 11 after his
digression about death in the city. An additional divine command is given to smash
to pieces all the buildings in the city, whether large or small. The reference is either
to the complete destruction of the land by the Assyrians or to the earthquake that
struck two years after Amos prophesied (1:1). That the new command follows the
previous reference to God delivering Israel into the hands of an enemy might argue
in favor of an Assyrian destruction, but the text need not be taken in chronological
order. The "large house" and the "small house" probably form a set of extremes,
with everything in between being implied (a merism).[59] The Targumic
interpretation that the two houses refer to the kingdoms of Israel and Judah is
unlikely.

Additional Notes

6:8 נְאֻם־יהוה אֱלֹהֵי צְבָאוֹת: The entire line is missing in the LXX. Wolff
suggests that it has been transposed from the end of v. 7.[60] The Syriac, Targum, and
Vulg. have it. Given the apparent difficulties the translator of LXX had with this
section in general, it is not impossible that he was working from a defective
manuscript.

מְתָאֵב: A unique spelling occurs here, the expected form being מְתָעֵב. The
root תאב means the opposite of "loathe," that is, "to desire." תאב occurs only three
times in the OT (also Ps. 110:40, 174) but is also attested in post-Biblical Hebrew.[61]
The ancient versions uniformly recognize the sense in v. 11 as "despise" or
"loathe." Note also that the biblical instances that clearly mean "desire" are in the
qal form of the verb, whereas Amos used the piel. Wolff feels that the form in the
text was probably altered by a scribe who was "affronted by the notion that Yahweh
'abhors.'"[62] Quite possibly the form was altered, but it seems more likely that the
reason lies in the object of the verb: "the pride of Jacob." Since the expression is
used as a divine title later in Amos (8:7), it would have seemed repugnant to a
scribe to say that the Lord abhorred Himself. Of course, Amos's deliberate play on
words occurs in a context where it is clear that in one case the "pride" is an attribute
of the people, while in the other case it characterizes the Lord. A similar scribal
alteration (or euphemism) seems to underlie the use of the term "bless" (בֵּרֵךְ)

[57] Thomas Edward McComiskey, "The Hymnic Elements of the Prophecy of Amos: A
Study of Form-Critical Methodology," in *A Tribute to Gleason Archer*, ed. Walter C. Kaiser,
Jr. and Ronald F. Youngblood (Chicago: Moody, 1986), pp. 112-13.

[58] Stuart, *Hosea-Jonah*, p. 364.

[59] Cf. Wolff, *Joel and Amos*, p. 283.

[60] Ibid., p. 273 n. m.

[61] See Marcus Jastrow, *A Dictionary of the Targumim, the Talmud Babli and
Yerushalmi, and the Midrashic Literature* (New York: Judaica, 1971), p. 1641.

[62] Wolff, *Joel and Amos*, p. 282.

where "curse" is expected from the context but the recipient would be God (1 Kings 21:10, 13; Job 1:5, 11; 2:5, 9; Ps. 10:3).

6:9 The LXX adds to the end of the verse "and the rest of them will remain" (καὶ ὑπολειφθήσονται οἱ κατάλοιποι). Stuart thinks of a corruption of a dittography of נשׂאו to נשׁארו, but Wolff suggests an attempt to temper the completeness of the judgment.[63] Wolff's idea is more likely because v. 10 suggests there are survivors. Amos probably surveys different scenes of damage: in one house all have perished, but there are still survivors to plod through the rubble.

6:10 וּנְשָׂאוֹ דּוֹדוֹ מְסָרְפוֹ: The LXX has "and their kinsmen [οἰκεῖοι] shall take (them) and use force [παραβιῶνται; var. παραβιωται] (to remove the bones)," which could reflect an interpretation of the consonants of MT.[64] Or perhaps it could be an inner-Greek corruption for παραβιβάζω (to remove).

C. A Rebuke For Injustice And Pride (6:12-14)

Translation

> Do horses run in a rocky area?
> Or can one plow (there) *with oxen?
> Yet you have turned justice into poison,
> and the fruit of righteousness to wormwood –
> [13]you who rejoice about *Lo-debar,
> who say, "Haven't we taken Karnaim by our own strength?"
> [14]"For consider this! I raise against you, house of Israel,"
> *declares Yahweh the God of Hosts, "a nation.
> And they will oppress you from Lebo-hamath
> all the way to the wadi of the Arabah."

Exegesis and Exposition

A theme of judgment by exile has run through these chapters (4:3; 5:5, 27; 6:7), and Amos closes his remarks in the first part of his book by returning to that theme. The section follows the familiar pattern of judgment as a result of injustice. In this case unrighteousness is highlighted through a rhetorical question concerning the impossibility of accomplishing anything useful in rocky, mountainous terrain. Even so, justice cannot be carried out; the Israelites render it ineffective. More than this, they even completely overturn its goals so that justice and righteousness themselves become deadly poison.

Consequently the Lord will afflict the nation through foreign conquest. The irony of the situation is heightened by the people's boast to have conquered others through their own military strength.

6:12 In a fashion reminiscent of the series of rhetorical questions by which Amos defended his right to preach judgment against Israel (3:3-8), he now directs two questions in v. 12 to focus attention on the absurdity of the way her rulers

---

[63] Stuart, *Hosea-Jonah*, p. 362; Wolff, *Joel and Amos*, p. 279 n. e.

[64] For further discussion of possible textual emendations based on LXX, see J. Alberto Soggin, *The Prophet Amos: A Translation and Commentary*, trans. John Bowden (London: SCM, 1987), p. 107.

behave. Horses cannot run where the hard, rocky ground will tear up their hooves. No one would be so foolish as to try to make a horse run in such an area; the owner would be responsible for ruining a fine animal. It would also be unthinkable to expect oxen to have the power to pull a plow through solid rock. (For a widely accepted emendation of the text, see Additional Notes). The form יְרֻצוּן (yĕruṣûn, "they run"), with suffixed *nun*, apparently intensifies the sense of anger with which Amos asks these questions.[65]

The contrast is made with a bold accusation.[66] Poison and wormwood are harmful things to be avoided, just like the rocky terrain for horses or plowing. Yet injustice is so prevalent in Israel that the court system is no less harmful.

The interesting parallel of "justice" (מִשְׁפָּט, *mišpāt*) with "fruit of righteousness" (פְּרִי צְדָקָה, *pĕrî ṣĕdāqâ*) shows how righteousness is the basic foundation for justice in a nation. Notice also how the line closely echoes 5:7. Amos characteristically repeats certain thoughts elsewhere in his book.

6:13 A lack of any sense of justice or righteousness combined in Israel with confidence in military might (v. 13). The two had become a deadly mixture for the nation, for it could only lead to ruin.

The city of Lo-debar is usually located somewhere in Gilead (cf. 2 Sam. 9:4-5; 17:27), possibly near Mahanaim. Amos is undoubtedly making another of his colorful word plays, for the Hebrew really means "nothing at all" (cf. LXX, οὐδενὶ λόγῳ, *oudeni logō*). Thus he evokes the memory of a military conquest which led to rejoicing in Israel, but in the sight of the Lord it is "nothing at all."[67]

Karnaim was located east of the Sea of Galilee, and the Israelites probably wrested it from Aramean control.[68] Since the name can also mean "horns," a common symbol for power (cf. Dan 7:7, 20, 24; Zech 1:18-21 [MT 2:1-4]), the prophet stresses even more the feeling of power the Israelites had. That, however, was a power soon to be crushed by the Lord.

6:14 Y. Aharoni identifies Lebo-hamath with Lebweh, located north of Baalbek in Syria.[69] If the phrase means "from the entrance of Hamath" (as in NASB), the combination of preposition *min* attached to *lamed* would be unique, though it does occur later in the Mishnah (BDB, 583*b*; 1124*b*). The "wadi of the Arabah," on the other hand, has to be found to the south of the Dead Sea. It forms part of the large rift valley of the Arabah which, geologically speaking, extends even into the Red Sea. No escape could be found from the enemy; they would pursue the Israelites from the farthest point north to the southernmost borders.

Jeroboam II managed to gain control of a broad territory east of the Jordan River, extending from the city of Lebo in the Beqa Valley of Lebanon on the border

---

[65] Cf. J. Hoftijzer, *The Function and Use of the Imperfect Forms with Nun Paragogicum in Classical Hebrew* (SSN 21; Assen, Netherlands: Van Gorcum, 1985), p. 61.

[66] The conjunction כִּי is contrastive after a negative clause. Here the rhetorical question expects a negative answer (cf. Ronald J. Williams, *Hebrew Syntax: An Outline*, 2d ed. (Toronto: Univ. of Toronto, 1976), par. 555.

[67] Cf. C. E. de Vries, "Lo-Debar," *ISBE*, rev. ed., 3:151.

[68] Wolff, *Joel and Amos*, p. 288.

[69] Aharoni, *The Land of the Bible; A Historical Geography*, 2d ed., trans. A. F. Rainey (Philadelphia: Westminster, 1979), p. 72.

with Hamath to the Dead Sea. Aharoni notes, "This would mean that he dominated the entire length of the King's Highway in Transjordan, from the border of Edom to that of Hamath."[70] The author of Kings makes it clear that Jeroboam II succeeded only because the Lord permitted it (2 Kings 14:25), yet he and his cohorts boasted of their military capabilities. Amos turns things around completely and promises "affliction" (cf. 2 Kings 14:26, where a different Hebrew term is used but the concept is similar) throughout the length of this territory by an unspecified "nation." Later prophets revealed that this nation was Assyria (cf. Hos. 11:5-6; Mic. 7:12), as confirmed by history (2 Kings 15-20).

Additional Notes

6:12 בַּבְּקָרִים: Many scholars assume that the Hebrew has been corrupted from an original בַּבָּקָר יָם: "Or will someone plow the sea with an ox?" The emendation would assume that a scribe accidentally combined two originally separate words into one. S. R. Driver gave two reasons for preferring this reading: "it avoids the unusual plural *bĕqārîm* and also obviates the necessity of mentally understanding 'there' in the second clause of the verse."[71]

The fact that the plural is rare (also found in 2 Chron. 4:3; Neh. 10:37) as against the common collective use of בָּקָר should have made it difficult for a scribe to neglect a word division if it were original.

In a poetic passage, the thought of one half-line often carries over into the second half. Thus, when Amos applies his rhetorical questions to the people of Israel, he does not repeat the verb in both halves. Therefore, it does not seem strange that the word "there" has to be assumed for the second half of the line.

The Targum supports MT, while the Syriac has "or does one plow with them?" (*'w dbryn bhwn pdn'*). There is a bare possibility that *bhwn* might represent בָּם, though the word order is against it. The LXX has "or will they keep silence among mares?" (εἰ παρασιωπήσονται ἐν θηλείαις). This reading, in common with the Syriac, has the horses as subject of both parts. Obviously the LXX took יַחֲרוֹשׁ in the sense of "keep silence," possibly with a metathesis of the *waw* and the *shin* to give a plural form. That idea probably then led to reading בַּבְּקָרִים as "among mares." Here again, though, there is a slight possibility that θηλείαις is an inner-Greek corruption of a form of θαλάσσα, "sea." If so, the LXX would support the conjectured change.

6:13 לֹא דָבָר: The city may be "Debir" of Josh. 13:26 (cf. NASB and NIV; JB/NJB has "Lo-debar"), where the Hebrew actually attaches a *lamedh* to the name, but the Masoretes have vowelled it as though it is the preposition, an understanding that is syntactically difficult. Thus, there are three spellings for the name: לוֹ דְבָר (2 Sam. 9:4); לֹא דְבָר (2 Sam. 17:27; Amos 6:13); and לִדְבִר (Josh. 13:26). In any event, the context of all four references indicates a northern location, and the city is distinct from the more commonly known Debir in Hebron.

---

[70] Ibid., p. 344.
[71] Driver, *Joel and Amos*, p. 198.

6:14 נְאֻם־יהוה אֱלֹהֵי הַצְּבָאוֹת: Part of the Greek tradition omits it (found only in B, V, 239, Syro-Hexapla and Armenian; Göttingen). The Syriac transposes the entire sentence to after the word "people" ('m'), the equivalent given for גוֹי.

8
The End for Israel
(7:1-8:14)

In the third part of the book Amos relates a series of visions that demonstrate the Lord's determination to judge (chaps. 7-9). Grace has been prominent in the past, but now the sinfulness of the nation has reached its full measure, though grace will be extended again after judgment.

The first two visions form a tight unit (7:1-6) and show how unwilling the Lord is to allow the nation to be consumed completely. In fact, they stand as a guarantee, along with 9:11-15, that Jacob will continue to exist. The visions of mercy set an underlying tone for the whole section, murmuring beneath the much louder theme of judgment that dominates the middle section.

The next two visions speak of a judgment that will not be turned back (7:7-9; 8:1-3). A plumb line reveals the necessity to destroy the "wall," which represents Israel, and a basket of summer fruit shows how ready the nation is to come to an end. Visions three and four are each followed by a response by the people and a further reply from the Lord.

The announcement of a coming famine in regard to the word of the Lord serves to close off the broader structural unit of the third and fourth visions (8:11-14). Those who refused to listen to the prophet will want a new word, but none will come.

In his last vision (9:1-15), to be discussed in the next chapter, Amos sees the Lord standing beside the altar at Bethel, ready to destroy the place and all the worshipers assembled there. Yet the grim scene is also balanced by a vivid picture of future salvation under the restored "booth of David."

Before turning to particulars about the visions, one should notice the role played by dialogue. In the first two visions Amos pleads with the Lord to pardon the sins of the people and hold back His wrath. And the Lord answers him by promising that He will stay the judgment. In the third and fourth, the Lord questions Amos about what he sees, and Amos merely restates the significant detail of the scene (a plumb line and a basket of summer fruit, respectively). This time he remains mute while the Lord announces the judgment to come.

Yet the visions of a plumb line and of a basket of summer fruit broaden the dialogue to include the people. The new revelation that the Lord will rise against Jeroboam's house with a sword (7:9) provokes an immediate rebuke from Amaziah, the priest of Bethel (7:10-13). He thereby becomes a type of those who have "commanded the prophets saying, 'You shall not prophesy!'" (2:12). Consequently Amos not only defends his role as spokesman for the Lord but also delivers a scathing word that Amaziah will personally go into captivity along with the rest of the nation (7:14-17).

A fresh call to "hear this" follows the vision of the basket of summer fruit. It opens with the people complaining about the new moon and sabbath (8:4-6), because at those times they cannot practice their dishonest dealings. Thus, they condemn themselves by their own words, even as Amaziah had done. The Lord's renewed promise of punishment is based on the "deeds" of those people and on His own authority (8:7-10).

The last vision contains no dialogue. Amos simply quotes the Lord's command to destroy the whole system of worship along with all the people (9:1-4). None will escape His wrath. This time no one makes a reply, because God's command to break down the temple cannot be changed. The closest thing to any kind of response is a hymn that affirms the power of the Lord, which He exercises alike in creation and judgment. This is the God Israel must "meet" in order to receive her just deserts (cf. 4:12).

The progression with relation to the prophet, then, is from active participation to silent bystander. But with relation to the people it is just the opposite. First, they do not participate; then they argue with the Lord; next they flee for their lives but can find no place to hide. Finally, the Lord's pronouncements increase from a terse "It shall not be" (7:3, 6) to a lengthy speech, which details the futile attempts of the people to avoid punishment (9:1-4).

Another feature of the structure is that the beginning of chap. 7 (visions one and two) and the end of chap. 9 (vv. 11-15) both speak of mercy. The Lord has been merciful in the past, and He will continue to be so in the future. The sins of Amos's generation cannot change the character of the Lord, and He has made an everlasting covenant with His people. The northern kingdom will cease to exist as a nation. However, the people of the covenant will continue through a small remnant. Then one glorious day the Lord will restore them to their land under the banner of David, the great monarch of the united kingdom era.

A. The Lord Has Spared (7:1-6)

Translation

Here is what the Lord Yahweh showed me:
*He was forming a swarm of locusts when the spring crop was just sprouting. *Now this was the spring crop that follows the king's cutting, ²and (I wondered) what would happen if the locusts were to completely devour the vegetation of the land.
So I said, "Lord Yahweh, please forgive! How will Jacob continue? For he is small in number."
³Yahweh relented about this. "It shall not be," says Yahweh.
⁴Here is what the *Lord Yahweh showed me:
The Lord Yahweh was calling *for a judgment by fire. Then it consumed the *great deep and was about to consume the fields.
⁵So I said, "Lord Yahweh, please stop! How will Jacob continue? For he is small in number."
⁶Yahweh relented about this. "This too shall not be," says the Lord Yahweh.

Exegesis and Exposition

First, the Lord shows Amos a locust swarm about to completely devour the vegetation in the land. Realizing the implications of this, the prophet intercedes, praying for pardon. When the Lord answers the prayer in a positive manner, the reader realizes God's desire to show mercy to sinners.

The second vision concerns drought, under the figure of a fire that consumes all the ground water that supplies the springs and wells so vital for the continuation of life and then stands poised to sear the fields completely. Once again Amos intercedes but this time only after the "great deep" has been consumed. So it is that Amos merely asks God to stop the judgment already in progress before it goes too far. For a second time, God listens to His prophet.

These visions are intended to focus attention on the issues of sin, judgment, and mercy. They also demonstrate the importance of the prophet as one who intercedes for the people in an effort to evoke mercy from the Lord. We see then that God is longsuffering and slow to anger. He is willing to hold back judgment so there will be time for the people to repent.

The first two visions promise that the Lord does not intend to destroy Jacob completely. That "shall not be." Judgment will continue only up to a predetermined point and then cease.

7:1-3 Amos reports in v. 1 a vision that the Lord showed him. When the prophet becomes aware that a swarm of locusts is about to completely overwhelm "Jacob" (v. 2), he cries out for the Lord to "forgive." But the Lord responds only with a promise that "this will not happen." He will have compassion and turn back the locusts, but He does not say anything about forgiveness.

7:1 The participle יוֹצֵר (*yôṣēr*) in v. 1 seems a bit abrupt. The Hebrew can be translated more literally: "Thus the Lord Yahweh showed me and behold! *One forming* a locust swarm." A parallel construction occurs in Isa. 29:8: "a hungry man dreams – and behold, one eating." In both cases the subject of the participle occurs in the introductory statement. Here the action of forming a locust swarm would be something that only God can do. The judgment of Israel comes directly from the Lord.

The unique term לֶקֶשׁ (*leqeš*) must refer to some type of crop. A related word (מַלְקוֹשׁ, *malqôš*) refers to the "latter rains," which fall during March and April (cf. Deut. 11:14; Jer. 5:24; Joel 2:23). A verb from the same root occurs in Job 24:6 with the meaning "glean." The Gezer Calendar, an ancient Hebrew inscription dating to about the tenth century B.C., mentions "two months" of *lqš*. The relation of these months within the document points to sometime around January and February.[1] Probably, then, the *leqeš* was a crop of hay planted so as to take advantage of the spring rains. Just as this crop was beginning to grow, Amos sees the locust swarm arriving. Another crop cannot be planted; by the time it came up there would be no rain to sustain it. The emphasis is upon lateness.

The impression of lateness becomes stronger when Amos refers to the crop taken after the king's harvest (גִּזֵּי הַמֶּלֶךְ, *gizzê hammelek*, "the cutting of the

---

[1] See S. J. De Vries, "Calendar," *IDB* 1:485.

king"). Apparently the king had first rights to the earlier plantings (cf. 1 Kings 18:5-6). Thus, the planting mentioned in the vision had occurred at the very last moment. Imminent disaster could only result if this crop were destroyed.

7:2 In v. 2 Amos gives a very dramatic acount of his response to the vision. Many have noted the unusual use of the verb וְהָיָה (wĕhāyâ, "and it will happen") to introduce the verse when וַיְהִי (wayĕhî, "and it happened") might be expected.[2] If the conjunction אִם ('im) is given its usual conditional force, it may be possible to take the sentence as an interrupted thought: "And it will happen if they finish devouring the vegetation of the land…" The sentence breaks off before the consequences are reported, though they are understood (cf. Gen. 3:22). LXX and Targum give a sense similar to that proposed in our translation. Consider also S. M. Lehrman's rendering: "And if it had come to pass, that when they made an end of eating the grass of the land – so I said."[3]

As he contemplates imminent disaster, Amos suddenly interrupts with a plea on behalf of Israel. The prophets are often thought of as strictly messengers, but intercession formed a major part of their duties as well. Abraham was called a "prophet" because he could intercede for Abimelech (Gen. 20:7). Jeremiah is noteworthy because the Lord told him *not* to intercede for Judah, whose sins were too great to forgive (Jer. 7:16; 11:14; 14:11). It was so unusual for a prophet not to pray for the people that the Lord had to issue a special command to prevent it.

Amos actually asks God to forgive (סְלַח-נָא, sĕlaḥ-nā'), not merely to stop the judgment. As Gary V. Smith so aptly states,

> Amos knows the nation has not repented to deserve God's
> compassion, he knows God's oath that Israel will be destroyed, and
> he himself has identified with God's decision to destroy Israel (3:1-
> 6:14). Yet a petition of compassion, a lament for mercy immediately
> springs forth from the prophet's mouth.[4]

God is the only one who performs the action of forgiveness or pardon, according to all the OT references for which the verb occurs. But there is no prophetic oracle of forgiveness in the divine response.

The question word מִי (mî) has been confusing for translators, because it normally means "who," not "how." LXX and Syriac interpreted the verb יָקוּם (yāqûm) as a causative: "Who shall raise up Jacob?" The Targum paraphrased, "Who will arise and pray for their sins?" The major Hebrew lexicons (BDB, KB) interpret the interrogative in an adverbial sense, "as who," which would be equivalent to "how." The parallel with Ruth 3:16 seems significant. Naomi asks Ruth, "How did it go?" (mî 'at, lit. "[as] who are you?") when she returns from her night encounter with Boaz.

Amos refers to the people of Israel by a variety of titles, but only a few times by "Jacob." That the patriarch's name can be used with primary reference to the

---

[2] Cf. Gary V. Smith, *Amos: A Commentary* (Library of Biblical Interpretation; Grand Rapids: Zondervan, 1989), p. 220 n. e.

[3] S. M. Lehrman, "Amos" in *The Twelve Prophets*, (Soncino Books of the Bible; ed. A. Cohen; London: Soncino, 1969), pp. 111-12.

[4] Smith, *Amos*, p. 226.

northern kingdom seems clear from Amos 3:13; 6:8; and 9:8 (against Cripps).
Even "Isaac" can be used in a similar manner (7:16). Wolff thinks that "Jacob"
may recall the divine election of the founder of the sanctuary of Bethel (Gen. 28:10-
22), or that it may "include acknowledgment of guilt for that Israel who haughtily
rebelled against Yahweh but nevertheless cannot escape him" (cf. Hos. 12:2-4 [MT
12:3-5]).[5]

7:3 Hebrew נָחַם (niḥam, root nḥm in the niphal or, less frequently, hithpael
pattern) is only rarely used of men who "repent" of their sins (Jer. 8:6; 31:19). שׁוּב
(šûb) more commonly carries the idea of repentance (cf. Isa. 6:10; Jer. 3:12; Hos.
3:5; 11:5). The frequent expression, "return to (Yahweh)," which uses šûb, implies
repentance. Correspondingly, "turn from (Yahweh)," which uses the same verb,
indicates apostasy. Niḥam seems to place more stress on the emotions, whereas
šûb emphasizes a change of mind and direction (i.e., repentance). Since judgment
is associated with the wrath or anger of the Lord, a staying of judgment
consequently occurs when His anger is stilled, whether by intercession or by the
repentance of the people.

Those passages that deny that God changes His mind (also using niḥam;
Num. 23:19; 1 Sam. 15:29) contain the parallel thought that He cannot lie.
Moreover, the reference is to a promise of God, whether to the entire people of
Israel (Num. 23:19) or to David (1 Sam. 15:29). When God promises something,
He cannot change His mind because that would make the promise a lie. However,
He can relent of His wrath in response to prayer and repentance.[6]

7:4-6 In the second vision Amos is shown a judgment by fire about the
consume the land. This time, however, he only asks the Lord to "stop" it, not to
forgive. The absence of forgiveness in the Lord's first reply and now in Amos's
question casts the issue in stark relief. The Lord can have compassion on the land
and relent from His judgment, but the issues of guilt and injustice remain. Thus, we
are prepared for the next series of visions, when Amos will announce the Lord's
more solemn verdict: "I will spare them no longer" (7:8; 8:2).

7:4 Amos once again sees the Lord directly involved in the preparation of
judgment. This time it is more awesome than before: the Lord is calling for fire.
Evidently the "fire" stands for the searing heat of a drought, since it first consumes
the "great deep" (תְּהוֹם, tĕhôm), that is, the underground water.[7] For tĕhôm in the

---

[5] Hans Walter Wolff, *Joel and Amos* (Hermeneia, trans. Waldemar Janzen, et al.;
Philadelphia: Fortress, 1977), p. 297; Richard S. Cripps, *A Critical and Exegetical
Commentary on the Book of Amos*, 2d ed. (Great Britain: S.P.C.K., 1960), p. 221.

[6] For a discussion of the theological issues, see John Calvin, *Commentaries on the
Twelve Minor Prophets* (Calvin's Commentaries 14; trans. John Owen; Grand Rapids:
Baker, 1981), p. 330.

[7] See BDB, p. 1062; Charles L. Feinberg, *The Minor Prophets* (Chicago: Moody,
1976), p. 112; Smith, *Amos*, p. 224. R. Laird Harris, *TWOT* 2:965-66, entry 2495, shows that
even though *tĕhôm* can sometimes mean deep waters that supply surface springs, it cannot be
used to support the idea that the Hebrews believed that the earth rested on the *tĕhôm*. For the
view that *tĕhôm* in the passage means the ocean or the Mediterranean Sea, consult Thomas
Edward McComiskey, "Amos," in *EBC*, ed. Frank E. Gaebelein (Grand Rapids: Zondervan,
1985), 7:321; and Douglas Stuart, *Hosea-Jonah* (WBC 31; Waco, Tex.: Word, 1987), p. 372.

singular compare Gen. 7:11; 8:2; 49:25; Deut. 33:13; Prov. 8:28. For the plural in
the sense of "springs," see Deut. 8:7; Prov. 8:24; Ezek. 31:4. On the other hand,
Amos may refer to a judgment similar to that against Sodom and Gomorrah (cf.
Additional Notes).

In the first vision Amos merely contemplated what the locusts might do to the
land. Now he actually sees the fire consume the source of the springs so vital for
the crops. Then he observes in horror as the fire turns to the "fields" (חֵלֶק, ḥēleq).

Perhaps Amos chose the term ḥēleq for the cultivated fields because it implies
the close relationship of the Lord to the land He had "apportioned" (the related verb
ḥālaq means "to apportion") to the Israelites (cf. Josh. 18:5). If so, it implies the
entire territory of the northern kingdom, but under the figure of fields with crops
about to be destroyed. God actually owned the land; the Israelites were merely
given their respective portions by tribes and families as a stewardship. The Levites
were not given any portion because the Lord Himself was to be their portion (Num.
18:20).[8] Amos has already said that the Israelites failed in their responsibility for
their portion by imposing "heavy rent on the poor" (see exegesis of 5:11).

Additional Notes

7:1 וְהִנֵּה: The particle typically introduces that which is seen in a vision (cf.
Gen. 15:17; Ezek. 1:4, 15; Dan. 8:3; Zech. 1:8), though it also occurs when certain
things in ordinary sight are brought into focus (cf. Gen. 22:7; 24:15; 29:2). The
listener or reader immediately senses something that will demand attention. The
translation is based on this grammatical function of the particle. The traditional
"behold" is archaic and therefore often subject to misinterpretation by English
readers.

וְהִנֵּה־לֶקֶשׁ אַחַר גִּזֵּי הַמֶּלֶךְ: Some propose to delete this line as a gloss that
explains the term לֶקֶשׁ more precisely.[9] Yet the passage is attested in the ancient
versions, and it would be strange to introduce a gloss with הִנֵּה. The unusual
reading of the LXX, "one larva (was) Gog the king" (βροῦχος εἷς Γωγ ὁ
βασιλεύς), came about through confusion of consonants and conjecture from the
context. The translator also had difficulty with the first part of the verse, "and
behold, a swarm [ἐπιγονὴ] of locusts coming early in the morning [ἐπχομένη
ἑωθινή]." Apparently the term לֶקֶשׁ was not understood.

7:4 אֲדֹנָי יהוה: The LXX has only κύριος both times the phrase occurs in
this verse and at the end of v. 6 (cf. Additional Notes on 1:8).

לָרִב בָּאֵשׁ: The traditional translation, "to contend with fire," would be the
only time the means of contention occurs with the verb רִיב, though if the term be
taken as a noun, one might compare רִבוֹת שְׂפָתַי (Job 13:6) and רִיב לְשֹׁנוֹת (Ps.
31:20 [MT 31:21]). D. R. Hillers proposed that the words be divided so as to give
the consonantal text לרבב אֵשׁ. The noun רְבִיבִים means "copious showers" (of
rain; e.g., Deut. 32:2; Jer. 14:22; Mic. 5:7 [MT 5:6]). The feminine form of the
verb וַתֹּאכַל points to "fire," not "showers," as the controlling noun. However, the

---

[8] M. Tsevat, *TDOT* 4:449.
[9] Cf. Wolff, *Joel and Amos*, pp. 291-92 n. d.

expression "a rain of fire" is a nominalized form for "fire rained (from heaven)." Hence "fire" would still be the controlling noun. The concept of fire raining down from the Lord is also found in Gen. 19:24 and Ezek. 38:22.[10] As a conjecture the reading must remain in the realm of unproven hypothesis. The rule of the more difficult reading does not apply to the MT, because "to contend" is a much more common word than the rare "copious showers."

תְּהוֹם רַבָּה: If the reading לְרִבב be accepted, perhaps "the great deep" should be understood as the ocean (Mediterranean Sea). The Lord hurls his fire, which burns up the sea and then heads for the dry land (cf. Rev. 8:10-11; also n. 7 above).

B. The Lord Will Spare No Longer (7:7-8:14)

The third and fourth visions belong together as a unit. The common framework (vision followed by a reply of the people and a further response from the Lord) highlights their similarity, as well as their similar meaning – the end for Israel has finally arrived.

1. The Vision Of The Plumb Line (7:7-17)

a) Presentation (7:7-9)

Translation

Here is what He showed me:
*The Lord was standing beside a *plumbed wall, with a plumb line in His hand.
[8]Then Yahweh said to me, "What do you see, Amos?"
So I said, "A plumb line."
Then the Lord said,
"Look! I am going to place a plumb line among My people Israel. I will spare them no longer.
[9]The high places of Isaac will be devastated, and the sanctuaries of Israel will be destroyed.
Then I will rise up against the house of Jeroboam with a sword."

Exegesis and Exposition

In this vision Amos learns how primed Israel is for judgment. The Lord stands beside a wall with a plumb line to see if it is straight. But Israel, which is the wall, cannot pass the test. When the Lord places the line within the nation, it will mean judgment. This time Amos does not plead for mercy. He recognizes the utter necessity for the end to come when God affirms that He can no longer spare the people.

7:7 The word translated "plumb line" (אֲנָךְ, 'anāk) appears in the Bible only in v. 7. Yet it forms a crux for the interpretation of the entire vision. LXX and the Peshitta have something like "adamant," indicating hardness. The Targum

---

[10] D. R. Hillers, "Amos 7, 4 and Ancient Parallels," *CBQ* 26 (1964): 221-25; cf. Wolff, *Joel and Amos*, pp. 292-93 n. i. Stuart (*Hosea-Jonah*, p. 370) and Smith (*Amos*, p. 220) follow Hillers.

interpreted the symbol by rendering "judgment" (דִּין, *dîn*) for each of the four occurrences of the term in the vision. Vulg. uses several terms and phrases that indicate the common meaning of "plaster" or "mortar."

The KJV has "plumb line," apparently on the basis of "the dialects and the Rabbins," referred to somewhat vaguely by Keil.[11] This latter translation has become commonly accepted in modern translations and commentaries. However, certain problems accompany it.

First, the etymology that produces the meaning "lead" and then "plumb line" is dubious. The standard Syriac lexicon gives the translation for *'ănāk* as "tin" (Payne-Smith), whereas the Akkadian equivalent is listed as *anāku* by von Soden's dictionary (*AHW*), with the meaning "tin" and "probably also 'lead.'" However, Benno Landsberger argued vigorously that the only possible meaning in Akkadian is "tin," not "lead,"[12] and the *CAD* lists the form *annaku* as only "tin." The evidence from the cognate languages, then, gives more support for "tin" than "lead."

A second problem is the phrase that is literally "a wall of *'ănāk*." Some have felt that the text is more easily explained if the word *'ănāk* is removed (as a dittography).[13] Yet the ancient versions all have some equivalent for it. A "wall of a plumb line" could be easily taken as "a plumbed wall," that is, a "wall that had been built true to plumb" (NIV). If the wall represents Israel, then its slant away from the vertical would be shown by the line that is hanging against it.

Even if *'ănāk* does mean "tin," it could still have assumed the derived meaning of "plumb line." Compare "the stone, the tin" (הָאֶבֶן הַבְּדִיל, *hā'eben habbĕdîl*) in Zech. 4:10, which the BDB lexicon takes as a plummet. Admittedly that passage is also problematic (cf. JB/NJB, "the chosen stone").[14]

Perhaps some help can be derived by comparison with the vision of the basket of summer fruit (8:1-3). There the idea is not only the phonetic similarity with קַיִץ (*qēṣ*, "end") but also ripeness for judgment. A similar meaning is obtained with "plumb line" for the present vision. When the Lord places the *'ănāk* in the midst of Israel, it reveals that the nation is primed for judgment. The people have not lived up to the standard of obedience expected on the basis of the covenant.

Another suggestion is that Amos sees the Lord standing beside (or on top of) a "wall of tin" and holding some tin in His hand. Then the tin might stand for the alloy needed to build weapons against Israel (Brunet) or for some threatening gesture derived from an ancient temple-building ritual (Ouellette). The "wall of tin" could perhaps be compared with the "wall of bronze" in Jer. 15:20. If there is some phonetic symbolism associated with *'ănāk*, it might be with *'ānōkî* ("I") or *'ānaḥ* ("sigh").[15]

---

[11] C. F. Keil, *Minor Prophets* (COTTV 10; Grand Rapids: Eerdmans, 1973), p. 310.

[12] Benno Landsberger, "Tin and Lead: The Adventures of Two Vocables," *JNES* 24 (1965): 285-96.

[13] See Wolff, *Joel and Amos*, pp. 293-94 n. r. See also under Additional Notes.

[14] See also Kenneth L. Barker, "Zechariah," in *EBC*, 7:630-32.

[15] Gilbert Brunet, "La vision de l'étain: réinterprétation d'*Amos* VII 7-9," *VT* 16 (1966): 387-95; Jean Ouellette, "Le mur d'étain dans Amos, VII, 7-9," *RB* 80 (1973): 321-

7:8 In his earlier visions, Amos responded to what he saw; now (v. 8) he remains silent until queried by the Lord. Perhaps at first Amos did not realize what the vision meant, or perhaps he feared its significance for Israel. The plumb line itself comes entirely into focus through the interrogation and Amos's response. The Lord's reply to Amos's admission confirms the meaning: the plumb line is there to measure "My people Israel." For the interrogation of the prophet in a vision, compare Jer. 1:11, 13; Zech. 4:2, 5, 13.

7:9 In v. 9 Amos seems to use the patriarchal name Isaac in the unique sense of the northern kingdom of Israel (also 7:16). Thus, "the high places of Isaac" is balanced in the next line by "the sanctuaries of Israel." Perhaps the mention of Isaac should be associated with the pilgrimages the Israelites made to Beersheba (Amos 5:5; 8:14), the only place where the patriarch is said to have had a vision of the Lord (Gen. 26:23-33).[16]

Amos's prediction of violence against the house of Jeroboam was fulfilled in the chaotic political conditions brought about after the king's death by the pressure from Assyria on Israel (see 2 Kings 15:8-31; 17). The explicit nature of the prophecy against the royal dynasty occasioned the official reaction to Amos's words by Amaziah, the priest of Bethel.

Additional Notes

7:7 וְהִנֵּה אֲדֹנָי: The LXX seems to have been based on a text arranged as "the Lord, and behold…" Taking the LXX order would yield a stronger parallel with the other two visions: "Yahweh showed me, and behold!" The MT could then be explained as a metathesis. Granted the structural dissimilarity of the MT, it could be more easily imagined that the LXX tradition was responsible for the metathesis. Dissimilarity may highlight a climax. In any case, the overall meaning is not changed much by either reading, though it would be possible to interpret the LXX's "one standing" as "a man standing" rather than "(the Lord) standing" (cf. JB).

חוֹמַת אֲנָךְ: Many prefer to omit the first occurrence of אֲנָךְ as a dittography (cf. *BHS*). The phrase "wall of a plumb line" is difficult anyway, and if it does mean a "vertical" wall it is hard to see how it fits into the vision. If the text reads simply "a wall," then we might imagine that it was in fact out of plumb, representing Israel's wickedness. On the other hand, the versions all attest to the reading, so it cannot be dismissed so easily. If "tin" is read instead of plumb line the difficulty is less severe, but then the wall itself becomes a problem for the correct interpretation.

b) Official Response (7:10-13)

31; R. P. Gordon, "Once More, "*anak*" = 'Tin,' Amos VII 7-8," *VT* 20 (1970): 492-94; Andor Szabo, "Textual Problems in Amos and Hosea," *VT* 25 (1975): 507; John H. Hayes, *Amos, The Eighth-Century Prophet: His Times and His Preaching* (Nashville, Abingdon, 1988), pp. 204-06. Hayes speculates about a metaphorical meaning for "tin."
[16] Cf. Cripps, *Amos*, p. 226; Wolff, *Joel and Amos*, pp. 110, 301-302.

Translation

> Then Amaziah the priest of Bethel sent word to Jeroboam the king of
> Israel: "Amos has plotted against you right in the house of Israel! The
> land is not able to put up with all his words. [11]For Amos has said this:
> 'Jeroboam will die by the sword, and Israel will certainly be exiled from
> its land.'"
> [12]So Amaziah said to Amos, "Seer, go flee away to the land of Judah.
> There eat bread and prophesy there. [13]But do not prophesy ever again in
> Bethel. For it is a sanctuary of the king and a royal temple."

Exegesis and Exposition

How quickly Amos stirred up controversy when he began to speak about the
king! Amaziah, the priest of Bethel, first complained to the king that Amos was
guilty of conspiracy and then confronted the prophet. Amaziah, on the basis of
royal and religious authority, then commanded Amos to go to Judah and earn his
living there as a prophet.

This official negative response to Amos plays an important role in the book.
The prophet has pointed out continually that the Lord is displeased with the
standard religion of the day, especially because it does not provide a context for the
Israelites to fulfill the demands of the covenant concerning love for their neighbors.
Typical for such a situation, the leaders strive to maintain the status quo and to
downplay the authority of those who challenge them. Amos, however, stands apart
from the official religious institutions, challenging them from the standpoint of the
very God who supposedly justifies their existence. The stage is thereby set for a
clash of authority.

Amos 7:10-17 is often treated as a parenthetical digression from the main line
of thought, or even as a unit that has been misplaced.[17] However, conservative
analysis seeks to find structural unity with the other visions.[18] The material is more
than mere biographical narrative. According to Jan de Waard and William A.
Smalley,

> There is important information about Amos himself here (vv. 14-15),
> but that is not the point in the story. In fact, it is Amaziah, not Amos,
> who is more important. Amos's experience with Amaziah shows the
> opposition of the religious leaders to the word of the Lord and gives
> Amos another chance to speak the word of the Lord, this time
> directly to a religious leader (v. 17). Amos tells him of punishment
> to come to him and his family, just as the stories about the visions
> end with the promise of punishment to the nation in general.[19]

It is precisely this disputational function that is stressed in the present analysis.
In this function it parallels Amos 8:4-10, though the latter passage is presented

---

[17] Cf. Cripps, *Amos*, pp. 310-11; Hayes, *Amos*, pp. 230-31. McComiskey, "Amos," p.
322, says that "Amos's visions are momentarily interrupted" by this passage.

[18] Smith, *Amos*, pp. 228-29, arrives independently at a similar explanation.

[19] Jan de Waard and William A. Smalley, *A Translator's Handbook on the Book of
Amos* (Helps for Translators; New York: United Bible Societies, 1979), p. 150.

THE END FOR ISRAEL (7:1-8:14)

poetically. If we assume that Amos authored 7:10-17 (see the discussion about the composition of Amos in the Introduction to Amos), then the distinctive form of the pericope may be due to the fact that it does include narrative and biographical material.

7:10 We can surmise from v. 10 that Amaziah acted as something like the "high priest" of northern Israelite worship. Bethel, as one of the two major centers of worship set up originally by Jeroboam I, played a role for the north comparable to that of Jerusalem for the south. Hence, Amaziah's reaction represents an official or institutional response to Amos's message.

Amaziah did not hesitate to make his case against Amos look as damaging as possible, even if it meant false accusations. Perhaps from Amaziah's perspective he was justified to fear conspiracy when Amos prophesied the downfall of the current dynasty, since a change of dynasty would almost certainly entail conspiracy and intrigue. Moreover, previous prophets had not only prophesied against a dynasty but even participated in its downfall (cf. 1 Kings 11:29-40; 2 Kings 8:7-15). However, the book of Amos nowhere hints that he ever participated in a conspiracy. In fact, by prophesying that doom would befall the "house of Jeroboam," Amos passed over the immediate political situation. Just as he did not function as a "professional" prophet (7:14), so he did not make any plans to assure that his predictions would come true.

Obviously when Amaziah complains that the land cannot endure Amos's words, he has missed the point. The words themselves are not as important as the authority behind them. The real issue is whether Amos speaks the truth about the Lord. That is why the present passage focuses on the encounter between Amaziah and Amos as a clash of authority. Amaziah claims to represent God, but so does Amos. They cannot both be right.

7:11 How Amaziah twists Amos's words in v. 11. Amos said that Yahweh (quoting Him) would rise against Jeroboam's *house* with the sword. Amaziah omits reference to either Yahweh, who would wield the sword, or to the fact that Amos spoke only of Jeroboam's "house" (i.e., his dynasty). As Feinberg rightly notes, the priest also failed to mention that Amos had on at least two occasions interceded for the people (7:1-6) and that he had held out hope if there would be repentance (5:4, 6).[20]

7:12 Amaziah probably does not use the term "seer" (חֹזֶה, *hōzeh*) in a negative sense. Rather, he seems to refer to the visions Amos had reported. Even the heading of the book (1:1) does not hesitate to say that Amos "saw" (*ḥāzâ*) his words. Amos himself viewed the designation as somewhat equivalent to the term "prophet" (נָבִיא, *nābî'*), as his reply to Amaziah demonstrates.[21]

Amaziah also implies that Amos prophesies in order to earn a living. That implied charge is what Amos reacts to so vigorously. He had other things he could do to earn a living; his prophesying was in direct response to the Lord's call. Notice as well the contempt for Judah that appears in what Amaziah says. Israel could not bear Amos's preaching, but it would be perfectly all right in Judah.

---

[20] Charles L. Feinberg, *The Minor Prophets* (Chicago: Moody, 1976), p. 114.
[20] Charles L. Feinberg, *The Minor Prophets* (Chicago: Moody, 1976), p. 114.
[21] Cf. A. Jepsen, *TDOT* 4:286.

7:13 בַּיִת (*bayit*, usually "house") in v. 13 should be taken as a parallel expression for "sanctuary" (מִקְדָּשׁ, *miqdāš*). NASB's "a royal residence" could mislead the reader into thinking of a capital city or a place with a royal palace. For other cases where *bayit* refers to a temple see Judg. 9:4; 1 Kings 7:12; 2 Kings 10:21; Hag. 1:8; and Zech. 3:7.

Amaziah wishes to make the point that the authority of the king stood behind worship at Bethel. Northern Israelite worship was instituted by Jeroboam I (1 Kings 12:26-33), and its authority was maintained by the reigning monarch.

c) The Lord's Reply (7:14-17)

Translation

Then Amos replied and said to Amaziah, "I am neither a prophet nor a disciple of a prophet, but I am a livestock (dealer) and a *grower of sycamore figs.
[15]Yahweh took me away from the flock and said to me, 'Go prophesy to My people Israel.'
[16]"So now hear Yahweh's word! You say, 'You must not prophesy against Israel, and you must not *preach against the *house of Isaac.'
[17]Therefore Yahweh says this:
'Your wife will become a harlot in the city,
and your sons and daughters will fall by the sword.
Your land will be divided up by the measuring line,
and you yourself will die on unclean soil.
Moreover, Israel will certainly go into exile,
(removed) from her land.'"

Exegesis and Exposition

Amos replied to Amaziah both with a defense of his prophetic authority and with a further prophecy of judgment on Amaziah and Israel. Essentially, Amos claims that his role as a prophet does not derive from traditional means but from the direct call of the Lord. His aim is not to make a living but to deliver a message.

Because Amaziah dared to silence God's prophet, the judgment of God will fall on him. It will fall on his wife, his children, his land, and his own person. The catastrophes that will happen to him are those that accompany an enemy invasion: the women are forcibly raped (cf. Zech. 14:2); the children are killed (cf. Amos 1:13); the land is parceled out to others; and captives are led away to a foreign land. Thus will Amaziah's doom come upon the entire country.

7:14 Amos's denial in v. 14 that he was a prophet has been much discussed. If he prophesied to Israel yet also believed the Lord had called him to prophesy, how could he say, "I am not a prophet"?

Some have stressed the ambiguity of a Hebrew sentence containing no verb (i.e., "am" has to be supplied in the above translation). Perhaps he was really saying, according to this view, "I *was* not a prophet *until* Yahweh called me to prophesy."[22] Comparable translations are already found in the LXX and Peshitta, though the Targum implies a present tense.

But to say that the Hebrew sentence without a verb can be supplied with a verb of any tense overstates the matter. Most (though not all) examples of sentences without a verb that are also contained within a *conversation* are best translated with a present tense.[23] In other words, the translator can assume that the sentence in such a case refers to the present tense unless there are special factors from the context to indicate otherwise. Some think, of course, that Amos' prophetic office is such a special factor. But using the past tense to translate v. 14 may be too restrictive, implying that while Amos was not previously a (professional) prophet, now he is one.

When Amos goes on to state his occupation, he apparently replies directly to Amaziah's implication that prophecy is the source of his food. In other words, Amos denies that he makes a living from prophecy, or at least that material gain in any way motivates his actions. Right now he is not making his living through the office of a prophet. The contrast can be brought out better, in my view, by the present tense translation: "I am not (nor have I ever been) a prophet (by profession)."[24]

The first word in v. 15 is a verb with *waw*-consecutive, pointing to a narrative situation, "*then* Yahweh took me." This may indicate that v. 14 should also be taken as a past narrative ("I was a livestock (dealer) ..., then Yahweh took me"). On the other hand, the narration of v. 15 could simply be a development from the occupation which Amos had at the time. In other words, "I am a livestock (dealer) ..., and Yawheh took me from my normal activities and gave me a message to proclaim."[25] The translation "I was not a prophet" correctly stresses that Amos now follows the Lord in a different manner than previously, but it misses the actual significance of the way he uses the term *nābî'*.

Simon Cohen sought to interpret the negative as an absolute denial, "No! I am indeed a Navi (prophet), but not a Ben Navi (professional prophet)."[26] In this case Amos objects to the title "seer" that Amaziah applied to him. He is not a "seer" (*ḥōzeh*), which would be more like a "disciple of a prophet"; rather, he is a "prophet."

The grammar of the proposed construction would not be impossible, but several factors weigh against the view. First, the evidence is too limited to

---

[22] E.g., Cripps, *Amos*, pp. 232-33.

[23] The author carried out some concordance study (Mandelkern and Even-Shoshan) to determine this observation, using the personal subject pronouns "I" and "you."

[24] Cf. Wolff, *Joel and Amos*, p. 313; Smith, *Amos*, p. 240.

[25] Cf. Wolff, *Joel and Amos*, pp. 312-13. He thinks the positive uses of *nābî'* in 2:11 and 3:7 are the product of a later editor, but in both passages the *nābî'* is directly connected with the Lord. Thus, Amos himself could have used the term in both a positive and a negative way. It is negative only in response to Amaziah's crass suggestion that Amos merely seeks to get material gain from his prophetic occupation.

[26] Simon Cohen, "Amos *Was* a Navi," *HUCA* 32 (1961): 177. Cf. also Ziony Zevit, "Expressing Denial in Biblical Hebrew and Mishnaic Hebrew, and in Amos," *VT* 29 (1979): 505-09; Stuart, *Hosea-Jonah*, p. 376.

demonstrate that Amos considered the office of a "prophet" (nābî') on a higher level than that of a "seer" (ḥōzeh) or a "disciple of a prophet." Second, the parallel structure of the three sentences of v. 14 would be broken up if the first "not" is taken in a way different from the second. Finally, the proposed structure has Amos objecting to the title by which Amaziah called him rather than to the command to cease his prophetic work.

Since the office of a prophet was not acquired by heredity, as was the priesthood, it is clear that the expression "son of a prophet" (בֶּן נָבִיא, ben nābî') implies membership in a prophetic guild or organization (cf. 2 Kings 2:3, 5, 15; 4:1, 38; 6:1; 9:1).

After a negative clause, כִּי (kî), normally translated "for" or "that," implies a strong contrast.[27] Rather than being a professional prophet, Amos has a normal profession by which he can earn his livelihood. Since he was prosperous in his business (cf. exegesis of 1:1), he was able to support himself. The only possible motive he had for acting as a prophet was that God told him to do it.

Both terms by which Amos describes his profession are unique to the present passage. The first, בוֹקֵר (bôqēr), seems clearly related to the common Hebrew noun bāqār, "cattle" or "herd." Normally the latter word implies oxen or cows, but Amos was following a "flock" (צֹאן, ṣō'n), that is, sheep and goats or other small cattle. Evidently the range of meaning for the root bqr could include sheep. The commentary translation "livestock (dealer)" stresses the greater significance of Amos' occupation than merely a "shepherd" or a "herdsman," though it cannot be proven that the term indicates this precise nuance (cf. comments on nōqēd, "sheep breeder," used in 1:1).

The only certainty about the phrase בוֹלֵס שִׁקְמִים (bôlēs šiqmîm) is that it shows that Amos had something to do with "sycamore figs." The Greek translations point to a nipping or scraping action performed on the figs. The only explanation that is botanically satisfactory is that gashing the figs at a certain period in their growth cycle releases ethylene, which hastens ripening. Sycamore figs in Israel today do not need this process, but it is not impossible that the trees in ancient times did need it.[28]

If the expression should be translated simply "grower" or "gatherer" of figs, it may be that Amos used the figs as fodder for his cattle. Presumably the figs would not be pierced if they were to be used for cattle food. This explanation has the advantage of explaining the relationship between Amos's two professions.[29]

As was mentioned above under Amos 1:1, sycamore figs do not grow in the area of Teqoa but only in lower elevations. The Targum recognizes this fact rather explicitly: "And I have sycamores in the Shephelah [low hill country])" (בשפילתא ושקמים לי, wešiqmîm lî bĕšāpēltā').

7:15 Amos received his commission to prophesy in the midst of his ordinary work. There is no suggestion of any explicit preparation he had received for his

---

[27] Ronald J. Williams, *Hebrew Syntax: An Outline*, 2d ed. (Toronto: Univ. of Toronto, 1976), par. 555.

[28] T. J. Wright, "Amos and the 'Sycamore Fig,'" *VT* 26 (1976): 363-65.

[29] Ibid., p. 367.

task. He could not have received the right kind of training from the corrupt religious structures in Israel. The Lord needed an outsider to deliver a prophetic message against an unholy system. Even though Amos did not hold the professional position of a prophet, he does not deny that he functions as a prophet. That is, he does what a *true* prophet does: he delivers God's message to God's people.

Amos does not make fine distinctions between the political entities of Israel and Judah. Here he traces his concern with Israel as God's chosen people to the call he received while taking care of his flocks. "My people" identifies Israel as the people of the covenant (see also 7:8; 8:2; 9:14).

7:16 It is unclear whether Amos quotes Amaziah directly or merely paraphrases his words in v. 16. One should consider, though, the close relation with Amos 2:12: "And you commanded the prophets saying, 'You shall not prophesy.'" Clearly Amaziah meant to force Amos to stop prophesying.

The terms "prophesy" (תִּנָּבֵא, *tinnābē'*) and "preach" (תַּטִּיף, *taṭṭîp*) occur together elsewhere only in Ezek. 20:46 (MT 21:2) and 21:2 (MT 21:7). Other passages where the root *nṭp* clearly refers to speaking include five instances in Micah (2:6, three times; 2:11, twice).

7:17 The contrast becomes complete in v. 17. Amaziah, acting as an official representative for the nation, demanded that Amos not prophesy. Now the Lord Himself has a further prophecy for both Amaziah and Israel.

Priests needed to be concerned about ritual purity. Therefore, a priest would find the thought of death on unclean soil particularly distasteful. That is, his body would be interred in pagan ground. אֲדָמָה (*'ădāmâ*) occurs three times in the verse. The second occurrence should be taken as "ground" rather than "land" because of the preposition "upon" (*'al*) rather than "in" (*b*; but cf. NIV). Either way, the ultimate sense is "in an unclean/pagan land."

The prophecy of exile for Israel was dramatically fulfilled by the Assyrian wars with Israel under Tiglath-pileser III, Shalmaneser V, and Sargon II. When Samaria fell in 722 B.C., the king of Assyria "carried Israel away into exile to Assyria" (2 Kings 17:6).

Additional Notes

7:14 בּוֹלֵס שִׁקְמִים: Stanley N. Rosenbaum suggests that the root בלס be connected with בלשׁ, making Amos some sort of government official in charge of sycamore trees. This ties in with Rosenbaum's belief that Amos was "a Northern civil servant."[30]

7:16 תַּטִּיף: Much is often made of the apparent etymological relationship with a Hebrew term meaning "to drip" (cf. note in NASB). It may be that it implies something like "make words drip or flow."[31] However, the meaning which occurs as an equivalent to "prophesy" is found only in the *hiphil* pattern, while the meaning "drip" normally occurs in the *qal*. Amos 9:13 contains the only instance

---

[30] Stanley N. rosenbaum, עָמוֹס הַיִּשְׂרָאֵלִי *Amos of Israel: A New Interpretation* (Macon, GA: Mercer University, 1990), pp. 48-50.

[31] Cf. Marvin R. Wilson, *TDOT* 2:576.

where the *hiphil* form means "drip" (cf. Joel 3:18 [MT 4:18], where the verb is *qal*). Job 29:22 contains the word in a *qal* form with reference to speech: "And my speech *dropped* on them." Yet Job goes on to say, "And they waited for me as for the rain" (v. 23). That is, Job uses "drip" in a figurative sense. Prov. 5:3 probably refers to kisses (cf. Song of Sol. 4:11; 5:13); thus the parallel term should be translated "palate" (as in NASB margin).

יִשְׂחָק בֵּית: The LXX has "house of Jacob," but the Targum and Peshitta agree with the MT. The Vulg. has *domum idoli*, "house of idols." Likewise, both the LXX and the Vulg. have a variant for Isaac at 7:9, the LXX reading "altars of laughter" (βωμοὶ τοῦ γέλωτος) and the Vulg. with "high places of idols" (*excelsa idoli*) for יִשְׂחָק בָּמוֹת. Apparently these versions had difficulty with the unusual spelling of Isaac's name.

2. The Vision Of The Basket Of Summer Fruit (8:1-10)

a) Presentation (8:1-3)

Translation

Here is what the Lord Yahweh showed me:
a *basket of summer fruit.
²Then He said to me, "What do you see, Amos?"
So I said, "A basket of summer fruit."
Then Yahweh said to me:
"The end has come for My people Israel;
   I will spare them no longer.
³The palace *songs will turn to wailing
   in that day," declares the Lord Yahweh.
"Many are the corpses!
   Everywhere they have cast them. Silence!"

Exegesis and Exposition

The vision of the basket of summer fruit has many similarities with the vision of the plumb line. In both, the Lord asks Amos, "What do you see?" Also, the message concerning judgment is the same in both: "I will spare them no longer." The advance in thought here is the stress upon the end for Israel, which is made through the word play between "summer fruit" (קַיִץ, *qayiṣ*) and "end" (קֵץ, *qēṣ*; see also under Additional Notes). Evidently the ripeness of the fruit also indicates the ripeness of the nation for judgment.

8:1 The term used for "summer fruit" (*qayiṣ*) in v. 1 can also mean simply "summer" (e.g., Gen. 8:22; Amos 3:15; Zech. 14:8). Other passages indicate a particular type of fruit, possibly figs.[32] The "basket" (כְּלוּב, *kĕlûb*) appears only to provide enough context to ascertain that Amos sees ripe fruit.

---

[32] Wolff, *Joel and Amos*, p. 319.

8:2 Once again the interrogation of Amos focuses attention on the central feature of the vision, in this case the basket of summer fruit. The effect is to slow down the action and linger over the mystery of what the vision might signify.

The connection between summer fruit and the meaning of the vision centers around a forceful play on words. The *qayiṣ* ("summer fruit") spells the *qēṣ* ("end") for Israel. The connection is strengthened even more by the use of the preposition *'el*, normally "to" or "unto," instead of the expected *l*. The English translation demands "for Israel," but the Hebrew makes it seem almost as though the "end" actually enters into the midst of Israel.

From a broader historical perspective we can easily connect Amos's prophecy with the fall of Samaria in 722 B.C. and the turbulent years leading up to it. Consider, however, Amos's perspective. He prophesies "the end," yet Jeroboam II continues to prosper on his throne for perhaps as much as a decade (or two or three years if Amos prophesied as late as 755 B.C.). Moreover, once "the end" arrived, it consisted of a process stretching out for an additional three decades.

The important fact, of course, is that biblical prophecy must be viewed from God's perspective. When He announces the end, there is no turning it back (cf. Amos 1:3-2:5). If He seems slow in bringing events into historical reality, it is because in His grace He is giving additional time for repentance.

8:3 Apparently Amos uses a strong figure of speech in v. 3: *songs will wail.* It would be unusual to personify "songs," but the verb for "wail" (הֵלִיל, *hēlîl*) cannot receive an object. One should imagine beautiful songs of joy and gladness that suddenly burst into somber wailing. Another possibility is that Amos uses abstract terms for the more concrete "singers."

We cannot know for sure whether the text refers to "palace songs" or to "temple songs." The term הֵיכָל (*hêkāl*), ultimately derived from a Sumerian term meaning "great house," could be applied to either a king's palace or the dwelling place of God. Probably Amos has in mind the unthinking revelry of the leaders, who "strum on the opening of the lyre" and compose "songs" for themselves (6:6). He also spoke earlier of temple songs (5:23), but they were representative of the worship the Lord would not accept.

In the last line the Lord evidently quotes the lamentation of the wailing songs. As Mays notes, such an interpretation best accounts for the use of the perfect of the verb "cast" (הִשְׁלִיךְ, *hišlîk*).[33] This would also help to explain the abrupt syntax of "silence!" (הָס, *hās*), the final word of the line. It functions as an interjection everywhere else it occurs, and the adverbial sense given it by the NASB, "in silence," would be unique. The NIV gives a better reading. The verb "cast" is often used when bodies are cast aside without a proper burial, especially after a violent death (cf. Josh. 8:29; 10:27; 2 Kings 9:25).

Additional Notes

8:1 קַיִץ: In the northern pronunciation of Hebrew the two words קַיִץ and קֵץ may have sounded exactly alike (*qēṣ*). Evidence from inscriptions (esp. the

---

[33] James Luther Mays, *Amos: A Commentary* (OTL; Philadelphia: Westminster, 1969), pp. 141-42.

Samaria Ostraca, roughly contemporary with Amos and Hosea) suggests that in the north the diphthong /ay/ was pronounced simply as /ê/. Thus, "wine" is spelled in the MT consistently יין, but in the Samaria Ostraca it is spelled ין.[34] Al Wolters recently proposed that the dialect difference is significant for the interpretation. The Lord pronounced in the Israelite dialect what Amos described in his own Judean tongue, turning the word for ripe fruit into that for disaster.[35] This is possible, though it is difficult to be certain since it is precisely the pronunciation of the words that has undergone the most change from ancient times to the era of the Masoretes (e.g., Wolters's reconstruction of the Judean pronunciation at that time should rather be /qayṣ/, not qayiṣ).

b) Popular Response (8:4-6)

Translation

Hear this, you who trample the needy
and do away with the afflicted of the land.
[5](You) say:
"When will the new moon pass so we may sell grain,
    and the Sabbath so we may open up the wheat,
making the ephah smaller, making the shekel heavier,
    and cheating with dishonest scales?
[6]Thereby (we) will acquire the poor for silver
    and the needy for the sake of a pair of sandals,
    and we will sell even the refuse of the wheat."

Exegesis and Exposition

Properly speaking, the present section does not contain a direct response to the vision, and it should also be tied together with the comments of the Lord following because of the command to "hear this." The division of the passage made here emphasizes, however, the broader structural similarity between Amaziah's reply and the words of the people. The material about Amaziah is a unit consisting of a response from the priest and a corresponding prophecy of judgment, and the present section has a similar structure. Amaziah condemned himself and so do the people by their hypocritical remarks. Consequently the Lord makes a further threat of destruction.

The complaining of the people ties together the two emphases in the book on social injustice and an ineffective religious formalism. The people lament the way the keeping of new moon and Sabbath prevents them from taking advantage of the poor in the marketplace! Obviously they care neither for their religion nor for their fellow Israelites. Yet the Lord considers proper treatment of the oppressed a prerequisite to true worship. The people themselves speak the last words in the book about their own injustice, and they eloquently summarize the dire need for

---

[34] See John C. L. Gibson, *Textbook of Syrian Semitic Inscriptions*, 2 vols. (Oxford: Clarendon, 1971), 1:7-8.

[35] Al Wolters, "Wordplay and Dialect in Amos 8:1-2," *JETS* 31 (1988): 407-10.

judgment to come. These final charges reiterate the accusations Amos first made against Israel (2:6-8).[36]

8:4 The expression "who trample the needy" in v. 4 repeats, in a modified form, the charge of 2:7. Here the details of how the action of trampling is carried out will be explained by the words of the oppressors (vv. 5-6).

A literal translation of וְלַשְׁבִּית (wĕlašbît) would be, "and to bring to an end (the afflicted of the land)." In a sentence of this type the infinitive can be translated as an additional finite verb (cf. Jer. 44:19).[37] Similar constructions occur in vv. 5b and 6. The Hebrew makes more explicit than the English that the actions expressed by infinitives are subordinate to the main verb. The destruction of the afflicted is a special case of "trampling" the poor.

8:5 "The new moon" (הַחֹדֶשׁ, haḥōdeš) in v. 5 refers to a festival time when no work was done (cf. 1 Sam. 20:5-6; 2 Kings 4:12; Ezek. 46:3). The merchants reveal their true motives toward the worship that ostensibly took place on the new moons and Sabbaths. They can hardly endure, because of their greed, the lack of commercial activity.

The merchant gains the advantage by using a smaller than standard measure of volume for determining the amount to give the customer. Also, since the purchaser would pay for his goods by a weight of silver as determined by the dealer's weights, the seller would also benefit from stones that weighed more than normal. Finally, the businessman could also tamper with the scales. Naturally these practices placed a heavy burden on the ordinary people, and they were soundly condemned in the Law of Moses (Lev. 19:36). The use of the infinitives in vv. 5-6 parallels the structure of v. 4. Here the subordinate clause shows result. The merchants are eager to open the markets so they can begin cheating the people.

8:6 When Amos turns his attention to the problem of debt slavery, the flow of the context is apparently interrupted. The immediately following sentence, "And we will sell even the refuse of the wheat," seems to continue the thought of dishonest business dealings at the wheat market. Some have proposed that the statement is a later gloss inserted into the text (so apparatus to *BHS*), while others have proposed rearranging the text so that selling "the refuse of the wheat" is in direct juxtaposition with the tampering with weights and standards.[38]

As for the relation of the section to v. 5, the Hebrew infinitive at the beginning of v. 6 does not have *waw* ("and") with it. The resulting break in syntax corresponds to the break in thought, and the connection should evidently be one of result ("so that" in NASB). The close relationship with Amos 2:6 is lessened by the use of the verb "buy" rather than "sell." The earlier passage dealt with debt slavery because the people were *sold* for money. Here the dishonest practices so impoverish the people that the merchants, in effect, *buy* the helpless and the needy. The reference to "a pair of sandals" heightens the sense of greed. Even for trivial sums the wheat sellers force the people into dependence.

---

[36] See the exegesis of that section for discussion of the important terminology which is repeated here.

[37] GKC, par. 114p.

[38] E.g., Wolff, *Joel and Amos*, p. 322 n. h.

When the verb form switches back from an infinitive (as in vv. 5b-6) to the imperfect "we will sell" (as in v. 5a), the entire section closes off neatly. Rather than being out of place, the final statement serves as a strong conclusion and forms an inclusio. Not only do the merchants use false weights, measures, and scales to draw the poor into a relation of dependence; they even dare to sell that part of the wheat that ought to be thrown away as of no value.

c) The Lord's Reply (8:7-10)

Translation

Yahweh has sworn by the Pride of Jacob,
"I will never forget all their deeds.
⁸Will not the land tremble because of this,
and every inhabitant in it mourn?
Indeed, all the land will rise up like *the Nile,
then it will roil *and sink down like the Nile of Egypt."
⁹"Now it will happen in that day,"
declares the Lord Yahweh,
"that I will make the sun go down at noon,
and darken the land in the brightness of the day.
¹⁰I will change your festivals into mourning,
and all your songs into dirges.
I will make sackcloth appear on every waist,
and baldness on every head.
I will make it like the mourning for an only son,
and the end of it will be like a time of bitter weeping."

Exegesis and Exposition

Amos has depicted a situation in Israel so bad that an immediate response from the Lord is expected. In fact, the Lord feels so strongly that He begins His response with an oath that He makes by Himself. He affirms that He is the true God of Jacob by calling Himself "the Pride of Jacob." Therefore, He has the authority to determine the destiny of His people.

Moreover, the Lord calls for a judgment that will cause complete destruction throughout the land, bringing bitter mourning with it. The cause of the devastation will be a mighty shaking of the land, and it will compare even with the awesome natural catastrophes that accompany the day of the Lord itself. On this day God will reverse the normal course of life that the Israelites had been enjoying. Day will become night; joyous festivals will become occasions of mourning; glad songs will become laments; ordinary clothes will be exchanged for sackcloth; and people will show their sorrow even in their physical appearance as they shave their heads. The depth of their sorrow will exceed the bitterest lamentations imaginable.

8:7 Since גְּאוֹן יַעֲקֹב (gĕʾôn yaʿăqōb) occurs in a negative context in 6:8, LXX translated "the Lord has sworn *against* [καθ, *kath*] the arrogance of Jacob." The Hebrew idiom, however, consistently means "swear by," not "swear against." Moreover, when the Lord swears "by" something, it is always by Himself or by one of His attributes (cf. 4:2; 6:8; Gen. 22:16; Ps. 89:36, 50; 95:11; Jer. 44:26).

Therefore, we must assume that "pride of Jacob" has a different sense here than in 6:8. In the former passage it signifies Jacob's own "god," their reliance on their own strength and on their own religious rituals. In the present passage, it means the Lord Himself, the one who is the true "Pride of Jacob." Parallel thoughts occur in the expressions "the Mighty One of Jacob" (Gen. 49:24) and "the Glory of Israel" (1 Sam. 15:29).

Many prefer to see here an ironic use of the phrase "pride of Jacob." In this interpretation the Lord swears by the assured fact that the nation is arrogant. As Wolff phrases it, "Yahweh's oath is just as unalterable as Israel's haughty arrogance is beyond reform."[39] However, one cannot find any other instance in the OT where the Lord takes an oath by a human attribute.

The second half of the line uses the oath formula to state as strongly as possible that the Lord will never forget Israel's deeds of iniquity. Yet the Lord also says through Amos that the nation will be restored (9:11-15). The sins of Israel were judged, and the process of refinement continues until the restoration will take place (9:9).

8:8a Regarding v. 8 Feinberg notes: "Some understand the verse to be speaking of an earthquake, but the thought is rather that the land will shake from the weight of the judgment it is called upon to bear."[40] Prov. 30:21 gives a parallel idea.

However, the introduction to the book speaks of an earthquake that occurred two years after Amos's prophecy. Some prophetic mention of the event is therefore expected. Surely the earthquake in Uzziah's reign, though undoubtedly severe and destructive, did not exhaust the words of judgment brought by Amos. Yet it did serve, apparently, as a foreshadowing of the total destruction to come. Moreover, it occurred in the midst of a very prosperous period. For years to come it would serve as a warning that the dire predictions of Amos would come to pass, regardless of how outward circumstances seemed to contradict them. Probably, then, we should understand the present verse to predict an earthquake. The verb translated "quake" (רָגַז, *rāgaz*) does not occur as often as רָעַשׁ (*ra'aš*) for an earthquake, but it does indicate frequently a trembling of the earth for one reason or another (cf. 1 Sam. 14:15; Joel 2:10; Hab. 3:7; Ps. 18:7 [MT 18:8]; 77:18 [MT 77:19]).

Josephus records an earthquake in Judea that took 10,000 lives (*Antiq.* 15.5.2). A tremor felt all the way from Hazor to Beersheba (cf. Introduction to Amos, n. 3) would have thrown the whole land into a period of mourning for the dead.

8:8b Since the rise and fall of the Nile is a gradual process, some interpreters feel that this image is not well-chosen for an earthquake.[41] Yet the point of comparison need be only to the rather dramatic difference between the high and low points of the river, not to the speed with which it occurs. Also the rolling and uplifting motion associated with many temblors could be described with reference to the rise and fall of a river.

---

[39] Ibid., *Joel and Amos*, p. 328; cf. also William Rainey Harper, *A Critical and Exegetical Commentary on Amos and Hosea* (ICC; Edinburgh: T. & T. Clark, 1979), p. 179.

[40] Feinberg, *The Minor Prophets*, p. 117; cf. Keil, *Minor Prophets*, p. 316.

[41] Cf. Mays, *Amos*, p. 145; Hayes, *Amos*, pp. 209-10.

One might still wonder why Amos chose a figure from Egyptian geography. The raging sea might have described a violent earthquake better. Possibly he intends the reader to go beyond the physical aspects of the earthquake to the terrors of chaos. No more would the land be a place of security; it would rise and fall continually, heaving its inhabitants around mercilessly in the process. Perhaps the mention of Egypt also foreshadows the thought of exile. The Targum offers an interesting paraphrase: "And a king shall rise up against it in its camps and become great like the waters of the river. And he will cover all of it and drive out the inhabitants, and [the land] will be immersed like the river of Egypt."

The line in v. 8*b* apparently has been taken by Amos from a hymn that he either used or composed, portions of which are found also in 4:13; 5:8-9; 9:5-6 (see also Excursus on the Hymnic Passages in Amos). In 9:5 the wording of the present passage is repeated almost verbatim. The former passage stresses the awesome power of God, while the present verse emphasizes the stressful nature of the judgment itself.

8:9 Does Amos mean in v. 9 the eschatological "day of Yahweh" (cf. 5:18), or does he simply refer to the approaching day of judgment for the nation of Israel? It may not be correct to try to distinguish these too finely. The earthquake in the days of Uzziah was a harbinger of the terrors of the Assyrians, and the terrors of the Assyrians foreshadowed the awesome day of the Lord, which will usher in the kingdom of God.

Amos speaks of a darkening of the daylight, a feature characteristic of the day of the Lord (Joel 2:31; Amos 5:18; Zeph. 1:15), yet he uses an unusual expression for it: "I shall cause the sun to enter at midday." From the viewpoint of the Hebrews, the sun would "enter" its nightly location at sunset (cf. Gen. 15:12). Hence, the noun from the root בוא (*bw'*) meaning "entrance" can also be used of the sunset (Ps. 104:19) and of the west (Deut. 11:30).

Some think Amos alludes here to an eclipse of the sun.[42] The Targum probably interpreted the Hebrew this way: "And I will cover the sun at midday," though the Syriac follows the Hebrew more literally. "Making the sun go down" could be a poetic way of saying "become dark." When the sun is eclipsed, it is like the darkness of night. In any case the parallel expression, "and make the earth dark in broad daylight" (NASB) could easily refer to an eclipse.

The terrors of the ultimate day of the Lord will undoubtedly include a literal darkening, perhaps through eclipse or volcanic activity (see comments on Joel 2:31 [MT 3:4]). The judgment in Amos's time may involve darkness more in a figurative sense, however, in that v. 10 stresses emotional gloom and sorrow. From another perspective, the dust raised by a major earthquake could cause some dimming of the light. Or victims trapped in collapsed structures would no longer be able to see the light of day.

8:10 Verse 10 speaks of deep grief and anguish. All the normal activities that bring so much joy to life will cease, and uncontrolled sorrow will follow. For sackcloth used in mourning see the comments on Joel 1:8. "Baldness" refers to shaving of the head as a further sign of grief (cf. Ezra 9:3; Isa. 22:12; Jer. 48:37).

---

[42] E.g., Erling Hammershaimb, *The Book of Amos, A Commentary*, trans. John Sturdy (New York: Schocken, 1970) p. 126.

Sons were highly valued in ancient Israel. To lose one's only son represented the deepest occasion of sorrow imaginable. Zechariah speaks of a great national mourning for sin that will take place when Christ returns: "and they will mourn for Him [i.e., for what they have done to Him], as one mourns for an only son" (Zech. 12:10). These images from the OT add force to the familiar words of John 3:16, "He gave His only begotten Son."

Additional Notes

8:8 כְּאֹר: The literal translation should be, "like the light," not "like the river." Yet 9:5, a clear parallel with 8:8, has כִּיאֹר, the only reading that makes sense in the context, especially in light of the parallel in both verses with "like the river of Egypt." Some Hebrew manuscripts also have כיאר here (apparatus to *BHS*), and it is presupposed by the ancient versions.

וְנִגְרְשָׁה: The LXX lacks any equivalent to the word, leading several commentators to omit it as a gloss (cf. JB).[43] It is not found in 9:5.

וְנִשְׁקָה: The *qere* is וְנִשְׁקְעָה, the identical reading being found in 9:5. It forms a suitable parallel to "rise up." The *ketib* apparently should mean something like "be inundated." It does not fit the context as well and occurs with a root that is not otherwise found in the *niphal* verbal pattern. The Targum rendering, "and it will be immersed" (וחשתקע), seems at first glance to support the *ketib*, but a cognate with the *qere* has been used.

3. Those Who Refuse To Listen (8:11-14)

Translation

"Look! Days are coming,"
declares the Lord Yahweh,
"when I will send a famine on the land.
It will not be a famine for bread
nor a thirst for water
but to hear the words of Yahweh.
[12]Then they will wander from sea to sea
and rove about from the north to the east,
searching for the word of Yahweh.
But they will not find it.
[13]In that day
the beautiful maidens will faint,
also the young men from thirst.
[14]Those who swear by *the guilt of Samaria
and say, 'Your god lives, Dan!'
    or 'By the life of the *way of Beersheba!' –
they will fall and not get up again."

---

[43] Cf. Wolff, *Joel and Amos*, p. 322 n. 1.

Exegesis and Exposition

As a conclusion to the series of two visions announcing the end in light of the people's own evaluation of the Lord, Amos speaks of a time when there will be no prophetic word to assure them. Amaziah had commanded Amos to cease his preaching; the wealthy merchants had expressed their inner feelings about even external efforts to worship the Lord. In the future the lack of the Word of God will be like a famine. A deep spiritual hunger and thirst that cannot be satisfied will cause the people to wander in search of nourishment and to "faint" from lack of water.

The visions reach a climax in the scene where God Himself stands beside the altar (9:1). Yet ironically, in the conclusion to the present section we see the people frantically searching for a word from God. The Lord's presence will be obvious only through acts of judgment, not by words of assurance and grace. The spiritual deprivation will only intensify the suffering of those under the judgment.

8:12 Verse 12 pictures starving and thirst-crazed individuals on a relentless quest for something to eat and drink. Less clear, however, is the extent of their wanderings. One viewpoint takes this as a universal picture: the Israelites will wander all over the world in their fruitless quest.[44] Parallel passages would then be Ps. 72:8 and Zech. 9:10. The latter couples "from sea to sea" with "from the River [Euphrates] to the ends of the earth" in its description of the universal Messianic kingdom.

Another possibility is to take "from sea to sea" in Amos in the sense, "from the Dead Sea to the Mediterranean Sea." "North" to "east" then represents the completion of the circuit. After the people journey to the Dead Sea they cross to the Mediterranean, then head back north, only to turn east again to complete the futile quest.[45]

The issue must be decided on the basis of the immediate context. The famine comes on the "land," a term that could mean the whole earth but here has the more restricted sense. The reference to Samaria, Dan, and Beersheba in v. 14 confirms this impression. Also, Amos consistently speaks of judgment against the land and people. Therefore, it does not seem that he speaks here of a hunger for the Word of God while the people are exiled from their land. The passage would apply best to the period of political upheaval during the time of the Assyrian monarchs Tiglath-pileser III (745-727 B.C.) and Shalmaneser V (727-722 B.C.). In these chaotic times the people would seek a word of assurance but find none.

Yet the ministries of Micah and Isaiah overlap the end of this period in history. Did they not have a word for Israel as well as for Judah? For Micah, though, Samaria comes into view only for the prophecy of 1:2-9, probably delivered during the reign of Ahaz and mainly for the benefit of Judah.[46] Isaiah also spoke briefly against the northern kingdom when it served his purpose with reference to Judah (cf. 9:8-10:11 [MT 9:7-10:11]).

---

[44] Feinberg, *The Minor Prophets*, p. 118; Wolff, *Joel and Amos*, pp. 330-31.

[45] Cf. Driver, *Joel and Amos*, p. 214; Mays, *Amos*, p. 149.

[46] Leslie C. Allen, *The Books of Joel, Obadiah, Jonah and Micah* (NICOT; Grand Rapids: Eerdmans, 1976), p. 265.

If the people of Samaria had wanted to, they could have listened to the preaching of these southern prophets. We might ask, however, just what they were seeking. During their quest they swear by "the guilt of Samaria," by the god of Dan, and by "the way of Beersheba" (v. 14). Even though they encompass the whole of the land from Dan to Beersheba (perhaps avoiding key Judean centers), they look in all the wrong places. Moreover, they are looking for words of comfort. Even Amos closed his book with a word of comfort, but it was found in the house of David, not in the kingdom of Israel (9:11-15). Israel would first have to repent before she could find solace in the Davidic dynasty. Of course, the Lord is always open to true repentance, but the obstinate northerners would have none of that. Hence, their quest was futile; they would never join the small remnant that God was preserving for himself. Nor would they ever find the "Word of the Lord."

8:13 The "beautiful maidens [בְּתוּלֹת, betûlōt]" and "young men" of v. 13 are not the only ones who go in search of a word from the Lord or who participate in the false worship described in the following verse. Being vigorous and healthy, they represent rather the extent of the famine and drought. If *they* cannot survive it, how much less the children or older people. The "maidens" are also "beautiful," further attesting to their youth and vigor.

8:14 The "guilt of Samaria" (אַשְׁמַת שֹׁמְרוֹן, 'ašmat šōmĕrôn) in v. 14 most likely refers to the golden calf worship set up in Bethel by Jeroboam I (but see Additional Notes).[47] Actually, two golden calves were set up to represent the Lord, one at Bethel and one at Dan (1 Kings 12:28-29). As discussed under 4:4-5, Amos was more concerned with hypocrisy in the worship of the Lord than with outright idolatry. Important also is that the second part of the present verse refers to Dan.

The idiom "by the life of X" would normally be filled in with a divine name or epithet. Since the calves at Dan and Bethel were probably intended to represent the Lord, we would expect "the way of Beersheba" (דֶּרֶךְ בְּאֵר־שָׁבַע, derek bĕ'ēršāba') to be an epithet of Him.[48] Otherwise the expression is quite obscure, and some textual emendations have been proposed (see Additional Notes). The KB lexicon explains Hebrew *derek* by Ugaritic *drkt*, meaning "dominion" or "power." The evidence for the connection is not clear, however. Some have pointed to the modern practice of Moslems who take an oath "by the sacred way to Mecca,"[49] but the parallel is too remote in time to be convincing. David Allan Hubbard suggests a reference to a religious pilgrimage to Beersheba.[50] This makes reasonable sense but still would be difficult in that the reference to the pilgrimage follows "by the life of."

In any case, the oaths represent attempts by the guilty Israelites to obtain a word from the Lord. Characteristically, their efforts are misdirected, still under the system of the "guilt of Samaria."

A future for Israel can be found only in the house of David. Those who stayed within the false system set up by Jeroboam I fell and perished forever

---

[47] Driver, *Joel and Amos*, p. 215; Feinberg, *The Minor Prophets*, p. 119.
[48] Cf. Mays, *Amos*, p. 150.
[49] Lehrman, "Amos," p. 119, citing G. Adam Smith.
[50] David Allan Hubbard, *Joel and Amos: An Introduction and Commentary* (TOTC; Downers Grove, IL: Inter-Varsity, 1989), p. 225.

(עוֹד יָקוּמוּ וְלֹא־, *weulō'-yāqûmû 'ôd*, "and they will not get up again") for lack of a word of mercy from the Lord. As Feinberg notes, Ezekiel promised restoration for the northern tribes of Israel (37:15-23),[51] but this restoration comes only in conjunction with Judah. As the Lord said to Ezekiel, "I will put [Israel] with it, with the stick of Judah, and make them one stick, and they will be one in My hand" (37:19).

Additional Notes

8:14 שֹׁמְרוֹן אַשְׁמַת: Some see the name of a goddess, either Ashimah (2 Kings 17:30) or Asherah.[52] For the exegetical reasons given above, plus the lack of evidence for an early cult of the goddess Ashimah in Samaria, the vowels of the MT are preferred. The reading Asherah (אֲשֵׁרָה) would have better historical evidence (1 Kings 16:33; 2 Kings 17:16), but there is no textual basis for emending *mem* to *resh*.

דֶּרֶךְ בְּאֵר־שָׁבַע: Since דֶּרֶךְ ("way") is difficult in this context, some have proposed to read דּדְךָ, "your beloved," or דּרְךָ, "your assembly" (interpreted as "your pantheon"). Wolff rejects these conjectures after a thorough discussion.[53]

---

[51] Feinberg, *The Minor Prophets*, p. 119.

[52] Cf. apparatus of *BHS*; Cripps, *Amos*, p. 317; Karl Budde, "Zu Text und Auslegung des Buches Amos (Schluss)," *JBL* 44 (1925): 95-97. Wolff (*Joel and Amos*, p. 323 n. x) discusses and rejects the emendation.

[53] Wolff, *Joel and Amos*, pp. 323-24 n. y. See Hammershaimb (*Amos*, pp. 129-30) for a more positive evaluation.

9
The Fallen Booth of David Raised Up
(9:1-15)

In the previous four visions Amos was shown symbols of destruction and the end of the northern kingdom. Here he sees the Lord Himself standing at the altar in Bethel, giving a command to smash the temple so that it falls on the assembled worshipers. Then the scene shifts to a relentless pursuit of any who would attempt to escape. The Lord even pursues them into exile to slay them. Finally the vision closes with a majestic hymn to the Lord who appears on earth with destructive judgment. The Lord's own words summarize the intent of the vision: "I will set My eyes upon them for calamity/ and not for good" (v 4).

Certainly the visions have moved a long way from the assurances accompanying the earlier scenes: "It shall not be" (7:3, 6). In the meantime the people have demonstrated their ripeness for judgment by their own words and deeds. The whole system of worship is so corrupt and false that the Lord must wipe it out utterly. Yet it is this very finality of judgment that lays the groundwork for the closing scene of salvation and restoration. The Lord's statement to Jeremiah is pertinent as a commentary on what Amos is trying to communicate:

> See, I have appointed you this day
> over the nations and over the kings,
> to uproot and to tear down,
> to destroy and to overthrow,
> to build and to plant.
> (Jer. 1:10)

Before God can restore the nation, He must first tear it down. Hope will rise from the ashes, but first the conflagration must come.

A. The Lord Will Spare None (9:1-6)

Translation

I saw the Lord standing beside the altar, and He said:
"Strike the capitals so that the thresholds shake.
  Yes, *cut them off on the heads of all of them.
The rest of them I will kill with the sword.
  Not a fugitive of them will flee,
  nor will any survivor from them escape.
²Though they dig into Sheol,
  from there My hand will take them.
Though they go up to heaven,
  from there I will bring them down.
³Though they hide on top of Mt. Carmel,

271

from there I will make search and take them.
Though they conceal themselves from My eyes on the bottom of the sea,
   from there I will command the serpent to bite them.
⁴Though they go into captivity before their enemies,
   from there I will command the sword to kill them.
Indeed, I will set My eyes upon them
   for calamity and not for good."
⁵Now the Lord Yahweh of Hosts –
Who touches the earth and it trembles;
   and all its inhabitants mourn;
   and all of it rises up like the Nile;
   and it sinks down like the Nile of Egypt;
⁶Who built His upper chambers in heaven,
   and founded His vault over the earth;
*Who called for the waters of the sea,
   and poured them over the face of the earth –
Yahweh is His name!

Exegesis and Exposition

9:1a-b In his final vision Amos views the Lord Himself. Isaiah reports a similar experience: "I saw the Lord seated on a throne" (6:1). The presence of the Lord should be an encouragement; perhaps the people expected a positive message at last from the prophet. Instead, God's presence becomes a terrifying experience. Amos had warned the people before not to hope for the "day of Yahweh" (5:18).

The altar almost certainly refers to the one at Bethel, though it stands for the whole system of Israelite worship that the Lord rejects. Amos was at Bethel when Amaziah encountered him (7:12-13), and the city was the center of Israelite worship of the Lord. Nothing in the text leads us to think that the geographical scene has suddenly shifted. However, the Targum obviously thinks of the Temple at Jerusalem. It even mentions the death of king Josiah of Judah. The translator may have assumed that Amos left Bethel after his session with Amaziah and continued to prophesy in the south.

Amos's strong words to the priest make us think, rather, that he continued to minister in the north. Moreover, he refers to the "house of Jacob" in v. 8 (cf. 3:13; 6:8; 7:2, 5). It is not impossible that the vision of the Lord beside the altar occurred prior to the events of chap. 7 (Jeremiah, e.g., is not arranged chronologically).[1]

The Hebrew leaves the issue of who receives the commands to "strike" (הַךְ, *hak*) and "break them" (בְּצַעַם, *bĕṣa'am*) unclear. A rhetorical effect is intended; the Lord emphasizes that judgment upon the temple will certainly come (cf. Hab.

---

[1] Calvin, *Commentaries on the Twelve Minor Prophets* (Calvin's Commentaries 14; trans. John Owen; Grand Rapids: Baker, 1981), pp. 383-84, agreed with the Targum that the altar was the one in Jerusalem. Ebenezer Henderson, *The Twelve Minor Prophets* (Grand Rapids: Baker, 1980), p. 178, responds directly to Calvin's arguments.

1:5).[2] A note to the JB explains that an angel was addressed, but no angelic beings appear in any of the other visions. The beginning of the action described may have been the earthquake two years later.

The term "capital" (כַּפְתּוֹר, *kaptôr*) occurs in the singular form, but perhaps it has a collective force (cf. NASB and NIV). We do not know what this temple looked like, but a thirteenth or fourteenth century B.C. temple excavated at Lachish had four columns positioned in the central area before the altar.[3] The capitals would be at the top of the pillars; when they are struck, the roof supported by them collapses. Moreover, the capitals are struck with such force that the "thresholds shake." Possibly the pillars themselves are at the thresholds, so that a sharp blow to the top sends tremors into the very foundations of the entrances.

When the Lord appeared to Isaiah, "the foundations of the thresholds trembled" because of the seraphim calling out to each other (Isa. 6:4). The parallel is important because in both cases the prophet receives a vision of the Lord's presence in a temple, and in both the Lord delivers a message of judgment. In Amos's vision the judgmental nature is more dramatic, in that the temple and the people assembled in it are completely destroyed. Jean Ouellette argues that the vision presents a scene where the Lord breaks into the temple at Bethel to reach the people who will seek refuge there in an attempt to escape the judgment.[4]

The structure of the Hebrew sentences needs careful analysis, since the terminology and syntax have proved difficult for interpreters and translators. The following diagram should help:

1b)	*Hak*	*hakkaptôr*	
	Smite	the-capital(s)	
1c)	*wĕyir'ăšû*	*hassippîm*	
	and-will-shake	the-thresholds	
1d)	*ûbĕṣa'am*	*bĕrō'š*	*kullām*
	And-cut-off-them	on-head-of	them-all
1e)	*wĕ'aḥărîtām*	*baḥereb*	*'ehĕrōg*
	and-rest-of-them	with-the-sword	I-will-slay

If the above analysis is correct, then imperative verb forms are expected where Hebrew *hak* ("smite") and *ûbĕṣa'am* ("and cut them off") occur. Moreover, the second part of each poetic verse indicates a further result of the first part. The thresholds quake because the capitals have been struck; the Lord Himself slays any who escape the destruction of the temple.

The combination "cut them off on the heads of" seems a bit awkward and does not occur elsewhere, but apparently it implies, "cut off the capitals (so that they fall) on the heads of" (cf. 1 Sam. 25:39; 1 Kings 8:32; Ezek. 16:43; Joel 3:4

---

[2] James Luther Mays, *Amos: A Commentary* (OTL; Philadelphia: Westminster, 1969), p. 153.

[3] G. A. Barrois, "Temples," *IDB* 4:563, fig. 44.

[4] Jean Ouellette, "The Shaking of the Thresholds in Amos 9:1," *HUCA* 43 (1973): 23-27.

[MT 4:4]).[5] The Peshitta renders the verb as a noun: "and their treachery will be on their own head." (See also Additional Notes.)

9:1c The announcement of the complete destruction of the people in 9:1c seems remarkable in light of 9:8b, which mitigates the judgment. Also, we know that some survived both the earthquake in Uzziah's day and the military activity of Assyria under Tiglath-pileser III, Shalmaneser V, and Sargon II. The message of doom is that the kingdom of Israel will be destroyed with no way to escape the disaster. The Lord intends to undermine any feeling that some might have that "it will never happen to us" or that "we will somehow escape." All paths of retreat will be cut off, and the all-inclusive language of the passage drives home the message of universal calamity. Even those who did escape with their lives still had to face a terrifying shake-up of their existence. In effect the Lord had reached them with "calamity" (v. 4).

The נָס (nās) will be someone trying to run away in the terror of the moment, while the פָּלִיט (pālîṭ) is a survivor left after the tragedy has occurred.

9:2 Many have noticed the correspondence between v. 2 and Ps. 139:7-9. David, as a believer, found assurance in the thought that he could not even flee from God's presence. When a guilty man has to face God, Amos says, he will find only a terrifying wrath.

The figure of "digging into Sheol" highlights the desperate attempt to escape. Of course, the people can no more enter Sheol with a shovel than they can climb up to heaven or hide on the bottom of the sea. The language is hyperbolic and represents all the desperate devices the Israelites can think of to escape from God.

The book of Revelation presents a similar theme in relation to the Great Tribulation. Then the inhabitants of the earth will hide "from the wrath of the Lamb" in caves and mountain crags, begging for the rocks to fall on them (Rev. 6:15-17). Later, at the judgment before the great white throne, "the sea" and "death and Hades" will surrender the dead in them, so that all may appear before God. The Lord's terrible wrath is taught in both Testaments, and it is to our peril to treat such teaching lightly.

Six times in vv. 2-4 the Lord says "I" will administer the punishment. Little wonder that the prophet warned the people, "Prepare to meet your God, O Israel" (4:12) or that he pronounced a "woe" on their longing for the day of the Lord (5:18).

9:3 The mention of Carmel in v. 3 transports the reader back to the opening verse of Amos's message. The hot breath of the Lord roaring like a lion will dry up the top of Carmel (1:2). Its dense forests and thickets provide no cover for Israel when God appears in her midst.

9:4 The force of Amos's message in v. 4 is, "I am not going to bless you; rather I intend to bring upon you the curses promised in the covenant as a result of disobedience."[6] Many translations have "evil" for רָעָה (rā'â), but here it perhaps means "judgment" or "calamity."

---

[5] A "pregnant construction"; see GKC, par. 119ee, gg.

[6] Cf. Mays, *Amos*, p. 155.

Actually the form עֵינִי (*ênî*) is singular: "My eye." This is idiomatic, however. The phrase "set one's eye on" requires the singular (though Jer. 39:12 is exceptional), whereas other expressions, such as "lift up one's eyes," require the plural.[7] Joseph used the first expression in an apparently neutral sense; he simply desired to see Benjamin (Gen. 44:21). In Jeremiah the phrase has the positive sense of watching or protecting someone (39:12; 40:4) and of the Lord blessing His people (24:6). Ezekiel uses a similar expression for God's judgment: "My eye shall have no pity" (5:11; cf. 7:4, 9; 8:18; 9:10; 20:17).

9:5 Wolff views the unique placement of the divine name at the beginning of the hymn in v. 5 as an intrusion.[8] However, a staircaselike effect patterns the three hymns. The first contains two parts, the next three, and the last four. Moreover, the final hymn highlights its subject by the device of closure (inclusio). That is, it begins and ends the same way. The first hymn began with the admonition, "Prepare to meet your God, O Israel." The last occurs in the context of a vision where the prophet actually sees the Lord present among His people for judgment. (See also the Excursus on the Hymnic Passages in Amos.)

NASB has "melts" for Hebrew מוּג (*mûg*), but something like "trembles" or "totters" is better. Only the Vulg. among the ancient versions renders "melts"; LXX, Peshitta, and Targum all indicate a shaking or trembling. Also, the usage of the term elsewhere fits well with this idea (cf. esp. 1 Sam. 14:15-16; Ps. 46:6 [MT 46:7]; 75:3 [MT 75:6]; Nah. 1:5). Some passages associated with water can be explained on the basis of a semantic development from the thought of trembling (cf. Job 30:22; Ps. 65:1; Nah. 2:7; Amos 9:13).[9] At 9:13 Amos uses the same root word (*mûg*) for the dissolving of the hills. However, there the root occurs in a different verb pattern (qal in 9:5, hithpolel in 9:13). Perhaps the most important argument for the translation "trembles" at 9:5 is Amos 8:8. There Amos adapted a line from the hymnic passage of 9:5-6: "Because of this will not the land *quake* / and everyone who dwells in it mourn?"

Since the Lord is said to "touch" the land, a theophany or appearance of the Lord in power is in view (cf. Ps. 18:7 [MT 18:8]; 97:4-5; 144:5). Perhaps this explicitly refers to the giving of the Law at Sinai or to some other specific occasion (cf. Judg. 5:20-21),[10] though the language could be taken as characteristic. The Lord is the One who appears with power for judgment (or salvation) whenever the circumstances call for it.

See the exegesis of 8:8 for וְשָׁקְעָה (*wĕšāqĕ'â*). The reference to the undulation of the ground supports the interpretation of Hebrew *mûg* as "tremble."

---

[7] Hans Walter Wolff, *Joel and Amos* (Hermeneia; trans. Waldemar Janzen, et al.; Philadelphia: Fortress, 1977), p. 335 n. i, has failed to recognize the idiom here.

[8] Ibid., p. 336 n. q.

[9] See BDB's "*Addenda et Corrigenda*," p. 1124b; cf. Walter C. Kaiser, *TWOT* 1:493, entry 1156.

[10] See W. Gross, *Verbform und Funktion. wayyiqtol für die Gegenwart?: Ein Beitrag zur Syntax poetischer althebräischer Texte* (Arbeiten zu Text und Sprache im Alten Testament 1; St. Ottilien: Eos, 1976), pp. 102-103.

9:6 At the center of the hymn (v. 6) the prophet declares that the Lord resides in heaven. From there He descends to the earth and sets it shaking or pours out water upon the land.

The participle בּוֹנֶה (bôneh, "builder") has a descriptive function: the Lord is a builder. The time when the building took place depends on the context. In this case, the reference seems to be to a part of the original creation, hence the past tense in the translation. The versions are divided about this; LXX uses the present, the Targum the past, and the Peshitta, in the absence of vowels, can be interpreted either way.

Klaus Koch argues that ma'ălôt (מַעֲלוֹתָיו, ma'ălôtāyw [qere], "His upper chambers") should have its more common meaning of "stairs" or "ascent," comparing the ladder between heaven and earth in Jacob's dream (Gen. 28:12).[11] However, none of the other clear instances of a theophany gives the image of a staircase for the Lord to descend. The ladder in Jacob's dream is probably meant as a temporary symbol, whereas Amos speaks of something "founded" in creation. For a discussion of textual issues see Additional Notes.

The Hebrew term וַאֲגֻדָּתוֹ (wa'ăguddātô, "and His vault") is obscure. 'ăggudâ occurs only here with this meaning; elsewhere it signifies "fetters" (Isa. 58:6), a "bunch" of hyssop (Exod. 12:22), and a "band" of men (2 Sam. 2:25; cf. KJV on the Amos passage). As a parallel to "upper chambers," it must indicate some kind of construction associated with the heavens. Since God "founded" the structure over the earth, something like the "firmament" or "expanse" of Gen. 1 must be intended.

The term founded (יָסַד, yāsad) is part of the vocabulary of divine creation (Prov. 3:19; Isa. 51:16; cf. Prov. 8:27, 28). Job 26:11 refers to "the pillars of heaven," evidently the high mountains thought of as undergirding the sky.[12]

Additional Notes

9:1 וּבְצַעַם: The vowel with the suffix would normally be tsere on an imperative. Gesenius cited Margolis in deriving the form from an "original" בְּצַעְמוֹ.[13] Many moderns prefer to read the verb as first person imperfect (cf. אֶבְצָעֵם in the apparatus of BHS), but we attempted to show above that the structure of the passage calls for an imperative.

9:6 מְעֲלוֹתוֹ: The ketib is attested already in the second century Hebrew Minor Prophets scroll found at Wadi Murabbaat.[14] The normal Hebrew for "his upper chamber" (singular) would be עֲלִיָתוֹ (cf. 2 Kings 1:2). Wolff suggests that the mem occurs by dittography, while a misreading would explain the waw where

---

[11] Klaus Koch, "Die Rolle der hymnischen Abschnitte in der Komposition des Amos-Buches," ZAW 86 (1974): 526-27.

[12] See Robert Gordis, The Book of Job (Moreshet Series; Studies in Jewish History, Literature and Thought 2; New York: The Jewish Theological Seminary of America, 1978), p. 279.

[13] GKC, par. 61g. This emendation would not change the meaning.

[14] Les grottes de Murabba'at: Texte (DJD 2; Oxford: Clarendon, 1961), text no. 88, p. 188.

the *yodh* belongs.[15] The textual errors he refers to are common, and his position helps to explain the strange form of the *ketib*. However, one could connect the general sense of "upper chambers" with the form with *mem*. Notice also that Ps. 104:3, 13 contains the plural form of the noun, though without the *mem* prefix.

וַיִּשְׁפְּכֵם ... הַקֹּרֵא: See exegesis of 5:8.

B. The Lord Will Restore His People (9:7-15)

Translation

"Are you not like the sons of the Cushites to Me,
sons of Israel?"
declares Yahweh.
"Did I not bring up Israel
from the land of Egypt –
and the Philistines from Caphtor
and Aram from Kir?"
[8]Look! The eyes of the Lord Yahweh
are on the sinful kingdom.
"I will destroy it
from off the surface of the ground.
Yet I will not completely destroy the house of Jacob," declares Yahweh.
[9]"For see how I give a command
to shake the house of Israel among all the nations,
even as (grain) is shaken in a sieve
and not a pebble falls to the ground.
[10]All the sinners among My people
will die by the sword –
those who say, '*You will not soon bring
the disaster upon us.'"
[11]In that day I will raise up
the fallen shelter of David,
and I will wall up *their breaches
and raise up *its ruins.
I will rebuild it as in the days of old,
[12]*so that they may possess the remnant of Edom
*and all the nations over which my name will be called,"
declares Yahweh who will accomplish this.
[13]"Look! Days are coming," declares Yahweh,
"when the ploughman will overtake the reaper,
and the treader of grapes the one planting seed.
Then the mountains will drip with sweet wine,
and all the hills will be dissolved.
[14]Then I will restore the fortunes of my people Israel,
and they will rebuild ruined cities and live (in them).

---

[15] Wolff, *Joel and Amos*, p. 336 n. u.

They will plant vineyards and drink of their wine.
They will make gardens and eat of their produce.
[15]Yes, I will plant them upon their land,
and they will never again be uprooted
from the land which I gave to them,"
says Yahweh your God.

Exegesis and Exposition

The closing section of Amos discusses the status of Israel as a chosen people. In light of the "end," which the Lord will bring to her, will there be any hope for the future? The answer has three parts. First, God asserts His sovereignty over the affairs of all the nations and His intention to destroy the "sinful kingdom" (9:7-8a). Second, He declares that the judgment with reference to individuals will be a sifting process (9:8b-10). A righteous remnant will be saved. Third, salvation is announced through the renewal of "the fallen booth of David" (9:11-15). This will be a joyous time of restoration and rebuilding. Also the new condition of Israel will be permanent: "they will never again be uprooted from their land" (v. 15).

9:7a With a bold stroke the Lord declares in v. 7 that Israel has been estranged from Him. The nation has no more claim on God than the Cushites who live in the extreme south, at the fringes of Israelite experience. Noteworthy here is the style of rhetorical questions for the expression of harsh reality, a device used by Amos earlier (3:3-8).

Some modern versions have "Ethiopia" for "Cush," but the reader should be careful not to confuse the biblical term with the modern nation. The Greek rendered "Ethiopia" (Αἰθιόπων, *Aithiopōn*), but there the term referred to any land to the south of Egypt with a dark-skinned population. The land of Cush included an area south of Egypt, extending along the Nile from about the third cataract and toward the east coast of Africa by the Red Sea. Modern Sudan would include most if not all of biblical Cush.[16]

9:7b In the same breath God says He intervened in the affairs of the Philistines and Syrians no less than in those of Israel. The feeling of comparison carries over from the first part of the verse also. To the Lord, Israel is like the Ethiopians, the Philistines, and the Syrians.

The point of the comparison concerns universal sovereignty from God's side and the lack of obedience from Israel's side. The people must not forget that it was God who chose Israel, not Israel who chose God. Just prior to the beginning of Saul's reign the people tried to manipulate the Lord through the ark of the covenant (1 Sam. 4:3-11). Yet as the ark could not save the people in battle, so the covenant itself cannot save the nation if the people will not obey.

Theologically, the passage asserts that God is in control of all the nations. The Philistines killed King Saul in battle, and though David and Solomon subdued them, they continued to cause problems for both kingdoms (see exegesis of 1:6-8).

---

[16] O. Wintermute, "Cush," in *IDBSup*, pp. 200-1; T. O. Lambdin, "Ethiopia," *IDB* 2:177; Yohanan Aharoni and Michael Avi-Yonah, *The Macmillan Bible Atlas*, rev. ed. (New York: Macmillan, 1977), maps 11, 14, 15.

Yet God also brought the Philistines up from Caphtor and allowed them to dispossess the Avvim (cf. Deut. 2:23). The Arameans (Syrians) began to goad Israel under David, and not very long before Amos's time they had been a major threat (see exegesis of 1:3-5). Yet God took them from Kir and placed them in the land that formed a part of David's empire. Israel spurned the relationship that alone made her role in God's plan unique.

Caphtor probably refers to Crete (and perhaps also the islands and coasts of the Aegean Sea), though no archeological evidence for Philistines has been found there. Perhaps Amos was aware of a situation where the Philistines were not originally from Caphtor, even as Israel was not originally from Egypt.[17] For the location of Kir, see the note on 1:5.

9:8 The expression "eyes of the Lord Yahweh" in v. 8 picks up the thought of v. 4. A negative sense is clear also from the following phrase which speaks of destruction. "Sinful kingdom" narrows the scope to the northern nation in particular (though Judah was hardly innocent; cf. Amos 2:4-5).

As the second half of the verse makes clear, with its "yet" (כִּי אֶפֶס, 'epes kî, a strong adversative), it is not God's intent to destroy completely the "house of Jacob."[18] The latter phrase focuses on the whole people of God, though Amos still has the northern kingdom primarily in view. Ever so gradually, though, the prophet sees before him a new vision of a people restored under the leadership of a new David. A remnant will survive a sifting process and experience the joy of the new kingdom the Lord will bring, in which all the sons of Jacob will be united.

9:9 The way of introducing the prophecy in v. 9 is unusual. The statement of command precedes not the content of the order but another statement that the Lord will do something ("I will shake"). A similar pattern occurs at Jer. 34:22 and Amos 6:11. Evidently the grammar follows a common Semitic procedure whereby a subordinate idea is expressed through coordination using "and."

The sifting process will be accomplished through exile among the nations. Here the people are referred to as "house of Israel," implying much the same thing as "house of Jacob." That is, the covenant people will be put to the test to separate the righteous from the unrighteous.

צְרוֹר (ṣĕrôr) can only mean "pebble," not "grain" (as in NASB; cf. 2 Sam. 17:13). As Wolff explains, the reference is to "a sieve with coarse meshing, such as is used on the threshing floor; the grains fall through, but that which is useless – straw, stones, clods of earth – is retained."[19] The Targum translates the term as "stone." The unrighteous Israelites will remain in the presence of the Lord as Judge.

9:10 In v. 10 the Lord makes plain that the goal of the sifting process is to destroy the "sinners" among the covenant people. The remnant will remain to

---

[17] Cf. K. A. Kitchen, "Philistines," in *Peoples of Old Testament Times*, ed. D. J. Wiseman (Oxford: Clarendon, 1975) p. 53; F. W. Bush, *ISBE*, rev. ed., 1:610-11.

[18] Cf. the discussion by John H. Hayes, *Amos, The Eighth-Century Prophet: His Times and His Preaching* (Nashville: Abingdon, 1988), pp. 220-21. He rightly argues for the genuineness and appropriateness of Amos's words of partial destruction.

[19] Wolff, *Joel and Amos*, p. 349.

inherit the blessings spoken of in the following verses. The "sinners" are not really God's people; that is why they must be weeded out. The NIV correctly takes account of this emphasis: "all the sinners among my people."

The term "My people" is otherwise qualified by "Israel" in Amos (7:8, 15; 8:2; 9:14). The shorter form deflects attention from the national aspect, concentrating on the very personal relationship between God and His chosen ones (cf. Isa. 5:13; Hos. 1:9).

The sinners maintain the obstinate position that was illustrated so often by their rejection of the prophetic word (2:12; 4:6-11; 6:3; 7:10-13). The *hiphil* form תַּגִּישׁ (*taggîš*) normally means "bring near" (also in Amos 5:25 and 6:3), but that sense does not fit if the subject is הָרָעָה (*hārā'â*, "the disaster"). The *qal* form ("draw near," "approach") would easily permit *hārā'â* to be the subject, and the BDB lexicon advocates emending the form to the *qal*.[20]

Wolff suggests, "You are not leading up the evil." This would mean that the guilty ones defy the Word of God directly, although Wolff further thinks the people are addressing the prophet, not God.[21] For the people to speak directly to the prophet, however, would be too abrupt in the context. If Wolff's rendering is followed, it would seem more natural grammatically that the people address God directly (see also Additional Notes). The TEV implies such an interpretation but softens the effect by making the reference to God indirect, "God will not let any harm come near us."[22]

The verb קָדַם (*qdm*) is rare in the hiphil (elsewhere only Job 41:3). Perhaps its close connection to the previous verb (with "simple" *waw*) warrants taking it adverbially, "You will not bring near *soon*." Usually this idiom requires the modifying verb to precede the main action, but there are exceptions.[23]

9:11 Many of the prophets often, though not always, use the expression "in that day" to signal a period of restoration for Israel that will occur after a refining judgment (cf. Isa. 4:1, 2; 10:20, 27; 12:1, 4; 25:9; 26:1; 28:5; 30:23; Ezek. 29:21; Hos. 2:16 [MT 2:18]; Joel 3:18 [MT 4:18]; Mic. 4:6). The prophets themselves did not know when the time would come, only that direct action of the Lord Himself would usher it in.

The events covered by the period specified as "that day" naturally depend upon the content of the prophetic word. Sometimes the judgment itself comes into view, as earlier in Amos (8:3, 9, 13; cf. Isa. 7:18-25; Jer. 4:9; Hos. 1:5; Mic. 2:4; Zech. 13:1-4), while other passages focus on the deliverance (cf. Jer. 30:8; Ezek. 39:11; Zech. 9:16; 12:3-11; 14:4-5). Hosea and Micah, like Amos, first detail the judgment (Hos. 1:5; Mic. 2:4) and then promise the restoration (Hos. 2:16-23 [MT

---

[20] An emendation followed by Mays, *Amos*, p. 161 n. c.; Douglas Stuart, *Hosea-Jonah* (WBC 31; Waco, Tex.: Word, 1987), p. 390 n. b.

[21] Wolff, *Joel and Amos*, pp. 344, 349. Wolff combines his view with an argument that the passage was inserted by later interpreters.

[22] Cf. also Jan de Waard and William A. Smalley, *A Translator's Handbook on the Book of Amos* (Helps for Translators; New York: United Bible Societies, 1979), p. 183.

[23] See A. B. Davidson, *Hebrew Syntax*, 3d ed. (Edinburgh: T. & T. Clark, 1964), p. 116, par. 83, rem. 5.

2:18-25]; Micah 4:6). Micah's pattern alternates: judgment – restoration – judgment – restoration.

On a theological level, the various predictions of judgment link together a chain that includes those under Assyria, Babylonia, Greece, and Rome, culminating in the Great Tribulation foretold in the NT (Matt. 24; Rev. 6-19). Promises of restoration have come about historically in the deliverance of Jerusalem from Assyria, in the return from Babylonian captivity, and in the victories of the Maccabees. The individual prophet, however, may be vague about the details or may make explicit reference to only one of these events. This does not mean, though, that even a restricted reference cannot represent a type or a foreshadowing of things to come.

Amos does not give historical details about the refining judgment, nor does he specify precisely when the blessings will follow. The item that does capture his attention, though, is the restoration of "the fallen shelter of David" (דָּוִיד הַנֹּפֶלֶת סֻכַּת, *sukkat dāwîd hannōpelet*).

It is hard to understand exactly what the "shelter" or, more traditionally, "booth" of David means. The plural of Hebrew *sukkâ* refers to the temporary shelters erected for the feast of booths (Sukkot). The word also is used of the hut that was occupied by a watchman in a vineyard (Isa. 1:8). These dwellings are humble and crude, but God's heavenly dwelling is also called a *sukkâ* (Job 36:29; Ps 18:11 [MT 18:12; the parallel passage in 2 Sam. 22:12 uses the plural]). The Lord also provides a *sukkâ* as a shelter for the righteous (Ps 31:20 [MT 31:21]).

Since v. 12 alludes to war with Edom (see below), the "booth of David" should perhaps be compared with the temporary shelter occupied by the king while he was at war (2 Sam. 11:11; 1 Kings 20:12, 16). Note that the passages that call God's pavilion a *sukkâ* occur in contexts depicting Him as Lord of the thunderstorm.

The previous verses detail a situation where Israel will be mercilessly assaulted by the nations. Hence, when God rebuilds David's booth, it means that once again the people will be delivered from their enemies. Further, David stands here as the greatest warrior ever known by the nation. If his "booth" has fallen, the people cannot defend themselves. It seems unlikely that the participle should be translated as either future ("which is going to fall") or as continuous ("which is falling").[24] It has simply a descriptive function, as NASB and NIV recognize. Moreover, if the reference is to the literal wartime shelter of the actual David, then it had in fact fallen by the time of Amos.

The promise to restore David's fallen booth signifies that the remnant will find new deliverance under the banner of David. The passage should be compared with Zechariah's later prophecy of a coming king who will defeat all the enemies of the people and establish a universal dominion (Zech. 9:9-11).

Other suggestions are that the booth represents the Davidic monarchy itself[25] or the empire of David.[26] Of course the monarchy and empire that had begun with

---

[24] Against GKC, par. 116d; Thomas Edward McComiskey, "Amos," in *EBC*, ed. Frank E. Gaebelein (Grand Rapids: Zondervan, 1985), 7:329.

[25] McComiskey, "Amos," 7:329.

David had deteriorated by the time of Amos, and he looks back to the former glory of the united kingdom as a model for God's future blessing. Hence, the shelter used by David during war may symbolize also the condition of his family and house. Yet Amos concentrates on what God will make of it in a day still to come.

From comparison with other Scriptures we can establish that God will act through the Messiah, Jesus Christ, to accomplish what has been promised by Amos. Therefore, the restoration of "David's booth" amounts to the setting up of the Millennial kingdom, and it will also fulfill the literal promise to David of an everlasting kingdom.

וַהֲרִסֹתָיו פִּרְצֵיהֶן (pirĕṣêhen wahărisōtāyw) actually reads "their breaches" and "his ruins." The text as it stands perhaps means for us to understand "their breaches" as the damage to the temporary shelters of David and the people or of Israel and Judah. "His ruins" is more difficult. Keil refers it to David,[27] but the grammar would be unusually abrupt. Possibly the reading "his" has arisen through the tendency for a masculine form to replace feminine forms (cf. Zech. 11:5 and Additional Notes).

According to Hubbard[28], "The choice of *booth* rather than 'house' to describe the re-establishment of the golden days of David may have been influenced by the negative ways in which palaces (or strongholds) and elaborate houses are treated in the book (cf. on 1:4; 3:11, 15; 5:11; 6:11)." This interpretation fits well with the book of Amos as a whole.

9:12 The mention of Edom in v. 12 should be connected with the name of David in the previous verse. David's conquest of Edom is detailed in 2 Sam. 8:14: "And (David) put garrisons in Edom. Throughout Edom he put garrisons, and all the Edomites became David's vassals." In the time of Amos, however, Edom was an independent kingdom. It is mentioned often in the eighth and seventh century Assyrian inscriptions. Amaziah of Judah, father of Uzziah, killed 10,000 Edomites in the Valley of Salt (2 Kings 14:7; 2 Chron. 25:5-14), but this does not necessarily mean that Edom became subservient to Judah at that time.[29] When David's booth is restored, then, the Lord will bring Edom back under the control of the nation, as in the days of David. There will be a return to the glory of the ancient days of David.

Walter Kaiser seeks to downplay the military nature of the incorporation of Edom into the Messianic Kingdom.[30] Yet Joel (3:19 [MT 4:19]) and Obadiah speak quite strongly of a future judgment on this nation. Moreover, as we have stated, Amos's language reminds the reader of the previous military actions of David against Edom. All this is not to deny that in the Millennium the remnant of Edom will ultimately receive a blessing because of their new association with Israel or

---

[26] Wolff, *Joel and Amos*, p. 353.
[27] C. F. Keil, *Minor Prophets* (COTTV 10; Grand Rapids: Eerdmans, 1973), p. 330. Cf. also Walter C. Kaiser, Jr., *The Uses of the Old Testament in the New* (Chicago: Moody, 1985), pp. 182-83.
[28] David Allan Hubbard, *Joel and Amos: An Introduction and Commentary* (TOTC; Downers Grove, IL: Inter-Varsity, 1989), p. 240.
[29] Cf. J. R. Bartlett, "The Rise and Fall of the Kingdom of Edom," *PEQ* 104 (1972): 32-33.
[30] Kaiser, *The Uses of the Old Testament in the New*, pp. 183-84.

that James drew a valid conclusion from the verse at the Jerusalem Council (Acts 15:14-19).

The idiom "be called by someone's name" (אֲשֶׁר־נִקְרָא שְׁמִי עֲלֵיהֶם, *'ašer-niqrā' šĕmî 'ălêhem*, lit. "who My name is called over them") expresses ownership or possession. The name of the Lord was "called over" Israel (Deut. 28:10), the ark of the covenant (2 Sam. 6:2), the Temple in Jerusalem (1 Kings 8:43), and the city of Jerusalem (Jer. 25:29). David spoke of the possibility that his name might be "called over" Rabbah, the Ammonite city, if he conquered it (2 Sam. 12:28).

Only in Amos do we hear directly of the special type of ownership the Lord had over Israel extending to other nations. Evidently Amos teaches that since the Lord will obtain these nations for Israel, they will be called by His name. The phrasing of the Hebrew could mean either that all the nations of the world will be included (Feinberg) or only the nations already called by His name (Mays). According to the latter interpretation, they are the nations brought into subjection to David.[31] The advantage of this view is that it fits with the mention of Edom. Since, however, the concept was never applied previously to any nation other than Israel, Mays's interpretation seems unlikely. The thought is rather that, as Israel under the Davidic banner possesses all the nations, the whole world will become God's kingdom (in keeping with the clear teaching of Scripture elsewhere).

When Amos says that the nations are called by the Lord's name, there surely has to be some element of salvation and benefit for the Gentiles as well as for Israel. The unique relationship that had been limited to Israel will be extended to all nations. As other passages teach, Israel will remain the focal point of the kingdom of God, but the nations will also worship the Lord and participate in the kingdom blessings (esp. Isa. 2:2-4; 11:10; Zech. 14:16). For James's use of Amos's prophecy at the Jerusalem council (Acts 15:15-19) see the Additional Notes.

9:13*a-b* The promise of restoration divides neatly into two parts at v. 13. The introductory phrase points to a new section, and the topic changes from Israel and the nations to Israel and her land. Interestingly this twofold sequence forms a nice closure to the book through a chiastic structure, which can be displayed as follows:

---

[31] Charles L. Feinberg, *The Minor Prophets* (Chicago: Moody, 1976), p. 123; Mays, *Amos*, pp. 164-65.

A Judgment on the Land (1:2)
>   B Judgment on the nations (1:3-2:3)
>   >   C Judgment on Judah and Israel (2:4 ff.)
>   >   C′ Restoration of Judah and Israel (9:11)
>   B′ Restoration of the Nations (9:12)
>   A′ Restoration of the Land (9:13-15)

Amos pictures a land so fruitful that the planting and reaping seasons lose their distinctiveness. The fields in Israel were plowed in the fall, followed by a spring harvest. Now immediately after the harvest the plowman will go to work, resulting in more frequent harvesting. Similarly, as soon as the grapes are picked and ready for treading, new seed will be planted.

The physical nature of the promised blessings should not be minimized. Israel will indeed be restored to her land, and the people will enjoy an unparalleled prosperity under the rule of the Messianic Kingdom. However, the physical blessings point beyond themselves to even greater spiritual blessings. In the Old Testament the condition of the land reflects the spiritual condition and well-being of the people. Even so, the great prosperity spoken of here mirrors a condition of forgiveness and wholeness that has been hitherto unknown in Israel or throughout the world.

9:13c Amos expresses himself in hyperbole to describe what cannot satisfactorily be described any other way. He went to the depths of emotion when he spoke of judgment; now he lifts his eyes to the hills and sees vines so bulging with ripe grapes that the wine is pouring off like torrents of water after a rainstorm. At last the call for justice to pour down in a never-ending stream is answered. Perhaps there is also the thought of a new "treading upon" the hills by the Lord, as a reference back to the hymn of 5:13. There the footfall of the Lord brought destruction; now the hills that had been judged bring forth new blessings.

9:14 For the idiom עַמִּי שְׁבוּת אֶת־שַׁבְתִּי וְשַׁבְתִּי (wĕšabtî 'et-šĕbût 'ammî, "then I will restore the fortunes of My people) see the discussion on Joel 3:1. The rest of the verse speaks of a reversal of the conditions Amos had predicted previously (5:11).

9:15 The final promise of the book shows that the blessing is just as certain and permanent for the remnant as the judgment for the sinners. Such a condition can only come about through the intervention of the Lord and through His continual supply of mercy. Hence, the passage aligns with so many in the OT that speak of the time when God will establish a new relationship with His people which will never again be severed (Hos. 2:23 [MT 2:25]; Joel 3:20 [MT 4:20]; Zech. 13:9).

Additional Notes

9:10 וְתַקְדִּים תַּגִּישׁ לֹא־: Many interpreters propose that the original vowels have been changed, making the forms *qal* instead of *hiphil*. Then the sinners would say only that they are not expecting the tragedy to "reach" (תִּגַּשׁ) or "overtake" (תִּקְדַּם) them. It may only be necessary to posit the single reading תִּגַּשׁ, since the *hiphil* of the root קדם occurs so seldom that the meaning "overtake" cannot be excluded.

One problem with this proposal is the presence of the vowel letter *yodh* in both forms. A more subtle suggestion is to change the order of the consonants on

חגיש so as to read חַשִׂיג ("it will overtake"). As a conjectural reading, this proposal seems more likely. A scribe could have been influenced (subconsciously) to reverse the letters because of the similarity in meaning between the two verbs. The LXX and the Peshitta support reading the forms as *qal*.

9:11 פִּרְצֵיהֶן וַהֲרֹסֹתָיו: The LXX translation "its" (αὐτῆς) for Hebrew "their" and "his," respectively, cannot be given any more textual weight than the modern versions, which similarly gloss over the difficulty. The Peshitta solved the problem by reading "their" in both cases. The Targum also supports the reading "their," but it does not help for the reading "his." If "his" has arisen through the tendency for a masculine form to replace a feminine, the MT might represent a conflation whereby the scribes chose the masculine from one tradition and the feminine from another. Only speculation is possible given the present state of knowledge about the text.

9:12 אֱדוֹם אֶת־שְׁאֵרִית אֶת־יִירְשׁוּ: The LXX has ὅπως ἐκζητήσωιν οἱ κατάλοιποι τῶν ἀνθρώπων, apparently reflecting יִדְרְשׁוּ for יִירְשׁוּ and אָדָם for אֱדוֹם. The LXX reading is presupposed in James' quotation at the Jerusalem council: ὅπως ἂν κατάλοιποι τῶν ἀθρώπον τὸν κύριον (Acts 15:17). In his Epistle James mostly followed LXX when quoting from the OT. James's interpretation of the text is an appropriate extension of the meaning of MT.[32]

וְכָל־הַגּוֹיִם: At the Jerusalem council, called to discuss whether Gentiles should be allowed into the Church without requiring circumcision, James appealed to Amos's words as agreeing with Peter's description of how God has taken "from among the Gentiles a people for His name" (Acts 15:13-18). Amos prophesied that God would grant to Israel a people called by His name. Even so He was now calling out Gentiles into the church as His own people. The remnant of the nations in the day of the Lord will be placed into the Kingdom as part of Israel's possession. In the present church age the Gentiles participate, through the body of Christ, in the spiritual blessings of the Kingdom (cf. Eph. 2:19-22). Thus, the use of Amos in Acts may be regarded as not just an illustration but as a fulfillment, yet only as a stage in the progressive fulfillment of the whole – the final and complete stage or fulfillment being still future.[33]

---

[32] F. F. Bruce, *The Acts of the Apostles: The Greek Text with Introduction and Commentary* (Grand Rapids: Eerdmans, 1975), p. 298.

[33] Cf. Kaiser, *The Uses of the Old Testament in the New*, pp. 185-94, who makes the connection between the "tabernacle [shelter] of David" and James's statement more direct than in our analysis.

Excursus on the Hymnic Passages in Amos

Three passages in Amos are often referred to as "hymns," because they draw together vivid descriptions of the Lord and each contains the refrain, "Yahweh (the God of hosts) is His name." Elements of poetic form and similar themes tie these passages together closely.

Poetic Form

Participle phrases are mostly used as epithets of the Lord, though other verbal forms also occur. All five participles in the first hymn are without the definite article, but two of the four participles in the second hymn and all three in the final hymn have it. Parallelism is grammatical only, not semantic, and it does not occur in every line.

The meter and strophic structure vary. The poems are divided into lines here by semantic criteria, with the basic unit of metrical structure taken to be the word. The first hymn (4:13) contains two lines with three segments each (tricola). Meter in the first line consists of two words in each of the first two segments but three in the last (2+2+3). The final line has three parts (a tricolon) with three words per segment (3+3+3). Sometimes a word that has a close grammatical connection with another is counted as one word. Such is the case with ʿal ("upon") and the construct phrase ʾĕlōhê ṣĕbāʾôt ("God of hosts") in the third line.

The second (5:8-9) and third (9:5-6) hymns have a meter with mostly three words per line segment. Both hymns begin with a three-part line (tricolon) when semantic factors are considered (3+3+3). The second hymn has three lines with the structure 3+3+3, 2+3+2, and 3+3; the last hymn has four lines that group as 3+3+3, 3+3, 3+3, and 2+3+2. The following diagram will summarize the metric and strophic patterns analyzed here.

Diagram Summarizing Metric And Strophic Patterns

First Hymn (4:13)

Line	1a:	*Yôṣēr hārîm*
		Former-of mountains
	1b:	*ûbōrēʾ rûaḥ*
		and-Creator-of wind
	1c:	*ûmaggîd lĕʾādām mah-śēḥô*
		and teller to-man what-is-His-thought
Line	2a:	*ʿōśēh šaḥar ʿêpâ*
		Maker-of dawn darkness
	2b:	*wĕdōrēk ʿal-bomŏtê ʾāreṣ*
		and-treader upon-high-places-of earth

2c: *YHWH 'ĕlōhê-ṣĕbā'ôt šĕmô*
        Yahweh God-of-hosts His -name

Second Hymn (5:8-9)

Line   1a: *'ōśēh kîmâ ûkĕsîl*
                Maker-of Pleiades and-Orion
        1b: *wĕhōpēk labbōqer ṣalmāwet*
                and-changer to-morning deep-darkness
        1c: *wĕyôm layĕlâ heḥšîk*
                and-day into-night He-darkens
Line   2a: *Haqqōrē' lĕmê-hayyām*
                The-caller for-waters-of the-sea
        2b: *wayyišpĕkēm 'al-pĕnê hā'āreṣ*
                and-He-poured-them upon-face-of the-earth
        2c: *YHWH šĕmô*
                Yahweh His -name
Line   3a: *Hammablîg šōd 'al-'āz*
                The-flasher-forth destruction upon-strong
        3b: *wĕšōd 'al-mibṣār yābō'*
                and-destruction upon-fortification comes

Third Hymn (9:5-6)

Line   1a: *Wa'dōnāy YHWH haṣṣĕbā'ôt*
                And-Lord Yahweh the-hosts
        1b: *hannôgēa' bā'āreṣ wattāmôg*
                the-toucher on-the-earth and-it-trembles
        1c: *wĕ'ābelû kol-yôšĕbê bāh*
                and-mourn all-inhabitants in-it
Line   2a: *wĕ'ālĕtâ kayĕ'ōr kullāh*
                and-rises like-a-river all-of-it
        2b: *wĕšāqĕ'â kî'ōr miṣrāyim*
                and-sinks like-the-river-of Egypt
Line   3a: *Habbôneh baššāmayim ma'ălôtāw*
                The-builder in-the-heavens His-upper-chambers
        3b: *wa'ăguddātô 'al-'ereṣ yĕsādāh*
                and-his-vault over-earth He-founded-it
Line   4a: *Haqqōrē' lĕmê-hayyām*
                The-caller to-waters-of-the-sea
        4b: *wayyišpĕkēm 'al-pĕnê hā'āreṣ*
                and-He-poured-them upon-face-of the-earth
        4c: *YHWH šĕmô*
                Yahweh His-name

The hymns gradually increase in number of lines from two to three to four. Also line 2 of the second hymn becomes line 4 of the third. An additional factor that unifies the compositions is the thrice-repeated confession, "Yahweh (God of hosts) is His name."

Alliteration figures prominently in these compositions. Especially noteworthy is the repetition of *resh* sounds in line 1*a-b* of the first hymn and of velar sounds (*kaph* and *qoph*) in the corresponding line segments of the second hymn.

Semantic Elements

Finally there are some key semantic elements that tie the individual poems together or serve to distinguish them. A creation theme runs through each one, with God depicted as Creator of earth ("mountains" and "wind," 4:13), sky (constellations and alternation between light and darkness, 5:8), and heaven as the divine dwelling place (9:6).

We also discern a theme of judgment running parallel to and even overlapping the creation theme. This idea of judgment finds expression in the concepts of dawn changing to darkness and God treading on the high places of the earth in the first hymn. When in the second hymn the Lord is said to pour out the water of the sea over the earth, there may be reference to the flood. The final line of the second poem, repeated in the third, describes God as the Judge who flashes forth destruction. The third hymn contains judgment at the beginning and the end, with the creation theme sandwiched between. "Who touches the earth so that it trembles" expands the language of the first hymn, "and treads upon the high places of the earth." The prophet Micah later placed these two ideas in close proximity (Mic. 1:3-4). The judgment occasioned by the touch of the Lord is itself expanded by detailed reference to the reaction of the inhabitants of the earth and even of the earth itself.

Integrity

Much discussion has centered around these three hymnic passages. Scholars have been concerned about whether the passages originated with Amos and whether they represent a single hymn split into segments or three separate hymns. The question of whether Amos composed the hymn himself or used one already in existence cannot be answered with certainty. If he did use an earlier composition, he was guided by the Holy Spirit to interweave it into his own prophecy. By doing so the words would have become his own, even as various prophets can draw on traditional phrases or motifs in their works (cf. the discussion of the relationship between Joel and Jeremiah in the introduction to Joel). No convincing evidence exists, however, for the view that the hymn was inserted into the book later than the period of Amos. According to Mays, "Nothing in the form or content of the hymn indicates that it could not have been current in Amos's day." Yet he feels that contextual reasons argue for its insertion shortly after the period of Amos.[1] On the other hand, Thomas McComiskey, arguing on the basis of elements of style and form that the passages share with the rest of the book, thinks Amos composed the hymn specially for his book.[2]

Structure within the Book

The most important issue is to understand how the various hymnic portions relate to each other and to the rest of the book of Amos. The discussion here has tried to show the tight interrelationship of these pieces, both poetically and semantically. The relationship of each with its context is discussed at the appropriate points in the exegesis.

Within the book of Amos, a hymn occurs at the climax to the first "word" that Amos called the people to hear (chap. 4), at the very center of the first rhetorical unit 5:1-17 in the second "word" (chaps. 5-6), and at the end of the vision of the Lord destroying the altar and temple at Bethel (9:1-4). As Jan de Waard and William A. Smalley have shown, the phrase "Yahweh is His name" in the second

---

[1] James Luther Mays, *Amos: A Commentary* (OTL; Philadelphia: Westminster, 1969), pp. 83-84. Hans Walter Wolff, *Joel and Amos* (Hermeneia; trans. Waldemar Janzen, et al.; Philadelphia: Fortress, 1977), pp. 217-18, places it in the period of Josiah; cf. also James L. Crenshaw, *Hymnic Affirmation of Divine Justice* (SBLDS 24; Missoula, Mont.: Scholars, 1975).

[2] Thomas Edward McComiskey, "The Hymnic Elements of the Prophecy of Amos: A Study of Form-Critical Methodology," in *A Tribute to Gleason Archer*, ed. Walter C. Kaiser, Jr. and Ronald F. Youngblood (Chicago: Moody, 1986), pp. 107-123.

hymn can be viewed as the center of the entire book.[3] Therefore, each of the three appears at a key point in the book, though they are not distributed evenly.

Since 5:1-17 contains the only direct calls to repentance and introduces the theme of Israel as already "dead," the placement of the hymn at its center adds to the pericope's climactic effect. The exhortations are both positive and negative. The people can "live" if they seek Yahweh, but if they stubbornly refuse to repent, they must die. The hymn reinforces the power and authority of the Lord who stands ready to execute the punishment.

The first hymn perhaps serves as an effective conclusion to the first half of the book. The Israelites have been indicted by the example of what God must do to their neighbors, by their deeds against the poor, by their breaking of the covenant, and by their past failures to repent. Their obstinate behavior can only lead to one thing: the appearance of Yahweh on earth as Judge. Yet the same theme also provides an appropriate transition to the second half of the book. The people must make a choice in light of the truth about who Yahweh is and what He expects from them.

The last hymn climaxes the startling vision of the Lord's judgment against the religious activities of Israel. Who is this One who will smash the altar and temple, and pursue the survivors all over the world? He is the One who has absolute, sovereign authority over everything that happens in heaven and on earth. Yahweh is His name. He has authority as Judge, but He also has the authority and the power to bring glory from the ashes and ruins of the Northern Kingdom; thus the hymn also serves as a bridge between the gloomy prophecies of 7:7-9:6 and the renewed hope (for the remnant) of 9:7-15. Yahweh is His name.

---

[3] Jan de Waard and William A. Smalley, *A Translator's Handbook on the Book of Amos* (Helps for Translators; New York: United Bible Societies, 1979), p. 192.

Excursus on Social Justice in Amos

Amos has so much to say about oppression and the plight of the poor in Israel it is only natural that his book has become a focal point for discussions about social justice.[1] At least three aspects of the issue dealt with by Amos concern the nature of God, the role of the individual, and the role of the social system.

For Amos, justice among people must begin with the Lord Himself. That individuals ought to behave in a certain way toward each other cannot be understood apart from a deep awareness of the character of the Lord, who alone can give definition to concepts such as "righteousness" ($\check{s}\check{e}d\bar{a}q\hat{a}$, 5:7, 24; 6:12) and "justice" ($mi\check{s}p\bar{a}t$, 5:7, 15, 24; 6:12).

The Lord expects justice first of all because He has created mankind on the earth. He can expect certain standards of conduct to be upheld by all nations (esp. 1:3-2:5) because of His sovereign power. He has appointed each nation to its own sphere (9:7), though He has reserved a place of special honor for His people Israel (3:2). Having formed the nations of the earth, He also has the absolute right to judge them (4:13; 5:8-9; 6:8; 7:1, 4; 9:5-6).

The figure of God as judge dominates the book of Amos, though the Lord is not viewed as a judge without mercy. At the very core of the message, the Lord holds out hope for any who will forsake evil and follow the good He desires (5:4, 6, 14-15). He sends His prophets and His punishments in an effort to stimulate repentance (3:6-8; 4:6-11). He will not destroy "the house of Jacob" completely but will preserve a remnant through much testing (9:9-10). In the end He will restore the former glory of the nation and even magnify it (9:11-15). The justice of God may demand judgment for wrongdoing, but His mercy searches for every conceivable way to bring about a stay of execution.

Then, too, the transgressions that require judgment are nearly entirely comprised of acts of oppression. It is hard to read the book of Amos and not conclude that the Lord is deeply moved when one nation deals cruelly with another, or when the weak and helpless in society are crushed by the powerful. Nowhere in Amos does the Lord ever make reference to poverty as the fault of the poor.

---

[1] See Thomas John Finley, "An Evangelical Response to the Preaching of Amos," *JETS* 28 (1985): 411-20; Richard Patterson, "The Widow, the Orphan, and the Poor in the Old Testament and the Extra-Biblical Literature," *BSac* 130 (1973): 223-34; J. David Pleins, *Biblical Ethics and the Poor: The Language and Structures of Poverty in the Writings of the Hebrew Prophets* (diss. for The Univ. of Michigan; Ann Arbor: University Microfilms, 1986), esp. pp. 163-81; Willy Schottroff, "The Prophet Amos: A Socio-Historical Assessment of His Ministry," in *God of the Lowly; Socio-Historical Interpretations of the Bible*, ed. Willy Schottroff and Wolfgang Stegemann, trans. Matthew J. O'Connell (Maryknoll, New York: Orbis, 1984), pp. 27-46; Mark Daniel Carroll, *Contexts for Amos: Prophetic Poetics in Latin American Perspective* (JSOTSup 132; Sheffield, England: JSOT Press, 1992).

Proverbs often teaches about the importance of industry and wisdom in making a man wealthy or poor (e.g., 6:1-11; 10:4-5, 26; 12:24, 27), but Amos and the other prophets do not speak of these issues. This does not represent a fundamental disagreement between the wisdom and prophetic perspectives on the causes of poverty,[2] but it illustrates two complementary ways of looking at the problem.

Amos desires only to uncover the evil that leads some to impoverish others for their own gain. Why is it evil? The Lord never deals with His creatures in that way, and therefore such behavior is offensive to Him. If the Lord shows compassion for the widow and the afflicted, He does not expect any less from His own people.

The individual aspects of this evil can be easily discerned in Amos's preaching. He presents his listeners with concrete images of those who tamper with scales (8:5), violate the slave girl who should be treated like a member of the family (2:7), or make exorbitant demands that cannot be met (2:6-7; 5:11). The individual merchants and wealthy landowners are dishonest and greedy for more money and power. If they would turn back to the Law of the Lord and meet His requirements, they would be righteous and merciful in imitation of Him.

However, one must also keep in mind the social setting in which Amos operated. The Law of Moses was given not merely for individuals to know right from wrong, but also to set up a social structure that would have a potential to express the Lord's character.[3] Thus, the Ten Commandments combine words about worship of the Lord with those about relating to family, neighbors, and slaves.

Amos was especially concerned because he could see the social system set up by the Lord disintegrating. "Joseph" was in ruins, having been thoroughly ransacked (6:6). The land tenure system provided at least a means for each individual to participate in the social process (see on 5:11), but Amos saw rather a rapidly expanding social class of poor people. They were incapable of making enough for even a subsistence, and they were forced to sell themselves into debt slavery (2:6-8). In stark contrast were individuals of wealth and privileged position who were securing greater riches and power by taking advantage of this poor class. As J. David Pleins puts it, "Amos spoke out against existing economic practices which were bleeding the life out of the peasant population. By these business practices and economic structures the members of the upper classes were guilty of taking property that rightfully belonged to others, be this land, grain, or clothing."[4]

The courts provide the setting for much of the illegal activity condemned by Amos.[5] The Lord had set up a system of judicial elders during the period of

---

[2] Contrary to Pleins, *Biblical Ethics and the Poor*, pp. 275-76.

[3] Leon Epsztein cites the difference between Israelite and Mesopotamian law, where the latter seeks justice "more for the economic and political advantages that it could present" but the former "justice for its own sake," citing Deut. 16:20; *Social Justice in the Ancient Near East and the People of the Bible*, trans. John Bowden (London: SCM, 1986), p. 107.

[4] Pleins, *Biblical Ethics and the Poor*, p. 173.

[5] John Andrew Dearman prefers to talk about an "administrative/judicial system" because "this system's officials had multiple duties and served differing social institutions," *Property Rights in the Eighth-Century Prophets: The Conflict and Its Background* (SBLDS 106; Atlanta: Scholars, 1988), p. 78.

wandering in the wilderness (Ex. 18), which later included the king and various advisors, as well as appointed judges (cf. 2 Sam. 15:3-4; 1 Kings 3:9; 1 Chron. 23:4; 26:29). The fatal disease that Israelite society had contracted becomes evident as Amos speaks of bribery (5:12), false testimony (5:10), inequitable rulings (2:8), and preventing injured parties from finding justice through the courts (2:7; 5:12).

The religious institutions as Amos was familiar with them, should also be examined in relation to social justice. Amos preaches that the Lord provided justice for all Israel when He brought them up from Egypt and gave them the land of the Amorites (2:9-10). He also raised up prophets and Nazirites to turn the people back (2:11-12), yet now the Lord finds Himself outside the established institutions of worship. Amos notes an insincerity about the way the people carry on at the various sanctuaries (8:5), in addition to a syncretism that mixes in elements opposed to the Lord's requirements (5:5, 26; 8:14).

Life is not divided into secular and sacred for Amos: all things stem from the sovereign Lord. The way people behave in the marketplace or how they judge in the gate directly relates to their religious practices. If the Lord demands fair and merciful actions, they must be as much a part of the worship as singing and sacrifice (5:21-24). When the Israelites defraud the poor, they just as surely defraud the Lord Himself.

Amos begins with the justice of God, then, and shows how that relates to justice in society. The entire book of Amos shines a powerful light on Israelite society, revealing its dishonesty, corruption, and violence. That being the case, God is perfectly right to bring the overwhelming disaster of which Amos speaks.

Obadiah

Obadiah tells a story of double betrayal. The nation of Edom, which should have been an ally, betrayed Judah when the Babylonians destroyed Jerusalem in 586 B.C. As punishment the Lord promises that Edom will likewise fall prey to a trap by its allies. Obadiah then takes this theme of "judgment through betrayal because of betrayal" and expands it to encompass all nations when the Day of the Lord comes and "the kingdom will be the Lord's."

Introduction to Obadiah

The book of Obadiah is not only the shortest book in the OT, it is also one of the least understood. Perhaps Obadiah's strong, sustained tone of vengeance against the nation of Edom adds to the feeling of distance many of his modern readers feel. Edom is of little concern to us. We do not have the same reaction to the name that Judeans in OT times had. Thus, while the prophet's language is vivid and lively, some of its effect is lost because of the unfamiliarity of its subject matter.

Yet it is important to study in detail the message of this brief prophetic book, if for no other reason than that it is a part of the canon of Scripture. This alone means it is profitable for "instruction in righteousness" (2 Tim. 3:16), but most readers may find it more difficult to find such instruction from Obadiah than from other biblical books. Our hope is that this commentary will establish a basis for arriving at valid spiritual insights into the lasting and universal truths of the book of Obadiah.

Historical Context

The Prophet Obadiah

Nothing is known about the author beyond his name and that he received a prophetic revelation. Some in the past have speculated that he was the same as Ahab's steward (1 Kings 18:3-16) or King Jehoshaphat's official (2 Chron. 17:7), but these traditions are historically improbable. [1]

The Date Of Obadiah's Book

When a book does not have information in the heading that helps to date it, it is necessary to analyze the contents for clues about the period of composition. Three sorts of evidence have been presented for the date of Obadiah: historical allusions, its position in the canon, and literary connections with other prophets. If a historical event mentioned in the book can be identified, it gives the most objective kind of evidence. Therefore, the historical allusions in Obad. 10-14 will be discussed first.

Historical Allusions.

A preliminary question is whether vv. 12-14 are historical or prophetic. They are introduced in the standard form used for prohibitions in Hebrew: "Do not gloat over your brother's day" (NASB). If Obadiah's words are in fact intended to convey a command not to do something to the Edomites, then they should be taken

---

[1] See Ebenezer Henderson, *The Twelve Minor Prophets* (Thorn apple Commentaries; Grand Rapids: Baker, 1980), p. 186.

299

as prior to any event to which they may refer.[2] It is more likely, however, that they are meant to have a rhetorical effect. In other words, the prophet portrays the past event of Edom's transgressions against Jerusalem more vividly by placing himself at the scene and demanding, as it were, that the Edomites cease their wicked behavior.

The validity of this interpretation is confirmed by vv. 10-11, which clearly depict a past event in which Edom became guilty, and by the overall context of the book. Edom is soundly condemned for what she has done, not for something she will do in the future. Finally, v. 15 refers only to the past behavior of the Edomites: "Just as you have done, it will be done to you." Thus, the *KJV* gives the correct sense, though in a less vivid manner: "Thou shouldest not have looked on the day of thy brother" (and similarly in the remainder of the passage; see also exegesis of v. 12). A similar literary device also occurs with reference to Edom in Lam. 4:21: "Rejoice and be glad, daughter of Edom... / The cup [of judgment] will come around to you as well." There the author sarcastically commands the Edomites to rejoice over Jerusalem's fall, even though that fall is a past event.

In highly picturesque language, then, Obadiah focuses on the actions of Edom at a time of great catastrophe for Jerusalem. The word "day" occurs ten times in vv. 10-14 of the disaster that befell the city, and it contrasts with the "day of Yahweh" in v. 15, at which time the tables will be turned for Edom. During this period the Edomites sat by and gloated while foreigners entered Jerusalem, looted it, and took captives. Some of the Edomites also participated in the looting (perhaps after the departure of the foreigners) and prevented some of the city's inhabitants from fleeing. The terrified refugees were either slaughtered by their former allies or captured by them and turned over to the enemy. The time is remembered as a period of "misfortune," "destruction," "distress," "disaster," and "calamity."

In searching the history of Judah for a similar great catastrophe, the fall of the city to the Babylonians under Nebuchadnezzar in 586 B.C. immediately presents itself. At this time the Edomites should have been allies of Judah (Jer. 27:1-11); instead they encouraged the Babylonians (Ps. 137:7; cf. Ezek. 25:12; 35:7). Moreover, despite the hostility of the Edomites some survivors did manage to make it to Edom (Jer. 40:11). The Judeans in Edom may have arrived there prior to the events of 586.

It is true, as Leon Wood notes, that Obadiah does not detail the complete destruction of the city brought about by the Babylonians.[3] However, the prophet intends to focus on the guilt of Edom more than the event itself. For that matter

---

[2] Cf. Gleason L. Archer, *A Survey of Old Testament Introduction*, rev. ed. (Chicago: Moody, 1975), p. 300.

[3] Leon J. Wood, *The Prophets of Israel* (Grand Rapids: Baker, 1979), p. 263. Cf. Walter Baker, "Obadiah," in *BKCOT*, ed. John F. Walvoord and Roy B. Zuck (Wheaton: Victor, 1985), p. 1454, who thinks the reference to "fugitives" in Obad. 14 would be incompatible with the events of 586 B.C. However, while 2 Kings 25, 2 Chron. 36, and Jer. 52 deal with Zedekiah's army (some of whom might have escaped; 2 Kings 25:5), they leave open the possibility of civilian refugees. The point of Obad. 14 is that the Edomites do not allow the refugees to escape but hand them over to the enemy.

Ezekiel gives even less detail about the destruction in his prophecy against Edom (25:12-15). One could wish Obadiah had been more explicit, but it was not necessary when his contemporaries remembered the particulars clearly.

The only other major contender for the historical incident underlying Obad. 10-14 took place during the reign of Jehoram (848-841 B.C.).[4] This king of Judah put down a revolt of Edomites who were seeking freedom from Judean control (2 Kings 8:20-21; 2 Chron. 21:8-10) but later suffered attack by the Philistines and Arabs (2 Chron. 21:16-17). About this attack we know very few details. The text says that the foreigners invaded "Judah" and "carried away all the possessions found in the king's house together with his sons and his wives ... except Jehoahaz, the youngest of his sons." From the mention of the king's house we can infer that Jerusalem was somehow involved, but the extent to which the kind of general looting Obadiah speaks of (casting of lots for Jerusalem) is unclear. Of course, despite this raid Jehoahaz continued as king in Jerusalem and the nation of Judah remained independent. The author of Kings did not even bother to include an account of it. It hardly seems like the kind of national catastrophe depicted by Obadiah.

Furthermore, the text of Chronicles remains silent about an Edomite role in this campaign. If anything, the Chronicler might have been expected to mention participation by the Edomites since only a few verses previously he had described how Jehoram subdued them. Amos speaks of Edom's pursuit of "his brother" with the sword, but his description is too general to be of any help (see exegesis of Amos 1:11).

In conclusion, the historical evidence points toward the Babylonian destruction of Jerusalem in 586 B.C. as the background for Obad. 10-14. Since the author describes this event so vividly, it seems likely that the book was composed not long after. The book of Malachi, written sometime in the fifth century B.C., shows that by then Edom had already fallen (Mal. 1:2-5). Some would date Edom's fall to near the end of the sixth century.[5] Since Obadiah predicts this event, it serves as a *terminus ad quem.*

Canonical Position.

One argument some have raised concerns Obadiah's position among the twelve Minor Prophets. Leon Wood felt that the location of Obadiah within these books argues for its pre-exilic date: "[Obadiah] falls among the first six of these prophets, all of which date to either the ninth or eighth centuries, while those that follow come from the seventh century, the exile, and finally after the exile. This placement would be strange if Obadiah were written as late as the time of the exile."[6]

---

[4] Cf. Archer, *Old Testament Introduction,* pp. 299-301; Wood, *Prophets of Israel,* pp. 262-63. For an exhaustive list of all the historical possibilities, see Carl E. Armerding, "Obadiah," in *EBC,* ed. Frank E. Gaebelein (Grand Rapids: Zondervan, 1985), 7:350-51.

[5] Cf. J. R. Bartlett, "The Rise and Fall of the Kingdom of Edom," *PEQ* 104 (1972): 36-37.

[6] Wood, *Prophets of Israel,* p. 264.

The issue of chronology as a criterion for the ordering of the Minor Prophets has been treated in the introduction to Joel. The reader may consult this for more details. Here let it be noted that Wood's objection assumes that chronology was a major controlling factor in the arrangement of the twelve Minor Prophets. Yet even among the first six books, the arrangement is not completely chronological, and the date of two of those six books (Joel and Obadiah) can by no means be clearly established as preexilic.

Literary Relations.

A comparison between Obad. 1-9 and Jer. 49:7-16 reveals some remarkable similarities in expression and thought. Many have argued that close analysis reveals that Jeremiah adapted the material from Obadiah and not the other way around.[7] If this was the case, Obad. 1-9 cannot be dated to after the fall of Jerusalem in 586 B.C., though some commentators (e.g., Rudolph) solve the problem by the unacceptable hypothesis that the passage in Jeremiah was inserted into the book at a much later time than Jeremiah himself.

The first argument for seeing Obadiah as the source of Jeremiah's oracle is that, as Keil put it, Jeremiah has a "peculiar characteristic ... namely, that he leans throughout upon the utterances of the earlier prophets, and reproduces their thoughts, figures, and words."[8] Actually, nearly all of the prophets lean to some extent on the writings of their predecessors. Thus, the comparison Amos made between the overthrow of Sodom and Gomorrah and the Lord's judgment of Israel is picked up by Isaiah and applied to Babylon (13:19), then by Jeremiah and applied to Edom (49:17-18) as well as to Babylon (50:40).

Each prophet was unique and original, of course, but various expressions tended to become part of a traditional stock in trade. Another example is the prophecy found in both Isa. 52:7 and Nah. 1:15 (Heb. 2:1). The great majority of Jeremiah's material in his prophecies against the nations (46-51) is unique, but occasionally he has expressions strongly reminiscent of earlier prophets (cf. 48:29-36 and Isa. 16:6-12; Jer. 49:1-6 and Amos 1:13-15; Jer. 49:27 and Amos 1:4). However, the postexilic prophet Zechariah also shows great dependence on Jeremiah, in addition to many other prophets (cf. 3:8; 6:12 and Jer. 33:15).[9] Thus, to say Jeremiah often borrowed from earlier prophets does not automatically exclude the possibility that Obadiah borrowed from Jeremiah.

Inspection of the two writings shows that while each one contains a separate oracle about Edom, certain phrases and longer passages are common to both. A

---

[7] C. F. Keil, *Minor Prophets* (COTTV 10; Grand Rapids: Eerdmans, 1973), 340-41, cites Caspari; more recently, see Wilhelm Rudolph, *Joel--Amos--Obadja--Jona* (KAT 13:2; Gütersloh: Gütersloher Verlagshaus Gerd Mohn, 1971), pp. 297-98. Julius A. Bewer, *A Critical and Exegetical Commentary on Obadiah and Joel* (ICC; Edinburgh: T. & T. Clark, 1974), pp. 3, 33-37, on the other hand, sees Jer. 49 as more original, though he posits an earlier oracle that underlies both.

[8] Keil, *Minor Prophets*, p. 340.

[9] For details, see Charles Henry Hamilton Wright, *Zechariah and His Prophecies, Considered in Relation to Modern Criticism* (Minneapolis: Klock & Klock, 1980), pp. xxxv-xxxviii.

basic difference is that the announcement of a message to the nations to attack
Edom occurs at the beginning of Obadiah but only in the middle of Jeremiah's
prophecy. In fact, the only real parallel in wording in the first part of Jeremiah's
oracle occurs in 49:9:

> If grape gatherers came to you,
>> would they not leave gleanings?[10]
> If thieves came by night,
>> they would destroy only until they had enough.

The order of this saying is inverted in Obad. 5, and it also contains an
additional statement: "How you will be ruined!" Apparently this is one place where
Archer feels that Jeremiah smoothed out "the rugged places in Obadiah's style of
expression."[11] It could just as easily, however, represent a reflection by Obadiah of
a traditional saying obtained from Jeremiah. In fact, the two main statements sound
like proverbs or popular sayings.

The major overlap between the two prophets concerns Jer. 49:14-16 and
Obad. 1-4. Again, however, while the language is close, each prophet has handled
the saying differently. Jeremiah gives the content of the message sent among the
nations: "Gather together and come against her,/ and rise up for the battle."
Obadiah, on the other hand, gives the response to it: "Arise and let us go against her
for the battle." Also Jeremiah says, "I have heard a report," whereas Obadiah
states, "We have heard a report." Obadiah used more archaic forms for "sent" and
"has deceived you," but Jeremiah seems more original in the use of כִּי (kî) before
"behold" and in the tightly parallel structure of his v. 15. Another place where
Obadiah gives a smoother reading is by omission of Jeremiah's "as for the terror of
you" (תִּפְלַצְתְּךָ, tiplaṣtĕkā, Jer. 49:16).

The description of Edom's pride possibly derives from real boasts made by
the Edomites themselves. Thus, the prophets could have known of sayings current
among them, such as "We live in the clefts of the rocks," or "We have made our
nest as high as an eagle's."

Even the concept of a message sent by the Lord among the nations could go
back to traditional language common among the prophets (cf. 1 Kings 14:6-9; Ezek.
3:5). Given that many prophets ministered in Israel whose writings did not get
recorded, it does not seem impossible that Obadiah and Jeremiah could have both
relied on earlier traditional language, reshaping their own unique prophecies under
the inspiration of the Spirit of God.

Another possibility was raised in the last century by Ebenezer Henderson. He
proposed that Obad. 1-8 was to be placed slightly before the fall of Jerusalem,
while vv. 11-14 were delivered shortly afterward. Then Jeremiah could have
borrowed from Obadiah, his near contemporary, while the unity of the latter
prophet's book can be maintained.[12] One might compare Isaiah and Micah, who
were close in time and shared an oracle about the Millennial Kingdom (Isa. 2:2-4;

---

[10] Actually, Jeremiah omits the interrogative particle here; notice that *JB* does not
translate as a question in Jer. 49:9: "If grape-gatherers come to you,/ they will leave no
gleanings behind them."

[11] Archer, *Old Testament Introduction*, p. 301.

[12] Henderson, *The Twelve Minor Prophets*, pp. 185-86.

Mic. 4:1-3). On the other hand, the events described in Obad. 10-14 form the basis
for the judgment predicted in vv. 2-9. Yet one could counter that Obadiah preached
vv. 2-9 prior to 10-14 but included both in his book to show a relationship between
them.[13]

Conclusion

The relationship between Jeremiah and Obadiah is the major positive
argument in favor of an early date for the latter prophet, but it is not strong enough
to overturn the historical and contextual evidence for placing the book after the fall
of Jerusalem. Still, since explicit indications of the date are lacking, one should not
be dogmatic.[14] Because it predicts the fall of Edom, 500 B.C. would be the latest
possible time for the book to have been written.

The Relations Between Edom And Israel

From the biblical point of view, the history of the struggles between Edom
and Israel began with the writhing of Jacob and Esau within Rebekah's womb. She
was so puzzled by the intensity of it that she asked the Lord about it, and He
replied:

> Two nations are in your womb,
> and two peoples shall be separated from your belly.
> One people shall be stronger than the other,
> and the older shall serve the younger. (Gen. 25:23)

The prophecy began to be fulfilled when Esau came out first with Jacob, the
"heel-grabber," clinging to his brother's heel.

Soon we learn that Esau is also Edom ("red") because he sold his birthright
for the red lentil stew (Gen. 25:27-34). Jacob's name becomes Israel after his
encounter with the mysterious figure at the Jabbok River near Peniel (Gen. 32:22-
32). Thus, the prophetic blessing that Isaac bestows on his two sons highlights the
great significance of the relationship between Israel and Edom.

Through a ruse Jacob deceives his father into giving him the blessing that
rightfully belongs to Esau. It calls for the Lord's favor, for fertility, and for mastery
over his brother and his descendants (Gen. 27:27-29). Later, Esau comes in and
both father and son realize the gravity of the situation. In response to Esau's strong
weeping Isaac can only speak of a lack of fertility, a life of violent bloodshed, and
service to his brother. Isaac does hold out one thread of hope, however:

> But when you become restless,
> then you shall break his yoke from your neck. (Gen. 27:40)

In light of subsequent history, it might be best to see the latter statement as
general rather than specific. On many different occasions Edom rebelled against
his servile condition and succeeded in breaking the yoke.

---

[13] Paul R. Raabe (*Obadiah: A New Translation with Introduction and Commentary*
[AB 24D; New York: Doubleday, 1996], pp. 22-23) presents detailed arguments for the
priority of Jeremiah to Obadiah.

[14] Cf. Frank E. Gaebelein, *Four Minor Prophets: Obadiah, Jonah, Habakkuk, and
Haggai; Their Message for Today* (Chicago: Moody, 1970), p. 15.

After the two brothers pass off the scene, the nations undergo their separate developments. The next time they come into contact Edom is strong enough to refuse passage to the Israelites who ask simply to journey by "the king's highway," promising not to turn right or left, "until we pass through your territory" (Num. 20:17).

Not until the period of the early monarchy does Edom come under Israelite control. Saul fought against Edom (1 Sam. 14:47) and Doeg the Edomite was his servant, acting as an informant against David (1 Sam. 21:7; 22:9, 18; cf. Ps. 52). David in turn subjugated the Edomites, placing garrisons in their land, so that "all the Edomites became vassals to David" (2 Sam. 8:14).

Solomon went so far as to build a fleet of ships in Ezion-geber "in the land of Edom" (1 Kings 9:26). Yet before the end of his reign the Lord had raised up Hadad the Edomite as his "adversary" (1 Kings 11:14-22).[15]

Some 60 or more years later we hear of Jehoshaphat of Judah (872-848 B.C.) and his control of Edom When Moab and Ammon rebelled against Jehoshaphat the Edomites apparently had a minor role in it (2 Chron. 20:10). On another occasion, when Jehoshaphat, did battle against Moab, the king of Edom accompanied him and Jehoram of Israel (2 Kings 3:9). Actually, the text informs us that the "king" of Edom was in reality only a "deputy" (נִצָּב, $ni\bar{s}\bar{s}\bar{a}b$; 1 Kings 22:47 [MT 22:48]). Perhaps this reflects the direct control Jehoshaphat exercised; his own appointed deputy served as ruler of the country.

A more serious Edomite rebellion occurred during the reign of Jehoram of Judah (848-841 B.C.; also known as Joram), Jehoshaphat's son (2 Kings 8:20-22). At this time the Edomites established an independent monarchy, which lasted right up to the time of the narrator of the passage. Amaziah was able to take Sela and rename it Joktheel, slaying 10,000 Edomites in the process (2 Kings 14:7).[16] Yet this does not seem to have resulted in a loss of independence for Edom (cf. Amos 1:11 and the Assyrian inscriptions).[17]

During the last days of the southern kingdom, Edom joined with Judah and numerous other allies in a rebellion against Nebuchadnezzar of Babylon (Jer. 27:1-11). Yet when Nebuchadnezzar appeared in Palestine and overran Judah, the allies deserted. For this Edom comes in for severe condemnation in the OT Scriptures. Psalm 137:7 depicts the Edomites as cheering on the Babylonians with "Raze it, raze it,/ to its very foundation!" Lamentations is equally vivid in its rebuke:

Rejoice and be glad, daughter of Edom,
who dwells in the land of Uz.
Also the cup will come around to you;
you will become drunk and stripped naked. (Lam. 4:21)

Ezekiel also castigates the Edomites for taking advantage of this opportunity to gain vengeance against their brother Judah (25:12; 35:5).

---

[15] Perhaps the statement "every male in Edom" (11:16) refers only to the royal line.

[16] John Gray suggests that Sela here does not refer to the capital of Edom but to some other place known by the same name, which means simply "rock, crag, cliff." *I & II Kings: A Commentary*, 2d ed. (OTL; Philadelphia: Westminster), p. 605.

[17] *ANET*, 3d ed., pp. 282, 287, 291.

Edomite behavior on this occasion, then, forms the backdrop to the condemnations of the prophet Obadiah (vv. 10-14). As a result of Edom's treacherous actions, the nation was able to occupy parts of southern Judah, especially in and around Hebron and the Negev. Recently Itzhaq Beit-Arieh proposed that various Edomite finds from the site of Horvat Qitmit in the Negev indicate that the site was "an Edomite cult-center, and the area around it must have been controlled by the Edomites." Beit-Arieh then cautiously concludes:

> From the Biblical evidence and the evidence from Qitmit, it may fairly be assumed that Edom invaded and conquered extensive territory that belonged to Judah in the eastern Negev some time near the fall of Jerusalem, either before or after, taking advantage of Judah's weakness. This Edomite invasion of the eastern Negev was a prelude to the further expansion of Edomite settlement into the Hebron highlands, the southern Shephelah and the northern Negev.[18]

Late in the sixth or early in the fifth century B.C. certain Arab groups displaced the Edomites from their homeland. Obadiah apparently prophesied of this event in vv. 7-9. Many Edomites did stay in southern Judah, however, mixing with the Arabs. Later, this mixed population became known as Idumeans, southern Judah being called Idumea. In the Maccabean and Hasmonean periods the Jews overwhelmed the Idumeans in this area. However, they were not able to drive them out completely, and a very astute Idumean, Herod the Great, eventually managed to become king of all Judea.[19]

Literary Context

Composition Of The Book Of Obadiah

One might think that such a short book as Obadiah would have to be the product of a single author, yet some have argued that certain verses were added by a later editor or editors. Early in the nineteenth century, J. G. Eichhorn posited that vv. 17-21 were appended in the time of Alexander Janneus, the king of Judah about 103-76 B.C. Eichhorn thought that vv. 1-16 were composed shortly after 586 B.C.

Near the end of the nineteenth century, J. Wellhausen proposed that vv. 1-14, 15b were the product of Obadiah, while the rest of the book was added later. Wellhausen's position has been quite influential in subsequent work on Obadiah, especially his bipartite division: vv. 1-14, 15b and vv. 15a, 16-21.[20] Otto Eissfeldt, for example, modified Wellhausen's conclusions only slightly: "It is thus more probable that we should deny vv. 15a+16-18 and 19-21 to the Obadiah who was

---

[18] Beit-Arieh, "New Light on the Edomites," *BAR* 14, no. 2 (March/April 1988): 41.

[19] See B. MacDonald, "Edom," *ISBE*, rev. ed., 2:20.

[20] Josef Wehrle, *Prophetie und Textanalyse: Die Komposition Obadja 1-21 interpretiert auf der Basis text linguistischer und semiotischer Konzeptionen* (ATAT 28; St. Ottilien: Eos, 1987), p. 6. For a discussion in English of the history of the criticism of Obadiah, see Leslie Allen, *The Books of Joel, Obadiah, Jonah and Micah* (NICOT; Grand Rapids: Eerdmans, 1976), pp. 133-35.

active just after 587, and attribute them to one or rather two later hands."[21] Hans Walter Wolff accepted Wellhausen's division but concluded that the second part was attached to the book by Obadiah himself in the sixth century B.C., though vv. 19 and 20 were insertions from the fifth century B.C.[22]

Wolff presents the following arguments for Obadiah's authorship of vv. 15a, 16-21 (exclusive of the alleged additions in vv. 19-20):[23]

1. The main subject in vv. 18, 21 is still Edom.
2. The legal principle of retaliation (*ius talionis*) found in the earlier part recurs.
3. Even though the second half of the book presents both Judah and Israel as instruments of Edom's judgment, some sayings from Ezekiel that date to the period of the exile (25:14; 35:10; 37:15-23) "already talk about Israel as Yahweh's instrument of judgment, and about the common cause of the survivors of the Northern and the Southern Kingdoms."

Leslie Allen accepted the unity of the entire book. With reference to vv. 19-20, Allen argues that "if Obadiah is placed toward the end of the sixth century he could have been an eyewitness of the fall of Jerusalem, which he so vividly describes, and still speak of Jewish exiles far away."[24] The same could be true even if Obadiah prophesied closer to 586 B.C. The mention of Sepharad is the main historical difficulty. Since the reference is so obscure, it is not possible to make any certain conclusions about the date of the passage (cf. the exegesis on v. 20).

The book is called "the vision of Obadiah," and this heading applies to the whole prophecy, stressing its unity. Even though the second half focuses on the Lord's judgment of the nations in addition to His judgment of Edom, this new theme has its motivation in the first half of the book. Edom participated with the nations in the downfall of Jerusalem. Obadiah first deals with the more immediate punishment that awaits Edom and then turns to the day of the Lord, the time when all the nations will have to undergo judgment. Moreover, the second half underlines the theme of just retribution and extends its scope to include all the countries that have participated in the scattering of Israel and Judah. With so much attention devoted to Edom's role in helping to drive Judah away from her land, does it not seem logical for Obadiah to devote several verses to the time when Israel and Judah will repossess their land?

Verses 15 and 16 have been the focal point of much of the controversy. Verse 15a introduces a traditional saying about the approaching "day of Yahweh" (cf. Isa. 13:6; Ezek. 30:3; Joel 1:15; 2:1; 3:14 [MT 4:14]; Zeph. 1:7, 14), but v. 15b reverts to the direct conversation with Edom. Yet v. 15a belongs right where it is as a transition. Obadiah speaks of Edom's downfall (v. 15b) immediately after he introduces the "day of Yahweh." Only then, in v. 16, does he talk about the nations as a whole. The eleven instances of the term "day" in vv. 8-14 find their perfect

---

[21] Otto Eissfeldt, *The Old Testament: An Introduction*, trans. Peter R. Ackroyd (New York: Harper and Row, 1972), p. 403.

[22] Hans Walter Wolff, *Obadiah and Jonah: A Commentary*, trans. Margaret Kohl (Minneapolis: Augsburg, 1986), pp. 18-19.

[23] Ibid., p. 19.

[24] Allen, *Obadiah*, pp. 133-36 (the quotation is on p. 135).

climax in the "day of Yahweh" of v. 15. The change to a plural pronoun "you" at v. 16 is somewhat abrupt, but it can be explained within the context of the unity of the book (see exegesis below).

The Message Of Obadiah's Book

Like the prophecy of Joel, Obadiah revolves around both history and the eschatological day of the Lord. Both prophets also predict judgment on the nations and a great deliverance for Judah. Yet Obadiah dwells on the fortunes of only one nation – Edom.

Edom's fate is presented in two parts, separated by a description of that nation's cruel treatment of Jerusalem. The first part (vv. 1b-9) concerns a future conquest of Edom by other nations. Therefore, this judgment will occur in the course of history, not as a part of the Lord's final judgment against all the nations. Since the center section of Obadiah (vv. 10-14) shows how the Edomites turned against Judah, their ally, it is fitting that the nations who subdue Edom will include her own friends. Just as Edomites stood at the crossroads and cut down the refugees from Jerusalem, so every one will be cut off from the territory of Esau in this first phase of the judgment.

A second outpouring of wrath awaits Edom in the great day of the Lord. Then Edom will share the sentence of all the nations, but Obadiah stresses the role of Israel in this final destruction. The Lord's people will be able to avenge themselves of the wicked nations' role in Judah's great catastrophe. This time Israel will be saved and possess the territories of her former enemies.

Notice, then, how each section makes reference to the participation of Edom in the fall of Jerusalem. The first prophecy concerns judgment by Edom's allies, the second is about judgment by Israel herself. Yet in both sections the personal participation of the Lord is also prominent. That the Lord will use the nations as instruments of wrath against Edom is clear from the message He has sent out among the nations (v. 1b). The Lord has summoned these peoples for battle; therefore all natural defenses are of no avail. The second prophecy is of the Lord's own day of vengeance against the nations. Then he will summon not the other nations but Israel as His tool to destroy Edom.

Outline Of Obadiah

I. Heading (1a-b)
II. Edom's Judgment at the Hand of the Nations (1c-9)
    A. The Nations Summoned for Battle (1c-d)
    B. The Defenses of Edom Breached by the Lord (2-4)
    C. The Treasures of Edom Plundered by Allies (5-7)
    D. The Resources of Edom Destroyed by the Lord (8-9)
III. Edom's Betrayal of Judah (10-14)
    A. Violence against His Brother Jacob (10)
    B. Participation in Jerusalem's Trouble (11-14)
IV. Edom's Judgment in the Day of the Lord (15-21)
    A. Edom and the Nations Judged According to Their Treatment of Israel (15-16)

B. Edom and the Nations Possessed by the Remnant of Israel (17-21)

Theological Context

J. Alberto Soggin says that Obadiah's book is "of little theological interest."[25] If one focuses on the apparently narrow perspective of a people's outrage against an ally that betrayed them and of their longing for vengeance, one might possibly concur. However, the themes of the book have a much broader theological interest.

Edom, first of all, stands as a type of all those who oppose the purposes of the Lord.[26] This is made plain by the shift in perspective at vv. 15-21, from Edom alone to Edom and all the nations. Descriptions of theophanies elsewhere in Scripture, when the Lord appears on earth for judgment, depict Edom in similar terms (Judg. 5:4; Isa. 63:1-6; cf. comments on v. 1a-b below). Edom's treachery against a brother nation and her unbounded confidence in her own invulnerability made her the perfect exemplar for the theological truths taught in the book. Whatever Obadiah says about Edom applies equally to any nation that sets itself against the Lord and His people.

The book of Obadiah also has much to say about the Kingdom of God. The closing statement proclaims, "The Kingdom will belong to Yahweh." The truth of this credo becomes increasingly plain throughout the book as we see that the Lord is ultimately in control of the nations. He issues the summons for the nations to assemble against Edom (v. 1b); He challenges the prideful security of the nation (vv. 2-4); He threatens to cut off all hope of rescue (vv. 8-9); and He promises a day for righting all wrongs, restoring Israel and Judah to their former territories (vv. 15-21).

Obadiah, in common with other prophets, sees the Messianic Kingdom established on the earth, with Mount Zion as the center of authority. The people of Israel, whether of the southern or northern tribes, will be rejoined to fight for their land and win it back with the Lord's aid. They will then have a position of prominence over the rest of the nations.

---

[25] J. Alberto Soggin, *Introduction to the Old Testament: From Its Origins to the Closing of the Alexandrine Canon*, 3d ed., trans. John Bowden (OTL; Louisville: Westminster/ John Knox, 1989), p. 399.

[26] Cf. Walter C. Kaiser, Jr., *Toward an Old Testament Theology* (Grand Rapids: Zondervan, 1978), p. 187. Douglas Stuart, *Hosea-Jonah* (WBC 31; Waco, Tx.: Word, 1987), remarks that the lengthy history of Edomite hostility to Israel, the "consistency and intensity of its enmity,' and "the 'treasonous' nature of its enmity" make the nation of Edom "function virtually as a paradigm" for Israel's enemies (p. 404). Stuart also has a helpful chart of "Prophetic Oracles against Foreign Nations" on pp. 405-6.

Exegesis and Exposition of Obadiah

A. Heading (1a-b)

Translation

> The vision of Obadiah.
> Here is what the Lord Yahweh has to say to Edom.

Exegesis and Exposition

The heading to Obadiah is surprisingly brief. Its first part identifies the book as an authoritative word from the Lord. Obadiah himself enters into it only as the recipient of a prophetic vision.

The second part lays out the setting within the vision by directing the words directly to Edom. This nation is to be the recipient of the entire prophecy, though strictly in a rhetorical sense. The Lord directs His words of judgment to Edom because of her treatment of "Jacob" or the "sons of Judah." No other prophet concentrates so exclusively upon the Edomites, though judgment against Edom is a familiar theme from many of the OT prophets (Isa. 34:1-15; Jer. 49:7-22; Ezek. 35:1-15; Joel 3:19; Amos 1:11-12; 9:12; Mal. 1:2-4). Also of interest is the old description of a theophany (appearance of the Lord on earth) in Judg. 5:4 in which the Lord comes from Mt. Seir and the territory of Edom to judge the nations. Similarly, according to Isa. 63:1-6 He comes from Edom and Bozrah, stained with blood from trampling the nations. Thus, Edom represents God's judgment against the Gentiles to its fullest extent. For a summary of the history of relations between Israel and Judah see the Introduction.

v. 1*a* In v. 1 חָזוֹן (*ḥăzôn*) refers specifically to a prophetic vision or revelation from God. The only other books called a *ḥăzôn* are Isaiah and Nahum. They share with Obadiah the characteristics of vivid imagery and animated divine speech. Only Nahum and Obadiah give no details about the prophet and his ministry outside the heading.

v. 1*b* The familiar prophetic "thus says Yahweh," in slightly expanded form, reinforces the divine authority of the message. It applies to the entire book. A syntactic break occurs between the identification of the Lord's words and the sudden statement by the nations. The translation above stresses both the authority of the statement and its syntactic connection with the rest of the book.

Why is the prophecy addressed to Edom (לֶאֱדוֹם, *le'ĕdôm*)? In its original setting Obadiah would have delivered his message directly to the Judeans who had recently witnessed their city burned to the ground and looted while the Edomites aided and abetted the enemy. It should be remembered that Edom is addressed within the vision. The deeds and fate of Jacob's brother serve as an example as well as an encouragement for Jacob's descendants. As a part of Scripture, though, this small book is both a warning to nations and individuals who do not serve the Lord and a lesson for those who do follow Him.

Josef Wehrle discerns three headings for three different "levels of communication" in the first verse. "The vision of Obadiah" is a first level, applying to the literary audience and including the whole book. A second level is the prophet's address to the Judeans (vv. 1c-e, 15a, 16-21), and its heading is given by v. 1c-d (see below). On the third level, the Lord communicates with Edom (vv. 1b, 2-3c, 5-14, 15b-d), and that is marked first by "thus says the Lord Yahweh to Edom." Then Wehrle introduces a fourth level that concerns Edom's discussion with the Lord, including only vv. 3c-4.[1] Within a canonical setting, of course, it must be remembered that communication between Edom and the Lord is given for rhetorical effect, levels one and two being essentially the same in intent.

B. Edom's Judgment At The Hand Of The Nations (1c-9)

Edom's punishment will come in two parts. First, in the general course of history the nations will rise up against her (vv. 2-9). Second, in the future day of the Lord, which will witness God's wrath against all the nations and the establishment of His kingdom on earth, the Lord Himself will blot out the descendants of Esau.

Within this first section of his book, Obadiah blends the divine origin of Edom's judgment with the actual performance of it by the nations. The armies destined to attack the Edomites are the Lord's instrument because He has summoned them. Edom smugly thinks itself impregnable by virtue of a geographical position that is easily defended, but the Lord will bring down the proud nation and open it up to marauders. This will be accomplished through a ruse by Edom's own allies. An ambush will be set and the Edomites will fall into it unaware. In this way the Lord will bring to nothing all the wise counsel of the nation's strategists and remove the Edomites completely from their territory.

1. The Nations Summoned For Battle (1c-d)

Translation

> *We have heard a report from Yahweh:
> "Now a messenger has been sent out among the nations:
> 'Arise!
> Yes, let us arise *against her for the battle.'"

Exegesis and Exposition

Obadiah sees a vision of a messenger who will go out with word that the nations should prepare for battle against Edom. All is well, for the message originates with the Lord Himself. He controls the counsels for this war, though the nations may make plans among themselves without realizing the true source of those plans. The language is a dramatic way of stating the theological truth that the

---

[1] Josef Wehrle, *Prophetie und Textanalyse: Die Komposition Obadja 1-21 interpretiert auf der Basis text linguistischer und semio tischer Konzeptionen*, Arbeiten zu Text und Sprache im Alten Testament 28 (St. Ottilien: Eos, 1987), pp. 34-42.

Lord will stir up the nations to do battle against Edom. Of course, there will be some political pretext, but the Lord stands behind all the plans of man.

1c-d The third part of v. 1 begins in a mysterious manner. The translation follows a suggestion by Michael B. Dick that the conjunction *waw* attached to the noun צִיר (*ṣîr*, "messenger") indicates the content of the Lord's report.[2] Obadiah then either uses an editorial "we" or possibly includes himself among other Judeans who will hear the message (cf. Wehrle's comment under v. 1b above). Others take "and a messenger has been sent out" as parallel to the "report from Yahweh" (cf. NASB). If so, it is even more difficult to understand the change in subject from "we" to "a messenger."

As the prophecy unfolds, it becomes clear that this council of war is future to Obadiah. He views the assembly in his vision and reports on it as though it has already happened, using the prophetic perfect. However, at the end of v. 7 ("they will set an ambush") and then in vv. 8-9 he returns to regular means for the presentation of future events.

After the Lord has initiated the action, a messenger goes out to alert the allies of the moment for action. The Hebrew text uses repetition to stress the urgency of the envoy's words: "Rise up! Come on, let's rise up against her for battle!" The confident expectation of victory then contrasts starkly with the picture of Edom's ensuing sense of security.

It seems unlikely that Obadiah expected Judah to participate in the action.[3] Immediately after the fall of Jerusalem in 586 B.C. Judah was hardly in a position to take military action. Obadiah's prophetic vision of a future war against Edom gives encouragement to his present audience, which still has bitter memories of Edom's treachery.

Additional Notes

1c שָׁמַעְנוּ: There is no need, with the JB, to follow the LXX and Jer. 49:14 in reading "I have heard." The LXX is possibly a harmonization based on Jeremiah. The two prophets do not give exactly the same oracle, and Jeremiah may have simply desired to stress that he had received the message himself. On the other hand, given the numerous textual problems connected with Jeremiah, his text may not have survived unaltered. In any case the MT of Jeremiah has the easier reading if one insists that he and Obadiah must have had the same text originally.

1d עָלֶיהָ: Throughout the remainder of the book Edom is referenced by masculine pronouns, making "against her" seem out of place. The feminine probably refers to the country, while the masculine refers to the people.[4] In this case Obadiah agrees with Jer. 49:14. Also, Mal. 1:4 uses a feminine verb with Edom as the subject (cf. Jer. 49:17; Ezek. 25:13; 32:29; 35:15).

---

[2] Michael B. Dick, "A Syntactic Study of the Book Obadiah," *Semitics* 9 (1984): 8.

[3] Contra Wehrle, *Prophetie und Textanalyse,* p. 25, who thinks the summons includes both Judah and the nations.

[4] See Ebenezer Henderson, *The Twelve Minor Prophets* (Grand Rapids: Baker, 1980), p. 189; Hans Walter Wolff, *Obadiah and Jonah: A Commentary,* trans. Margaret Kohl (Minneapolis: Augsburg, 1986), p. 33.

2. The Defenses Of Edom Breached By The Lord (2-4)

Translation

"Look! I have made you small among the nations;
you are very despised.
³The arrogance of your heart has deceived you,
you who live in the cleft of the rock,
whose dwelling place is *lofty,
(you) who say in your heart,
'*Who can bring me down to the ground?'
⁴Though you soar like the eagle,
and though your nest be placed among the stars,
from there I will pull you down,"
declares Yahweh.

Exegesis and Exposition

Edom was located south of the Dead Sea, being bounded on the north by the Wadi Zered. The other borders are uncertain, but the country did encompass much of the rugged terrain between the deep Arabah depression on the west, the desert on the east, and the Gulf of Aqaba on the south. According to Yohanan Aharoni:

> It is a difficult area, not easily accessible, and its many crevices and natural strongholds provide excellent places of refuge for the population in time of emergency. A chain of fortresses on the fringe of the desert gave added protection. Thus in both early and later periods it enjoyed considerable strength and independence.[5]

The blessings of geography made the Edomites confident they could maintain their independence, but the Lord declares that the highest place imaginable cannot save the proud nation from judgment. Wherever they are the Lord will personally bring them down and open them up to the plundering of foreign armies.

v. 2 Though many modern versions (cf. NASB and NIV) translate v. 2 as though the Lord anticipates his judgment of Edom at this point, it is possible to see the verse as referring to the nation's present condition. Then a better contrast results with the secure pride that Edom feels. Compare the Targum, "I have made you weak [חלש, *ḥallāš*]." The nation thinks she is important and secure, but the Lord has actually given her a reduced position among the world powers. She is no Babylon or Assyria. Moreover, the Lord later promises to reduce the nation to nothing (vv. 9, 18). The force of these threats seems greater than the threat alleged to be present in v. 2.

v. 3 As the following verses explain, Edom's arrogance consists of thinking she is immune from the swift destruction that can so easily befall other nations. Later the prophet will also make explicit what his audience already knows – Edom is arrogant because she thought to plunder God's people and get away with it. A deep undercurrent of divine sovereignty underlies v. 3. A nation only deceives

---

[5] Yohanan Aharoni, *The Land of the Bible: A Historical Geography,* 2d ed., trans. A. F. Rainey (Philadelphia: Westminster, 1979), p. 40.

itself if it hopes to ensure its own safety through human effort. Nothing can stop God's arm from reaching anywhere to pull down arrogant strongholds. Verse 3 closes with a concrete illustration of Edom's self-deception: "Who will bring me down to earth?" The reader knows the answer: the Lord will do it.

The term translated "rock" (סֶלַע, *sela'*) is also the name of the capital city, Sela. Previously this had been identified with modern Petra (which also means "rock" in Greek), but more recent archaeological research places it farther to the north at the modern village of Sela, about two and a half miles northwest of Bozrah.[6]

The phrase שִׁבְתּוֹ מְרוֹם (*měrôm šibtô*) is difficult to translate. Literally it is something like, "the loftiness of his dwelling place." NASB understands the phrase adverbially ("*in* the loftiness of"), but this seems awkward. The translation given here takes "his" to refer back to "who dwells." An adjective in the construct state should be epexegetical: "lofty with respect to his dwelling place."

v. 4 The Edomite boast of v. 4 seems absurd next to the power of the Lord. No eagle can fly high enough to escape His hand. If a people were capable of building even among the stars, could they elude there the God whose own dwelling place is in heaven (cf. Amos 9:2-4)?

An interesting parallel occurs in the Lord's speech to Job: "Is it at your command that the eagle soars/ and that he makes his nest in a high place?" (Job 39:27). In light of the use of the same verb for "mount up" or "soar" in both passages (גבה, *gbh*; in the hiphil), NASB's "you build high" seems less appropriate. Also the rendering given here reflects an understanding of שִׂים (*śîm*) as a passive (cf. Num. 24:21).[7]

Additional Notes

v. 3 מְרוֹם: Wilhelm Rudolph prefers to emend the vowel so that the form would be absolute ("the height is his dwelling place").[8]

בְּלִבּוֹ: The pronoun reference has been changed in the translation from "*his* heart" to "*your* heart" because vocative constructions in Hebrew frequently exhibit an interchange between first and third persons (cf. Amos 6:1; Zech. 3:8).[9]

מִי יוֹרִדֵנִי: The context of boasting supports the nuance of ability for the Hebrew imperfect (cf. NIV).[10]

---

[6] C.-M. Bennett, "Edom," in *IDBSup*, pp. 251-52.

[7] Leslie C. Allen, *The Books of Joel, Obadiah, Jonah and Micah* (NICOT; Grand Rapids: Eerdmans, 1976), p. 146.

[8] Wilhelm Rudolph, *Joel--Amos--Obadja--Jona* (KAT 13:2; Gütersloh: Gütersloher Verlagshaus Gerd Mohn, 1971), p. 304.

[9] Cf. Delbert Hillers, "Hoy and Hoy-Oracles: A Neglected Syntactic Aspect," in *The Word of the Lord Shall Go Forth: Essays in Honor of David Noel Freedman* (ASOR Special Volume Series 1; Winona Lake, Ind.: Eisenbrauns, 1983), pp. 185-88.

[10] Various nuances of the Hebrew imperfect are listed in Ronald J. Williams, *Hebrew Syntax: An Outline*, 2d ed. (Toronto: Univ. of Toronto, 1976), par. 167-75.

3. The Treasures Of Edom Plundered By Allies (5-7)

Translation

> If thieves came to you
> or those who plunder at night –
> oh, how she will be destroyed! –
> would they not steal only until they had enough?
> If grape gatherers came to you,
> would they not leave some gleanings?
> ⁶Oh, how Esau will be ransacked,
> his treasures searched out!
> ⁷They will expel you to the border,
> all the men who are your allies.
> They will deceive you and overpower you,
> the men who are at peace with you.
> *Those who eat with you
> will set a trap for you
> without your knowing it.

Exegesis and Exposition

Having been pulled down from the heights by the Lord, the Edomites will find the wealth of their kingdom opened up to foreign invaders. The passage first describes the stripping bare of the nation so thoroughly as to provoke astonishment. Then it describes how, in human terms, the deed will be possible. Edom's own trusted allies will set an ambush and rout its army.

v. 5 Obadiah portrays the Lord's judgment on Edom as total and thorough. Thieves and grape gatherers would not devastate the nation so completely as the Lord. *They* would leave something behind, but nothing will remain after the Lord brings Edom down from the lofty heights.

The speaker, suddenly struck by the horror of Edom's plight, interrupts the discussion about thieves and robbers with an astonished exclamation: אֵיךְ נִדְמֵיתָה (*'êk nidmêtâ*, "Oh, how you will be ruined!"). To paraphrase, "If mere thieves came to you – but oh, how much worse it will be for you when the Lord Himself sends judgment!" Hebrew *nidmâ* ("be cut off, destroyed") usually refers to a violent end (cf. Isa. 15:1; Jer. 47:5; Hos. 4:6; Zeph. 1:11). The tense of the verb is prophetic perfect.

Literally דַּיָּם (*dayyām*) means "their sufficiency." The JB renders "they would steal to their heart's content." That is a possible interpretation of the Hebrew, but one must remember that the statement occurs as part of a condition. JB requires the reader to begin the announcement of punishment with the conditional clauses.[11] Rather, the contrast is between what might happen if only men are involved and what will happen when the Lord intervenes. Also, the comparison with the gleaners stresses that something is left, even if it is suitable only for poor people.

---

[11] Cf. Allen, *Obadiah*, pp. 148-49, who has a translation similar to that of JB.

The JB further finds it necessary to transpose "Oh, how you will be ruined!" to v. 6. The intrusiveness of the latter sentence can be explained better if it contrasts with, rather than reinforces, the main thought.

v. 6 Verse 6 explains that it will not be like mere robbery or a harvest with gleanings for Esau. Nothing will remain; every last piece of wealth will be found and brought out.

v. 7 Since so little is known about Edomite history, it is difficult to discern the precise incident referenced in v. 7. Assuming that Obadiah writes soon after the fall of Jerusalem in 586 B.C., he would be predicting the displacement of the Edomites from their homeland by the Arabs. The allies might be the Persians or even the Arabs themselves. The dislocation itself probably occurred near the end of the sixth century B.C.[12] The Hebrew implies a forceful expulsion from the country. לַחְמְךָ (laḥmĕkā, lit. "your bread") and מָזוֹר (māzôr, "trap"?) are difficult to place properly in context. Since "your bread" is obviously not a suitable subject for "they will set," it is necessary either to change the text or to find some figurative meaning. Armerding has an excellent discussion of the problem and gives good support for taking laḥmekā as "(those who eat) your bread." This agrees with the ancient versions (Targum, LXX, Vulg., Symmachus) and gives a plausible poetic structure to the entire verse. Also, "those who eat your bread," that is, "your friends who sit down to a meal with you," corresponds to "all the men allied with you" and "the men at peace with you."[13]

The term māzôr is also unclear. It should probably be derived from the root mzr, "to weave" or "twist," attested in post-biblical Hebrew. Then it would be possible to adopt the meaning of "trap" or "net" given in the ancient versions. "Wound" is another meaning for the same word (Jer. 30:13; Hos. 5:13), but it hardly makes sense as something to be placed under the Edomites (yet it is the reading of KJV).

Recently P. Kyle McCarter proposed to follow Symmachus's Greek version by reading, "They have established a place of foreigners in your stead."[14] While the preposition can mean "instead of," it makes for an awkward connection. This is because the expression "A instead of B" expects "A" and "B" to be semantically similar. But McCarter's reading makes "A" a place and "B" a people. Instead, one would expect, "they will make your land a place of foreigners." Or, "they will establish foreigners (in your land) instead of you."

A literal rendering of אֵין תְּבוּנָה בּוֹ (ʾên tĕbûnâ bô) would be "there is no understanding in it." The Edomites will fall into the trap completely unawares. A trap cannot work unless the victim does not know about it. The line makes a nice transition to v. 8. Edom, which was noted for wisdom (cf. Eliphaz the Temanite in Job 2:11; Jer. 49:7), will lose all sense and be deceived by her enemies.

---

[12] P. Kyle McCarter, "Obadiah 7 and the Fall of Edom," *BASOR* 220 (1975): 87-91. McCarter uses the historical evidence to date the book of Obadiah in the late sixth or early fifth century; but the statements are prophecy, not historical description.

[13] Carl E. Armerding, "Obadiah," in *EBC,* ed. Frank E. Gaebelein (Grand Rapids: Zondervan, 1985) 7:345-46.

[14] McCarter, "Obadiah 7 and the Fall of Edom," pp. 87-88. He does not take the perfects as prophetic.

Additional Notes

v. 7 לַחְמְךָ: Some prefer to emend to a participle לֹחֲמֶיךָ, but this is
unnecessary and is not obviously the reading in the Hebrew texts used by the
versions. They could either have followed a similar reasoning process as here or
have supplied an unpointed text with the vowels of the participle. The MT surely
represents the more difficult reading.[15]

4. The Resources Of Edom Destroyed By The Lord (8-9)

Translation

> "Will it not be in that day,"
> declares Yahweh,
> "that I will make wise men perish from Edom,
> and understanding from the mountain country of Esau?
> ⁹Then your warriors will panic, Teman,
> so that each one will be cut off from the mountain country of Esau *by
> slaughter."

Exegesis and Exposition

Obadiah's discussion nicely interweaves the themes of divine intervention and
human instrumentality. He began with a council of war by the nations, but the
message to commence the battle came from the Lord Himself. Then the Lord's
personal role in pulling Edom down from its lofty position came into focus,
followed by a description of a plundering made possible by an ambush set by the
nation's allies. At the end of the passage the prophet returns to the theme of the
Lord as the initiator of the judgment. Will the Edomites fall into the trap unawares?
That is only because the Lord will destroy wise counsel from the nation. The army
will look for capable guidance in a crisis but find none. This will lead to a
wholesale slaughter of the population.

v. 8 "That day" (v. 8) often refers in the prophets to the day of the Lord at the
end of the age. Here it continues the prophecy of the attack by other nations begun
in v. 1c, but it also highlights the Lord's personal role in the judgment. It will have
the quality of a day of the Lord against Edom, though she will also be present for
that final judgment along with all the nations (v. 15). נְאֻם יְהוָה (*nĕ'um-YHWH*; lit.
"utterance of Yahweh") brings the "day" into close association with the Lord.

v. 9 Teman may refer to a region rather than a city, possibly to the southern
extent of Edom. Yet Aharoni still regards it as a specific site, possibly Tawilan.[16]
In v. 9 it stands for the whole nation (as in Jer. 49:20). When battle strategies fail,
the warriors panic.

Some of the Edomites would be expelled across the borders, the rest were to
be slaughtered in fierce fighting. The country would become completely empty of

---

[15] For the opposite view, see Allen, *Obadiah,* p. 150 n. 27. Note also McCarter,
"Obadiah 7 and the Fall of Edom," p. 88, who sees "your peace" as a gloss to explain an
original "men of your bread."

[16] Bennett, "Edom," p. 252; Aharoni, *Land of the Bible,* pp. 40, 442.

its original inhabitants. It is evidently from the offspring of those who were exiled that a new coalition of Edomites will arise against Israel and be judged in the great day of the Lord (v. 15; cf. Joel 3:19).

Since Edom will again face judgment in the day of the Lord to come, it is evident that some must have escaped the historical judgment referred to in these verses. Therefore it is only in the end time that the full force of the prophecy will be realized. Consider also that in the time of the end Edom will be assailed by the King of the South (Dan. 11:41); the Edomites will experience trouble from other nations as well as from Israel.

It must also be noted, however, that in Hebrew thought to speak of "all" or "every" (אִישׁ, 'îš, in v. 9 indicates "each one") often means a majority or a very large number. For example, David struck down "every male in Edom" (1 Kings 11:15), yet the nation of Edom continued. Notice also that Amos, uniquely among the prophets, speaks of a "remnant" for Edom that will continue into the Millennial Kingdom (9:12). Even this remnant will be Israel's possession, but it must consist of individual Edomites who will profess the name of the Lord (cf. Joel 2:32 [MT 3:4]). Exactly how God will raise up the descendants of Edom for a renewed battle against Israel in the end times remains a mystery. Yet He surely is capable of accomplishing it just as He will bring all Jews back to their land.

Additional Notes

v. 9 מִקֶּטֶל: LXX and Peshitta join "because of slaughter" with "because of violence" in v. 10, adding a conjunction to the second term. Many have accepted this as more original because it gives better poetic balance to v. 9 to shorten it by one word. The apparatus to *BHS* proposes that מִקֶּטֶל be deleted as a gloss. The text of Obadiah in the Hebrew scroll of the Minor Prophets supports the lack of a conjunction as in the MT.[17]

C. Edom's Betrayal Of Judah (10-14)

A long history of bitter relations between Judah and Edom culminated with Edom's role in the Babylonian capture and destruction of Jerusalem in 586 B.C. (see Introduction to Obadiah and Amos 1:11-12). Edom should have fought alongside the Judeans; instead they stood aloof, helped themselves to the spoils, and actively prevented refugees from escaping. The Jews became especially bitter because they believed they had been betrayed. The Lord's response assured His people that justice would be done. Edom, according to vv. 7-8, will itself fall prey to treachery.

1. Violence Against His Brother Jacob (10)

Translation

Because of violence against your brother Jacob,
shame will cover you
and you will be cut off forever.

---

[17] *DJD* 2:189 (text 88).

Exegesis and Exposition

Obadiah takes a family perspective on the relationship between Judah and Edom. The two nations began in the brothers Jacob and Esau. Yet the word "violence" summarized the long history of relations between these two peoples. On many occasions Edom acted cruelly toward his brother, but the culminating act of violence was in his betrayal of Judah at a time when the two countries were allies. Because of this violence Edom will be cut off as a nation.

The grammatical structure of מֵחֲמַס אָחִיךָ (*mēḥămas 'āḥîkā*, lit. "because of the violence of your brother") is that of an objective genitive. That is, "your brother" functions as the recipient of the violence.[18] Amos had earlier depicted the Edomites as a bloodthirsty people bent on venting their anger against a brother nation (1:11).

A close connection exists between a nation's "shame" (בּוּשָׁה, *bûšâ*) and its destruction. Thus, Joel urged the priests to entreat the Lord not to make His "inheritance a reproach, a byword among the nations" (Joel 2:17). Later, the Lord responded: "My people will never be put to shame." Here the contrast is with Edom's haughty pride (v. 3). The once-proud people will be put to shame because they will have lost everything. As Horst Seebass puts it, "*bosh* expresses the idea that someone, a person, a city, a people, a professional organization, or the like, underwent an experience in which his (or its) former respected position and importance were overthrown."[19]

2. Participation In Jerusalem's Trouble (11-14)

Translation

> *On the day when you stood aloof,
> on the day when strangers carried off his forces,
> when strangers entered his gates
>   and cast lots for Jerusalem,
> you too were like one of them.
> [12]So do not gloat over the day of your brother,
> over the day of *his misfortune.
> And do not be glad about the sons of Judah
> on the day when they perish.
> And do not boast
> in a day of distress.
> [13]Do not enter the gate of my people
> on the day of *their disaster.
> Do not gloat, yes you, over his calamity
> on the day of his disaster.
> And let not your hands *reach out for his wealth
> on the day of his disaster.

---

[18] See Williams, *Hebrew Syntax*, par. 38.
[19] Horst Seebass, *TDOT* 2:52.

[14]And do not stand at the crossroads
to cut down his fugitives.
And do not hand over his survivors
in a day of distress.

Exegesis and Exposition

A certain progression occurred in Edom's behavior at the time of Jerusalem's downfall. First, they simply stood by and watched while the Babylonian forces took the city. In this they also became guilty. The Edomites were allies of Judah at this time and should have come to their brother's aid (cf. Jer. 27:1-11). They could have stayed their distance and watched in horror, but instead they also rejoiced and boasted about what was happening to the people of Jerusalem. Next they actually entered the city to take whatever share of the loot they could. At the same time they also made sure none escaped, handing over all survivors to the Babylonians. This was the behavior that finally filled up their guilt and brought on the stinging denunciations of Obadiah, Jeremiah, Ezekiel, and Joel.

This progression of watching, gloating, entering, looting, blocking escape, and handing over refugees to the enemy is reinforced by the structure of the passage itself. In vv. 10 and 11 Obadiah reports the scene objectively, while in vv. 12-14 he directly admonishes the Edomites. These verses, in turn, have a structure that highlights the sequence that moves from outside (v. 12) to inside (v. 13) and then back outside the city (v. 14). The prophet focuses our attention on the scene (entering and surveying the shameful destruction that has taken place) by a type of chiastic structure. The first three and the last three prohibitions are introduced by *waw* ("and"), but the two warnings in the middle are without a conjunction. Furthermore, in this center section, along with the first line of the concluding triad of lines, Obadiah repeats much of the previous vocabulary ("enter the gate," "disaster," "gloat," "wealth" [="forces" of v. 11]), thus slowing down the action that takes place in the city itself.

v. 11 All of the biblical references to Edom's participation in the fall of Jerusalem agree, or at least do not disagree, that the nation did not enter the city directly with the Babylonians (Ps. 137:7; Lam. 4:21; Ezek. 25:12-14; Joel 3:19 [MT 4:19]). Rather, they watched nearby and waited for their opportunity (v. 11), much like vultures waiting to feed on a carcass until after the lions are finished. One of the apocryphal books (1 Esdr. 4:45) has the Edomites actually burning the Temple, but this is evidently due to later reflection and amplification of the biblical statements.

Since חֵילוֹ (ḥêlô, "his forces") can mean either "his wealth" or "his army," commentators are divided over which sense best fits the context. The term "carry off" is normally connected with people, though Allen cites 2 Chron. 21:17 and Jer. 43:12 as exceptions.[20] However, the former verse uses רְכוּשׁ (rĕkûš), not ḥayil, for "possessions," while Jeremiah probably means that the idols, which represent gods, are taken captive.

---

[20] Allen, *Obadiah,* p. 154 n. 1.

In Obad. 13 *ḥayil* does mean "wealth," but that does not preclude a different meaning in its first occurrence. The context of v. 13 (see exegesis) is a sufficient clue that a different sense is present. Finally, one must consider that the defending army would have to be captured or killed before the invaders could enter the gates. This last argument, however, cannot carry too much weight since the events are not necessarily arranged chronologically. For the present verse the Targum translates "wealth" (נכסוהי, *niksôhî*), while LXX (δύναμιν αὐτοῦ, *dynamin autou*, "his army" or "his wealth") and Syriac (*ḥylh*) maintain the same ambiguity found in the Hebrew.

יַדּוּ גּוֹרָל (*yaddû gôrāl*, "they cast lots") might mean that lots are cast for the *people* of Jerusalem (cf. Joel 3:3; Nah. 3:10).[21] More likely the reference is general. The conquerors cast lots to divide the spoils, whether for things or persons (i.e., for slaves).

When a man stands by and watches an enemy attack and plunder his brother, he also (גַּם־אַתָּה, *gam-'attâ*, "you too") becomes guilty. Yet if he then seizes the opportunity to steal from his brother while he is down, he has failed to show any normal sense of family responsibility or human compassion. Verses 12-14 go on to describe how Edom took advantage of a bad situation for Judah.

v. 12 As discussed in the introduction, it is best to take the prohibitions in vv. 12-14 as rhetorical. The prophet places himself alongside the Edomites, as it were, and tries to stop them from doing what they did. The KJV has "thou shouldest not have" for each verb. While this translation has drawn much criticism, one does wonder just how Hebrew would express this idea. Perhaps the KJV was on the right track (cf. Hos. 4:14-19; the commands of v. 15 occur in the midst of a description), though the rhetorical explanation seems more likely. In the final analysis very little difference may exist between the two interpretations.

Carl Armerding argues that the commands stress the hostile attitudes of the Edomites rather than their actions.[22] They participated with the Babylonians in their minds, all the while watching from afar. Yet attitudes can only become known through deeds, and in any case when Obadiah commands the Edomites not to cut off the escape of refugees or hand over fugitives (v. 14), he must have a real event in mind.

The Hebrew term for "gloat" would more commonly mean "look at" (using the verb רָאָה, *rā'â*). The context of "looking at" somebody's misfortune indicates the more specific idea of "gloating" (cf. Judg. 16:27; Ps. 22:17 [MT 22:18]; Ezek. 28:17). A closely related idea is to "look at" an enemy that one has triumphed over (Ps. 54:7 [MT 54:9]; 112:8; 118:7; Mic. 7:10). The idiom also occurs in the inscription on the Moabite Stone (*ANET*, 3d ed., p. 320). Albright's translations, "caused me to triumph" (1. 4) and "I have triumphed" (1. 7), are literally "caused me to look on" and "I have looked on" (cf. Ps. 59:10 [MT 59:11]). The verse in Obadiah draws out the description of the gloating: "And do not be glad. ... And do not boast."

---

[21] So Rudolph, *Obadja*, p. 309.

[22] Armerding, "Obadiah," p. 349.

"And" (MT *waw*) connects v. 12 with v. 11, indicating a continuation of the thought: "You became like the nations when you stood by and gloated." With v. 13 the prophet accuses Edom of a more active participation, and the conjunction is dropped from the prohibition (cf. also the comments on the structure of vv. 12-14 above).

Five terms are used in vv. 12-14 to describe the "day" (יוֹם, *yôm*) of disaster that befell Judah. The first one, נָכְרוֹ (*nokrô*, "his misfortune"), occurs elsewhere only in Job 31:3, where it parallels אֵיד (*'êd*, "disaster"), the fourth of Obadiah's terms (three times in v. 13). When the prophet refers to "the day of his misfortune," he singles out a specific period of time when great calamity came upon Judah and Jerusalem. Because of the similar terminology (using *yôm*, "day"), this time should be identified with the "day" when "strangers entered his gate" (v. 11).

The second term, אָבְדָם (*'obĕdām*, "when they perish"), is quite strong and makes it unlikely that Obadiah means an event prior to the destruction of Jerusalem by the Babylonians in 586 B.C. Lamentations also speaks sarcastically of the joy the Edomites felt when Jerusalem fell, "Rejoice and be glad, O daughter of Edom" (Lam. 4:21).

The third term, צָרָה (*ṣārâ*, "disaster"), occurs at the end of v. 12 and again at the end of v. 14. It is used in Jer. 30:7 of the "time of Jacob's trouble," that forms a part of the eschatological day of the Lord (cf. Zeph. 1:15).[23] In Jer. 15:11 the term parallels רָעָה (*rā'â*, "disaster"), used for the fifth of Obadiah's terms (v. 13), and several other times in Jeremiah *ṣārâ* refers to the anguish that accompanies a painful childbirth (Jer. 4:31; 6:24; 49:24; 50:43).

Obadiah forbids the Edomites to "boast" over Judah's misfortune. The Hebrew is quite expressive: "And do not make great with your mouth" (וְאַל־תַּגְדֵּל פִּיךָ, *wĕ'al-tagdēl pîkā*, cf. Ezek. 35:13). Allen translates, "Do not talk so big." He also suggests a close relationship between the boasting here and that of v. 3.[24] The boasting would include belittling and taunting Judah so as to make the boasters seem superior. The Edomites felt that what happened to Judah could never happen to them.

v. 13 First, the Edomites stood at a safe distance and joked and laughed about Jerusalem's misfortune. When it appeared prudent to do so, they entered the city for a closer look (v. 13). Within the walls of Jerusalem itself they see the effects of the great disaster everywhere, but rather than aid the victims they continue to gloat. Finally, they begin to pick through the rubble to obtain their own spoils.

The first line of v. 13 concludes with the refrain, בְּיוֹם אֵידָם (*bĕyôm 'êdām*, "in the day of their disaster"), while the other two lines end with the slightly varied בְּיוֹם אֵידוֹ (*bĕyôm 'êdô*, lit. "in the day of his disaster). The two forms comprise the fourth of Amos's terms for qualifying the terrible "day" when Jerusalem was destroyed (see above). The verse is framed by two scenes of the Edomites standing outside the city. The effect is to focus on the disaster within the city itself. *'êdām*

[23] Cf. Charles L. Feinberg, "Jeremiah," in *EBC*, 6:560.

[24] Allen, *Obadiah*, pp. 156-57.

("their disaster") may be a deliberate variation in order to make an intricate word play on Edom (see also Additional Notes).[25]

The fifth of Obadiah's terms for the conquest and destruction of Jerusalem is בְּרָעָתוֹ (bĕrāʿātô, "over his calamity"). It is the only one that does not directly modify yôm ("day"), but "in the day of his disaster" immediately follows it. Thus, the dual expression, "over his calamity in the day of his disaster," underlines the shameful guilt of the Edomites: they are gloating even while they survey the ruins of the city.

In the final prohibition of the verse, וְאַל־תִּשְׁלַחְנָה בְחֵילוֹ (wĕʾal-tišlaḥnâ bĕḥêlô, "and let not your hands reach out for his wealth"), a plural feminine verb is used for the first time (everywhere else a masculine singular). Evidently the noun "hands" is the unexpressed subject (cf. Additional Notes for other explanations). The idiom "stretch out the hand" means to touch something or someone with a view to disturbing the object in some way (e.g., Ex. 22:7; 1 Sam. 24:6; Esther 2:21; 9:10). Since the Edomites would not have entered Jerusalem until after the Babylonians were through, Obadiah must forbid them to put their hands to the plunder. Also, the cowardice they displayed would make it unlikely they tried to capture any Judean soldiers (though ḥêlô in v. 11 probably means "his army").

v. 14 Once again the scene shifts in v. 14 to outside Jerusalem. Refugees are fleeing the Babylonian army, but the Edomites stand in their way and cruelly cut them down. The action could have been simultaneous with the looting depicted in v. 13 if it was done by additional Edomites who did not enter the city. More likely, however, it was simultaneous with standing at a safe distance and gloating. The arrangement of the verses is not chronological but for its rhetorical effect of making the inside of Jerusalem the center of the stage. Just as Edom "cut down" Judean fugitives, so shall Edomites be "cut off" by slaughter when the Lord judges them (v. 9).

It is difficult to arrive at certainty for the meaning of פֶּרֶק (pereq). Its etymology would indicate a splitting. Some take it to refer to a split in the road, as here, while others prefer to see a reference to a mountain pass.[26]

The Edomites slaughtered some of the refugees but captured others to turn over to the Babylonians for a reward. The hiphil of סגר (sgr) here means "deliver up" (cf. 1 Sam. 23:11; Amos 1:6).

Additional Notes

v. 11 בְּיוֹם עֲמָדְךָ: BHS prefers to emend to "because of your standing" (מֵעָמְדְךָ). Yet this would disturb the continual repetition of "day" throughout vv. 11-15.

v. 12 נָכְרוֹ: From its etymology (which must play a subordinate role to its use in context) the term signifies something "strange," an unusual experience. In the Mari Texts, nukru was used of "a strange piece of work" (CAD "N," 2:328). The

[25] Cf. Dick, "A Syntactic Study," pp. 7, 9.
[26] Henderson, The Twelve Minor Prophets, pp. 194-95. More recently Rudolph (Obadja, p. 305) refers it to the narrow entrances into Edomite territory itself.

pattern of the noun in Job 31:3 is *nēker*, whereas the MT of Obadiah presupposes *nōker*. The HALOT lexicon relates the word in Obadiah 12 to *neker* and translates with "misfortune."

v. 13 אֵידָם: Despite the note in *BHS*, the LXX offers no real evidence for the sequence, "his trouble [אוֹנוֹ] ... his distress [אֵידוֹ] ... his destruction [אָבְדוֹ]." Apparently the translator of the LXX, like the modern versions, smoothed out the pronominal references. Also, different terms were chosen to give more variety than the Hebrew. The MT is preferred because of the impact of repetition on the passage and the word play on Edom.

וְאַל־תִּשְׁלַחְנָה: *BHS* suggests emending to וְאַל־תִּשְׁלַח יָד, also found in the Targum (וְדַראוֹשִׁיטְתָא יְדָךְ, "and that you stretched forth your hand"). This seems suspiciously like a smoothing out of a difficulty. Wolff proposes that the ending נָה was a misreading of נָא, while Douglas Stuart thinks of an energic ending.[27] Once again the manuscript from Murabbaat fully supports the MT.

D. Edom's Judgment In The Day Of The Lord (15-21)

Edom's judgment is twofold. First, the nation will suffer at the hands of other nations (vv. 1b-9). Later, however, it will suffer at the hands of the Lord and at the hands of His people. It is this later judgment that is in focus in vv. 15-21.

The first half of this section (vv. 15-16) contains a general reference to the judgment against Edom and the nations, based on the way they have dealt with Israel. That is, their judgment will be in the same measure and in the same manner as their mistreatment of Israel. The second half (vv. 17-21) develops the salvation of Israel and their return from captivity. Consequently they will take possession of the same lands from which Edom and the nations exiled them.

The Lord is active throughout this period. It is His "day" when He brings the era of the control of the world by the nations to an end. He pours out His wrath, rescues and restores His people, and finally establishes His kingdom on earth.

1. Edom And The Nations Judged According To Their Treatment Of Israel (15-16)

Translation

> For the day of Yahweh is near
> upon all the nations.
> Just as you have done it will be done to you;
> your deeds shall return upon your own head.
> [16]For just as you (Edomites) drank upon My holy mountain,
> so all the nations will drink continually.
> Yes, they will drink and swallow
> and become as though they had never been.

---

[27] Wolff, *Obadiah and Jonah,* p. 37; Douglas Stuart, *Hosea-Jonah* (WBC 31; Waco, Tex.: Word, 1987), p. 413.

Exegesis and Exposition

The first (v. 8) and last (v. 15) occurrences of "day" in Obadiah have reference to the time when the Lord acts against the enemies of His people. All the references in between are to the "day" of distress and anguish experienced by Judah and Jerusalem. Edom alone stood under the Lord's judgment the first time; now all the nations, including Edom, will have to suffer the full force of the Lord's fury.

v. 15 If Judah, the Lord's people, had a "day of distress" at the hands of the Edomites and Babylonians, an even greater "day" looms on the horizon, according to v. 15. This day belongs to the Lord, and He will pour out His wrath on all the nations of the earth (cf. on Joel 1:15; 2:1, 31 [MT 3:4]; Amos 5:18-20). Edom cannot expect to escape this judgment, and the prophet's announcement brings to a halt the sounds of merriment and boasting.

The justice of God demands that unrighteousness in a nation be punished. As is so often the case in the prophets, Obadiah here announces that the punishment will fit the crime. The Edomites betrayed Judah; the nations will betray Edom (v. 7). The Edomites killed or betrayed the refugees; the Lord will cut off all Edomites from their land (v. 9). They boasted against Judah; their shame will last forever (v. 10). Edom dealt violently with his brother; Jacob and Joseph will be like fire burning among the Edomite chaff (v. 18). Edom took the possessions of his brother; the whole nation of Israel will dispossess Edom. For the pronouncement in the last verse segment, "your deeds [גְּמֻלְךָ, *gĕmûlĕkā*] will return on your own head," see the exegesis of Joel 3:4 (MT 4:4).

v. 16 One might expect looting to be accompanied by heavy drinking of wine (v. 16), but there is also something figurative about the expression. In this regard, the statement in Zech. 12:2 (cf. Isa. 51:22) indicates that Jerusalem is a "cup that causes reeling to all the peoples around." In other words, Jerusalem herself is like a cup filled with a drink that will be intoxicating to all the nations. Furthermore, God's wrath is often described as "wine" in Scripture (Ps. 60:3 [MT 60:4]; 75:8 [MT 75:9]; Jer. 25:15; 51:7; Rev. 14:10; 16:19; 19:15). Evidently the nations become drunk with God's wrath when they attack Jerusalem or His people. More precisely, the attack makes them deserving of wrath just as surely as wine makes its abusers stagger and fall.

Edom's judgment will correspond to its deed. The people made a mockery of God's holy hill by their drunken actions against defenseless Judah. In so doing they became drunk with the wrath of God. The wrath was not expressed immediately, but the Edomites are still filled with it. In the future all the nations will imbibe heavily of this wrath. They will even drink more as they again attack Jerusalem and Judah, until at last the wine itself will destroy them.

Some argue that the Lord addresses Judah, not Edom in this verse.[28] In this case it means that just as Judah suffered the wrath of the nations, so the nations will suffer God's wrath. It is true that the Hebrew for "you" is singular in v. 15 and plural in v. 16, but for cases where a nation is viewed as an individual, such

---

[28] See Henderson, *The Twelve Minor Prophets,* p. 195; Rudolph, *Obadja,* pp. 311-12; Armerding, "Obadiah," p. 353; Wehrle, *Prophetie und Textanalyse,* pp. 34-35; Allen, *Obadiah,* p. 161.

alternation between singular and plural is not unusual (cf. also "their distress" and "his distress" in v. 13).[29] In any case, it is very difficult to accept linguistically that Judah is suddenly introduced with only a pronoun. The ancient versions continue to make Edom the center of attention.

The rare verb וְלָעוּ (wĕlāʿû, "and they will swallow") occurs also with the meaning "speak rashly" or "wildly" (Job 6:3; Prov. 20:25). No other passages contain the sense of "swallow," but a related noun has the meaning "throat" (Prov. 23:2). A Syriac cognate means "lick" or "sip." Since there is no special reason to stress rash speech as the outcome of the drinking, it is better to follow the traditional sense of "swallow," as in the Targum. LXX and the Peshitta contain the thought of staggering.

The verse apparently precludes any trace of the nations remaining (וְהָיוּ כְּלוֹא הָיוּ, wĕhāyû kĕlôʾ hāyû, "and become as though they never had been"), yet there will be a remnant of various nations in the Millennium (Isa. 2:2-4; Amos 9:12; Mic. 4:1-3; Zech. 14:16-19). How are these two ideas to be reconciled? The answer perhaps lies in the difference between the concept of nations before and during the Millennium. Before the golden age of Messiah's rule on earth the nations consider themselves sovereign and fight to maintain their individual rights. When Christ returns, however, only those from the nations who have called on the Lord's name will enter. Also, they will be under one King and no longer a threat to Israel's existence. Therefore, the nations as we presently know them will exist no more once the Millennium begins. In any case, Obadiah dwells only on the destruction of the old order as far as the nations are concerned.

2. Edom And The Nations Possessed By The Remnant Of Israel (17-21)

Translation

But on Mount Zion there will be those who have been delivered,
and it will be a holy place.
Then the house of Jacob will take possession of *their possessions.
[18]Now the house of Jacob will be a fire,
and the house of Joseph a flame,
with the house of Esau as stubble.
So they will ignite them and consume them,
and there will be no survivor for the house of Esau.
For Yahweh has spoken!
[19]Also (Judeans from) the Negev will possess the mountainous area of Esau,
and (Judeans from) the Shephelah the (territory of) the Philistines.
Also (the Ephraimites) will possess the territory of Ephraim
and the territory of Samaria,
and Benjamin (will possess) Gilead.

---

[29] Dick thinks the change of pronouns is stylistic, the "grammatical tension" contributing to the "dramatic" element ("A Syntactic Study," p. 10).

[20]And the exiles of *this company of the sons of Israel
will *possess the (territory of) the Canaanites as far as Zarephath,
and the exiles of Jerusalem who are in Sepharad
will possess the cities of the Negev.
[21]Then deliverers will ascend Mount Zion
to judge the mountainous territory of Esau,
and the Kingdom will belong to Yahweh.

Exegesis and Exposition

The day of the Lord will dawn with judgment for the nations but salvation for Israel. At the end of his book Obadiah turns to the changing fortunes of God's chosen people in that day. The two parts of the nation will be reunited and possess their former territories, expanding into what was formerly Edomite land. Thus, a complete reversal of the situation in Obadiah's own day, when Judah and Israel were scattered and Jerusalem was humbled, will occur.

v. 17 At the fall of Jerusalem in 586 B.C. the survivors were cruelly killed or delivered to the enemy. When the Lord returns, however, there will be survivors (v. 17). He will see to it that all who call upon His name will escape (see comments on Joel 2:32 [MT 3:5]; cf. also Zech. 14:1-5). A strong contrast begins here as Obadiah now turns to the role played by Israel in that future day.

The "house of Jacob" stands for all Israel, north and south (v. 18), but it also emphasizes Edom as the brother of Jacob (v. 10). In its present form the text means that Israel will regain its former land, which was its "possession" or inheritance (cf. Ex. 6:8; Ezek. 11:15). It seems unusual that here more than one possession is mentioned, but perhaps the one land is thought of as the various possessions of the individual tribes or groupings of tribes, as in vv. 19 and 20. A significant textual variant yields, "And the house of Jacob will possess those who had possessed them" (see Additional Notes).

v. 18 Some passages, like v. 18, speak of a military participation by Israel in the judgment of the nations just prior to the Millennium (Zech. 12:1-9; Mal. 4:3), while others depict the Lord carrying out the judgment on behalf of His people (Joel 3:12; Zech. 14:3-5; cf. Matt. 25:31-46). It is difficult to reconstruct the precise order of events. In any case much of the material is evidently not strictly chronological. Zechariah 12-14, for example, opens with the events surrounding the establishment of the Millennial Kingdom (12:1-13:6), suddenly switches back to the rejection of Christ at the first Advent (13:7), continues with the separation of a righteous remnant of Jews through their trials among the nations (13:8-10), and finally returns to the events that usher in the Millennium (chap. 14).

Tentatively, it would seem that when the nations come against Jerusalem they are at first victorious (Zech. 14:2). Then the Lord gives His people divine strength in battle, followed shortly by the pouring out of the Spirit (Joel 2:28 [MT 3:1]; Zech. 12:10) and Christ's personal presence in the company of angelic hosts (and saints?; Zech. 14:3-5). It is not impossible that the Spirit is poured out more than once during the Tribulation period, even as He was poured out more than once during the foundational era of the Church (Acts 2; 10:44-48). In any case, when Christ returns He will perform a final judgment of the nations that will determine those to be included in or excluded from the Millennial Kingdom.

The name "Jacob" would include the entire family of Israel, but the "house of Joseph" is added to make it clear that even the northern kingdom, which had been destroyed by the Assyrians, will be reassembled by the Lord to inherit their former territory (cf. Amos 9:8-9). For the figure of Israel fighting its enemies like a flame among highly combustible material, see Zech. 12:6.

For the problem of the "remnant of Edom" in Amos 9:12, see the comments on Obad. 9. Armerding finds a preliminary historical fulfillment in the defeat of the Idumeans by Judas Maccabaeus in 166 B.C. and in their subsequent subjugation under John Hyrcanus, which was completed by 125 B.C. Armerding goes on to state: The Idumeans "continued to haunt the Jews, however, for the family of Herod the Great was of Idumaean descent; but after the second century B.C., they had virtually been consumed by the house of Jacob, to which they lost their national identity and autonomy."[30]

Idumea is the name for the territory of Edom found in LXX and Josephus. After the conquest of Judah the Edomites began to occupy parts of southern Judah itself, especially in and around Hebron and the Negev. Various Arabian groups (eventually the Nabateans) took over the former territory of Edom, but some Edomites managed to maintain their identity in southern Judah.[31] Therefore, one could speak of a partial fulfillment of Obadiah's oracle when the Maccabeans and Hasmoneans reclaimed these areas for Israel.

Several factors should be kept in mind, however. First, Obadiah speaks of the final day of the Lord when all the nations shall be judged prior to the setting up of the Messianic Kingdom. Second, a remnant from the exiles of the Ephraimites must play a large role in the fulfillment of the prophecy. Third, the term Idumea can be vague; not all Idumeans are necessarily "of the house of Esau." Finally, Armerding is correct to note that Herod and his descendants still plagued Israel even after the assimilation of the Idumeans.

v. 19 Verses 19 and 20 go through the Israelite territory possessed before the exile, expanding on the statement at the end of v. 17. The only territory that becomes Israelite that did not formerly belong to them is Edom.[32] Only Obadiah refers to Edomite land as the "mountain" (i.e., mountainous area) of Esau.

The Negev in OT times included only the area currently categorized as the northern Negev. It included territory east and west of Beersheba and north of Kadesh Barnea.[33] As discussed in the Introduction under Relations between Edom and Israel (esp. n. 18), Edom may have conquered much of Judean territory in the Negev around the time the Babylonians destroyed Jerusalem.

The Shephelah, a geographical area in Palestine, is characterized by low hills and broad valleys between the Philistine territory along the coastal plain and the

---

[30] Armerding, "Obadiah," p. 354-55.

[31] J. R. Bartlett, "The Moabites and Edomites," in *Peoples of Old Testament Times,* ed. D. J. Wiseman (Oxford: Clarendon, 1975), pp. 243-44.

[32] Cf. Jeffrey L. Townsend, "Fulfillment of the Land Promise in the Old Testament," *BSac* 142 (1985): 320-37, esp. the map on p. 327. He does not discuss this important passage from Obadiah.

[33] A. F. Rainey, "Negeb," *ISBE,* rev. ed., 3: 511.

Judean hill country. An expansion from previous territory is in view, then, but not beyond the boundaries allotted to Israel (Josh. 15:45-47).

From the Hebrew (וְיָרְשׁוּ, wĕyārĕšû, "and they will possess") it is difficult to determine who is to possess Ephraim and Samaria. NASB seems to imply that it would be those of the Negev and shephelah. Yet if "the house of Joseph" (v. 18) is a participant, it is hard to imagine why Judeans would take over their territory. The text probably means that exiles from Ephraim and Samaria will possess their former territories. This assumption would provide a balance between vv. 18 and 19, as the translation given above stresses.

The last part of the verse turns to Benjamin. Saul, the first king of Israel and a Benjamite, won Jabesh-gilead for Israel from the Ammonites (1 Sam. 11:1-11). Later, Abner set up Ish-bosheth, a son of Saul, as king over Gilead and Israel (2 Sam. 2:8-11). Perhaps this background helps explain the expansion of Benjamin into the territory across the Jordan which would otherwise have belonged to Manasseh.

Verses 19 and 20 seem so overloaded with words, especially in comparison to the previous verses, that some of the phrases might be considered glosses. That is, comments originally reserved for the margins of the manuscript eventually worked their way into the text.[34] While such proposals are highly speculative because of the lack of manuscript evidence, it is also true that these verses are exceptionally difficult to interpret and translate. It is possible, however, to discern the general flow of the argument despite any corruption that may have occurred in ancient times.

v. 20 From the standpoint of the Hebrew text, v. 20 is the most difficult in the entire book of Obadiah to interpret. The text may have undergone alteration during the process of transmission by scribes, but if so, an original text cannot be recovered with any confidence (see Additional Notes).

The NASB (also the ancient versions) assumes that the text singles out those exiles who are living among the Canaanites as far as the town of Zarephath (צָרְפַת־עַד, 'ad-ṣārĕpat, "as far as Zarephath"). The NIV, on the other hand, indicates that the exiles living in Canaan will have a separate inheritance which will extend as far as Zarephath (see also the KJV). This latter interpretation seems more likely because of the emphasis in the passage on an extension of territory.

Zarephath was a Phoenician coastal town roughly midway between Tyre and Sidon. It is best known as the site where Elijah lived at the house of a widow and her son until the Lord was ready to remove a great drought from Israel (1 Kings 17:8-24). The term "Canaanites" here might mean the Phoenicians (cf. Isa. 23:11-12).[35]

The most obvious reading of אֲשֶׁר־כְּנַעֲנִים (ʾašer-kĕnaʿănîm) is "who are Canaanites." It is difficult to imagine, however, that the prophet actually meant that the "sons of Israel" are Canaanites. The NASB supplies the word "among" in front of "Canaanites" (cf. NIV, "who are in Canaan"), but this translation makes it appear that Israelites in Canaanite territory as well as citizens of Jerusalem who are

---

[34] For details see Allen, *Obadiah,* pp. 169-71; Wolff, *Obadiah and Jonah,* p. 61.
[35] See A. Haldar, "Canaanites," *IDB* 1:494.

residing in a distant country will together take possession of the cities of the Negev. That assumption is problematic in light of the immediately surrounding context, though it does seem to be the implication of the stress markers in the MT (the *athnach* being placed on the word immediately before *yirĕšû*, "they will possess").

The real crux of the issue is that "they will possess" (*yirĕšû*) occurs only once at the end of the verse. The NIV ("This company of Israelite exiles who are in Canaan will possess the land as far as Zarephath") apparently assumes that the thought of possessing carries over from v. 19. However, all the other instances of the verb "possess" in vv. 19 and 20, whether actual or implied, have an object marked with אֵת (*'et*), whereas the NIV supplies "the land" as an object before "as far as Zarephath." Many moderns have assumed that an original "they will possess" became corrupted to "who" (*'ăšer*).[36] This makes excellent sense in the context but assumes that the Hebrew text was severely corrupted prior to the time of the early versions (also the Murabbaat text supports the MT). This view also has the problem of explaining the lack of the marker *'et* before "Canaanites." On balance it seems best to assume some type of textual corruption yielding an original meaning close to that given in the translation. MT is the more difficult reading, but it hard to give it a meaningful interpretation as it stands.

Obadiah predicts that the former inhabitants of Jerusalem (and possibly also the Israelite exiles) will expand into the Negev (אֵת עָרֵי הַנֶּגֶב, *'ēt 'ārê hannegeb*, "the cities of the Negev"). One problem is that v. 19 already speaks of Judeans in the Negev who will possess Edomite territory. Since the Edomites began to take over the area of the Negev shortly after the fall of Jerusalem, however, the text simply explains that the returned exiles will not only inhabit old territories but also extend into those of their enemies. Also, there seems to be some distinction between the Negev in general and the "cities" of the Negev. Perhaps there is thought of Levites in Jerusalem taking possession of the towns of the Judean southland (cf. Josh. 21).

Sepharad is quite difficult to identify. The Peshitta and Targum already refer to it as Spain, but many modern interpreters prefer Sardis in Asia Minor.[37] The latter view might entail moving the date of Obadiah into the Persian era (or perhaps only of a gloss added to the text), though the historical problems are too complex to preclude an earlier Judean colony at Sardis.

Another interesting suggestion is Saparda, an area of ancient Media where Sargon II settled prisoners from Syria-Palestine.[38] One problem is that the term "captivity of Jerusalem" makes us think of the mass deportations by the Babylonians between 605 and 586 B.C. rather than a much earlier deportation by the Assyrian king Sargon II (for which there is no independent biblical evidence).

---

[36] See Allen, *Obadiah,* pp. 170-71 n. 38; Wolff, *Obadiah and Jonah,* p. 61 (but he thinks only of the verb having fallen out). JB seems to presuppose this emendation.

[37] Cf. George M. A. Hanfmann and Jane C. Waldbaum, "New Excavations at Sardis and Some Problems of Western Anatolian Archaeology," in *Near Eastern Archaeology in the Twentieth Century: Essays in Honor of Nelson Glueck,* ed. A. Sanders (Garden City, N.Y.: Doubleday, 1970), pp. 317-18. See also Allen, *Obadiah,* p. 171; Raabe, *Obadiah,* pp. 267-268.

[38] M. C. Astour, "Sepharad," in *IDBSup,* p. 807.

v. 21 Who are these "deliverers" (מוֹשִׁעִים, *môš'îm*) in v. 21 who "judge" (לִשְׁפֹּט, *lišpōt*) the Edomites from Mt. Zion? In the period between the conquest and the monarchy, the Lord would raise up a "deliverer" when the Israelites cried out because of foreign oppression (Judg. 3:9, 15). Some of these deliverers also acted as judges or leaders for the people of Israel. (Nehemiah 9:27 refers to all the judges collectively as "deliverers"). Evidently Obadiah intends to make some reference to this period of the Judges. Just as the Lord raised up the judges of old to rescue His people, so in the future similar leaders will arise to save Israel from the oppression of the nations. Here "the mountainous territory of Esau" is intended as a type to include all the enemies of God's people.

In this way the verse harks back to the promise that "on Mt. Zion there will be those who escape" (v. 17). Mt. Zion is the place where the Lord will deliver His people and then enable them to conquer their enemies. Perhaps there is also the additional thought that these saviors will continue to exercise authority over the nations in the Millennial Kingdom.

When the day of the Lord arrives and the nations are judged and Israel delivered, a kingdom will be set up that will endure forever (cf. Dan. 7:26-27). Obadiah seems strange to some because it draws out the theme of judgment on Edom. Yet Edom is only one of the nations that will feel the Lord's wrath. It stands out for its pride and violent treatment of the covenant people. In the overall picture, then, the struggles between Edom and Israel highlight a broader theme of good against evil, of the people of God against the people of Satan (cf. Gen. 3:14-15). That struggle finally culminates in an earthly kingdom set up by Christ when He returns to rule all the nations from Jerusalem. In the NT the book of Revelation picks up these encompassing topics and develops them in terms of Babylon as the great representative of evil on earth (Rev. 17-18).

Additional Notes

v. 17 מוֹרָשֵׁיהֶם: The Peshitta and the LXX agree in reading, "and the house of Jacob will take possession of those who had taken possession of them." The Targum expands this: "and the house of Jacob will take possession of the properties of the nations which had taken possession of them." For years some commentators preferred to reconstruct an original Hebrew text with different vowels but the same consonants, yielding *môrišêhem*, "those who dispossessed them."[39] Then in 1952 an exploration of some caves in the wilderness of Judah near Wadi Murabbaat produced a fragmentary Hebrew scroll of the Minor Prophets which dates to the early second century (A.D.). Its text is remarkably close to what later came to be known as the Masoretic Text (MT), but for our passage it has the significant variant, מורישיהם. The *yodh* surely indicates, for the first time, a Hebrew text suggested by the versions.

Some feel that the variant fits the context better because of the emphasis in v. 18 on taking the land by force from the Edomites. On the other hand, the MT does not disturb the context. The verse simply states that the Israelites will regain their

---

[39] E.g., Julius A. Bewer, *A Critical and Exegetical Commentary on Obadiah and Joel*, (ICC; Edinburgh: T. & T. Clark, 1974), p. 29.

former possessions; then v. 18 tells how it will happen. On the whole, the MT seems the more difficult reading. That is, it cannot be explained easily except on the supposition that it is the original text (possibly one could assume that one of the two *yodhs* was omitted by a copyist). The Targum may be a conflation of two traditions: 1) a reading of "their possessions," which was interpreted as the possessions of the nations; and 2) a reading of "their dispossessors," which makes it clear that the nations are in view.

v. 19 הַר עֵשָׂו: Some (cf. *BHS*) argue that "the mountain of Esau" is a gloss to "the Negev." Then the text would read, "They (the house of Jacob and of Ephraim) will possess the Negev." Yet there is no textual evidence for the conjecture, and several other phrases also have to be taken as glosses if the view is adopted. The point is rather that the Israelites who had formerly inhabited only the Negev will expand into Edomite country.[40]

וְיָרְשׁוּ: Because there is no clear subject, Rudolph proposes that the consonants ירוש were used to abbreviate Jerusalem.[41] The suggestion is ingenious, but it is hard to imagine those who used the abbreviation not being aware of the likely confusion with "and they will possess." In any case, it would still be necessary to assume a metathesis, and the text stresses the actual presence of the "house of Joseph." Why, then, should Jerusalem be mentioned here?

v. 20 וְגָלֻת הַחֵל־הַזֶּה: The term translated "company" is presumed to come from חַיִל. Since it does not contain the letter *yodh*, one must also assume a contraction of the sound /ay/ to /ē/. Yet this should not happen when the form contains the article. The two other occurrences in Obadiah (vv. 11, 13) have the contraction, but it is expected by the rules of Hebrew grammar (a pronoun suffix is used). Moreover, they do contain *yodh* as a vowel letter. On the basis of Hebrew grammar, then, it seems unlikely that הַחֵל can be related to חַיִל. In any case, the latter term means "army," whereas the context of Obadiah requires a reference to the general population.

The second part of the verse speaks of the "captivity of Jerusalem." Therefore, we expect a place name after the term "captivity" in the first part. The LXX and the Peshitta interpret הַחֵל as "first" or "former." That is, Israel was the first part of the covenant people to go into captivity. There are also difficult grammatical problems with this translation.

Some have suggested that הַחֵל might be a corruption of חלח, the area of Halah in Assyria, where Israelite captives were settled after the fall of Samaria (2 Kings 17:6; 18:11; 1 Chron. 5:26).[42] The problem is that "captivity of X" normally means "those who have been taken captive *from* X," not "*to* X" (Isa. 20:4; Jer. 24:5; 28:4; 29:22; 40:1). This problem could be solved by taking Halah as a gloss (Rudolph), but it would be odd for an explanatory gloss to become so corrupted.

---

[40] For more details in favor of textual emendation, see Allen, *Obadiah,* pp. 168-71.

[41] Rudolph, *Obadja,* p. 315.

[42] See John D. W. Watts, *Obadiah: A Critical Exegetical Commentary* (Grand Rapids: Eerdmans, 1969), p. 63; also discussed but not accepted in Allen, Obadiah, p. 170 n. 38. See also the HALOT lexicon under חַיִל.

v. 21 מוֹשִׁעִים: LXX and Peshitta read a passive: "the saved ones will rise up." Some prefer to follow this reading, assuming the original text was either מוּשָׁעִים (*hophal*) or נוֹשָׁעִים (*niphal*).[43] A problem with the former suggestion is the lack of a *hophal* for this verb otherwise. The latter idea presupposes an unlikely change of the consonant *nun* into *mem.*

---

[43] See Allen, *Obadiah,* p. 163 n. 12.

Abbreviations

The following abbreviations supplement the list adopted by the *Journal of Biblical Literature:*

233′	A cursive (minuscule) LXX ms. (Rome, Bibl. Vat., Vat. gr. 2067; written 10th cent.) plus the related cursive 410 (Jerusalem, Patr. Bibl. 36; 13th cent. palimpsest)
239	A cursive (minuscule) LXX ms. (Bologna, Bibl. Univ., 2603; written 1046)
A	Codex Alexandrinus
B	Codex Vaticanus
bis	Twice
BKCOT	*The Bible Knowledge Commentary: An Exposition of the Scriptures by Dallas Seminary Faculty; Old Testament*
C-68	A group of four cursive (minuscule) LXX mss., as in Göttingen ed. of LXX, 13: 90-91
CBSC	Cambridge Bible for Schools and Colleges
COTTV	Commentary on the Old Testament in Ten Volumes by C.F. Keil and F. Delitzsch
EBC	*The Expositor's Bible Commentary*
GTJ	*Grace Theological Journal*
HALOT	*The Hebrew and Aramaic Lexicon of the Old Testament* by Ludwig Koehler and Walter Baumgartner; revised by Walter Baumgartner and Johann Jakob Stamm; translated and edited under the supervision of M. E. J. Richardson; 5 vols. (Leiden: Brill, 1999).
NAC	The New American Commentary
Syh	*Syro-Hexapla*
TOTC	Tyndale Old Testament Commentaries
TWOT	*Theological Wordbook of the Old Testament*
V	*Codex Venetus*

Commentaries and Special Studies

General Works on the Minor Prophets

Calvin, John. *Commentaries on the Twelve Minor Prophets*. Calvin's Commentaries, vol. 14. Translated by John Owen. Reprint. Grand Rapids: Baker, 1981.

Feinberg, Charles Lee. *The Minor Prophets*. Chicago: Moody, 1976.

Henderson, Ebenezer. *The Twelve Minor Prophets*. 1858. Reprint. Thornapple Commentaries. Grand Rapids: Baker, 1980.

Keil, C. F. *Minor Prophets*. COTTV, col. 10. Reprint. Grand Rapids: Eerdmans, 1973.

Rudolph, Wilhelm. *Joel-Amos-Obadja-Jona*. KAT, vol. 13, no. 2. Gütersloh: Gütersloher Verlagshaus Gerd Mohn, 1971.

Stuart, Douglas. *Hosea-Jonah*. WBC, vol. 31. Waco, TX: Word, 1987.

Joel

Hans Walter Wolff and Douglas Stuart (listed) have detailed bibliographies in their commentaries. Some of the more significant works cited in the present commentary on Joel are listed here.

Ahlström, G. W. *Joel and the Temple Cult of Jerusalem*. VTS, vol. 21. Leiden: E. J. Brill, 1971.

Allen, Leslie C. *The Books of Joel, Obadiah, Jonah and Micah*. NICOT. Grand Rapids: Eerdmans, 1976.

Bewer, Julius A. et al. *A Critical and Exegetical Commentary on Micah, Zephaniah, Nahum, Habakkuk, Obadiah and Joel*. ICC. Edinburgh: T. & T. Clark, 1974.

Chisholm, Robert B., Jr. "Joel." In *BKCOT*, edited by John F. Walvoord and Roy B. Zuck. Wheaton: Victor, 1985.

Driver, S. R. *The Books of Joel and Amos*. The Cambridge Bible for Schools and Colleges. Cambridge: University, 1907.

Hubbard, David Allan. *Joel and Amos: An Introduction*. TOTC. Downers Grove, IL: Inter-Varsity, 1989.

Lehrman, S. M. "Joel." In *The Twelve Prophets*. Soncino Books of the Bible. Edited by A. Cohen. London: Soncino, 1969.

Patterson, Richard D. "Joel." Vol. 7 in *EBC* edited by Frank E. Gaebelein. Grand Rapids: Zondervan, 1985.

Price, Walter K. *The Prophet Joel and the Day of the Lord*. Chicago: Moody, 1976.

Thompson, John Alexander. "The Date of Joel." In *A Light unto My Path: Old Testament Studies in Honor of Jacob M. Myers*. Gettysburg Theological Studies, no. 4, edited by Howard N. Bream, et al., pp. 453-64. Philadelphia: Temple Univ., 1974.

Wolff, Hans Walter. *Joel and Amos*. Hermeneia. Translated by Waldemar Janzen, et al. Philadelphia: Fortress, 1977.

Wood, Leon J. *The Prophets of Israel*. Grand Rapids: Baker, 1979.

Amos

The works by Gary V. Smith, Douglas Stuart, Adri van der Wal, and Hans Walter Wolff give detailed bibliography on Amos. Included here are some of the more significant works cited in the present commentary on Amos, with an emphasis on recent studies. The studies by Max E. Polley and Gary V. Smith appeared too late for detailed treatment in the present work.

Achard, Martin. *A Commentary on the Book of Amos*. International Theological Commentary. Edited by George A. F. Knight, et al. Grand Rapids: Eerdmans, 1984.

Barton, John. *Amos's Oracles against the Nations: A Study of Amos 1.3-2.5*. SOTSMS, vol. 6. Cambridge: Cambridge Univ., 1984.

Barstad, Hans M. *The Religious Polemics of Amos*. VTSup, vol. 34. Leiden: E. J. Brill, 1984.

Boyle, Marjorie O'Rourke. "The Covenant Lawsuit of the Prophet Amos: III 1-IV 13." *VT* 21 (1971): 338-62.

Coote, Robert B. *Amos among the Prophets: Composition and Theology*. Philadelphia: Fortress, 1981.

Cripps, Richard S. *A Critical & Exegetical Commentary on the Book of Amos*. 2d ed. N.p.: S.P.C.K., 1960.

Davies, G. Hinton. "Amos – The Prophet of Re -Union: An Essay in Honour of the Eightieth Birthday of Professor Aubrey R. Johnson, F. B. A." *ExpTim* 92 (1981): 196-200.

Dybdahl, Jon Lee. *Israelite Village Land Tenure: Settlement to Exile*. Diss. for Fuller Theological Seminary, School of Theology. Ann Arbor: University Microfilms, 1981.

Driver, S. R. *The Books of Joel and Amos*. CBSC Cambridge: University, 1907.

Fendler, Marlene. "Zur Sozialkritik des Amos." *EvT* 33 (1973): 32-53.

Finley, Thomas J. "The *Waw*-Consecutive with Imperfect in Biblical Hebrew: Theoretical Studies and Its Use in Amos." In *Tradition and Testament: Essays in Honor of Charles Lee Feinberg*, edited by John Feinberg and Paul Feinberg, pp. 241-62. Chicago: Moody, 1981.

Hammershaimb, Erling. *The Book of Amos, A Commentary*. Translated by John Sturdy. New York: Schocken, 1970.

Harper, William Rainer. *A Critical and Exegetical Commentary on Amos and Hosea*. ICC. Reprint. Edinburgh: T. & T. Clark, 1979.

Hasel, Gerhard F. *The Remnant: The History and Theology of the Remnant Idea from Genesis to Isaiah*. Andrews Univ. Monographs; Studies in Religion, no. 5. 3d ed. Berrien Springs, Michigan: Andrews Univ., 1980.

Hayes, John H. *Amos, The Eighth-Century Prophet: His Times and His Preaching*. Nashville: Abingdon, 1988.

Hubbard, David Allan. *Joel and Amos: An Introduction*. TOTC. Downers Grove, IL: Inter-Varsity, 1989.

Kaiser, Walter C., Jr., "The Davidic Promise and the Inclusion of the Gentiles (Amos 9:9-15 and Acts 15:13-18): A Test Passage for Theological Systems." *JETS* 20 (1977): 97-111.

Kaiser, Walter C., Jr. *The Uses of the Old Testament in the New*. Chicago: Moody, 1985.

Koch, Klaus. "Die Rolle der hymnischen Abschnitte in der Komposition des Amos-Buches." *ZAW* 86 (1974): 504-37.

Koch, Klaus. *The Prophets: Volume One, The Assyrian Period*. Translated by Margaret Kohl. Philadelphia: Fortress, 1983.

Lehrman, S. M. "Amos." In *The Twelve Prophets*. Soncino Books of the Bible, edited by A. Cohen. London: Soncino, 1969.

Mays, James Luther. *Amos: A Commentary*. OTL. Philadelphia: Westminster, 1969.

McComiskey, Thomas Edward. "Amos." Vol. 7 in *EBC*, edited by Frank E. Gaebelein. Grand Rapids: Zondervan, 1985.

Motyer, J. A. *The Day of the Lion: The Message of Amos*. Downers Grove, Ill.: InterVarsity, 1974.

Paton, Lewis B. "Did Amos Approve the Calf-Worship at Bethel?" *JBL* 13 (1894): 80-90.

Paul, Shalom M. "Amos 1:3-2:3: A Concatenous Literary Pattern." *JBL* 90 (1971): 397-403.

Paul, Shalom M. "A Literary Reinvestigation of the Authenticity of the Oracles against the Nations of Amos." In *De la Torah au Messie: Melanges Henri Cazelles*, edited by Maurice Carrez, et al., pp. 189-204. Paris: Desclee, 1981.

Paul, Shalom M. "Amos 3:3-8: The Irresistible Sequence of Cause and Effect." *Hebrew Annual Review* 7 (1983): 206-16.

Polley, Max E. *Amos and the Davidic Empire: A Socio-Historical Approach*. New York: Oxford Univ., 1989.

Schottroff, Willy. "The Prophet Amos: A Socio-Historical Assessment of His Ministry." In *God of the Lowly: Socio-Historical Interpretations of the Bible*, edited by Willy Schottroff and Wolfgang Stegemann, translated from the German by Matthew J. O'Connell. Maryknoll, N.Y.: Orbis, 1984.

Seilhamer, Frank H. "The Role of Covenant in the Mission and Message of Amos." In *A Light unto My Path: Old Testament Studies in Honor of Jacob M. Myers*, Gettysburg Theological Studies, no. 4, edited by Howard N. Bream, et al., pp. 435-51. Philadelphia: Temple Univ., 1974.

Smith, Gary V. *Amos: A Commentary*. Library of Biblical Interpretation. Grand Rapids: Zondervan, 1989.

Soggin, J. Alberto. *The Prophet Amos; A Translation and Commentary*. Translated by John Bowden. London: SCM, 1987.

Sunukjian, Donald R. "Amos." In *The Bible Knowledge Commentary: An Exposition of the Scriptures by Dallas Seminary Faculty, Old Testament*, edited by John F. Walvoord and Roy B. Zuck, pp. 1425-52. Wheaton: Victor, 1987.

Van der Wal, Adri. *Amos: A Classified Bibliography*. Applicatio, vol. 3. 3d ed. Amsterdam: Free Univ., 1986.

Wolff, Hans Walter. *Joel and Amos*. Hermeneia. Translated by Waldemar Janzen, et al. Philadelphia: Fortress, 1977.

Wright, Christopher J. H. *An Eye for an Eye: The Place of Old Testament Ethics Today*. Downers Grove, Ill.: InterVarsity, 1983.

Wright, T. J. "Amos and the "Sycamore Fig"." *VT* 26 (1976): 362-68.

Obadiah

Included here are some of the more significant works cited in the present commentary on Obadiah, with an emphasis on recent studies.

Allen, Leslie C. *The Books of Joel, Obadiah, Jonah and Micah*. NICOT. Grand Rapids: Eerdmans, 1976.

Armerding, Carl E. "Obadiah." Vol. 7 in *EBC* edited by Frank E. Gaebelein. Grand Rapids: Zondervan, 1985.

Baker, Walter L. "Obadiah." In *BKCOT*, edited by John F. Walvoord and Roy B. Zuck, pp. 1453-59. Wheaton: Victor, 1985.

Bewer, Julius A. *A Critical and Exegetical Commentary on Obadiah and Joel*. ICC. Edinburgh: T. & T. Clark, 1974.

Gaebelein, Frank E. *Four Minor Prophets: Obadiah, Jonah, Habakkuk, and Haggai; Their Message for Today*. Chicago: Moody, 1970.

McCarter, P. Kyle. "Obadiah 7 and the Fall of Edom." *BASOR* 220 (1975): 87-91.

Watts, John D. W. *Obadiah: A Critical Exegetical Commentary*. Grand Rapids: Eerdmans, 1969.

Wehrle, Josef. *Prophetie und Textanalyse: Die Komposition Obadja 1-21 interpretiert auf der Basis textlinguistischer und semiotischer Konzeptionen*. Arbeiten zu Text und Sprache im Alten Testament, vol. 28. St. Ottilien: Eos, 1987.

Wolff, Hans Walter. *Obadiah and Jonah: A Commentary*. Translated by Margaret Kohl. Minneapolis: Augsburg, 1986.

Selected Works Published Since 1989

These are works that have appeared since the publication of the commentary in 1990 (with a few works from 1989 that were not available before the manuscript was submitted). They have not been fully integrated into the study, but on occasion an insight from one or more of them will be added to the commentary.

Andersen, Francis I. and David Noel Freedman. *Amos: A New Translation with Introduction and Commentary*. AB 24A. New York: Doubleday, 1989. In this massive volume (979 pages) on Amos the authors try to work as much as possible within the framework of the Masoretic text rather than propose many conjectural emendations. They also see a "structural unity of the completed book" that must stem either from Amos himself or an editor who "must have been very close to his teacher" and worked with Amos's own prophecies (p. 5).

Barton, John. *Joel and Obadiah: A Commentary*. OTL. Louisville: Westminster John Knox, 2001. Life Hans Wolff before him, Barton thinks that chapters 3 and 4 of Joel were written later than chapters 1 and 2. Barton even refers to "*Deutero-Joel*" (p. 7). He dates the completed book to somewhere in the fifth century B.C. in the "mid-Persian period." Chapters 1 and 2 "could be somewhat earlier but still probably postexilic" (p. 16). Barton likewise divides Obadiah into two, with verses 1-14 after the fall of Jerusalem in 587 B.C. and verses 15-21 consisting of "eschatological passages added to older passages" (p. 123). This later part would have been added in the late Persian or Hellenistic period.

Carroll, Mark Daniel. *Contexts for Amos: Prophetic Poetics in Latin American Perspective.* JSOTSup 132. Sheffield, England: JSOT Press, 1992. This work explores "how to use the Bible in moral reasoning within a given context" (p. 20). The central chapters explore (from the table of contents) "sociological studies and the Old Testament," "religion and morality in context," "the moral authority of Scripture and the call for a responsible poetics," "poetics and the social imagination in Amos," and "Amos in the modern context." Carroll intends "to offer alternative approaches to those of Latin American liberation theologians" (p. 9).

Crenshaw, James L. *Joel: A New Translation with Introduction and Commentary.* AB 24C. New York: Doubleday, 1995.

Finley, Thomas J. *Joel, Obadiah and Micah.* Everyman's Bible Commentary. Chicago: Moody, 1996. This popular work follows my earlier work on Joel and Obadiah closely but with a few updates.

Garrett, Duane. *Hosea, Joel.* NAC 19A. [Nashville]: Broadman & Holman, 1997. Garrett prefers, (somewhat tentatively) a 7th cent. date for the book (p. 294). It contains much helpful information.

Hubbard, David Allan. *Joel and Amos: An Introduction and Commentary.* TOTC. Downers Grove, IL: Inter-varsity, 1989. Like most of the works in this series, this brief commentary is basically conservative in its approach and offers many helpful insights on the biblical books covered.

McComiskey, Thomas Edward (ed.). *The Minor Prophets: An Exegetical and Expository Commentary.* Volume 1: "Hosea, Joel, and Amos." Grand Rapids: Baker, 1992. "Joel" was done by Raymond Dillard and "Amos" by Jeffrey Niehaus. Volume 2: "Obadiah, Jonah, Micah, Nahum, and Habakkuk." Grand Rapids: Baker, 1993. "Obadiah" was done by Jeffrey Niehaus.

McQueen, Larry R. *Joel and the Spirit: The Cry of a Prophetic Hermeneutic.* Journal of Pentecostal Theology Supplement Series 8. Sheffield, England: Sheffield Academic Press, 1995. McQueen's book "grows out of a desire to bring the book of Joel and especially the text of Joel 3.1-5 (Eng: 2.28-32) into conversation with emerging Pentecostal scholarship" (p. 11). He accepts the unity of the book and dates it to 500-450 B.C. In the first part of his study McQueen sees three movements in the book of Joel (p. 21): lamentation (1:1-2:17); salvation (2:18-3:5); and judgment (4:1-21). He then interweaves these themes with the "Day of Yahweh," "Zion," and the "Promise of the Spirit" as thematic issues in Joel. In the second part, McQueen traces these same themes of lament, salvation, and judgment through the New Testament. Then he follows this up by tracing how these themes have been appropriated in the modern Pentecostal movement. In the final chapter McQueen describes his personal struggles in writing his book, one which arose out of his own experience of lament. McQueen's book is a fascinating read.

Paul, Shalom M. *Amos: A Commentary on the Book of Amos.* Ed. Frank Moore Cross. Hermeneia. Minneapolis: Augsburg Fortress, 1992. A notable feature of this second Hermeneia commentary on Amos is that Shalom Paul argues for the genuineness of passages that Hans Wolff (author of the first Hermeneia commentary on Amos) had previously argued were secondary. For example, Paul brings forward detailed reasons to attribute to Amos the oracles against the Philistines (1:6-8), Tyre (1:9-10), Edom (1:11-12), and Judah (2:4-5). Also, he argues that the final oracle of the book concerning the restoration of "the fallen booth of David" (9:11-15) is a genuine prophecy given by Amos. These two commentaries on Amos in the same Heremeneia series, then, are miles apart in terms of their conclusions concerning the critical analysis of the book.

Raabe, Paul R. *Obadiah: A New Translation with Introduction and Commentary.* AB 24D. New York: Doubleday, 1996. Raabe's detailed commentary on Obadiah deals in some depth with the style of Obadiah (poetry and prose, imagery, parallelism, terseness; pp. 6-14). The book is to be dated to the early exilic period (ca. 585-555 B.C.) and finds its unity in it view of Judah's downfall from two different perspectives, one historical and the other theological (p. 15).

Rosenbaum, Stanley N. עָמוֹס הַיִּשְׂרְאֵלִי *Amos of Israel: A New Interpretation.* Macon, GA: Mercer University, 1990. Rosenbaum argues that Amos was from the north (Israel), not the south (Judah) as most commentators think. In fact, Amos became an exile in Judah, settling in Tekoa (p. 100). Rosenbaum also assumes that the book is a unified whole and was written by Amos himself (pp. 3-7).

Smith, Billy K. "Amos, Obadiah." In *Amos, Obadiah, Jonah.* NAC 19B. by Billy K. Smith and Frank S. Page (Jonah). Ed. E. Ray Clendenen. [Nashville]: Broadman & Holman, 1995. As is true of other volumes in this conservative series, Smith's work on Amos and Obadiah is generally sound and helpful.

Printed in the United States
1403000004B/1-18

9 780737 500189